THE LIFE INSURANCE ENTERPRISE, 1885-1910

A PUBLICATION OF THE CENTER
FOR THE STUDY OF THE HISTORY OF LIBERTY
IN AMERICA · HARVARD UNIVERSITY

THE LIFE INSURANCE ENTERPRISE, 1885-1910

A STUDY IN THE LIMITS OF CORPORATE POWER

by Morton Keller

THE BELKNAP PRESS OF
HARVARD UNIVERSITY PRESS

CAMBRIDGE, MASSACHUSETTS · 1963

DISTRIBUTED IN GREAT BRITAIN
BY OXFORD UNIVERSITY PRESS, LONDON

LIBRARY OF CONGRESS CATALOG CARD NUMBER
63-10868

PRINTED IN THE UNITED STATES OF AMERICA

TO PHYLLIS

FOREWORD

Voluntarism was one of the weighty forces that preserved liberty in the United States. The fact that not every desirable social end had to be pursued through the use of the coercive instruments of government gave Americans a choice of means of cooperative action. They could sometimes work through the polity; but they could also use other means of association when they deemed it desirable to do so. The forces that kept the capacity to choose alive since the colonial period are among the essential elements in the preservation of freedom in the United States.

The business corporation was among the most important of these alternatives to the state. Originally an agency of the government, it slowly achieved independence of political control and established its private character. By the end of the nineteenth century it was an autonomous institution governed by its own stockholders and their elected officers and subject only to general regulation by law. The nineteenth century expansion of the American economy gave many such corporations enormous power. The necessity of confining that power to socially acceptable uses while still leaving the corporation free within the areas of its own competence became one of the continuing issues of American policy. The accumulation of power in institutions that were defined as private was tolerable only when qualified by the assurance that they would not serve as a means of establishing the dominance of those who controlled them.

The history of the great life insurance enterprises that took form during the last quarter of the nineteenth century dramatically exemplified these tendencies. These corporations performed a vital function in the life of an urban, industrial society. They grew rapidly in strength and amassed enormous resources, for the nature of their business made them custodians of the savings of millions of people. The very magnitude of their strength raised serious questions about the place in a free society of private institutions that served a public purpose.

Significantly Professor Keller's study shows the importance of self-limiting factors in the structure of American corporations that prevented their growth from becoming socially dangerous. Even before any state intervention, the great life insurance companies were themselves adjusting to the obligations of the kind of society in which they operated. They were therefore able to survive government investigation and, purged of abuses, continued to grow as private enterprises. This experience forms an instructive contrast to that in many contemporary European countries where the inability to achieve the same ends by voluntary means created a vacuum into which the government moved.

Oscar Handlin

PREFACE

Few artifacts of this corporate age are more impressive than the buildings of the large life insurance companies. Their local offices stand in a thousand communities. Regional headquarters share the skylines of a dozen American cities; Hartford, Boston, and Philadelphia house major firms. And in and about New York stand the home offices of the long-established giants: the Metropolitan at Madison Square; the New York Life just to the north; the Mutual and the Equitable in new midtown monoliths; the Prudential in Newark.

These are corporations at the highest level of the nation's business structure. If size counts, and money talks, they should be among the most potent institutions of this society. Yet the large life insurance companies play a curiously limited role in American life. They control increasing amounts of corporate stock, but they do not systematically and purposefully use their voting strength. Their officers do not figure largely in the interplay of business and politics. In many ways, they are giants without power.

This was not always so. Around 1900 the great life firms were among the lustiest of American corporations. No business had more, or more highly visible, elements of power. The large insurance companies freely used their substantial assets to control their investment and regulatory milieus; they had uniquely sophisticated corporate, managerial, and marketing structures; theirs was an executive leadership unusually dedicated to the quest for power and place.

The nature of this quest, and the complex of forces that transformed the enterprise of life insurance, is one concern of this book. Another is with the life insurance business as a social institution. The nature of the enterprise permitted a rich and diverse rendering of the possibilities of corporatism as a form of social organization to a degree matched, perhaps, by no other business group. Indeed, there seems to have been a positive relationship between the baroque vigor with which this society of companies made its way and the extent to which it was finally contained.

This work places greater emphasis on the limits of American corporate power than on its possibilities, and suggests (as an adjunct to John K. Galbraith's concept of countervailing power) that there are internal as well as external checks to the force of the corporate institution. But it does not intend to imply that only inconsequential problems stem from the rise of large organizations in American life. The real perils of bigness in America—flaccidity, mediocrity, inertia, and sterility—continue to demand the society's full attention and concern.

I have many favors to acknowledge and obligations to record. Grants from the Social Science Research Council, the John Simon Guggenheim Memorial Foundation, and the Center for the Study of the History of Liberty in America smoothed the way for my research and writing. The officers and staffs of the Equitable, John Hancock, Metropolitan, Mutual, New York Life, and Prudential insurance companies were immensely helpful; I want to thank these firms, too, for permission to quote from their records. My thanks go also to Alice B. Beer, Charles B. Bradley, R. Carlyle Buley, Arthur Hunter, Alvin Levin, Richard V. Lindabury, and William N. Parker. Thomas C. Cochran has been a constant source of encouragement. I owe a special debt of gratitude to the kindness and wisdom of Oscar Handlin and have drawn heavily on my wife's good judgment and editorial skill. I also want to thank Robin and Jonathan, who endured.

Morton Keller

Moylan, Pennsylvania

CONTENTS

PART FIVE: THE COMPANIES AND THE COMMONWEALTH

PART SIX: THE LIMITS OF POWER

ILLUSTRATIONS

Unless otherwise noted, photographs and drawings are by courtesy of the respective companies.

TABLES

Grown to tremendous proportions, there may be said to have evolved a "corporate system" — as there was once a feudal system — which has attracted to itself a combination of attributes and powers, and has attained a degree of prominence entitling it to be dealt with as a major social institution.

Adolph A. Berle and G. C. Means,
The Modern Corporation and Private Property

Part One * A Society of Companies

Insurance is one of the most venerable of business enterprises. Its development touched on major themes of eighteenth and nineteenth century economic change: the rise of the business corporation, the ebb and flow of government regulation, the entrepreneurial response to industrialization and urbanization.

In the United States, the life insurance business came to be dominated at the end of the nineteenth century by a small group of great firms: the New York Life, Equitable Life, Mutual Life, and Metropolitan Life insurance companies of New York, and the Prudential Insurance Company in Newark. The managers of these companies assumed more than strictly entrepreneurial roles. They defined themselves not only as sellers of insurance but as men of standing and power in the community; and they claimed for their corporations equally prestigious, quasi-public functions. In consequence, this self-contained society of companies took on an unusual ideology of corporate purpose and power.

I * The Life Insurance Enterprise

When man's economic activities moved beyond the demands of simple subsistence, insurance came into being. After capital broke away from its immemorial stagnation on the land, and assets became fluid and hazardously placed, the desire developed for some protection against sudden disaster. Systematic guarantee against loss — of produce, of ships, of slaves — crops up in ancient Greece, classical Rome, medieval Europe. As natural as the movement of goods by ship was the insurance of their safe arrival; when fire threatened the buildings and products of urban commerce coverage by organized underwriting developed.

Life insurance was the last and most sophisticated of insurance forms. It began with underwriting on the lives of slaves, the most literal possible translation to humans of the principle of property protection. Coverage in the modern sense came only after the Renaissance made viable a strong sense of the intrinsic importance of human life. The first known life insurance policy appeared in Elizabethan England, where the glory of man, prospects of material gain, and the identification of property and person were well advanced.[1]

The general appeal of life insurance made it a lucrative enterprise and an apt tool for the fund-raising purposes of burgeoning national states. The France of Louis XIV first plumbed its possibilities for public finance. The government, financially straitened by war and extravagance, adopted the scheme of Italian physician-banker Lorenzo Tonti for a state loan with both gambling and insurance features. Subscribers made payments, parts of which were set aside yearly for annuities; and those participants who lived longest within their age group benefited most. The scheme's success in 1689 and 1695 led to its imitation elsewhere in Europe, generally by private parties, but with results always disastrous for the participants.

As private speculation on a mass scale became a fixed feature of European life, insurance schemes gained in prominence. Wager policies, where one could insure the life of another without the insured's knowledge, spread rapidly through the sixteenth and seventeenth centuries. The murders that too often resulted from this form of enterprise led to its abolition in Genoa, Spain, and Germany. But in the world of John Law and the Mississippi Bubble, societies offering wager or speculative assessment annuities flourished mightily. It was possible in England to take out insurance on the lives of statesmen and noblemen, and on a multitude of other things besides: against the occurrence of divorce; against loss of virginity; even, in one case, against an individual's failure to return from Lapland with two reindeer and two female natives.[2]

But such extravagances eventually were judged improper. The *London Chronicle* protested in 1768: "when policies come to be opened on two of the first peers in Britain losing [their] heads . . . or on the dissolution of . . . parliament within one year . . . and underwritten chiefly by Scotsmen . . . it is surely high time to interfere." In 1711 a statute prohibited insurance on marriages, births, and christenings. Finally in 1774 an antigambling act required that the policyholder have an insurable interest in the project or person underwritten.[3]

As wager ventures collapsed under the weight of their impropriety, the tools of a more rational system of life insurance came to hand. The mathematics of Blaise Pascal, Edmund Halley, and others led to the first life expectancy tables; they would be improved through the eighteenth century. Lloyd's of London combined a reasonably respectable maritime insurance business with more speculative ventures. By the end of the eighteenth century it had a fixed policy form which suggested the possibilities of contractual regularity in life insurance as well. And in 1762 The Society for Equitable Assurances on Lives and Survivorships — London's "Old Equitable" — appeared as the first modern life insurance firm, mutual rather than joint-stock in organization, selling long-term life insurance on a plan of level, annual premiums.[4]

The Equitable stood in an almost unbroken line of unincorporated eighteenth century insurance ventures. After the Bubble Act of 1720 Parliament rarely granted charters of incorporation to any enterprise. But this did not prevent a vast accumulation of entrepreneurial experience and technique; and in that development insurance firms played a conspicuous role. Fire companies desiring to expand into the life insurance field worked out an early form of holding company organization. Insurance ventures, more than most, wrestled with the problem of limited liability, for although the creditor-policyholder posed a special danger, there was a salient need to appeal to him as a customer with the promise of guaranteed recovery. The opposition to the Equitable on the part of the Royal Exchange, the London Assurance Corporation, and the Amicable Society was a prime example of the struggle between established, chartered companies and new, unincorporated firms. A 1782 statute licensing unincorporated insurance companies was one of the major legislative victories of burgeoning new enterprise in late eighteenth century England.

By the end of the century the safeguards and opportunities inherent in incorporation strongly attracted entrepreneurs. Insurance firms were prominent in the fight to gain access to this form of business organization. A legal action involving an insurance company was the occasion for an early judicial characterization of the corporation as a device appropriate to private enterprise. Fire and marine insurance was included — with banks, canals, and water works — in Adam Smith's select tally of enterprises suitable for incorporation because of their social utility and capital needs. Nineteenth century English insurance charters pioneered in the development of the concept of shareholders' limited liability, although Parliament would not allow this privilege to insurance firms chartered under an act of general incorporation until 1862.

Through the late eighteenth and early nineteenth centuries mutual friendly societies were formed in England by "almost every distinct religious sect, by every interest where the members of it congregated in particular haunts, every class of professional and commercial life." A 1793 act recognizing the societies' legality marked the first official divergence from the anticorporation policy set in the Bubble Act almost seventy-five years before. On the ground that their "dealings are admitted to be of general utility, and need more money than partnership can supply," these firms fought a long and ultimately successful battle for the right of free incorporation.

The nineteenth century efflorescence of laissez-faire seemed to divest chartered enterprise of its fundamental identification with the public interest. But the belief persisted — if anything, grew — that the business of insurance had special responsibilities. An English Parliamentary committee decided in 1853 that the public function of insurance transcended the generally accepted "principle of [governmental] non-interference" in matters of trade. Income tax remittances were granted to life insurance policyholders on the ground that they reduced pauperism and crime.[5] The relatively late application of limited liability to insurance incorporation also suggested the special public concern with the business.

2

Insurance ventures played a prototypal role in early American business history as well. The first American life insurance company, the Presbyterian Ministers' Fund of Philadelphia, got its start in 1759. The Philadelphia Contributionship for Insuring Houses from Loss by Fire, dating from 1768, was the only chartered private business corporation in colonial America. Numerous fire and marine firms, including the Insurance Company of North America, emerged after the Revolution as part of the new country's expanding commercial structure.[6]

Insurance companies joined with banks to play a leading role in gathering and applying the capital necessary for the rapid development of the American economy in the early nineteenth century. Bank charters often bore the title of a combined insurance and trust company, for insurance incorporation was among the most familiar and most flexible of chartering forms. Prominent in the often chaotic banking history of pre–Civil War America were the New York Insurance and Trust Company, which had a particularly active life insurance department during the 1830's; the Massachusetts Hospital Life Insurance Company; and the Ohio Life and Trust, whose failure ignited the panic of 1857. As incorporation spread, the banking-insurance company served as a model for canal, railroad, and manufacturing charters.[7]

Yet in the midst of this unshackling of corporate enterprise, the special nature and perhaps the very venerability of the insurance business induced continuing, even increasing, checks upon it. State regulations were early and numerous. Pre–Civil War litigation involving insurance or insurance and trust companies often led to decisions that increased the power of the states over foreign (out-of-state) corporations.[8]

American life insurance at first continued to operate in the tradition of the Presbyterian Ministers' Fund: as the province of special, limited groups. But during the 1840's it emerged as a full-fledged enterprise. Only twenty-nine life companies were formed up to 1840; in the next decade thirty-seven new firms appeared. Of this group twelve survived into the twentieth century, including such bulwarks of the industry as the New York Life, the Mutual of New York, the Mutual Benefit of New Jersey, the New England Mutual, the Connecticut Mutual, and the Penn Mutual. The country's growing economic independence and maturity made this expansion possible. The new companies began in a prosperous decade by appealing to commercial and professional men in the booming Eastern cities of New York, Philadelphia, Boston, and Hartford.[9]

As dramatic as the number of new and successful companies was their dependence on the mutual form of corporate organization. Up to 1841 three mutual life insurance companies had been established in America; in the subsequent decade at least eighteen more appeared. Several factors accounted for the dramatic change, which extended to all forms of underwriting. For fire and marine companies, the decisive factor was a disastrous fire in 1835, which turned new commercial insurance ventures to mutualization as a means of obtaining capital without exposing a small group of stockholders to heavy, concentrated loss. Life company organization was most affected by the panic of 1837 and the ensuing depression, which dampened the stock-buying enthusiasms of investors. Yet the demand for life insurance in the prosperous cities of the 1840's was patent enough, and entrepreneurs were anxious to tap the market. Mutualization was the ideal solution: it enabled companies to begin with relatively small initial capital guarantees, and had the marketing advantage of luring commercial-minded policyholders with the prospect of sharing the dividend rewards of ownership.

The success of mutualization created a vested interest of established companies which would not encourage the indefinite multiplication of their breed. In 1849 a New York law required insurance firms to place a $100,000 security deposit with the state, thus raising the initial capital needs of a new company to a level mutualization could not reach. But though the life insurance firms of the 1840's choked off the form of capitalization that had created them, they could no more exclude new entrants into their enterprise than could canal, bridge, or railroad companies. Their success gave them power; but it also gave the business an aura of promise which attracted other entrepreneurs.

The organization of the Equitable Life Assurance Society in 1859 as a stock company marked the opening of a new period of insurance expansion. The Civil War gave notable stimulus to the insurance business; it focused attention on the transience of life in the most dramatic possible way. After the war, capital sought fresh investment outlets, among them the life insurance enterprise. Between 1865 and 1870, 107 new companies appeared, almost all stock in form. Most spectacular was the National Life Insurance Company of the United States, organized by the Civil War's leading financier, Jay Cooke, with a congressional charter. In New York alone, companies increased from 14 in 1860 to 69 in 1870; policies from 50,000 to 650,000; insurance in force from \$140,000,000 to \$1,800,000,000; assets from \$20,000,000 to \$229,000-000. The amount of life insurance issued in 1868 was larger than the national debt; and the New York insurance commissioner did not exaggerate when in 1870 he noted that "life insurance has become one of the great business interests of the country." [10]

Such vigorous expansion evoked attempts to impose order on the industry. American Life Conventions were sponsored by the Mutual of New York in 1859 and 1860, and a movement for Federal regulation occurred in the late 1860's. Actuaries such as Sheppard Homans and particularly Elizur Wright played a role as stabilizing influences. Mathematician and actuary, Massachusetts insurance commissioner, and doughty fighter for meaningful regulation and equitable nonforfeiture and valuation laws, Wright more than any other man brought restraint and regulation to a chaotic business.[11]

But though the state of the business called for order, the spirit of the time did not. The New York insurance commissioner, however committed to the interests of the established companies, could not bring himself to support restrictions on the formation of new ones. Multiplication and cutthroat competition remained the unwanted but unavoidable characteristics of the life insurance business. Elizur Wright impatiently looked for popular pressure to check the boom, but Charles Dana of the New York *Sun* astutely concluded: "Sometime, probably after a general crash in life insurance, we can get the public to take an interest . . . It does not do it now." [12]

Then came the panic and depression of the mid-1870's, with an inevitable flood of failures (seventy-five between 1871 and 1877) and heavy declines in insurance in force. Investigations (New York, 1870, 1872, 1873, 1877; Ohio, 1885) denoted the public pressure for reform. The survivors, primarily well-established companies going back to prewar times, had an important stake in a more settled order. During the 1880's, in clear reaction to the anarchy of the preceding decade, came the first signs of meaningful cooperation. Twelve beneficiary societies formed a National Fraternal Congress in 1886. In 1889 the Actuarial Society of America and the Association of Life Insurance Medical Directors conferred the aura of professionalization on important elements of the business; in the following year the organization of the National Association of Life Underwriters did the same for agents. By the end of the century life insurance had attained the capsheaf of respectability with lectures on the subject at Harvard and Wisconsin.[13]

3

The life insurance business took on new forms and qualities suitable to the age. A complex industrialized economy meant rapid urbanization and growing numbers of commercial and professional people. Both developments strengthened the appeal of life insurance in the late nineteenth century. The rise of the cities created an ever growing mass of people detached from the relationships and environment that once had provided security. Previously, on the farm or in the small town, the clan-family or one's neighbors provided social stability and economic safety; property was landed, permanent, protected. In the shifting, expansive, uncertain life of the city, where assets were more fluid and more in jeopardy, the immediate family unit had to seek out its own security. In a world of changing residences, jobs, and friends, life insurance could be a tangible expression of family continuity, responsibility, and security.[14]

Increasingly, certain urban groups were ready to pay for relatively expensive insurance, not only to protect the gains they had made in an unstable society but also, if possible, to add the fillip of speculation to the provision of security. Deferred dividend policies, which combined insurance protection with the possibilities of investment profit, grew greatly in popularity among urban professionals, businessmen, and the more prosperous white-collar workers during the late 1800's. Direct agent selling, accompanied by a growing paraphernalia of advertising, swelled the volume of insurance bought. The result was a striking growth rate. The assets of life insurance companies rose by 12,000 percent during the second half of the nineteenth century. Per capita holdings went from $40.69 in 1885 to $179.14 in 1910. By 1890 more life insurance was held in the United States than in the entire British Empire; soon American holdings easily surpassed the rest of the world's total.[15]

New forms of underwriting arose to meet changes in the nation's economic and social structure. A growing number of people came to handle large sums of money in the complex financial transactions of a mature capitalistic society. During the 1880's surety companies bonding such employees against loss or defalcation came into existence. In 1894 Congress allowed these firms to bond Federal employees; thereafter the expansion of the surety insurance business was rapid.[16]

The most spectacular of the new types of insurance touched upon the millions unable to afford the relatively high price of regular life insurance. The same industrialization and urbanization that created business, professional, and white-collar markets also gathered masses of industrial working families ready to pay, if not for survivors' well-being, at least for the decencies of burial. Especially responsive were the immigrants, who particularly needed the perquisites — social- and self-respect — that insurance could offer.

Special insights and techniques, not common in the American corporate lexicon, were necessary to reach this market. The first successful entrepreneurial response came from the people themselves, in the form of fraternal societies. Usually assessment-plan organizations, the societies had a manifold appeal. They offered the attractions of lodge and clubhouse, of ritual and organization, of familiar faces and customs; and they shut out the hostile new environment. At the same time the fraternal societies offered burial insurance (and occasionally more extensive coverage) which gave them formal, if not real, reason for being. All peoples on the move — Negroes and whites going from rural to urban America, immigrants swelling the industrial and agricultural ranks — cushioned the social and, less successfully, the economic shock of their displacement with these fraternal associations. The great age of the fraternals began in the 1870's, and they grew with the ensuing decades of industrialization and immigration until by 1895 their insurance in force surpassed that of the regular life companies. Although their assessment method of payment was fiscally inferior to the fixed premium plan of most regular companies, it was highly appropriate to the cooperative spirit which gave them meaning. Fraternal insurance vied with regular life insurance in volume at the turn of the century, but its very nature prevented individual societies from attaining considerable size: their essence was exclusivity.[17]

The application of large-scale business methods to the mass insurance market of the poor was not long neglected. Companies selling small, fixed-premium, weekly payment policies to working people serviced the industrial population of mid-nineteenth century England. The Prudential Assurance Company of London, organized in 1854, played the same pioneering role for industrial insurance that the "Old Equitable" of the eighteenth century performed for ordinary life. The English Prudential's success stimulated American emulation. In the same decade in which fraternal societies emerged in force, the 1870's, United States industrial insurance was launched. The requisite heavy urban concentrations of industrial workers had appeared during the Civil War period; the hard times following the 1873 panic created among men of substance a consciousness of the plight of the urban poor and of the moneymaking possibilities in selling burial insurance on a mass scale.

The industrial insurance business prospered despite the fact that its prime markets lay among the same groups which the fraternals served. As substantial corporations with fixed premiums, the industrial firms had an air of stability and business efficiency denied fraternals which too often were at the mercy of dishonest secretaries and an unworkable assessment plan. A fundamental difference in appeal also separated fraternals from industrials. The former offered, in essence, protection from the surrounding milieu; the latter, adjustment to it. To go from the familiar if uncertain protection of the fraternal society to the Americanized, routinized product of the industrial company must have marked, for immigrants and natives alike, a step forward in their adaptation to an urban, industrial society.[18]

So the business of life insurance, long a significant form of corporate enterprise, found in late nineteenth century America substantial fulfillment of its entrepreneurial possibilities. The Massachusetts insurance commissioner commented in 1897 with some awe on the "extraordinary extent [to which] life insurance has come to enter into the business affairs, fortunes and homes of the people. It is no longer considered as a speculation or a luxury, but as an absolute essential to the modern forms and habits of living and business." [19] Out of this juncture of a society and an enterprise emerged a group of great life and industrial insurance companies, which by the end of the century held a towering place among American corporations. These firms were the cumulative product of an entrepreneurial and corporative experience stretching back three hundred years to William Gibbons' first halting attempt to protect the most fundamental of all equities — his life.

II * A Society of Companies

Henry Hyde showed good judgment in 1859 when he called his new firm the Equitable Life Assurance Society. For by 1900 the largest life insurance corporations were complex and consequential enough to be considered major social institutions. In their structure, functions, and interrelations, they took on the attributes of a society of companies.

1

Other well-established enterprises — railroads, steel, oil — were moving steadily toward concentration and consolidation. In so doing, they created the pools, trusts, and monopolies that by 1900 were a central fact of the nation's economic structure, and a major concern of its people. To some extent the same development occurred in life insurance. Under the impact of hard times, the number of companies shrank from 129 in 1870 to 55 in 1882. The Metropolitan Life occasionally absorbed insolvent firms. By the turn of the century smaller companies were raising the complaint, also familiar in other businesses, that the capital necessary to compete effectively with the giants impeded the start of new or the continuation of existing competition.

But monopolistic consolidation was not the keynote of the life insurance industry. From the 1882 trough of 55, the number of companies rose to 126 in 1905. No equivalent of Standard Oil or United States Steel came to dominate the business. Rather, a group of roughly equal corporate giants, and an expanding group at that, dominated the field by 1900. The largest established firms — the Mutual Life Insurance

Company, the Equitable Life Assurance Society, the New York Life Insurance Company — grew steadily and impressively. In addition, two relatively new corporations, the Prudential Insurance Company and the Metropolitan Life Insurance Company, rose to eminence in industrial insurance and began to figure prominently in regular life insurance as well. From the vantage point of 1900, then, the business was as much the province of large corporations as any American enterprise, but it did not seem to be heading toward concentration and monopoly. Instead, the great firms dominating the industry resembled what a later generation would call a corporate oligopoly — modified by the coexistence of a number of smaller but still substantial companies.

The central factor in the life insurance business of the latter part of the nineteenth century was headlong, unchecked growth. At the core of this expansion were the "Big Three" of the industry, the Mutual, the Equitable, and the New York Life. All were New York corporations organized before the Civil War; each struggled with the others for supremacy. The Mutual was America's largest life insurance company from 1855 until the Equitable supplanted it in 1886; the New York Life shouldered aside the Connecticut Mutual Life Insurance Company and the Mutual Benefit Life of Newark to stand third in size in 1885, and surpassed the Equitable in 1899.

In their ceaseless striving for primacy, the three "racers" increasingly dominated their field. By 1890 they did 86 percent of the business handled by New York life insurance companies; and in that year they boasted a collective insurance in force of $2,000,000,000, greater than the next twenty-two American companies combined. Insurance opinion around 1890 often concerned itself with the great companies' size and prospects; for some, corporations of such magnitude already were overextended. But one journal accurately caught the firms' animus when it declared: "Whatever has the element of evolution in it lives. Only so far as the principle of insurance is capable of development is it entitled to continued existence." [1]

The depression of the 1890's did not seriously impede this purpose. Unlike the 1870's, the new period of economic hardship affected only the rate of growth — not the factor of growth itself — of the large companies. The Mutual's president gratefully, if perplexedly, remarked: "How people should have money . . . to spend in life insurance policies under the prevailing conditions is more than I can explain." In 1899 each of the Big Three passed the billion-dollar mark in insurance in force; in 1905 their combined premium income was over $200,000,000. Their growth rate accelerated dramatically: the New York Life's first billion dollars' worth of insurance policies came after fifty-four years; its second came in six.[2]

As the companies blossomed — their assets in 1904 totaled a billion dollars, with two million people holding policies — grandiose comparisons proclaimed the achievement. It was noted that their funds were greater than the amount of currency in circulation within the United States; that their 1904 assets equaled the national wealth of Greece or Norway, or one-tenth the value of the United States' railroad system, or twice the bullion of Great Britain; that their 1906 surplus could pay the interest on the national debt. It was thought to be "the greatest wealth ever concentrated in the control of a few persons for beneficent reasons." The New York Life's John McCall, pressed in 1905 to put a reasonable ceiling on the companies' growth, spoke casually of the "limit of . . . human capacity."[3]

Although the magnitude of the three regular life companies made the heaviest claim on the popular imagination at the turn of the century, industrial companies more than matched the others in the rapidity of their growth. In insurance in force, the Metropolitan stood fifth and the Prudential eighth in 1890; by 1900 they were fourth and fifth; in 1905 the Metropolitan was second to the New York Life. The John Hancock of Boston, far smaller than the two giants, nevertheless figured with the Prudential and the Metropolitan in political matters and questions of industry policy. By 1909, two out of every nine people in the United States were covered by industrial policies, and the three leading companies had 95 percent of the business. They had 3,750,000 policyholders in 1890; 15,750,000 in 1905. In their growth they burst the bonds of localism and specialization. Quickly the Prudential and the Metropolitan developed a national business and, by the turn of the century, had rapidly growing straight life departments which appealed with great success to a lower middle class market untouched by the Big Three.

More than size drew the five largest insurance companies into a corporate society of special intimacy and commonality of interest. Geographical proximity played a part: with four of the firms in New York, and the Prudential nearby in Newark, they were bound by a thousand subtle but real ties of daily executive contact.[4] Common markets and common interests — the complex interplay of competition and cooperation — created highly correlated business techniques. Proximity to the New York investment and money markets guaranteed closely interrelated investment experiences. Equivalent corporate ideologies and the spurs of competition sent the three straight life companies on extensive marketing adventures overseas. Shared regulatory problems made for joint political action.

One measure of the cohesiveness of this society of companies was the degree to which the rest of the industry stood outside. Around the great pentad of the New York–Newark companies stood clusters of lesser, regionally oriented firms. The John Hancock of Boston shared New England insurance market dominance with Hartford's Aetna and Connecticut Mutual. In New Jersey the Mutual Benefit of Newark, fifth in size among American companies during the 1880's, still was a substantial firm by 1900, as was Philadelphia's Penn Mutual. The giant of the West was the Northwestern Mutual of Milwaukee, sixth in insurance in force at the turn of the century.

Significant differences aside from size and geographical propinquity set these lesser firms apart from the leaders. Generally they were more committed to conservative, restrained ways of business. Company spokesmen such as Jacob L. Greene of the Connecticut Mutual and the Mutual Benefit's Amzi Dodd protested against the techniques and the tendencies of large-scale corporate expansion. In 1867 Dodd warned Elizur Wright: "Unless more sobriety be maintained in making promises or raising expectations it would seem that the whole business will be brought down to a level where plain and honest men will not wish to stand." And at the end of the century, when the great companies developed sophisticated and productive liaisons with the state and national political structures, Greene fretted over "the disposition of those concerned in various enterprises to turn to the state for aid." President John McCall of the New York Life contemptuously regarded him as "so ultra-conservative that I think he would oppose anything he did not originate." [5]

Differences cropped up in the specifics of business, too. Greene and Dodd and their companies, as well as the New England Mutual, staunchly fought deferred dividend policies. The Northwestern Mutual stopped offering these speculative but profitable contracts in the early 1900's. While the Penn Mutual had a respectable third of a billion dollars' worth of insurance in force in 1905, its president earned a salary of $25,000, paltry by Big Five standards. Although the Northwestern's selling methods yielded nothing in vigor to the larger companies, the firm nevertheless had no desire for business outside of the United States. And though the Aetna's Morgan Bulkeley was a United States Senator from Connecticut, he did not share the bold enthusiasm of Prudential president and fellow Senator John F. Dryden for Federal regulation of the life insurance business.[6]

2

For the corporate institution, as for any other, the most readily discernible continuum of historical development is the story of its leadership. A distinctive group of managers dominated the great life insurance companies during the latter half of the nineteenth century: Henry Hyde of the Equitable; Frederick S. Winston and Richard McCurdy of the Mutual; William H. Beers and John McCall of the New York Life; John F. Dryden of the Prudential; Joseph F. Knapp and John R. Hegeman of the Metropolitan. These men shared a hearty enthusiasm for growth at almost any cost, an enthusiasm fed in part by prospects of pecuniary reward and, in the reluctant words of a competitor, "more, perhaps, for the pride in doing it than otherwise."[7] Aggressive, self-confident, filled with a desire for large and momentous achievement, they were the conflux of the forces that turned their enterprises into massive corporations; they were the necessary agents of the firms' maturation into a society of companies at the century's end.

Henry B. Hyde was the prime mover and best embodiment of the post–Civil War life insurance business. Authoritarian and hard-driving, immensely able and energetic, full of self-esteem, in the habit of viewing his company as his own property, he belonged to that select group of late nineteenth century entrepreneurs which included Andrew Carnegie, James J. Hill, John D. Rockefeller. This most masterful of insurance entrepreneurs made his way in a business already well established. Hyde's father had been the most successful agent of the Mutual, America's largest pre–Civil War company. Henry Hyde himself was an employee of the Mutual when he chose to strike out on his own. Only twenty-five years old in 1859, he took rooms directly over his former employer (this was, he said, a natural "sentiment" for him), and from his window projected a thirty-foot sign — which dwarfed the advertisement below — proclaiming the existence of his new company, the Equitable Life Assurance Society.[8]

Hyde's special qualities brought him rapid success. By 1886 the

Equitable had insurance in force surpassing its rival, the Mutual; it had become the world's largest life insurance company. Intensive, imaginative — and expensive — marketing and agency techniques, and, most important, the introduction of deferred dividend policies were the means by which Hyde wrought his achievement. With sure instinct, he satisfied the speculative-protectionist yearnings of multitudes of middle class Americans. Thus he identified the life insurance business with the most vital economic drives of the time.

The Mutual reacted to the challenge like an uncertain but still powerful old giant. Frederick Winston, the company's president since 1853, was a cold, overbearing, often arrogant executive. His was the fundamentally undaring leadership of a man at the head of an established, dominant corporation. He never fully apprehended the tremendous appeal of life insurance to the business and professional classes of an urbanizing, industrializing America.

Winston's first response to the Equitable's growing success was vigorous, often brutal opposition. A spectacular competition between the two companies flowered in the late 1860's and the early 1870's. Hyde pitted his salesmanship and deferred dividend policies against the older, richer Mutual's dividend power and established organization and reputation. Above the grim, persistent, unrecorded struggle between the companies' agents, paid insurance journalists engaged in boisterous verbal dogfights. One of these journalists, when not in jail for criminal libel, profited from the impartial sale of his favors to both companies.[9]

But Winston did not, in the last analysis, share Hyde's ruthless commitment to business volume. He once predicted, "In the future, the struggle will be between conservatism and audacity"; and his ultimate allegiance lay with the former value. In 1874 Hyde reported to Elizur Wright: "We have buried the hatchet with the Mutual Life, & trust there will be no more 'war,' & consequently no more expenses." While premature, the statement presaged a change in the Mutual's reaction to the rise of the Equitable: opposition gradually gave way to acquiescence. Winston was afraid that deferred dividend policy lapses made the issuing company unpopular, and after a halfhearted attempt at marketing them he abandoned the experiment. He turned instead to premium reductions as a competitive device. But this dangerous innovation shocked the rest of the insurance business, while it failed to pique the speculative interests of the policy-buying public, and it soon was dropped. Winston in effect conceded defeat when in 1873 he proposed that the Mutual limit its size to 100,000 policyholders. Thereafter he and Hyde became friendly once again, and the Equitable moved more easily toward parity with its rival.[10]

Winston's death in 1885 put at the head of the Mutual a man ready to renew the struggle for primacy. Richard McCurdy did not, perhaps, have Hyde's executive and selling abilities, but he easily matched the other in his commitment to the aggressive pursuit of business. Like Hyde he came naturally to the insurance business; his father had been the Mutual's leading director. But his upper class upbringing and a Harvard College and Law School education gave his business drives a more sophisticated tone. Publicity, notoriety — for his company, for himself — repelled him. He was readier to rationalize (often, it seemed, hypocritically) his business impulses. It was as though his social and educational advantages made it necessary for him to mask a ravenous entrepreneurial lust. He looked with some scorn on Hyde as a parvenu, and with heavy contempt rejected Winston's surrender to the Equitable. The Mutual's alternatives, as he saw them, were meekly to "subside into the position of the Connecticut Mutual, the Mutual Benefit, and New England Mutual — good second and third class companies — with only its age and its respectability to rest on, or . . . bravely take up the work which it practically laid down ten years ago." His choice was clear: "As population and wealth increase, so must the volume of our business." With revealing imagery he spoke of the company's reinvigoration: "Now . . . you see the fires burning brightly under boilers that are no longer cold, and the wheels not only beginning to move but actually gaining speed at every revolution, the great machine developing new energy with every stroke of the piston and the huge mass moving with increasing speed and power." [11]

The New York Life did not figure at first in the consuming struggle between the Equitable and the Mutual for leadership. As late as 1890 the company's expenses were lower, its executive force smaller, than those of the other two firms. Morris Franklin, its president from 1848 until 1885, embodied far more than Winston a conservative business attitude that Hyde and McCurdy had rendered antiquarian. But Franklin's successor, William H. Beers, shared the others' zest for expansion and size. Suggestively he came to office in the same year as McCurdy. Not as forceful as Hyde and McCurdy, Beers nevertheless quickly swung his company into the swift-flowing stream of competition dominated by the others.[12]

But a scandal in the early 1890's led to Beers's sudden departure from the New York Life. Its revelation suggested that the reckless quest for size was not without its penalties. The New York Life's cashier, Theodore M. Banta, was an outspoken critic of Beers's administration; he disliked the president's emphasis on rapid growth. In late 1887 and 1888, Banta made a series of charges regarding the improper placement of company investments, fiscal irregularities, and an overlarge reserve. The charges, at first shunted by a directors' committee, took on added weight in 1891. The New York *Times*, possibly instigated by the other firms, exposed administrative troubles within the company, fixing especially on defalcations in its Spanish American department. Banta publicly supported these attacks. The New York Life responded by filing suit for libel against the *Times* and firing the cashier.[13]

Reactions to the scandal were numerous and swift. A policyholders' committee formed, and the New York insurance department launched a special examination of the company. Even a board of directors' committee admitted that "the business of the Company has outgrown the methods and checks now in use." Beers bowed under the pressure: he spoke of the strain on his health ("it is only a matter of time as to how much longer I can exist under it") and gave way in 1892 to a new president, John McCall.

No great alteration in company policy seemed likely to come from McCall. He did cancel an overgenerous contract given ex-president Beers as a New York Life adviser, and ended the company's libel suit against the *Times;* but the directors who selected him noted his "willingness to do as little as possible to disturb present arrangements." McCall's presidency did, however, mark the introduction of a new element into life insurance management. Though sharing the devotion of Hyde and McCurdy to untrammeled expansion, he was committed also to new and more sophisticated concepts. The New York Life executive committee later characterized the company's troubles in the early 1890's as a deficiency "in that part of its organization which touched the public." McCall, active in New York Democratic politics, had been a state insurance commissioner and then comptroller and political liaison man for the Equitable. Clearly, the New York Life chose him for his public relations value and political skills as much as for his ability at life insurance marketing.[14]

At the time of McCall's appointment, the leading industrial insurance firms were just beginning to enter the select circle of great corporate enterprises. They had already undergone a process of managerial development strikingly similar to that of the Big Three. The Prudential's first president, Allen L. Bassett, was forced out of office in 1879 primarily because of his inability to secure the increased capital needed by an expanding company. But even he had verbally committed the Prudential to participation "in the grand race for success across the Continent." In 1881 John F. Dryden, from the beginning the active managerial force in the Prudential, became president. His perception of the marketing possibilities of industrial insurance and his devotion to unlimited expansion put him in the same class with Hyde, McCurdy, and Beers; his polish and sense of politics, which took him eventually to the United States Senate, gave him much in common with McCall.[15]

The Metropolitan and the John Hancock, not very successful as straight life companies, established industrial departments in 1879. The impact of the depression of the 1870's convinced the Metropolitan's management that lesser companies stood little chance against the older, wealthier, larger ones. Thereupon it "turned its attention from this uneven competition . . . toward a distinctive form of business." Joseph F. Knapp, president of the company from 1871 to 1891, brought to this change in business purpose the drive and determination of the other pioneers in life insurance growth. He and Dryden engaged in a bitter competition during the 1880's which closely resembled the Hyde-Winston struggle a decade before. And Knapp's longtime assistant and successor, John R. Hegeman, had harmonizing and mediating abilities similar to those of McCall and Dryden. Appropriately his presidency began almost contemporaneously with that of the New York Life chief executive.[16]

The John Hancock in its smaller business environment shared the managerial experiences of the industrial giants. Stephen H. Rhodes came to its presidency from the Massachusetts insurance commissionership in 1879. He immediately established an industrial insurance branch, whose success took the company into undisputed third place in that field and to occasional confederation with the Metropolitan and Prudential.[17]

3

The struggle for primacy raged unabated among the great life and industrial insurance companies at the turn of the century. If anything, the rise of the New York Life and the industrial companies' growing interest in the possibilities of the regular life insurance business should have intensified the competitive atmosphere. The Prudential created an ordinary insurance branch in 1886 which did 3 percent of the company's business in 1890 and 37 percent by 1905. The Metropolitan revived its regular policy business in 1892, the John Hancock in 1902.

Nevertheless, during the 1890's values and aspirations quite at odds with those common to the competitive ethos began to appear within this society of companies. Traces of these changes were everywhere, but executive leadership reflected the evolution with particular clarity. McCall of the New York Life and Hegeman of the Metropolitan had managerial qualities not directly germane to life insurance marketing. Even the great figures of the late nineteenth century expansion — Hyde, McCurdy, Dryden — were, by the 1890's, interested in more than the race for size. Hyde, sated with success, declared in 1890: "My first ambition was to make the Equitable . . . the biggest life insurance company in the world. Henceforth it will be my ambition to make it the best." McCurdy retained the appearance of aggressiveness; when the Mutual's 1890 business failed to reach the goal he set for it, he pugnaciously announced that "there is no intention on the part of the Executive to steer the ship ashore or anywhere near it." But he spent much of the century's last decade maintaining an uneasy truce with the Equitable. Several times he responded to competition with attempts to get the New York legislature to establish legal limits on the companies' yearly business — an essentially negative and restrictive approach more in line with the Winston of the 1870's than the McCurdy of the 1880's.[18]

Aspects of the business other than insurance sales came to demand the magnates' attention. This was due in part to the growing complexity of life insurance. Under investigation in 1905, McCurdy revealed a woeful ignorance of his firm's operations. The agency business had "not been under my particular observation for a great many years." He declared, "I have never overruled one of the heads of the executive departments in my life"; for so authoritarian a man, this was an admission of lack of technical knowledge rather than a proclamation of administrative policy. Hegeman, too, confessed that "the business some time ago outgrew me."[19]

The leaders increasingly were concentrating on their companies' investment activities. With its boundless possibilities of corporate influence and personal gain, the placement of life insurance assets piqued the interest of executives for whom, perhaps, the appeal of marketing competition had become passé. McCurdy liked to talk of the "pure banking" role of life insurance, and considered "legitimate methods of increasing accumulation systematically employed" at least as important a business attribute as "management freed from antiquated precedent and dead tradition." James Hazen Hyde, the son of the Equitable's founder, said of his preparation at the turn of the century to assume command of the company, "my attention had been specially directed toward finance and general executive work." [20]

As a result, this period saw the rise of men who took over the business end of company operations from chief executives whose real interests lay elsewhere. George W. Perkins was brought into the New York Life by McCall as "my right-hand man in the agency business," and with ardent assistants (Darwin P. Kingsley, Thomas A. Buckner) vitalized the company's selling force. In the Equitable, James W. Alexander, longtime and not overly dynamic assistant to Henry Hyde, took the presidency upon the latter's death in 1899. The assumption was that Henry Hyde's son James Hazen, upon coming into full control of a majority of the Equitable's stock in 1906, would accede to his father's place. But vice-president Gage Tarbell quickly emerged as the man in charge of agency and marketing matters. For all practical purposes, the Equitable's insurance selling activities were under Tarbell's control after the elder Hyde's death. Business operations in the Metropolitan rested not so much with president Hegeman as with vice-president Haley Fiske ("I . . . have charge of the whole company, except the financial end"). Only in the Mutual and the Prudential did McCurdy and Dryden maintain the tradition of the strong-handed president. But as finance and politics absorbed their attention, men of specialized business skills and interests came to play roles of importance: first vice-presidents Robert A. Granniss and Dr. Walter R. Gillette in the Mutual, agency director Leslie Ward in the Prudential. By 1905 much executive power had come into even more sophisticated and specialized hands. Corporation lawyers Richard Lindabury in the Prudential and Bainbridge Colby and Elihu Root in the Equitable took significant parts in company decision-making.[21]

Powers behind the scenes — Warwicks — had existed before: McCurdy, Beers, Dryden, had been prime movers in their companies for years before each became president. But previously, figurehead chief executives and strong-minded Warwicks alike had been dedicated primarily to their companies' marketing activities. Now a functional distinction had arisen between hard-driving assistants in charge of the firms' business machinery and presidents concerned more with high finance, public relations, and politics. By the 1890's, the channels of responsibility and authority were sufficiently organized, the pattern of the life insurance business sufficiently defined, so that it was possible to dispense with the heavy-handed entrepreneurial leadership characteristic of the decades following the Civil War.

More personal features of the managerial elite bespoke the quick maturity of the life insurance business. Physical prepossession counted heavily in an enterprise so dependent upon salesmanship. Henry Hyde, tall and domineering, the heavy-set McCall and McCurdy, the towering and long-maned Hegeman, the immaculate Dryden, commanded respect and confidence as much by their appearance as by their abilities. George Perkins' manner exuded the easy *expertise* which characterized his executive performance.

Relatively high educational levels and familial backgrounds far from the image of the self-made man were commonplace among the insurance leaders. Richard McCurdy boasted in 1893: "Probably in no other business are so many educated intelligences brought into the service of the participants in its success." Hyde and Perkins did not go to college, but both were the sons of successful agents in the companies that first employed them. McCurdy, son of a leading Mutual trustee, was a product of Harvard College and Harvard Law School; McCall had a politically prominent father and an education at Albany Commercial College; Darwin P. Kingsley, long Perkins' closest associate in the New York Life and the company's president from 1907, had a B.A. and an M.A. from the University of Vermont; Haley Fiske was graduated from Rutgers; Gage Tarbell was a lawyer; John F. Dryden had gone to Yale for several years (and was capable of chastizing a Senatorial colleague with his feet on his desk: "Come come, Senator. Take down your feet, this isn't the House of Representatives, you know").[22] With style and flair the chief executives of the society of companies took themselves, often in clusters, to palatial country estates: McCurdy and Dryden to the New Jersey countryside near Morristown and Bernardsville; Hegeman and several of the New York Life's chieftains, including George Perkins, to Westchester; Hyde to Bay Shore in Long Island; McCall to "Shadow Lawn" at West End, New Jersey.

These were intensely vocal and articulate men — McCall, McCurdy, Perkins, Fiske, and Dryden especially so. In a national magazine, McCurdy commemorated a recuperative trip in the West with a poem written in the form of a Greek choral ode.[23] The willingness of Dryden, Perkins, McCall, and Fiske to communicate with the public was notable at a time when big businessmen, with the conspicuous exception of Andrew Carnegie, were not particularly responsive to this demand upon their time and talents.

Henry Hyde's son, James Hazen, educated to a high degree of affectation at Harvard and destined by his doting father to take over the Equitable, was at once the epitome and the most disastrous example of the cultivated insurance man. A big business apologist had argued in 1902: "Even when . . . fortunes pass by inheritance into the hands of degenerate descendants their influence for good is but little impaired; since their wealth is in corporations under the control of the 'Fittest.' " But the younger Hyde's place in the Equitable seemed to many the very embodiment of irresponsible and untrammeled control. The hauteur so impressive in Henry Hyde or Dryden or Fiske or McCurdy became comic in this young dilettante who enjoyed such alien pleasures as violet boutonnieres and sweeping through New York's financial district in his coach-and-four. In a *Harper's* article he commented on the joys of coaching through France: "To me, these simple country people are never-failing sources of interest, and their wonderment and open curiosity were most amusing." A special commitment to a public consciousness, if not conscience, was a characteristic of all the insurance leaders. But James Hazen Hyde's social perceptions were an almost satiric distortion: "To me it has always seemed that women are better off if they have a little house-work to do. During a recent trip in Texas, I visited one of the largest lunatic asylums. There I found that a large percentage of insane women were wives of farmers, the chief cause of their insanity being simply *ennui*." It may well have been that the younger Hyde was a luxury possible only in a mature corporate elite.[24]

Much of the underlying transformation of the life insurance business was summed up in the career of the New York Life's George W. Perkins. A highly successful agency manager in Chicago, Perkins was summoned to the home office to be McCall's liaison man with the company's agents. He quickly became the driving force behind the swelling insurance business of the New York Life, the prime creator of agency, managerial, and marketing policy. With McCall he vitalized the company's overseas business, and by the late 1890's was shaping its investment policy as well. The two men skilfully used politics and publicity to further the company's well-being. The contacts and reputation derived from this diverse corporate experience impelled Perkins into close relations with, and then a partnership in, J. P. Morgan and Company; from there he went to the finance committee chairmanship of United States Steel, to a central role in the creation of the International Harvester Company, and to an important advisory place in Theodore Roosevelt's Progressive party.

Here was a new man in corporate enterprise, in investment finance, in national politics: in all of the loci of power in the United States at the turn of the century. He was an ideologue, a man driven by a vision of the corporation as an institution of great social and political and economic power. He was, in a latter-day phrase, the first of the business generalists of the new, complex, twentieth century capitalism — men whose ability to apprehend and manipulate power enabled them to move easily through the worlds of business, finance, politics.[25]

Yet Perkins was not a man of power in the sense of consummated control. All of his skill and influence in the insurance world did not prevent the Armstrong investigation of 1905, which ended the kind of corporation he envisaged and created. All of his money and place did not win the presidency for Theodore Roosevelt in 1912. He died in 1920, limited in influence and mentally shattered. Perkins' career of impressive and diverse powers, and ultimately decisive limitations, epitomized the corporate group that produced him: the turn-of-the-century society of life insurance companies.

III * An Ideology of Power

The evolution of executive leadership was but one expression of a maturing society of companies. The burgeoning life insurance giants also took on an ideological commitment to public service and private power not common to corporate enterprise. The need for self-justification apart from the profit motive stemmed from the palpable public interest in life insurance as "essentially a *social* economy." President James W. Alexander of the Equitable put the proposition in its classic form: "assuredly, an institution which exists for the benefit of widows and orphans . . . is one which ought not to be conducted on a low plane of competition." Legal and legislative precedents underscored the fact that life insurance companies bore to a special degree the public obligation that belonged to all chartered corporations.

Nor did insurance men shy from the opportunity of articulating their business' *raison d'être*. Indeed, a quasi-public role had a positive business value: it was as useful to emphasize the social duty to sell insurance as it was to stress the social obligation of buying it. The head of the nation's largest insurance agency found "abundant indications" that churches and social organizations "hold that any man not having life insurance should not be permitted by public opinion to marry." [1]

Thus the prevailing doctrine had it that life insurance was an instrument of peculiar social benevolence; its dispensers, bearers of a special social responsibility. The conservative president of the Connecticut Mutual, Jacob L. Greene, compared a life insurance company to a university and its officers to trustees. Vice-President George W. Perkins of the New York Life, at the antipodes of business policy from Greene, referred to his company's assets as a "trust fund" and to its officers as "trustees." The Equitable's Gage Tarbell spoke of "trustees of the most sacred trust . . . on earth"; the Mutual's McCurdy, of "a great and sacred trust."

Trusteeship implied responsibility (Oliver Wendell Holmes thought that life insurance "should be . . . the most secure of all enterprises"), and insurance officers in theory assumed the burden. Hegeman uprightly declared of the business: "Of all things its methods and conduct must surpass all the wives of all the Caesars — in being *beyond suspicion.*" Company contributions to flood, depression, and yellow fever sufferers gave testimony to a rudimentary social consciousness.[2]

The theme of social responsibility drew strength from the rise of industrial insurance. The values attached to life insurance had a special poignancy when applied to the underprivileged. The "thrifty cottager" and the "honest poor" (as opposed to the "indigent pauper") joined the pantheon of beneficiaries previously dominated by the widow and the orphan. Industrial insurance, which "performs a mission not covered by any other institution in the world's affairs," inculcated thrift, patience, courage, morality, and industry in its policyholders; was "a beneficent and conservative force that can hardly be over-rated"; and was thought to lower the rate of pauper burials, thus assuaging taxpayers too.[3]

In one sense this was a return, after a long night of entrepreneurial irresponsibility, to the Adam Smithian mystique of public good emerging from private gain. John McCall described his business as "a form of communism that allows unrestrained individualism," and Richard McCurdy reveled in the thought that life insurance was "an occupation which combined business with pleasure, business with sentiment, business with philanthropy, business with great and ennobling ideas of humanity." The Metropolitan's John Hegeman admitted to being impelled by "purely business motives," but could not see that "these motives . . . in any degree detract from the inherent beneficence of the business itself."

These sentiments had little weight when set against the ideological commitment to growth and the force of competition. Thus, Richard McCurdy spoke of policyholders "participating in a great movement for the benefit of humanity at large." But when pressed on the fact that the Mutual's advertising stressed policyholder moneymaking, not philanthropy, he blamed it on "very swift competition from very strong and active and ingenious competitors." Nevertheless, the image of Emersonian self-reliance encouraged and set to work through life insurance was a compelling one. It added substantially to the unusual prestige of the insurance enterprise.[4]

The special qualities of the insurance business set it apart from the rest of the corporate economy. A New York Life official noted that no other enterprise had its own press and literature, and McCurdy majestically reminded his board: "It should be recognized always that we are a *Life Insurance Company* . . . and that we are not a bank, a railway company or an industrial corporation that we own and can do with as we can with our own property." Here, too, was a business with a special relationship to the element of time. The nature of the policy contract, and of the investments supporting it, presupposed a considerable corporate longevity. McCurdy in 1894 held forth on the prospects of the Mutual a half-century hence. Declaring that the company's record to date marked "an epoch in the history of human progress," he boldly predicted that it would have three billion dollars' worth of insurance in force in 1940.[5]

It was not surprising that the magnates of an enterprise so consequential turned often to institutional imagery. As one spokesman put it, the life insurance business performed the functions of family, church, and state. Identification with religion came readily. McCurdy liked to speak of his business as a missionary activity. Henry Hyde, too, spoke easily of an Equitable agent's "missionary work" in developing a life insurance market in Spain, and George W. Perkins assured a correspondent: "Our profession requires the same zeal, the same enthusiasm, the same earnest purpose that must be born in a man if he succeeds as a minister of the Gospel." Darwin P. Kingsley of the New York Life found signs of grace everywhere: "What a picture of belief — I had almost said of faith — is presented by the securities that center in the vaults of the . . . companies doing an international business." He compared insurance agents to preachers, and thought that the deferred dividend policy resembled a religious doctrine of rewards and punishments in its effectiveness in spreading the gospel — the gospel of life insurance.[6]

By the turn of the century more mundane comparisons seemed appropriate to the burgeoning size, wealth, and influence of the business. Company sales booklets distributed in the Civil War era stressed life insurance's protective, beneficiary function; those issued around 1900 emphasized the success of particular companies in accumulating surplus, issuing dividends, earning profits. It became customary to consider, along with "the people's appreciation of its beneficent mission," the "commanding place" life insurance "has suddenly gained in American business and finance." One insurance leader described the change in emphasis more explicitly: "We have heretofore thought almost exclusively of [life insurance's] . . . moral and beneficent side; hereafter we shall think more of what we may call its physical side, of the enormous force which it will be compelled . . . hereafter to exercise in the affairs of men." [7]

The enormity of the business became a ponderable factor in the ideology of life insurance. A company attorney pointed out that "as an institution" it "collects more money each year than the Government itself, disburses more than the receipts of all the custom-houses, and administers an accumulated treasure greater than all the money now in circulation in this country or the entire capital of our national banks." John McCall was impressed by his business' "colossal proportions" and the "still more enormous proportions which, by the operation of natural laws, it must assume in the future." Size and wealth were thought to add force to the beneficent purpose of the enterprise. The concentration of large blocs of securities in companies acting for millions of policyholders, rather than in the hands of "the very rich," excited one insurance man: "What a powerful influence for health, for financial and political peace!"

Benevolence and power thus fused into an integrated corporate purpose. As John McCall put it: "The life insurance companies of to-day cannot be truthfully described either as money-making or local institutions; for there is neither profit in, nor limit to, their benefactions." Although the business did not participate in the corporate consolidations common at the turn of the century, its leaders upheld the prevailing values of concentration and harmony; one of them considered the growth of the great insurance companies to be "the most striking feature in an age full of remarkable activities." "Great is the power of system, order and discipline," declared Henry Hyde; and James Alexander approvingly observed: "This is the day of concentration in business." Although McCurdy warned his board lest the time's industrial consolidation and expansion "befog our perceptions and lead to confused notions of our own powers," he vigorously espoused "the substitution of the accumulative idea" (in the form of deferred dividends) for "distribution—dispersal—dissemination of assets." [8]

The ideology of life insurance reflected also the ethos of national expansion prevailing around 1900. Insurance men, no less than imperialists, hopefully looked beyond America's borders. Darwin P. Kingsley proclaimed: "Life insurance to-day is the very spirit of the Anglo-Saxon race; its methods are masterful; it seeks to melt and mingle with all men; it learns and it teaches; but chiefly, it has an ideal for which it strenuously labors." His interpretation of the Big Three's foreign business was that life insurance now had "more serious work": the development of "a community of interest with all men." Soaringly he proclaimed: "The strong boxes of these companies are a prophecy of the parliament of man." John McCall, too, was impressed by American life insurance "as a beneficent enterprise which has assumed international proportions." [9]

As parallels with religion seemed most appropriate to convey the beneficence of life insurance, so did the metaphors of statecraft suggest the strength and influence of the society of great companies. Mutual's president McCurdy spoke to his board as "your prime minister"; Perkins called the New York Life's foreign business division the company's "State Department"; a Washington lobbyist referred to himself as the "Confidential Agent" of his firm. Even so mundane a factor as business competition became cloaked in the language, and the hypocrisies, of war. Hyde took up the patois with particular ease, complaining to McCurdy that "although our guns are silenced we are still under fire," or piously denying "that I had under conditions of peace taken any hostile action against you or your Company, [but] . . . of course under pressure of continuous attack I cannot but protect the interests of the Equitable. Under all circumstances in the past my voice has been for peace." To his consulting actuary, Sheppard Homans, he declared: "I always listen to overtures of peace from any quarter, but if the companies do not desire peace, I am prepared for war, and I think on the whole I rather like war" — which, if understated, was true enough. The imagery of nationalism came readily to Darwin Kingsley; exhorting a group of agents to greater efforts, he concluded: "If you are the best kind of a New-York Life man, you feel much as the old Roman felt when his loyalty and his pride of nationality had taught the world that in some sense every Roman was a King." [10]

All of the artifacts of a political order were at hand: an often venal press; wars between sovereign companies; agent armies in the field. The great companies' leadership was deeply involved in state, local, and national politics by the turn of the century, and abundant evidence suggested that political skills were necessary for success in the enterprise. Stewart L. Woodford, United States ambassador to Spain during the tense years preceding the Spanish-American War and former counsel for the Metropolitan, found his insurance experience distinctly applicable to his new situation. He wrote to Hegeman of his first meeting with the Spanish Foreign Minister: "I talked pretty plainly. I fancy that I copied your suavity and [Haley] Fiske's directness." Political experience was a notable element in the background of several leading life insurance men. Stephen H. Rhodes, president of the John Hancock, had been mayor of Taunton, Massachusetts, as well as a member of the state's Senate and its insurance commissioner. John McCall grew up in the intensely political atmosphere of his father's Albany tavern, and made an early career in the Democratic party of New York. He was the state's insurance superintendent when the Equitable hired him in 1886 as its comptroller. Darwin P. Kingsley was Colorado's superintendent of insurance when in 1888 he began an association with the New York Life which led eventually to the company's presidency.

Successful insurance men, if not originally politicians, sometimes eventually became so; and again the connection between their business and public careers seemed more than casual. One year after Morgan G. Bulkeley was elected president of the Aetna Life Insurance Company of Hartford, he became the city's mayor. From 1888 to 1903 he was governor of Connecticut, and in 1905 was elected to the United States Senate. John M. Pattison, who had been an Ohio legislator, state senator, and United States congressman before becoming president of the Union Central Life Insurance Company, later was elected governor of Ohio (in the same year that Bulkeley went to the Senate). A complaisant New Jersey legislature made the Prudential's John Dryden a United States senator in 1902. And George W. Perkins, after a long period of behind-the-scenes activity, emerged on the political stage as Theodore Roosevelt's adviser and confidant in the 1912 Bull Moose campaign.[11]

The intimacy between politics and life insurance was natural. The business, more than most at the time, was involved in, and had demands to make upon, an extensive state regulatory structure, and stood to gain by drawing capable men from that system. But there was another, more positive, factor at work. The nature of the business itself always placed a high premium on the political arts; by 1900 this was particularly true of the society of great companies. The institutionalization that came with pandemic growth lessened the need for chief executives who were primarily insurance technicians and salesmen. An extensive regulatory structure and growing corporate emphasis upon organization, morale, and public relations put a premium on the skills of politically minded executives.

It was not surprising that companies so led and motivated treated government regulation with something other than the easy contempt of their corporate peers. Supervision sometimes was welcomed as a prop to life insurance's reliability rather than feared as a drag on its capacities. James Alexander boasted — where an executive in another business might have complained — that an "electric searchlight is ever directed on all the transactions of American life assurance companies. There is no other enterprise which is subjected to such public scrutiny." The size and importance of life insurance, he thought, made it "worthy of the best endeavors of the best people in the community to keep it decent, pure, and dignified." A number of leaders — including McCall, McCurdy, Dryden, Perkins, Kingsley, and Alexander — interested themselves in a movement for Federal regulation of the life insurance business: national control, a matter of concern to other corporate groups, seemed a safeguard and an opportunity to the executives of the great companies. When the clouds of the 1905 scandals began to gather, the reaction of the New York Life's executive committee was to speak of "our increasing sense of responsibility in the administration of a business which comprehends the whole civilized world in its activities," and to commend "the policy of an open ledger . . . the value of international supervision." [12]

In a speech to Boston's Commonwealth Club in October 1905, Louis D. Brandeis handed down a classic indictment of the large life insurance companies. He recognized their marketing achievements, and noted that they were "the creditors of our great industries with all the power which that implies." But his conclusions — that their power was exercised so "selfishly, dishonestly . . . inefficiently" that they had become "the greatest economic menace of to-day"; that "these large insurance companies through the power which inheres in the control of quick capital expose the community to dangers which no other kind of corporation presents to so great an extent" — turned the companies' strengths into a prime social menace.[13]

Brandeis' denunciation underlined a home truth: that ideologies had consequences. By proclaiming the social importance of their enterprise, the life insurance magnates earned the advantages of quasi-public status. But they also assured that they would be subject to countering restraints. The same complex of tensions — between opportunity and responsibility, between power and diffusion — appears in every sector of the great companies' business — their corporate structure, their domestic and overseas marketing, their investment and political influence. With unparalleled purpose and skill the managers sought to control their business environment; but everywhere their efforts came into conflict with limiting factors which finally put significant checks upon their power and altered the face of the life insurance enterprise.

What still remains is to look at business as a social system.

Paul Lazarsfeld, "Reflections on Business"

Part Two * The Business of Life Insurance

Rapid growth and impressive size were the determinants that shaped the companies' corporate structure and their domestic business technique. Giantism produced great wealth, which made control of the large firms a tempting goal. Yet purposeful domination of companies so committed to an image of public service was difficult; and the gap between ambition and fulfillment generated the evils of nepotism and managerial irresponsibility. In addition, the size of the great firms led to increasingly complex and sophisticated business techniques, which blunted purposeful decisionmaking. Thus growth provided the companies with the sinews of power; but it also raised a need for bureaucratized system and order which acted as a constraining force.

IV * Growth and the Corporate Structure

As the substantial life insurance firms evolved into a corporate institution, their internal organization changed. Functions of increasing scope and complexity led to the bureaucratization of the corporate structure: a New York Life trustees' committee concluded in 1892 that "the business of the Company has outgrown the methods and checks now in use." [1] Home office staffs grew to impressive size: the Prudential's staff went from 89 employees in 1883 to 250 in 1890; the Metropolitan employed 1081 in 1897; the Mutual employed 645 in 1906. The Mutual's 1903 home office organization had a policy loan department; treasurer's (investment) department; law department; agency department; cashier's department; auditor's department; department of supplies, printing, and advertising; actuary's department; medical department; department of revision; secretary's department; policy department; records and mails department; and foreign department. By the beginning of the new century the Metropolitan was well on its way to becoming one of the twentieth century's prime symbols of corporate vastness and efficiency. Its president, John R. Hegeman, appropriately was called "a business machine"; its home office had more typewriters than any other office building in the world.[2]

As company departments proliferated, authority became more centralized: bureaucratization intensified the pressure for decisionmaking at the highest managerial level. The New York Life's trustees in 1887 formally gave President Beers and his vice-presidents receipting and endorsing authority over company bills and notes. Two years later the rapidity and intensity of the competitive struggle for size led Beers to ask for authorization to take such measures "as he should consider best from time to time to protect and advance the interests . . . of the Company." [3] The 1890's saw steady delegations of power by the directors to the Prudential's officers. The top managers could convey company-held real estate and report to the board later; could open business in any state and file the necessary papers without specific authorization; could assign mortgages and deliver releases and quitclaims; could sell stocks and bonds. In 1901 the executive committee's bill-paying was systematized so that the committee would not have to give its detailed approval; in 1904 the board formally delegated broad authority to the president and the three leading vice-presidents.[4]

Boards of directors, once sources of capital, business acumen, and decisionmaking, sank to rubberstamp roles. By 1905, Mutual trustee George S. Haven did not know that he was a member of the salary committee, or what salary was paid to President McCurdy. A director's chief function came to rest in public relations: to appeal to prospective customers by his regional or other representation, or to reassure existing policyholders by his respectability and stature. Trustees such as David Ames Wells, who had served on the New York Life's board because he was the best equipped man of his time to deal with tax matters, were no longer necessary in institutionalized corporations that had employees, even departments, to handle such affairs.[5]

Committee minutes, once evocative records of company life and development, became after 1900 empty, formal things, fitting chronicles of the ritualistic meetings that produced them. As executive decisionmaking concentrated in top management by authority as well as in fact, secrecy became easier in practice and seemed more necessary in theory. With remarkably unfortunate imagery, Richard McCurdy discussed the problem: "Civilized men cannot perform all the offices of nature upon the sidewalk, however proper and necessary they may be in themselves. So the inner workings of the machinery of any technical business cannot be exposed to the observation of the public with propriety." George W. Perkins asserted: "you have got to give men authority . . . you have got to give them latitude." [6]

The growth and centralization of the corporate structure expressed itself materially, too, in the expansion of home office buildings. A sentiment quite independent of the need for space impelled the company chieftains to vie with each other in erecting impressive edifices. Grandiose as geometric increases in size and wealth may have been, they lacked the satisfying corporeality of shining rails, roaring blast furnaces, busy refineries. Men of great consciousness of place such as Hyde, McCurdy, McCall, Dryden, and Hegeman looked for — and found in elaborate home offices — the sort of physical expression that their unmaterial business otherwise denied them.

In 1887 the Equitable enlarged and renovated its building at 120 Broadway, and the stamp of Henry Hyde was everywhere: in the stained-glass portrait of his dead son dominating the front; in the select club and restaurant that he partially owned; in the great flagpole boldly commanding the surrounding skyline; in the size and grandeur of the building itself. The New York Life embarked on a nation-wide building program during the late 1880's, and in 1895–96 added a twelve-story annex, designed by McKim, Mead, and White, to its office at 346 Broadway. The Mutual, too, expanded its home office at 34 Nassau Street in 1892.

The industrial firms, comparative newcomers to expansion and prosperity, blossomed forth with particular éclat. The Prudential opened an elaborate new structure in 1892. Its cathedrallike quality reflected the active intercession of President Dryden; he told his board that "the idea is to construct a building which shall typify and symbolize the character of the business of the Prudential, exemplify its all-pervading spirit of beneficence and its ingrained love of the golden rule." (The New York Life building, too, had an entrance resembling "an ancient temple — and a temple it is — a Temple of Humanity.") In 1893 the Metropolitan occupied the first portion of what would come to be the most distinctive of home offices. The Madison Square structure boasted a staircase inspired by the Paris Opera, a president's office furnished at a cost of $90,000 and — by 1909 — the famous tower (supposedly Hegeman's idea), then the tallest on earth. Even the generally restrained John Hancock occupied a new home office in 1889 which featured an impressive triptych of Time and Death, Prudence succoring Misfortune, and Wisdom subjugating the Spirit of Flame; Fame and History supported the company's coat of arms.[7]

By 1900 several firms had invested heavily in office buildings in other cities. Although generally these were unsatisfactory investments, the Metropolitan's Hegeman spoke for all when he outlined their real purposes: "for the sake of inspiring local pride, getting a local hold, securing the local business."[8]

2

Evils in the business structure — insider control, excessive salaries, nepotism — flourished in the midst of corporate maturity and drew nourishment from growth and institutionalization. Mutual companies such as the New York Life and the Mutual supposedly were governed by the votes of their policyholders, but policyholders showed little inclination, and got less encouragement, to be active in the choice of officers.[9] Proxies were an ever ready, but rarely needed, weapon against policyholder revolt. Legend had it that Beers of the New York Life had a trunkful in his house; that Winston and McCurdy of the Mutual had 20,000 to 30,000 proxies — called their "children of Israel" because they were too numerous to count — in their possession. Sporadic policyholder outbursts were put down with ease. In 1869 the Mutual leaders compelled voters to write their names on the backs of their ballots as a form of intimidation. The end result of a New York Life policyholders' committee roused by the Beers scandals of the early 1890's was the election to the board of a "reform" director who thereupon pledged to support the incumbents.[10]

Although the activities of minority stockholders in the Prudential and the Equitable were more substantial than the occasional stirrings of the mutual firms' policyholders, the pattern of executive control was not essentially different. The minutes of the Prudential and the Metropolitan boards of directors show consistently unanimous votes for the existing officers; and the Metropolitan's newspaper announcements of stockholders' meetings were anything but conspicuous. Prudential policyholders could vote until 1880, but received no notice of meetings; after 1880, a New Jersey law deprived them of the franchise. The company's caution was superfluous; in the early 1900's the Metropolitan gave the vote to all of its policyholders, but in 1904 only 38,000 of some 8,000,000 bothered to use it.[11]

With weak boards of directors and minimal stockholder and policyholder voting influence, high executive salaries and nepotism flourished. The restricted nature of the rewards open to the companies' managers encouraged these abuses. Commission arrangements were widespread up to the 1890's, but as business volume reached astronomical proportions these were replaced by straight salaries.[12] There were only limited opportunities for stock speculation, and dividends were restricted by the charters of incorporation. In mutual companies, not even the gratifications of stock ownership were available. Just as impressive home offices satisfied the executives' need for material manifestations of their corporate success, so did inflated salaries, the patronage of nepotism, and affiliated personal investments compensate for the difficulties that stood in the way of profit accumulation.

The salaries of the companies' top officials were among the highest in the United States. Solemn rituals enacted by modest executives and insistent boards accompanied each new boost. Richard McCurdy, earning $100,000 in 1901, disarmingly left the matter of his salary to his board's discretion; they asked him to leave the room and increased his remuneration to $150,000. With simple frankness, he noted that no other insurance executive received so much, and took the increase as the board's fair appraisal of his worth. The New York Life's John McCall also earned $100,000 by 1901. George W. Perkins, weighing a tempting partnership offer from J. P. Morgan and Company, went through a salary-raising ritual very similar to McCurdy's for an increase to $75,000. Hegeman, close to $100,000 a year on a commission plan in the early 1890's, voluntarily switched to a fixed salary. Although he rested content with $90,000, his board in 1905 awarded him a $10,000 bonus. However, he modestly refused to draw the supplement.[13]

Justification of such substantial compensation to the executives of eleemosynary institutions raised certain difficulties. The Mutual Life's counsel tried to relate proper salary size to the amount of a company's insurance in force, but was not convincing.[14] Chauncey Depew argued that Henry Hyde's remuneration was necessary to keep him from the temptation of selling his Equitable stock, the dividend earnings of which were only $3500 a year. McCurdy said of his executives' salaries: "I do not think any one of them is overpaid, for the conditions in which they live and move and have their being and for the character of the business which they do." Dryden, too, defended his salary by reference to the big business milieu: "The ability to achieve, the ability to produce, the ability to do something, is a commodity that commands its price in the market." Pressed with the example of relatively low-paid senators and Supreme Court justices or, for that matter, presidents of the United States the Prudential chieftain argued that the prestige and honor of high government position compensated for the lack of financial reward.[15] If he left unresolved the conflict between high salaries and the quasi-public ideology of his business, the fault was not his.

The same growth in size that justified large salary increases made it easier to fit relatives into lucrative company positions. Clusters of brothers, nephews, cousins, and sons-in-law of top executives appeared everywhere. Company presidents were especially solicitous of their sons. James Hazen Hyde recalled: "I had always been brought up to consider my legitimate life work to succeed my father in the Equitable." He became a director while still in Harvard; entered the company upon his graduation in 1898; and in five years was chairman of the executive and finance committees, vice-president of the company, and the recipient of a $100,000 annual salary. Forrest Dryden served an extensive, if not distinguished, apprenticeship in the Prudential, and succeeded his father as president in 1910. Richard McCurdy's dapper son Robert drew about $110,000 in salary and commissions as director of the company's foreign business department during the early 1900's. John McCall's oldest son served more modestly as the secretary of the New York Life; his son-in-law, Darwin P. Kingsley, eventually became the company's president. Anthony R. Kuser, Dryden's son-in-law, was a director of the Prudential.[16]

This sort of managerial irresponsibility was endemic in the insurance business. Many smaller firms were at least as culpable. None of the great company presidents, for instance, could match the arrant nepotism of the head of the Security Mutual of New York: this worthy admitted that his wife, son, wife's nephew, son-in-law, "and my wife's sister's husband" were on the payroll.[17] Nor did these failings depend upon the form of corporate ownership. Flamboyant, expensive, near corrupt management existed in mutual and stock companies alike. The evils of growth and the life insurance business' peculiar restraints upon profitmaking cut across most divisions of the corporate structure.

3

The conflict between checks on profit and the temptations presented by towering assets was particularly severe in the large stock companies. For here was the same framework of ownership which, at the turn of the century, was yielding a profit of tens of millions in other enterprises. Yet charter restrictions limited the dividend yield of Metropolitan and Equitable stock to 7 percent and that of the Prudential to 10 percent. Nor was the companies' stock capitalization subject to indefinite expansion.

The Metropolitan's original capitalization was $200,000, half of which it retired during the doldrums of the 1870's. But in 1883, when its new industrial insurance business was beginning to catch on, capitalists invested $400,000 to bring the company's stock total to $500,000. As the Metropolitan prospered, it created another $1,500,000 in capital out of its surplus. Joseph F. Knapp, its president until 1891, had over $700,000 and his successor, John R. Hegeman, had $275,000 of the company's final capitalization of $2,000,000. Knapp's more than 28,000 shares paid him annual dividends of almost $50,000; a combined salary and commission arrangement gave him another $112,000 in 1891. But no additional stock supplements were forthcoming, and although the Metropolitan continued to expand, Hegeman's stock and salary earnings did not surpass Knapp's total. Indeed, from 1897 the Metropolitan, in conjunction with the Prudential, paid dividends to its industrial policyholders, although the policies' terms did not require it to do so. From that time, the company's practice was to keep the surplus at 10 percent of its assets, and to distribute the remainder to its policyholders. Only $140,000 a year went for stockholders' dividends. Hegeman and the Knapp heirs, who implicitly supported the management, together controlled a majority of the stock, and although financier groups made attempts to buy control of the company, no further changes in capitalization occurred. But the paradox of a stock company that paid no significant dividends remained. Mutualization was a logical step, would strengthen the company's public image, and promised to be the only way for the stockholders to get a substantial return for their securities. Hegeman contemplated such a move in 1902, but his legal advisers dissuaded him. In 1905 the company was still almost a decade away from mutualization.[18]

The clash of values inherent in the position of the great insurance companies both as private corporations and as quasi-public institutions wracked the Prudential. The company's initial capitalization in 1875 was $100,000; but the stockholders had actually contributed only $91,000. In the first ten years of the firm's existence its capital slowly increased; on January 1, 1885, it totaled only $115,000. A potential crisis in control arose at the beginning of 1880. Policyholders, who according to the Prudential charter could vote for directors, now could outvote stockholders. But on March 3, a complaisant New Jersey legislature passed an abbreviated piece of legislation, known as The Bill of a Hundred Words, which abrogated the voting rights of the policyholders.[19]

As in the case of the Metropolitan, stockholder enrichment came primarily through increased capitalization. The surplus of the company, which rose from $6,115 in 1877 to $13,324,000 in 1904, provided new capital funds. The Prudential's stock increased by 30 percent to $149,-500 in 1885; by 40 percent to $209,300 in 1887; by 100 percent to $418,800 in 1889; again by 100 percent to $837,200 in 1890; by 40 percent to $1,162,800 in 1892; and to an even $2,000,000 in 1893. Substantial profits accrued to the stockholders who shared in these increases. The Massachusetts insurance commissioner commented in 1903 that the Prudential's stockholders "have already received enrichment beyond what avarice could have dreamed of when the Company started," and by 1909 over $5,500,000 had been earned in dividends on the original $91,000 investment.[20] Yet compared to the hundreds of millions that Carnegie and Rockefeller and, later, Ford took out of their companies, or to the tens of millions in fees and stock earnings derived from the organization of United States Steel, or to the exploitation of railroads, utilities, and other quasi-public corporations, the Prudential's earnings were not spectacular.

It soon became clear that the peculiar nature of the business set limits even upon stock expansion. Neither the company's growth nor its well-being were dependent upon stock increases; the capital supplements of the 1880's and the 1890's represented withdrawals from surplus earnings, not the injection of new funds. In 1898 a group of Prudential stockholders proposed a bold new capital increase (out of the surplus) from $2,000,000 to $5,000,000. Dryden, who had supported the previous stock supplements, now drew the line, warning that so large an expansion would be harmful to the company and unfair to the policyholders. Considerable outside pressure supported him. Hegeman and Fiske of the Metropolitan wrote to Dryden strongly protesting the move as one which "would result in serious attacks upon Industrial Insurance generally" and would contribute further to the already high cost of policies. They argued that "in this country the business of insurance is looked upon as a public, and not a private, business; and . . . managers of companies are looked upon as trustees for the policyholders rather than for the stockholders." The public, policyholders, and insurance commissioners shared these sentiments, the Metropolitan executives warned. The state insurance officers of Connecticut, where Hegeman lived and wielded much influence, and of Ohio confirmed this threat.[21]

Dryden's volte-face may also be explained by the development of the

Prudential. As the company became, in size as well as function, an institution of manifest social importance, Dryden the insurance officer took precedence over Dryden the stockholder. A significant portent was his 1897 agreement with the Metropolitan to distribute some of the company's huge surplus to its industrial policyholders. The ideology of life insurance made the normal acquisitiveness of stockholders seem alien, out of place. In the Prudential directors' minutes of January 5, 1899, the "voluntary" dispersal of dividends to policyholders took symbolic precedence in place and attention over the usual 10 percent capital distribution to the stockholders. The close juxtaposition of ownership and management had not changed; here, as in the other stock insurance firms, the leading stockholders served as officers or as directors. But the managers inevitably were more engaged in business expansion than in earning legally circumscribed dividends or exploiting limited possibilities of stock expansion.

These restraints on profitmaking were countered by the potential of the companies' great investment capital. Just as the prospects of business growth took precedence over a restricted stock-earning capacity, so did managerial enterprise give way to the greater stimulations of large-scale fund placements in the securities market. When the Prudential's directors gave Dryden, Leslie Ward, and Edgar Ward, the company's leading stockholder-directors, authority to vote the Prudential's security holdings, they gave a prize more pleasing than an increase in Prudential dividends — or, one suspects, than a triumph in insurance marketing.[22]

This evolution of emphasis underlay Dryden's 1903 arrangement for perpetuation of Prudential stock control by his group of insiders. According to this agreement, a majority of the firm's stock would be sold by the major Prudential stockholders to the closely allied Fidelity Trust Company of Newark. In turn, a new issue of Fidelity Trust stock, increasing its capital from $1,500,000 to $3,000,000 and sufficient for control, would be taken by the Prudential. Annual meetings, and other details, would be so arranged that the group controlling both the Prudential and the Fidelity Trust would act first in its capacity as directors of the insurance company, and thus ensure that that corporation was the senior partner of this strange and highly entangling alliance.[23]

Dryden later explained that he had been led to the exchange of stock by fear of "the attempts of any selfish interests to get control of [the] company for selfish purposes," by his own emotional commitment ("the company has been my own life work, and I had my pride in it"), and by his desire to prevent further stock increases which would heighten the possibility of the firm drifting into unsafe hands ("I had concluded that the company had reached its length, that it had gone as far as it ought to go"). Whatever the validity of Dryden's justifications, a manifest result of the arrangement was to put under the control of one group of insiders an insurance company with great investment potential and a trust company with great investment flexibility. For not least among the frustrating constraints inherent in the insurance business were those surrounding its investment practices; and the earning capacity of trust company stock was not as circumscribed as that of an insurance company. Finally, sale of the Prudential stock and the increase in Fidelity stock would have given the participants the advantage, "not ordinarily associated with such control," of an estimated $6,000,000 profit. Dryden's plan was a significant thrust against the profit limitation that so paradoxically accompanied the expansion of the great life insurance firms.[24]

No less revealing was the reaction to the plan. As in the case of the 1898 attempt to enlarge the capital stock, insurance commissioners and the Metropolitan rose in protest. Twelve state insurance officers opposed the Fidelity-Prudential merger. The Massachusetts commissioner in particular was aroused: only a few years before he had got the Prudential to agree to reduce its already existing investment in Fidelity stock on the ground that that investment surpassed the insurance company's surplus and capital. Bluntly the commissioner declared: "Such concentration of authority, so far removed from the reach of the individual stockholders, is contrary to public policy." In 1904 he extracted, on the threat of withdrawing the company's Massachusetts license, an agreement by the Prudential to limit its trust company holdings to 50 percent or less of its surplus. Wisconsin's commissioner refused to issue a state license to the Prudential until a court order required him to do so.[25]

Once again Hegeman and Fiske spoke up: "This proposed compact revives the memories of [the proposed capital increase of] 1898." They saw legal complications, commissioners' protests, hostile legislation, and denigration of the reputation of industrial insurance resulting from the scheme, which "savors strongly of reprehensible stock-jobbing methods." It was "unbecoming to a Life Insurance Corporation whose repute should be like Caesar's Wife." Prudential minority stockholders, too, objected to the plan, and brought suit in the New Jersey courts. The

Court of Chancery granted an injunction blocking the Prudential's purchase of Fidelity Trust stock, declaring that the insurance company's managers "were not elected to revise the laws of New Jersey, or to devise schemes for evading those laws." [26]

In response to this pressure, the Fidelity limited its stock increase to $2,000,000, and sold eight shares of its Prudential stock to ensure that it did not have a majority. But the holdings of the interlocked insurance company–trust company officers, combined with the two institutions' blocs of each other's securities, made for "an effective if not a technical control." And most of the new Fidelity stock was purchased by the Equitable, which was in close managerial alliance with the Prudential.[27]

So Dryden adhered to his great plan for internal, interlocking control of trust company and insurance company; for plumbing the investment possibilities of the insurance company's assets; for imaginative exploitation of the potential value of the Prudential's stock. But the reaction — from court, competitor, commissioners — made full implementation of the arrangement hazardous indeed. The Armstrong investigation of 1905 and an inquiry by New Jersey in 1906 heightened public awareness and disapproval of the merger, and the fundamental awkwardness of manipulating the stock of a quasi-public corporation remained. As in the case of the Metropolitan, mutualization — eliminating the company's stock capitalization — was the long-run solution to the problem.

4

More dramatic than the controversy over the Prudential-Fidelity merger, but stemming from the same dichotomy between corporate giantism and the restrictions of the insurance business, was the Equitable's time of troubles in 1905. The conflict in that company was a major struggle for managerial and stock control. The ultimate consequences included substantial changes in both management and ownership, and New York's Armstrong investigation of the life insurance business.

From the beginning, Henry Hyde defined the Equitable's purpose as business growth rather than stockholders' profits. He insisted that the company charter limit investors' earnings to 7 percent on the $100,000 worth of $100 par value shares. As the Equitable prospered, Hyde gathered together a majority of 502 shares. Little as the stock was worth in direct earnings (Hyde's portion brought yearly dividends of $3,514), it had an immense value as the ultimate basis of its owner's authoritarian direction of the Equitable. As Jacob H. Schiff, a director, put it, the company was "at the mercy of one man"; at "the very bottom of the whole question, of the whole system" was the fact that "Mr. Hyde had a majority of the stock." In 1902 the Metropolitan commented on reported attempts by Wall Street magnates to secure control of the Equitable's stock. Vigorously it warned that such an occurrence "will be the severest blow ever dealt to the business of life insurance." [28]

Henry Hyde died in 1899, confident that the company would pass on as a piece of property to his son James Hazen Hyde. He expected James W. Alexander, long his chief assistant, to act as tutor and prop while the younger Hyde prepared to become the Equitable's chief executive. In 1895 he put the majority bloc of stock in trust for his son, with Alexander one of the trustees.

The younger Hyde became a voting trustee of the stock in 1897, and was to come into complete control in 1906 when he reached his thirtieth birthday. As that time approached, his relations with Alexander grew strained. The latter dropped his trusteeship in 1903, and by early 1905 was openly at odds with James Hazen Hyde. He criticized the young man's "public coaches, special trains, elaborate banquets, costly and ostentatious entertainments, accompanied . . . by continuous notoriety of a flippant, trivial, cheap description." Alexander and those supporting him called for Hyde's removal from active management in the company and for the inclusion of policyholders in the election of company directors.[29]

The struggle between Alexander and Hyde was a classic example of the ineluctable antagonism between corporate management and a relatively detached corporate ownership. The critics of James Hazen Hyde's frivolity and irresponsibility, the exponents of a system of policyholder voting which meant greater control for the managers, were the men most closely associated with managerial power, or who desired such association. Alexander himself, with his years of close association with Henry Hyde, could not help but look upon the injudicious son as an impertinent upstart and resent the outright control which would so easily come to the young man. Gage Tarbell, like Perkins of the New York Life and Fiske of the Metropolitan, was very much the driving force in the Equitable, the agency man most responsible for the firm's operation as an insurance-selling enterprise. Strong-minded, arrogant, jealous of Perkins' growing power in the worlds of insurance and finance, full of the sense of his indispensability to his company, aware of the check to his ambitions that James Hazen Hyde's supremacy might mean, Tarbell firmly resisted the interloper. Bainbridge Colby, rising corporation lawyer and a behind-the-scenes power in the Equitable, cast his lot with Alexander and Tarbell.[30]

A third factor — control of the Equitable's assets — added another dimension to the conflict between management and ownership. An extraordinary value attached to the possession of a majority of the Equitable's stock. Individual shares brought one to three thousand dollars on the market — a value out of all proportion to their dividend earnings and book value. Surely nothing but his stock holdings, in temporary trust though they were, earned for James Hazen Hyde an Equitable vice-president's salary of $100,000 a year and directorships in forty-five banks, trust companies, railroads, and other firms. Hyde claimed that extravagant cash offers were made to him for his stock rights: $4,000,000 from George J. Gould, $5,000,000 from Henry C. Frick, $7,000,000 from George W. Young, $10,000,000 from George Haven and James Stillman.[31]

Clearly, interests greater than those of Alexander and his associates were involved. Frick headed an Equitable directors' committee which took the statements of Hyde and Alexander and presented a report damning both sides. Reports circulated that a group of financiers — Stillman of the National City Bank, Jacob Schiff of Kuhn, Loeb and Company, Edward H. Harriman of the Union Pacific, Frick of United States Steel — were pressing to obtain control of the company. The offers of Young and Haven represented attempts by the Mutual to take over its old rival. Finally, in 1905, James Hazen Hyde gave in to these manifold pressures from the financial community. Apparently angered by Harriman's efforts to pry loose his stock control, he suddenly sold his shares to Thomas Fortune Ryan, a free-lance corporate organizer and stock speculator, for a comparatively modest $2,500,000.[32]

The utmost circumspection surrounded Ryan's acquisition of the Equitable. In accordance with the purchase agreement he put the voting power of his holdings into the hands of three trustees of impeccable respectability: former President Grover Cleveland, the inventor George Westinghouse, and New York Supreme Court justice Morgan J. O'Brien. Paul Morton, a former Secretary of the Navy who had been in charge of Ryan's New York street railway consolidation, replaced Alexander as president of the Equitable. Modestly Ryan explained that a sense of "public duty" — and the desire, as a longtime political admirer of

Grover Cleveland, to give that worthy a position appropriate to his eminence — moved him to obtain the stock. To unfriendly contemporaries, however, Ryan's interest in the Equitable's great surplus and its immense investing powers seemed a more likely explanation. Yet Ryan already had strong connections with such substantial sources of investment capital as the Bank of Commerce and the Morton Trust. There was talk, too, of the psychological pleasures to be derived by a stock manipulator of uncertain reputation from control of so immense and respectable a corporation as the Equitable. "How much is it worth to a very wealthy man to come in a day to be regarded as the greatest of financiers?" one observer asked.[33]

Ryan may well have had less grandiose expectations. His fortune of between twenty-five and thirty-five millions was founded on the profits of corporate reorganization: the American Tobacco Company and the Metropolitan Transit Company were his creations. Among Ryan's holdings was the Washington Life Insurance Company, which was in financial and managerial trouble. It is possible that he expected the Equitable to take over the lesser firm in an arrangement profitable to its stockholders. It may be, too, that he had an eye to an advantageous settlement with the Equitable should it mutualize and buy in its stock.[34]

But his tenure of Equitable ownership brought him no apparent gains. The glare of publicity attending the Equitable crisis, the Armstrong investigation in late 1905 and the rigorous New York legislation that followed, the very probity of the trustees, made any untoward action by Ryan all but impossible. Grover Cleveland declared in 1908 that Ryan never "offered a suggestion nor has he approached the trustees directly or indirectly." In December 1909 the financier sold his Equitable stock to J. P. Morgan — for the same price (plus interest) that he had paid more than four years before.[35]

Whatever Ryan's underlying intentions were, like Dryden in the Prudential-Fidelity Trust merger he found the nature of the business a substantial hindrance to his aspirations. The Equitable's stock, commonly supposed to bestow great power upon its majority holder, turned out for James Hazen Hyde, and then for Thomas Fortune Ryan, to be instead a conveyer of weighty, unavoidable, and fundamentally not very profitable corporate responsibilities.

Thus growth had unexpected consequences for the corporate structure of the great companies. Managerial practices of questionable propriety developed because of the disparity between corporate size and compensation. Even stock ownership, the keystone of corporate worth, did not open the sluicegates of profitmaking. The growing size and wealth of the companies opened vistas of great financial remuneration; but the same process tended to put the corporate structure beyond purely entrepreneurial considerations. The resulting tensions and frustrations help to account for the special ardor with which the life insurance chieftains sought satisfaction in varied forms of corporate power.

V * Growth and the Business Technique

Growth had no less distinctive consequences for the companies' business technique. The fundamental development in the change in corporate structure had been an unresolved — and heightening — tension between the companies' responsibilities as quasi-public institutions and their temptations as private corporations. In the area of insurance marketing, too, growth brought problems — and prospects — more than purely entrepreneurial in nature.

One disturbing phenomenon was the stubborn association of growth with high, and rising, costs. True, "expensive" insurance fitted into the magnates' business ideology. Richard McCurdy drew a lesson for his board: "Gentlemen, Herter grows rich on the Fifth Avenue, and his widow has her box at the Opera. Tiffany . . . sells articles of the highest cost that can be made or imported, and builds a palace on Madison Avenue. 'Cheap John' and 'The Original Jacobs' sell cheap goods on the Bowery — and live and die in Hester Street." In 1898 he announced with pride that life insurance companies no longer were "the custodian of the savings of those of slender resources but thrifty habits"; rather, they had become "the bulwark and defense of large fortunes and large ventures." [1] Ideology and attitudes apart, giantism and corporate maturity raised the companies' expense ratio. One measurement of the expense rate of the ten largest life insurance firms set it at 11.8 percent of income in 1870, 14.8 percent in 1883, and 19.2 percent in 1903. By the early 1900's the Mutual was surpassing its loading (estimated expenses) with disturbing frequency. Industrial companies were particularly bedeviled by costs considerably higher than those of the ordinary life companies. The operating expenses of the Big Three in 1904 were 49 percent of the total paid to policyholders; for the Metropolitan the figure was 119 percent. Smaller companies generally subsisted on lower expense ratios. But even they felt the pressure of the operating standards set by the giants.[2]

Nor did the "expensive" insurance sought by the Big Three's leaders prove proportionately profitable. The great increase in number of policies at the turn of the century did not yield commensurate gains in the amount of insurance in force, or in premium income accruing to the companies (see Table 1).

TABLE 1. The growth of the Big Three, 1899–1904 (percent)

Company	Number of policies	Insurance in force	Income
Equitable	60.65	42.34	47.73
New York Life	114.00	83.15	65.47
Mutual	66.23	48.07	45.91
Average of four other American companies	36.74	34.08	34.08

Source: Equitable, *Supplemental Report in the Investigation of the Equitable. . . , March 15, 1906*, pp. 59–60.

The great companies showed concern over costs as early as 1891, when the Mutual and the Equitable pledged themselves to cut expenses. The problem heightened in intensity during the 1890's. The panic of 1893 and the ensuing depression caused a decline in new business and a fall in security values, but no discernible cut in costs. McCurdy braced his board for a disappointing annual statement at the end of 1893, and thought it an appropriate time "to look more closely into general expenditures than we have been accustomed to in the past." But no improvement came; and in 1898 he ordered audits of Mutual departmental expenses and appointed a confidential committee of officers to examine company costs. Though the New York Life and the Equitable were not "models of economical management" the Mutual's expenses were "decidedly heavier," and McCurdy wanted to know why. (George W. Perkins' explanation was that "they liked to live pretty well down there.")[3] Still the problem resisted solution. In 1900 McCurdy chastized his son for the foreign department's high expense ratio; wanted advertising and luncheon costs cut; and importuned his subordinates to "begin the new Century by showing that the acquired experience and momentum of the last ten years has enabled us to reasonably increase our productiveness and to diminish the rate of expenses." By this time the New York Life's officers, too, thought it imperative that the expense ratio show a rapid and marked improvement. But, as the Armstrong investigation demonstrated, none of the great firms had come close to solving the cost problem by 1905.[4]

Explanations of this unsatisfactory experience varied, and in their diversity underlined the fact that the phenomenon was an integral part of rapid growth. Rising agency and managerial expenses (as one executive put it: "It costs more to live"); the decline in interest rates on investments; rising taxes; deferred dividend policyholders lapsing (canceling) their policies less frequently than expected; industrial policyholders lapsing *more* frequently than was desirable; expanding policy benefits — all of these were explanations of the stubbornly high cost, the disappointingly low dividend returns, of life insurance at the turn of the century. The costs of a burgeoning, sophisticated, bureaucratized enterprise — what Dryden called "the general toning up and elevating of the entire operation of the company's business" — canceled out the potential savings of greater size.[5]

Competition, as well as growth and size, worked to increase the cost of the business: a state of affairs which Burton Hendrick oversanguinely thought unique to life insurance. James Alexander blamed heavy — and expensive — policy cancellations on "the competition in the business"; ambitious agents enticed (or, as the trade put it, 'twisted') policyholders to drop one company's insurance and take up the supposedly more attractive offerings of another. An executive of a small company observed that "competition has brought out many liberal features that ought not to be put in a contract"; and those policy improvements were a cause, or at least a justification, of continually high premium rates.[6]

Just as the problems of management and the corporate structure stemmed from growth alone and not from the nature of ownership, so was high cost a product of the expansion of business itself. Thus, whether one proceeds from an analysis of the companies as competing entrepreneurial units, or from a view of them as bureaucratized corporate institutions, unsatisfying and stubborn cost ratios were the unavoidable and logical development.

The failure of the managers to cope with the cost problem suggested that the companies' business technique would not easily come under strong executive control. As the firms developed into an institutionalized society of corporations, their business techniques became subject to considerations more complex than simple and direct profitmaking. And complexity, no matter how much the product of growth and wealth, put restraints on the exercise of corporate power.

2

Of most direct concern to policyholders were premium rates. These rose very slightly between 1860 and 1910.[7] But in view of the steady climb in life expectancy, and the decline in policy dividends, price stability reflected the rising operating costs of a highly competitive, expensive, institutionalized business. Premium rates early became rigid under this stabilizing influence. Mutual president Frederick Winston's attempt in the 1870's to meet the Equitable's competition with a substantial premium reduction was blocked by widespread and concerted opposition from the rest of the industry. In 1896 another Mutual president, Richard McCurdy, interested himself in premiums — but this time in the form of a call for a Big Three meeting to discuss raising the rates on policy classes that he considered insufficiently remunerative.[8]

Formalized and noncompetitive ratemaking also involved certain responsibilities. Rebating — the return of part or all of a premium to a policyholder as an inducement to the purchase of the policy — was a popular competitive device. However, its explicit conflict with stabilized premium rates made it indefensible in the eyes of the public, the legislatures, and eventually the companies themselves. The industrial companies' attempts to establish different premium rates for white and Negro policyholders, no matter how justified by actuarial computations, so clashed with accepted notions of the role of life insurance that several states forbade the distinction.[9]

During the Civil War the then less trammeled industry raised its rates on soldier policyholders. The Mutual's reaction to the Spanish-American War was to require permits and extra premiums from policyholders joining the military. McCurdy, with his customary brusqueness, had said in 1895: "Whatever sympathetic interest we may feel for the defenders of our country in time of war, as a business proposition they are not worth any special effort to secure their patronage." The New York Life, the Prudential, and the Metropolitan, however, set no additional premium requirements for members of the armed forces. Several considerations may have shaped this decision: the ratemaking rigidity of the time, the lack of actuarial danger, public relations advantages. George W. Perkins gleefully compared the New York Life's approach to the "stupid, laborious" position of the Mutual. The institutionalization of premium rates meant not so much the end of decisionmaking in that area as the injection of factors more subtle and less controllable than direct and immediate profit and loss.[10]

3

Nothing was more fundamental to the business growth of the Big Three, or more evocative of the values that governed them, than the deferred dividend policy. This contract required the policyholder to forego dividends for five, ten, or twenty years. In return he had the prospect of benefiting from the more flexible investment powers thus afforded the company, and from the lapses and policy surrenders of fellow policyholders unable to maintain premium payments. The policies resembled Lorenzo Tonti's seventeenth century annuity schemes for Louis XIV, which gave them the popular name of tontines. In the age of Social Darwinism, the tontine policy rewarded in the most direct manner the fittest who survived. As New York Life's President Beers put it: "That is the law of every business enterprise — free choice at the outset; risk in any course and the greater prospective gain attended by the greater risk . . . It is neither new nor wrong to link duty to others with profits to one's self." At a time when the heady promises of speculation intermingled with the sober realities of rapid social and geographical displacement, tontines satisfied both the desire for gain and the need for security. When the traditional entrepreneurial concern with expenses was giving way to expansion at any cost, an ideal "absence of accountability" inhered in the deferred dividend policy, for the effect of "growth at undue cost . . . is not felt by the policyholder until . . . it is too late for his unavailing protest." [11]

The policy fit the business views of magnates who, with all the hard-headed attributes of Rockefellers and Carnegies, dealt in so intangible a product as life insurance. John McCall observed that "the average man will not insure through sentiment"; his actuary with greater pungency spoke of the tontine policy's appeal to "the commercial man's natural selfishness." To heighten this quality, the companies gave their policies labels evocative of sound yet profitable investment: "bonds," "gold bonds," "consols." The *Commercial and Financial Chronicle* began in the 1890's to treat tontines as investments more than as insurance, for it considered that "[i]nsuring life has become business, and is put on the 'business' basis at once and primarily." "What," it asked, "is there . . . in the line of pure investment of the very highest class, which can be bought to run twenty years and do as well?" The answer, it would turn out, was: almost anything.[12]

It was appropriate that Henry Hyde, the most daring and inventive insurance man of his time, should be the first to fix successfully upon this revolutionary insurance device. Trammeled by a charter requirement for dividend payments at least once every five years, Hyde obtained from the New York legislature a misleadingly titled Law Authorizing the Payment of Annual Dividends. This act provided that any life insurance company might pay its dividends annually "or at longer intervals," and thereby gave Hyde the legal permission he needed for deferred dividend policies.[13]

Once the Equitable's rapid growth proved the efficacy of the tontine policy, the other companies fell into line. The New York Life adopted it in 1871; the Mutual, in 1885. By 1888, only 0.5 percent of the Mutual's new business was on an annual dividend basis. Indeed, annual dividend policy solicitation was positively discouraged. Actuary Rufus Weeks of the New York Life bluntly declared: "We do not want the annual dividend business." The Mutual offered its agents a higher commission rate for deferred dividend policies. Its actuary argued that without the differentiation its "indoctrinated" solicitors would be "confused" and hence less effective. The Prudential in 1886 and the John Hancock in 1896 emphasized the sale of tontines in their ordinary life departments. Only the Metropolitan, whose vice-president, Haley Fiske, looked upon deferred dividend policies with distrust and distaste, refused to succumb to the prevailing trend.[14]

Deferred dividends became a special target of insurance men opposed to the corporate values of the great companies. Elizur Wright, deeply committed to the eleemosynary role of life insurance, roundly denounced tontine policies as "life insurance cannibalism. It is as if a temperance society should endeavor to promote its cause by establishing a liquor saloon under its lecture-room, or a church should support its minister by a lottery." Tontine investigations in New York (1877) and Ohio (1886) suggest that Wright's unease was widely shared. The leading managerial opponents of deferred dividend policies were Colonel Jacob L. Greene of the Connecticut Mutual and Amzi Dodd of the

Mutual Benefit of New Jersey. Both business traditionalists, they condemned tontines as unsound and dishonest.[15]

But these were ineffective voices, overwhelmed by the appropriateness of deferred dividend policies to their market and their time. Wright's criticisms were muted by an Equitable retainer until his death in 1885, and Greene's indignation could not easily be separated from the fact that his company, second in size in the 1870's, slipped badly until in 1904 it wrote only 1 percent of the business of the Big Three.[16]

Yet the tontine device was a prime source of the troubles that led to the Armstrong investigation of 1905. The inaccuracy of the companies' glowing predictions of ultimate returns caused considerable policyholder wrath by the beginning of the new century. Even earlier, the high lapse rate forced the initiation of semitontine policies, which preserved some of the contract's equity for the defaulting policyholder.

Strikingly, industrial insurance policies fell heir to the same ills that afflicted the deferred dividend system. Plagued by high costs and a heavy lapse rate, the Metropolitan and the Prudential tried to make their policies more attractive by paying dividends — just as the straight life firms turned to semitontines.

Both the high costs and the heavy lapse rate of pre-1905 tontine and industrial insurance seemed at the time to be inevitable accompaniments of large-scale insurance marketing. After 1905, legislation ended deferred dividend policies and the need to assuage public opinion forced the reduction of industrial operating expenses. But neither development injured the business; quite the contrary. In retrospect, then, the high costs and deferred dividend policies of the great companies were an organic part of the business only because they accorded with the prevailing managerial ideology.

4

The pressures of competition that made the deferred dividend policy the standard by 1900 also led the companies to vie with each other in liberalizing policy terms. If Hyde's tontines marked the apogee of bold and dynamic insurance marketing, rapid and often imaginative policy liberalization toward the end of the nineteenth century suggested a more mature and sophisticated business technique.

In line with their deification of growth and size, the companies allowed ever larger individual insurances. The New York Life's trustees noted in 1883 that because of the decline in the general interest rate capitalists were turning to "Life Insurance as an investment," and approved of an increase in the maximum insurance on a single life from $50,000 to $75,000. At the end of 1884 the ceiling reached $100,000. The Mutual in particular relished large insurance holdings. In 1891 Theodore A. Havemeyer and four members of his family had five $100,000 policies, the industry's largest familial holding. By 1905 Rodman Wanamaker alone held $2,000,000 worth of insurance. The Mutual in fact reinsured all but a quarter million of this insurance with other firms, but the total had an obvious public relations function, and in McCurdy's company contributed to a cherished image of corporate grandeur.[17]

The New York Life under Perkins' aegis boldly experimented with new policy techniques. During the 1890's it pioneered in extending its coverage, at heightened rates, to substandard risks, and even attempted group coverage plans. From the 1880's on, various employers and industries discussed or implemented insurance plans to benefit struck firms; and the Mutual became involved in this extension of the underwriting principle. In 1896 it issued endowment policies on selected employees in a firm, with compensation adjusted to length of continuous employment. "It may be that we have accidentally hit upon an effective means of counteracting the machinations of the Trade Unions in promoting strikes," McCurdy wrote hopefully. But he shied from insuring large groups of workmen on the ground that the industrial companies were more experienced in that line. In any event, the opposition of the *Commercial and Financial Chronicle* to an antistrike insurance plan suggested that such an application of insurance seemed improper to many even at the turn of the century.[18]

Of more significance than these experiments was the liberalization of the terms of ordinary and industrial policies. Beginning in the 1870's, and furthered by an intricate complex of competitive emulation, legal interpretation, and legislative requirement, policy liberalization reached its greatest intensity in the 1890's. By the early twentieth century, the benefits of the insurance contract extended to substandard risks and hazardous occupations; restrictions on travel and exemptions based on the manner of death were dropped; nonforfeiture and incontestability features had been developed and expanded; a liberal interpretation of application statements was becoming common; and greater surrender values and borrowing equity added to the policy's financial worth.[19]

The growth of policy loan provisions illustrated the strong impetus that competition gave to policy liberalization, and the way in which the values of the managers determined their business techniques. The New York Life began to grant policy loans in 1892, after the revised New York insurance law permitted it. As the device proved popular, Hyde set Tarbell to examine the New York Life's lending machinery, and told his company's agents that the Equitable was willing to lend on its policies. Although McCurdy informed Hyde that he could not follow suit "without stultifying myself," the Mutual temporarily joined its competitors. The popularity of the loan provision, like deferred dividend policies, reflected the investment orientation of policyholders and of company marketing practices. When the ordinary life business turned to the less affluent in the 1920's, policy loans sharply decreased.[20]

5

Even the seemingly abstract and objective area of actuarial computation reflected prevailing corporate values. No phase of the business was more enmeshed in arcane technicalities than the reserve. Level (equal-sized) premiums made necessary an invested reserve fund to compensate for the steady decline in the insured's life expectancy. Several variables entered into the requisite calculations: the proportion of the premium to be charged against the reserve; the assumed mortality rate; and the interest that the invested reserve might be expected to earn.

The first variable was controlled in 1858, when Elizur Wright induced Massachusetts to require that reserve calculations be based upon a net premium (premium less loading) rather than upon a gross premium. The immediate effect was to raise the amount needed for the reserve, a fact of significance to borderline companies. The question of the assumed mortality rate also seemed to be settled early. Actuary Sheppard Homans, with Wright's approbation, had the Mutual use the American Experience mortality table in the 1860's, and all American companies followed suit. This, too, increased the reserve requirement, for the new table listed longer life expectancies than did the English tables previously used. When adopting the American Experience table the Mutual assumed that reserves thus accumulated would earn 4 percent in interest, a long-term factor of some consequence in determining the size of the reserve itself. The New York law allowed up to 4.5 percent in reserve valuation. The large companies that used the 4 percent rate thus demonstrated their financial soundness, since the lower the earning rate the larger the reserve would have to be. When in 1888 New York adopted the companies' 4 percent rate as the legal maximum many firms had to lower their reserve valuations, and thus increase their reserves by a total of thirty million dollars.[21]

Reserve size, and the valuation rates which helped to determine that size, could be of concern to companies teetering between solvency and bankruptcy or anxious to bend their resources to business expansion. For example, the Metropolitan in the early 1880's found Massachusetts' strict reserve valuation an onerous requirement. But the reserve had no such import for large and financially secure firms. Rather, their major interest in the reserve rested on subtler considerations: whether the valuation system would inspire or detract from public confidence; whether the valuation rate corresponded in a satisfactory way with investment earning rates. Now a larger reserve meant not a greater guarantee of corporate solvency, but a greater accumulation of capital available for investment by company managements. New York Life cashier Theodore M. Banta, attacking his company's extravagant management in the late 1880's, criticized the firm's reserve for being wastefully large, not for being dangerously small.[22]

These considerations came into play when, in 1893, a New York law allowed the use of varying tables of mortality, not just the American table, in computing reserve rates. The purpose of the law clearly was to allow companies to substitute mortality tables that would allow a lesser reserve. It was supported by the Mutual's McCurdy, who retained an old-fashioned distaste for large reserves and complained about "the blind cult of a net reserve and a single standard." But the Missouri insurance department responded to the law by demanding detailed lists from the New York companies of all policies in force, with a view to making its own valuation of the appropriate reserves for these firms — and charging the companies heavily for the service. Every other state, presumably, could undertake the same expensive process. The New York Life led the city's major firms in filing notice of their intention to retain the former valuation standard, and induced the Missouri commissioner to withdraw his revaluation threat.[23]

Indeed, the companies came to welcome the opportunity to emphasize their fiscal conservatism and at the same time to increase the size of their invested reserves. As general interest rates declined, they pressed for a lowered valuation. The Prudential dropped to a 3.5 percent rate in 1897, and to 3 percent in 1899. The Equitable, too, went to 3 percent, and after New York State scaled down its maximum valuation rate to 3.5 percent, the Mutual in 1907 also went to the 3 percent level. Valuation levels became entangled in competition as well; an intercompany agreement to keep the rate at 3.5 percent broke down in 1897 when Hyde brought out a policy based on a 3 percent reserve valuation. McCurdy, who considered a return to the 4 percent rate logical, decided that the views of the other companies and "the possible course of legislation" made the 3.5 percent standard the most viable one.[24]

Yet the Mutual's own actuary was confident in 1905 that the companies would continue to earn 4 percent on their investments, perhaps a little more. It seems clear that the function of the reserve, and company policy toward it, had moved far from their original purpose of guaranteeing long-term insurance policy commitments. For example, a valuation rate lower than actual investment earnings would help to cover unconscionable expenses. It was suggestive that by 1905 John McCall of the New York Life publicly stated his belief that the policyholder, who could break his insurance contract while the company could not, was not entitled to the full face value of his reserve. And the actuary of the Mutual, which persisted in regarding the reserve as a troublesome imposition, thought it desirable to allow the companies to use most of a policy's first premium for the expenses of obtaining the business. In practice, he declared, the companies dipped into their surpluses to make up the substantial first-year reserve that the law demanded.[25] Thus did the reserve, onetime bulwark of the insurance contract, become a factor in the business technique of companies for whom it was a nuisance or a convenience, but not a burden.

6

Since life insurance companies generally received more money in premiums and investments than they disbursed in policy payments and expenses, a surplus usually existed. The ideology of insurance equity and the dictates of competition committed most of the surplus to the policyholders. Even the stock industrial companies, which had no legal obligation to disburse the surplus to their insured, found it necessary to do so. Of course, in law and by charter the mutual companies' surplus belonged to their policyholders.

Deferred dividend policies eliminated the obligation for rapid distribution of the surplus. The undistributed surplus, particularly of the Equitable, grew larger and larger (see Table 2). The surplus became an

TABLE 2. Undistributed deferred dividend surpluses of the Big Three, 1880–1904 (millions of dollars)

Year	Equitable	Mutual	New York Life
1880	6.5	6.3	6.7
1885	12.9	6.9	9.8
1890	21.5	9.9	15.1
1895	39.4	26.9	24.0
1900	65.9	56.6	46.0
1904	80.5	74.4	47.5

Source: Spectator Company, *Insurance Year Book*, years cited.

expression of the companies' size and soundness; a source of fluid capital for investment; an inducement to managerial extravagance and irresponsibility. The reserve satisfied the legal definition of insurance-company solvency, leaving the surpluses untrammeled as a source of and an incentive to wasteful managerial practices. Yet the great sales of deferred dividend policies in the late nineteenth century depended in part on grandiose promises of accumulated dividend returns upon maturity. By 1900 large numbers of those policies were maturing, and it had become necessary to weigh the effect upon current business of "awfully disappointing" dividends on the older contracts.[26]

As a result, the companies' actuarial computations became something more than statistical exercises. Equitable and Mutual loading figures included a substantial factor based on the judgment or inclinations of the management. The New York Life's trustees set up a special fund at the beginning of 1896 so that despite poor business conditions the company's expense ratio (from which loading, surplus, and dividend calculations were made) would be at least as favorable as in the preceding year. In 1900 they established an Annual Dividend Equalization Fund, based on undivided surplus and designed to secure a steady return for annual dividend policies.[27]

Guesswork and subjective computations were particularly endemic in the preparation of deferred dividends. The panoply of mathematical complexity was impressive enough. Richard McCurdy frankly said of his company's dividend appraisal method: "It is quite complicated, and I cannot say that I understand it very well myself." But Mutual actuary Emery McClintock clarified the process. Generally he tried to keep dividend fluctuations at a minimum, since then it was "most easily explainable to the public." When in 1903 the company's investments fell heavily in market value, he seized the opportunity to make a substantial cut in returns to annual dividend policyholders, even though "I don't think [the market fall] . . . made any difference in the figures at all." Nor did the market's recovery in 1904 lead to a dividend increase; it only "influenced me not to make a further reduction." McClintock's technique in determining the 1904 dividend rate was to modify the previous year's return "in accordance with what appeared to be the way business was running." Especially figurative were his general criteria for annual policy dividends: "First, whether they progress with a reasonable closeness to the year before, so as not to produce violent jerks in the figures up or down, and secondly . . . the moral liability which [the company] . . . ought to hold for the deferred dividend." On grounds of marketing policy it was advisable to favor deferred over annual dividends; Henry Hyde asked the Equitable's actuary to raise out of hand the figures that determined deferred dividend rates.[28]

7

The growth of the insurance companies into great corporate institutions thus infused the most technical aspects of their business with complex and far-ranging policy considerations. It had even more dramatic effects on the key components of the marketing process: advertising, agency structure, and business competition.

A sense of publicity and of the power of advertising inhered in the business from its beginning. But the most active function of public relations in the years following the Civil War was not so much the development of policyholder acceptance and loyalty as effective intercompany warfare. During the 1870's, particularly, the great struggle between the Equitable and the Mutual often took the form of claims and promises unfavorable to the other company, or of fulminations by paid newspaper and insurance journal hacks.[29]

The existence of an active insurance press reflected the highly verbal nature of the business, and the maturity of the enterprise. But the often scurrilous nature of insurance journalism betrayed a general inclination to use public relations as a weapon rather than as a tool. The Big Three, at much expense, set insurance periodicals against Jacob Greene and the Connecticut Mutual, the great opponent of deferred dividend policies. The Mutual had an arrangement with the *Insurance News,* which McCurdy planned to supply with lead articles "in the right direction." He thought it important that the Mutual's relationship with the journal be a muted one; otherwise, criticisms of other companies appearing there could too easily be blamed on his firm. When the Equitable's James Alexander complained about an item in the *Insurance Record,* another journal temporarily in the Mutual orbit, McCurdy denied controlling the editor, but thought he could make him "understand" that the piece was inaccurate. Each of the Big Three became the object of the special — and paid-for — animosity of an insurance periodical: the Mutual, of the *Guardian*; the Equitable, of the Chicago *Investigator*; the New York Life, of the *Record*.[30]

Henry Hyde fully shared McCurdy's willingness to use public relations for pejorative purposes. The Equitable's house organ tangled fiercely with its opposite number in the Mutual, and Hyde set actuary Sheppard Homans to work on charts comparing the two companies' growth to the Mutual's disadvantage. On the eve of the appearance of a new Mutual premium rate book, an accepted means of demonstrating the inferior quality of competitors' policies, Hyde readied his company to "attack the Mutual to the same extent as they attack us in their book — in case it does attack us." [31]

Companies schooled in this warlike approach to public relations were inclined to use *sub rosa* methods in all of their advertising efforts. They often gave their sales messages the guise of news rather than advertising matter. During the late 1880's Hyde engaged numerous journals to print favorable material in their news columns, and found the results satisfactory. In 1888 he paid $3000 to Charles Dana's *Sun*; in return, the *Sun* agreed to print "any general articles about the Equitable or about life insurance, if they are not too partisan." Impatiently he prodded James Alexander to feed copy to the compliant newspaper: "It is a pity to pay them the money without getting some benefit out of it." The Mutual, too, actively placed publicity material masquerading as news, and rewarded friendly journals with paid advertising. One of its publicity specialists recommended applying the technique to religious papers: "they put anything in there." At one point a dummy news agency called the Mutual Press Association fed paid-for fillers to a national list of publications. The going rate was suggested by the sobriquet of one of the company's publicists: "Dollar-a-Line" Smith.[32]

But there were signs by the turn of the century that public belaboring of one's competitors, and heavy dependence on subventions to the insurance press, was passing out of style. For one thing, the bought would not stay bought. Hyde complained in 1888 of the ingratitude of New York insurance editors who seemed to be in combination against the Equitable, and McCurdy noted that the New York Life seemed to be able to get better treatment at less expense from the insurance press than did either of its competitors. The cost, too, could become oppressive: a New York Life lobbyist reminisced in 1910 about "how many insurance journals there were which the president of any one of the big three companies had to pay blackmail to every month, or else have himself caricatured and ridiculed unmercifully." The imaginative George W. Perkins first broke from accepted publicity techniques. In 1900 he told insurance journal editors that the New York Life no longer would run formal ads, but would maintain its subsidies if in each issue an article on the company appeared. "In effect," he hoped, "this will mean that we will pretty nearly control every insurance journal . . . so that it cannot say anything against us." In a year, once the journals were committed to constant endorsements of the New York Life, he planned to halve their allowances. This process could, of course, be copied by the other firms, and thus vitiate the force of bought insurance journalism.[33]

Perhaps most decisively, these older public relations methods came to seem out of place in a sophisticated corporate group. McCurdy grandly rebuked his subsidized English journal's attacks on John McCall of the New York Life: "Badly as I think of the means which Mr. McCall has seen fit to adopt in making wholly unprovoked warfare upon my Company . . . [c]haracter is something and will prevail in the end." The early years of the twentieth century saw agreements among the Big Three not to attack each other in advertisements and to restrict invidiously comparative literature put out by agents.[34]

As the leaders' blood lust lessened with the emergence of a sophisticated society of companies, new techniques of public relations came into favor. By 1904 the Mutual's advertising budget was $330,000; it devoted $42,000 to direct appeals for policyholders in magazine ads, and wrote $13,000,000 worth of insurance through them. The Metropolitan showed some reluctance to plunge heavily into advertising, Hegeman discounting it as "an expensive luxury." But the Prudential embarked on broad-scale publicity campaigns in the mid-1890's, and was probably the first insurance company to use a full-time advertising agency, J. Walter Thompson. An agency man devised the most successful of all insurance symbols and slogans: "The Prudential Has the Strength of Gibraltar." The Equitable used similar motifs in its advertising: a towering mountain to suggest the company's huge surplus; beckoning lighthouses and sturdy bridges to symbolize the security that life insurance afforded. The distance between this institutionalized, socially conscious advertising technique and the emotional, competitive public relations of earlier decades was another measure of the degree of maturity attained by the great life insurance companies at the century's turn.[35]

8

Large, aggressive selling forces were critically important in the expansion of the life insurance business. This marketing element dramatically reflected the corporate institutionalization that came with growth.

The dominant selling structure in the late nineteenth century was the general agency system. Companies in the early stages of national expansion found it useful to turn over their insurance solicitation to regional agents. These general agents hired corps of insurance solicitors, paid their own operating expenses (often out of substantial advances from the mother company), and sent a due proportion of their receipts to the home office. Agent compensation rested almost wholly on commissions.

It was significant that by 1905 one of the few defenders of the general agency system was the Equitable's Gage Tarbell. Unlike most of his peers, he interested himself exclusively in life insurance marketing. In his agency days in Chicago, he had been known as the "prince of rebaters." For Tarbell the advantages of commissioned general agents and subagents over centrally controlled, salaried solicitors lay in the commission system's incentives to large producers. The system was "more economical and more American." But so simplistic an insistence on entrepreneurial essentials had become old-fashioned by the turn of the century. For one thing, the expenses and profits of the larger agencies were embarrassingly high to cost-conscious companies, the justification that "large rewards" were due "large achievements" notwithstanding. In addition, size alone made the system cumbersome: the Big Three had between ten and fifteen thousand agents apiece by 1905.[36] Inevitably the decentralized general agencies clashed with the consolidating tendencies of the booming companies. For a society of mature, institutionalized corporations, the domains of the general agents became as much an irritant as the fiefs of great lords had been to rising national monarchs.

The first sign of this clash of interests was the introduction of special agents directly responsible to the home office. Free-lance supersalesmen who specialized in securing large policies roamed from city to city in search of men of affairs who could be induced to take substantial amounts of insurance. McCurdy got authority from his board in 1888 to send out such agents, and created a special department which dispatched flying squads of solicitors — Executive Specials — to sign up large policyholders. The most spectacular of these special agents were the Dinkelspiel brothers. Sam worked for the New York Life, William for the Equitable. A third brother, the New York Life's general agent in New Orleans and less avaricious than the others, was known as the "good Dinkelspiel." In every large city the brothers were notorious for their flamboyant selling techniques. To wealthy customers they airily promised rebates, company investments in local hotels and office buildings, directorships in their insurance firms, and, in Boston, commissions on all other insurance sold in the city. Far from discouraging such recklessness, the companies advanced huge sums of money to the brothers and accommodated them in other ways: when they lost $50,000 in one day at the Saratoga race track, the New York Life made good $30,000; the Equitable, the remainder. Sam Dinkelspiel left the New York Life in 1887 owing the company $348,000.[37]

More important than the spectacular but essentially anarchic and transitory special agent was the development of branch office systems to replace general agencies. Headed by salaried superintendents directly responsible to the home office, the branch offices reflected the tendency toward centralized, rationalized organization. McCurdy's declaration that "there is no place for 'general utility' on our stage. The day of the . . . amateur is gone" expressed the soliciting viewpoint which eventually spelled the end of the general agency system.

George W. Perkins, who pioneered in installing a branch office system in the New York Life, was aware of its psychological impact on the fabric of agency loyalty and reward. He devised an accompanying agents' association, Nylic, which through badges and awards, picnics and conventions, songs and contests, and profitable trust funds, riveted solicitor loyalty to the company itself. It was much as if a rising king attempted to preserve the fealty of his nobility through the creation of a monarchical order. By 1905, the New York Life had 215 domestic and forty foreign agency directors, all salaried, all Nylic men, all presumably loyal to the home office.[38]

The Mutual moved more slowly than the New York Life from general to branch agencies. McCurdy found it a difficult, twenty-year job to uproot the established general agencies. He was restrained, too, by the fact that his son-in-law was a partner in the C. H. Raymond Agency, which had the lion's share of the rich New York City market. But by 1905 the company's changeover to centrally controlled branch agencies was close to completion. Only Tarbell's Equitable continued to adhere to the old way.

Although the industrial companies always exercised direct control over their agency forces, the growing size and complexity of their operation required organized morale-building. The Prudential, with over 3200 agents in 1890 (it would have more than 10,500 by 1905) established an Old Guard association of long-term agents which played much the same role as Perkins' later Nylic.

The evolution of the agency structure was yet another reflection of the change wrought by growth. Although the comparative efficiency of the general agency and branch office systems was unresolved (at least for the Equitable) for decades to come, the attraction of a centralized organization was powerful indeed. Even the Equitable, which resisted the trend, strove for a more professional force by beginning, at the turn of the century, a summer training school for college-educated prospective agents.[39]

9

The institutionalization of the society of companies came up against the very heart of the insurance business technique when it modified traditional patterns of intercompany competition.

Surely competition was as strong in life insurance as in any other American enterprise in the late nineteenth century. The "Thirty Years War" between the Equitable and the Mutual was a classic case of intercompany battle. Nor did the onrushing quest for size toward the end of the century suggest any diminution of conflict. Vigorous competition made for spectacular marketing methods. The New York Life moved to the top of the industry during the 1890's with a panoply of selling drives. Agents were incited to new heights of sales volume to celebrate such events as John McCall's return from a European trip in the summer of 1897, or, in 1902, his tenth anniversary as president of the New York Life. Imaginative as George W. Perkins was in his business methods, he was of an old tradition in his fierce commitment to his company's ultimate supremacy. In this he was much like his political friends Albert Beveridge and Theodore Roosevelt, who never let their visions of sophisticated imperialism and nationalism interfere with a staunch, self-seeking political partisanship. Beveridge feelingly congratulated Perkins on a New York Life annual report which trumpeted the company's successes over its peers: "I think it very appropriate that you bind your reports in alligator. I understand that that animal devours everything in sight."

The mutual dislike of Hyde and McCurdy, and the vigor infused into the New York Life by Beers, McCall, and Perkins, made the last decade of the nineteenth century a time of frenetic competition among the Big Three. Perkins reported with no visible reluctance in 1890 that competition in the West "is certainly going to be extremely bitter." Two years later McCurdy observed that "at no time within my recollection have I found the indications of relentless struggle for supremacy clearer than I now find them."

Henry Hyde piously complained that "the unwise competition that exists on the part of the Mutual and the N.Y. Life make the business more difficult than ever to conduct — that is, if you wish to adhere to strict business principles." But he easily surmounted his scruples, assigning an Equitable man to go through the Mutual's annual reports for evidence on how that firm "oppressed the South" during the Civil War, and aggressively declaring: "I do not think any existing agreements with the New York Life, are good for anything." James Hazen Hyde's eccentricities seemed fair game to the New York Life's executives, and they made plans to distribute a photograph of the younger Hyde in foppish attire.[40]

Much bad blood stemmed from agent-stealing. "Shall the auction go on or not?" McCurdy dramatically asked Hyde over one such incident in 1893. Clearly it would, for soon after the Mutual head hoped that his Chicago general agent had "scanned the Equitable list of representatives with a view to employing those who prefer to come with us." In 1900 the Equitable substantially reduced its agents' commission rates, and the New York Life swung into action. Abruptly terminating an 1894 agreement against hiring another firm's agents, it tried to entice to its employment as many Equitable agents as possible. But Gage Tarbell was not one for passive acceptance of such tactics. Confidentially of a Sunday, he met with Robert J. Mix, the New York Life's general agent for the Manhattan department, and with the inducement of a $250,000 to $300,000 advance won him and all but 3 of his 170 agents to the Equitable. "It was a good job, and I thought it would not do any harm to do it on a good day," Tarbell complacently remarked.[41]

As the Prudential and the Metropolitan rose to dominate the industrial field, competition burgeoned between the two firms. Overzealous industrial agents attacked each other's companies as early as 1879, with Hegeman philosophically observing to Dryden that "now and then a little elbow-jostling will be inevitable." In this friendly spirit, the firms signed an agreement not to hire agents that the other had fired. But Knapp of the Metropolitan soon complained that the Prudential had violated the pact. Dryden replied that the agreement applied only to men dishonorably discharged, and pugnaciously declared that "[w]e desire peace" but would fight if necessary. "Words! Words! Words! A mass of special pleading, contradiction, inconsistency and nonsense," was Hegeman's reaction, and the fight was on. Through the 1880's complaints of agent-stealing flew between the two companies. One Prudential agent thought that an article in a Camden paper accusing his company of refusing to pay on an insured child's death had been planted by the Metropolitan. Nor did the John Hancock escape unscathed: when a "break up" of its Philadelphia agents threatened, that city's Prudential agent eagerly told his home office: "I can see opportunities that . . . will never occur again." [42]

The Big Three also turned on lesser companies in their competitive vigor. Assessment firms were a special target. Hyde had his consulting actuary, Sheppard Homans, prepare material illuminating the all-too-patent fallacies of assessment insurance, and put pressure on the New York legislatiure for action against that system. The increasingly numerous cooperative fraternal companies disturbed the Equitable head. He told vice-president James Alexander in 1887: "We must make a sharp attack upon co-operatives, as we are being troubled by them a good deal," and planned to work with the other two companies in the dissemination of circulars attacking fraternals.[43]

The society of great companies concerned themselves with more direct competitive threats as well. When a promoter of direct-mail insurance attempted to place advertising in national magazines, he found these outlets blocked by a "combination" including the Equitable, Mutual, and Prudential. Hyde waged a long and ultimately successful war against the Connecticut Mutual during the late 1870's and early 1880's. By the turn of the century the Northwestern Mutual of Milwaukee, next to the Big Five in size, had become a special object of attack. "If you can get up little slips against [the Northwestern] . . . do so, as they are pursuing a pretty tough course towards us," Hyde counseled Equitable attorney William Alexander. The New York Life, expanding into Minnesota in 1890, tried to capture a crack Northwestern Mutual agent there. Perkins was afraid that the Milwaukee firm had got wind of his company's operations, and that they would counter by selling insurance to Minnesotans "upon almost any terms at all." Such competition could be nothing more than a minor annoyance to the giant companies. But the John Hancock, junior member of the industrial Big Three and more of a size with the Northwestern Mutual and the Mutual Benefit of New Jersey, felt the competition of the lesser firms.[44]

10

The great companies thus preserved a striking competitive vigor as growth took them to new levels of corporate maturity and sophistication. But despite their staunch commitment to the ethos of competition, the virtues of cooperation were increasingly attractive. In the 1890's the belief grew that the intercompany struggle was demoralizing, wasteful, at odds with the major tendencies of the corporate structure and the business technique. Consequently, continuous efforts were made to impose order within the society of companies.

Ephemeral declarations of peace and good feeling always had provided a muted counterpoint to the clash of the giants. As early as 1884 the three leading industrial companies entered into agreements on premium rates and business methods. Coincident with the last decade of the nineteenth century there appeared evidences of what the *Weekly Underwriter* optimistically called the "beginning of a new epoch in life insurance practice in the United States." In this spirit Hyde, who by the 1890's was extolling the virtues of quality over corporate size, grandly observed to McCurdy in 1892 that he was opposed to a "system of controversy which ought to be buried with rebates and bonuses and huge brokerages and extraordinary expenses." [45]

The firms early agreed on the need to do something about rebating. From 1885 attempts were made to curtail the evil. Jacob Greene of the Connecticut Mutual, which was suffering badly from the energetic rebating of Big Three agents, took the leading role in the movement. Hyde felt obliged to go along with Greene (in a tone of injured concern he complained to the Connecticut Mutual head about the indifference of

McCurdy and Beers), but privately he was "confident it never can be carried out."

Even pressure so indifferently applied was enough to extract an anti-rebate law from the New York legislature in 1888. Other states followed; Massachusetts with an especially severe statute. The New York Life in 1889 introduced a policy allowing the equivalent of a 50 percent rebate on the first premium. The Massachusetts insurance commissioner declared the policy illegal under the state's new law. The company angrily withdrew, but soon dropped the offending policy provision and returned to the state. In general, however, the legislative movement against rebating proved ineffectual. Hyde complained righteously that rebating was the major evil in the insurance business, and McCurdy showed no real willingness to abandon the practice.[46]

Rebating was only part of a complex of business problems including high costs, the need to keep agents in line, and the competitive interests of the several companies. One expression of the interplay between competition and cooperation was the attempt during the 1890's to put some limit on the amount of insurance that a company wrote yearly. The Mutual seized the initiative in this movement, clearly not because of a change of heart by the expansionist McCurdy but out of a desire to check the growth of oversuccessful competitors. The continued superiority of the Equitable led McCurdy in 1891 to propose a sales limit to Hyde. This, he argued publicly, could produce regulated competition which offered the only effective way of cutting the companies' heavy costs. Not surprisingly, Hyde showed no great enthusiasm for the scheme. Nor did Jacob Greene of the Connecticut Mutual, who objected to the limitation because of its threat to free enterprise, and because it so obviously was a device in the Mutual's war with the Equitable. After a special committee of the National Convention of Insurance Commissioners made limitation proposals, Hyde reluctantly supposed that a one-billion-dollar maximum was the least objectionable; he thought, nearsightedly, that no company would ever have more insurance in force. But he doubted if the courts would sustain such a law, and argued that a lapse rate equal to or surpassing new business was a natural limiting factor. When a limitation bill was introduced in the New York legislature, Hyde decided not to support it, and the measure got nowhere.

In 1900 McCurdy tried again, this time with the rapidly rising New York Life as his target. McCall, who had approved of the previous, anti-

Equitable limitation attempt, felt obliged to support a Mutual-sponsored bill setting a maximum of one and a half billion dollars. But the ambitious Perkins quickly converted his chief to opposition and the measure was defeated.[47]

Nevertheless, it became increasingly clear that concerted action was necessary to do something about the anarchic competition which so obviously contributed to the high cost of life insurance. In 1891 Hyde fathered a conclave of insurance companies designed to stop the raiding of agents. In the following year the Equitable and the New York Life agreed more specifically to the same thing, and in 1893 Hyde, McCall, and McCurdy met to discuss the coming year's agent commission rates.

By 1895 the New York Life could afford to take the lead in attempts at cooperation. Spurred by that company, the Big Three in October 1895 signed a formal antirebate agreement at a meeting chaired by Massachusetts insurance commissioner Horace Merrill, and appointed former Massachusetts governor William Russell the arbiter of the compact. Representatives of twenty-eight companies, without the by now disillusioned Jacob Greene, signed this Magna Charta of reputable business practices. The fine political hand of John McCall made this an impressive achievement. The participation of officials from Massachusetts, the state thought to be most rigorous in its regulation practices, gave the compact an air of solidity and worth. When ex-Governor Russell gave up his arbitership, former speaker of the house Thomas B. Reed was his replacement.[48]

But rebating quite evidently persisted in airy disregard of the compact. Perkins reported in 1896 that the Equitable and the Mutual offered discounts of up to 80 percent to secure new business, and in 1899 McCall found that rebating "is on by . . . agents everywhere." The Equitable pulled out of what it termed a useless agreement, and the Mutual's board seriously questioned the agreement's value.

Attempts to control agent-stealing were just as frequent, and just as unavailing. The companies agreed that an agent could transfer from one firm to another only with his original employer's permission. Personnel officers had an informal arrangement whereby letters of recommendation from an agent's previous company were typed on a pink slip if he had been "honorably" discharged. Nevertheless, mass raids on agents continued into the early 1900's.

Other agreements, too, seemed to be distinguished primarily by the ease with which they were broken. The Big Three combined to fix the reserve valuation rate at 3.5 percent, but Hyde soon put out a policy with a 3 percent valuation. He graphically portrayed the pressures for disunity: "One of the companies to this . . . agreement has . . . dissolved its relations to it; another . . . has come to a deadlock with its neighbor as to the understanding of a simple statement of facts . . . I have done everything in my power to reconcile matters, but cannot . . . consider the agreement other than at an end." Only limited arrangements, such as the simultaneous payment of dividends on industrial policies by the Metropolitan and the Prudential, or the Big Three's agreement to place the burden of the Spanish-American War policy stamp tax on their policyholders, stood up reasonably well.[49]

Yet even by 1896 McCurdy discerned a great change in the nature of the business: "Competition between leading companies is much modified and the former aggressive and propagandist methods, at least so far as my own Company is concerned, have practically fallen into disuse," to be replaced by the "strictly business presentation of life insurance as an investment." The growing commonality of interest among the great corporations, the growing discordance between untrammeled competition and the needs of a mature, institutionalized society of companies, forced constant, if unsuccessful, attempts at cooperation in every sphere.

A display of managerial good fellowship was the most impressive evidence of the transformation. Some old antipathies continued — Hyde wrote of his "utter contempt" for McCurdy, and Perkins saw the Mutual president as a "cold-blooded villain, caring nothing on earth for anybody or any thing except himself and those connected with him." But the coming of John McCall to the New York Life began a new day of easier intercompany executive relations. The New York Life trustees, in choosing McCall as the company's president, spoke of his good relations with the other firms, and hoped that "he would be able to harmonize the animosities resulting from the intense business competition of recent years . . . and thereby effect a saving of many hundreds of thousands of dollars in their annual expenses." Even McCurdy welcomed McCall as bringing a new era of peace and goodwill to the life insurance business.[50]

McCurdy's delayed payments on a $15,000 personal loan from Hyde occasioned some strain in 1888, but such difficulties disappeared when loans between the chieftains came from company funds. Hegeman and McCall, who was a Metropolitan director, exchanged notes for $150,000 at the more than reasonable interest rate of 1.5 percent. As Hegeman explained it, "I consulted him as business men and professional men consult each other, frequently on matters of common interest . . . On the other side, I have perhaps acted in the same spirit towards him." And when Gage Tarbell took out a New York Life policy from his opposite number George Perkins, it was only common and reciprocal courtesy for Perkins to allow the Equitable official the agent's commission on the policy.

Toward the turn of the century, gestures of respect and courtesy seemed to be increasing, as though the great corporations were settling down to peaceful coexistence. When Henry Hyde weakened and then died, McCurdy found it easier to be on good terms with the Equitable. In 1898 he politely complimented James Alexander on the Equitable's annual statement ("It is great in any sense. Worthy of the great men and the great abilities which have created such results.") and invited Alexander to examine the Mutual's display for the Paris Exhibition of 1900. He welcomed James Hazen Hyde at the beginning of that young man's ill-starred insurance career, and supported the junior Hyde in his 1904 attempt to gain appointment as ambassador to France. Hyde responded to these gestures, telling McCurdy with cloudy enthusiasm that the companies should use their "immense moral influence as well as material means" to further their own ends. McCurdy's relations with Hegeman of the Metropolitan were excellent, and in his new-found mellowness he stopped a proposed attack on the New York Life, declaring that the Mutual would not criticize other companies.[51]

The fullest expression of the amity that corporate institutionalization brought came in company alliances — and, some hoped, in the actual consolidation of the firms. Rumor had it that the New York Life was so close to the Metropolitan, and the Equitable to the Prudential, that the Mutual also "deems it necessary to have such a side partner" and planned to convert the Washington Life Insurance Company into an industrial insurance firm. The Mutual, through some of its affiliated banking organizations, apparently made efforts in the early 1900's to purchase James Hazen Hyde's controlling bloc of Equitable stock. The close identification of the Equitable and the Prudential was common knowledge; a false report of their amalgamation circulated in 1902. As James Hazen Hyde put it in 1902: "The Equitable and the Prudential in every way — in finance, in banking and in insurance — are on the most friendly terms possible."

But these alliances had their limits. Perkins, McCurdy, and Alexander met in Paris in 1901 to discuss the tripartite financing of an English insurance paper, and Perkins responded to McCurdy's hope for "better things in the future" by suggesting that the Big Three amalgamate into one giant insurance company. His competitors did not respond to his enthusiasm. "The Steel Trust and the Standard Oil have suggested it," reported Alexander, who sarcastically summarized Perkins' intentions:

> Amalgamate. Become the arbitrator of life assurance in the world. Be so large as to be able to cope with foreign governments. Cut down expenses to the quick. Make everything purely mutual, and be the exponent of real and justifiable socialism. Buy out . . . everybody's stock for some millions. Buy out all general agents commissions . . . Form an executive control . . . have the whole under immediate management of one competent man. Perkins would consent to be this man.[52]

As great as the pressure for cooperation was the difficulty in achieving it. For while the growth of the companies made the rationalization, even the elimination, of competition seem logical and desirable, the increase in corporate worth — in the stakes involved — made its attainment correspondingly difficult. Growth and the consequent development of a society of mature, sophisticated corporations raised new vistas of business efficiency and control. But high costs, hard-to-justify dividend computations, and fervid competition remained the unwanted accompaniments of growth and size. Well might the Mutual's actuary muse that "prosperity has many meanings." [53]

Power is not a brick that can be lugged from place to place, but a process that vanishes when the supporting responses cease.

Harold D. Lasswell, *Power and Responsibility*

Part Three * The Venture Overseas

The aggressive ideology and the domestic business triumphs of the Big Three persuaded them to look overseas for new markets to conquer. In consequence, they built up by 1900 a foreign business venture of unparalleled magnitude. The sophisticated techniques which served them so well at home worked with equal effectiveness abroad.

But the very dynamism of their venture evoked substantial counterforces. The American companies were successful enough to stir foreign firms and governments to vigorous restrictive action. Although the Big Three claimed to be the evangels of a benevolent, international commerce, they could not escape the stigma of their foreignness. Everywhere they were treated as threats to domestic enterprise and national sovereignty. An international insurance business was a logical extension of American marketing triumphs, but the power of the great companies ultimately proved unexportable.

VI * The Dynamics of Foreign Expansion

In 1900 a French magazine charged that the Belgian manager of the Mutual Life Insurance Company of New York planned to engage the Pope as a general agent for his firm. The Pontiff's district would, of course, be the world, and he would receive 38 percent commission on initial premium payments.[1] This flight of fancy was stirred by a business venture whose dramatic success and precipitous decline constituted a revealing chapter in the history of the great life insurance companies.

American life insurance abroad involved companies other than the Big Three, and went back in time to the Civil War era. A scattering of lesser firms — the Germania of Madison, Wisconsin; the Union Mutual of Portland, Maine; the United States Life of New York; the New England Mutual; the Mutual Benefit — ventured into other countries at diverse times. But only the Germania developed a durable and substantial foreign market. The Equitable had rudimentary agencies in Europe and Asia from the early 1860's, and along with the New York Life did a serious business in the major European nations during the 1870's.

The American life insurance venture overseas took on substantially greater importance between 1885 and 1905. The New York Life, the Equitable, and the Mutual dominated the field; the Prudential and the Metropolitan, apart from some activity in Canada, did not seek business beyond the United States. The foreign business of the Big Three became extensive enough to amount to a sizable portion of their total insurance in force. By 1900 the Equitable was active in almost a hundred nations and territories the world over; the New York Life, in almost fifty; the Mutual, in about twenty. The volume of the New York Life's Paris office alone equaled the company's entire business of a few years before, and surpassed all American life insurance firms except the other two giants. The Big Three had almost three quarters of a billion dollars' worth of insurance in force abroad — overwhelmingly in Europe — with a quarter of a million policyholders. The three companies' 1905 premium income of almost $50,000,000 was about one eighth of the total value of the United States' finished manufactured exports.[2] (See Table 3.) This, then, was a uniquely dynamic American corporate venture overseas. It eloquently attested to the vigor of the special drives that animated the turn-of-the-century society of life insurance companies.

2

The American companies found in Europe a domestic life insurance business which, though substantial, did not match their own in size or marketing techniques. The business in Germany was "very primitive" when the Big Three entered, although several companies dated back to the 1830's and 1840's and had considerable sums of insurance in force by the end of the century. In England, the domestic business was sapped by "fraud, extravagance, dishonesty, bankruptcy, and amalgamation." Outworn tradition also weighed heavily; the venerable Equitable of London had no soliciting agents, and sold insurance only to those who sought it. French companies appealed effectively to lower income groups, but offered no equivalent to the American companies' deferred dividend policies. A European authority epitomized the clash set off by the arrival of the American firms: "From the beginning there was intense competition. It was as if two worlds had entered the lists . . . [The European companies] had been moving along the old outworn paths, tied up with red tape and bureaucratic methods. The superiority of the American methods of doing business and capacity of organization, backed up by unlimited resources, made the competition fearful.[3]

In 1899 John McCall judged that of 190 companies in continental Europe, only one, the Gotha, approached the Big Three. Of 92 in Great Britain, the Prudential, an industrial firm, alone exceeded the American companies' volume totals. The Mutual's French business went from 5.2 percent of that country's total in 1893 to 12.2 percent in 1895. Only in Australia and Canada were domestic firms able to outdo the marketing challenge of the United States corporations — although the

TABLE 3. The foreign business of the Big Three (excluding Canada), 1890–1905

	New York Life		Equitable		Mutual	
Year	Premiums	Insurance in force	Premiums	Insurance in force	Premiums	Insurance in force
			Dollars			
1890	8,008,174	172,351,422	8,639,173	215,979,331	1,435,586	33,091,053
1895	10,965,201	233,720,641	9,705,427	261,597,161	4,899,266	111,692,607
1900	12,813,382	285,161,655	10,571,755	275,878,296	7,920,573	181,729,271
1905	22,765,641	494,383,349	12,251,755	310,734,187	11,968,462	289,792,263
			Percent of total business			
1890	5	30	5	30	1	5
1895	7	29	8	29	3	12
1900	5	24	5	25	4	16
1905	15	24	9	21	7	18
			Number of foreign policyholders			
1890	40,625		54,109		8,841	
1895	59,697		74,427		40,399	
1900	98,891		86,964		74,969	
1905	201,645		105,681		122,037	

Sources: Spectator Company, *Insurance Year Book*, 1896, 1901, 1906; *Hayden's Annual Cyclopedia of Insurance in the United States*, 1911; N.Y., *Test.*, VIII, Ex. 253, 458.

Big Three kept about 30 percent of the Canadian business after 1885 while presumably better advantaged English firms were down to 13 percent of that business by 1890. Nor could European companies successfully enter the American market. Life, and particularly fire, insurance organizations tried often enough; but the pressures of competition caused 53 foreign firms to leave the United States between 1865 and 1914. Only Canada's Sun Life and a few English fire insurance companies had substantial and permanent success in the United States.[4]

The Big Three's overseas success had its source in world-wide social developments in the late nineteenth century. The business, professional, and white-collar groups which made up the bulk of the American life insurance market had counterparts elsewhere. John McCall observed that "the conditions of life abroad among the insuring classes, especially in Europe, are quite as favorable as they are in the United States." Sturdy German burghers, English doctors and businessmen, French tradesmen, commercial men and business-minded aristocrats everywhere, responded to the marketing appeal of the Big Three. In Edinburgh the American companies were strong "among professional men, especially." In Stettin their business was with "well-to-do merchants and landowners"; in Solingen, with the "better class of local business men"; in St. Étienne, with "the educated classes, who grasp their business-like methods." [5]

The deferred dividend policy had a special attraction for the world's bourgeoisie. Although tontines had been under a cloud of disrepute in Europe since the eighteenth century, the policies of the American companies seemed somehow to be free of that taint. The offerings of the New World firms exuded the heady aroma of sound investment commonly attached to American securities. Aggressive, imaginative, and successful moneymaking was considered an American trait, a national characteristic as distinguishable as British restraint or Dutch stubbornness. The United States consul in Athens reported that "the word 'American' attached to any business enterprise here inspires a certain degree of confidence." When, early in its British career, the New York Life quickly paid a doubtful policy claim, newspapers reporting the incident spoke admiringly of "Yankee Enterprise." The Big Three, as "the strongest types of American enterprise and business aggressiveness," impressed and drew the patronage of tens of thousands of foreigners attuned to these fresh new winds of entrepreneurship.[6] The bourgeoisie everywhere participated vicariously in the same homage to American freshness, opportunity, and enterprise which led so many of their peasant and artisan contemporaries to come to the golden land.

The companies took overseas techniques that had stimulated the domestic life insurance business, and found a ready response in their new markets. The aggressive, questing agents in the employ of the American firms were as effective as they were novel. In type they were much like their American counterparts. They looked upon American life insurance with the same sense of release and opportunity that animated their customers, even though salaries rather than commissions were the normal mode of payment. A German periodical spoke respectfully of the "tact and energy" of the Equitable's agents. When the American companies left Prussia in the 1890's some of their agents withdrew from the insurance business altogether: "they had been accustomed to the liberal and businesslike methods of the American companies and could not, or would not, accommodate themselves to the bureaucratic and old-fashioned system which prevails among the German insurance societies." The Equitable's Russian director, Sydney S. Schmey, built up his business by entertaining in St. Petersburg with "immense sums" of the company's money. When it became necessary to replace him because of trouble over his accounts, high Russian officials interceded for him.[7]

Flexibility of organization also characterized the companies' overseas venture. The New York Life had a separate Latin American department in the 1880's, and in 1893 established a European branch office in Paris which was independent of the home office in all but broad policy and investment matters. By 1899 George W. Perkins was ready to install a branch office system in Russia. A German office of issue was added in 1903, and in 1905 the company had 129 European branches with 278 agency directors and 292 salaried agents. Branch managers served the Equitable in Great Britain and France, although Henry Hyde kept an especially close watch on his foreign business. The Mutual's McCurdy, alert to possible improvements, considered adopting for his Russian agency the International Bell Telephone Company's system of appointing agents and collecting money. The company's foreign department was under the direction of Robert McCurdy, son of the president, who operated it as an extension of the firm's domestic general agent system. The younger McCurdy drew a 5 percent commission on the overseas business until his earnings ($40,000 to $60,000 a year) became too much even for a notably avaricious management.[8]

As in America, the companies supplemented their policy, agency, and managerial techniques with a variety of subtler weapons. In 1888 Henry Hyde thought it a good idea "to have a man go around among the representatives of the foreign nations in this city, as I believe they are often written to for information about the American companies." The distribution of printed material was heavy. The Equitable lavishly disbursed "blue books" documenting the superiority of the company and its deferred dividend policies. Elizur Wright was called on to prepare material for translation. George Perkins noted in 1899 that the Mutual spent a great deal of money on advertising in Europe, and a Swedish journal spoke of the American companies' "energetic and often ruthless propaganda." [9]

The insurance press, so often a competitive battleground in America, was not neglected abroad. Harry S. Homans, the New York Life's first English general agent, became a close associate of Cornelius Walford, the leading British insurance publicist. Hyde, as usual, was particularly skillful and alert. As early as 1880 he confidently (and overoptimistically) predicted that there would be no more attacks on the Equitable in the British press. When French periodicals criticized his company, he planned to answer with material printed in French in New York and shipped abroad; thus no one could be arrested if a libel suit resulted. "That is the way the thing is done by people who understand it," he knowingly observed.

In 1888 and again in 1894, Hyde sought to "have confidential relations with" or to "get hold of" insurance journals in England, Austria, and Germany which would "be friendly to us" and "print editorial matter in the right way." He proposed to the other companies in 1884 that each pay $5,000 to gain the "assistance" of newspapers in Great Britain's major cities. In 1901 Presidents Alexander of the Equitable and McCurdy of the Mutual met with Perkins of the New York Life in Paris to discuss the purchase of *The Review,* an English insurance journal. They agreed to lend $10,000 each to the periodical, which would "be conducted in the interest of American insurance and financial ideals." [10] Though controlled insurance media offered no immediate marketing advantages, the security and prestige of the American venture would be enhanced.

As important as proper press relations were personal contacts. A member of the Russian government's insurance regulation commission was in the Equitable's employ. In the early 1900's, James Hazen Hyde worked with the Mutual "to interest in behalf of the American companies prominent persons connected with the press, and people who were influential in moulding public opinion." Well-known customers such as Joseph Chamberlain were prized publicity assets. The New York Life sought to broaden the base of its public support by establishing resident boards in cities throughout the world; the Equitable had a "board of directors" in England.

The companies sought to ensure the friendship of appropriate American diplomatic representatives. Hyde supported the appointment of Jared L. Rathbone as American consul-general in Paris: the diplomat had been useful to American business interests there. The Equitable head reminded Chauncey Depew of the importance of having ministers to Brazil, Russia, and Switzerland who "were strong friends of ours, and willing to go outside of their official duties to help us, if necessary." He asked the Equitable director and politico to secure such appointments, or at least to see that the diplomats were "made friendly" to the company before going abroad. When Stewart L. Woodford went to Madrid as the American envoy on the eve of the Spanish-American War, Hyde reminded him that "in case of trouble arising between the Spanish Government and ourselves, advises [*sic*] from you to our [Spanish] Manager might be of the greatest importance." William I. Buchanan, ambassador to Argentina from 1894 to 1900, subsequently represented the New York Life in its dealings with foreign governments.[11]

Fierce competition typified the formative years of the great companies' venture overseas. Periodicals and pamphlets, such as the Mutual's 1898 circular to Spanish policyholders calling Perkins and McCall "arch-fiends of war," concentrated on intercompany feuding as much as they extolled the American life insurance enterprise. The achievements of one company stirred the competitive fire of another. In 1882 Hyde was aroused by the knowledge that the New York Life was "quite running away from us in the Spanish countries," and with jocular aggressiveness warned Beers: "I do not know that you own Russia or have a lien upon it." McCurdy justified the Mutual's entry into a foreign business on the ground that the greater volume of his rivals was due entirely to their sales overseas.[12]

But the injury of untrammeled competition spurred attempts at mollification and cooperation. McCurdy cautioned against too exuberant attacks on his competitors by English journals controlled by the Mutual, and in 1895 the firms entered upon a shaky agreement to restrain the competitive ardor of agents and periodicals in the South American market. Hyde attempted to end feuding with his rivals, observing that "it injures us . . . and helps everyone else." He pointed out: "Nothing is calculated to do us more harm in foreign countries than public controversies or hostilities of any kind among the American companies." After John McCall became president of the New York Life in 1892 he told his board of his hopes for overseas cooperation among the Big Three. The appointment of General George S. Batchellor as a roving "tontine ambassador" serving the interests of the three companies was a sign of this development. The 1901 Paris meeting to discuss a joint sponsorship of *The Review* also testified to the trend of cooperative effort — a trend encouraged by the difficulties then besetting the overseas venture. James Alexander hoped in 1903 that the prevailing domestic agreements on agent employment and "decency in competitive literature" might be expanded to include premium rates and policy forms throughout the world.[13] The tendencies that characterized the domestic marketing technique also affected the international business of the great companies.

3

The Big Three's foreign insurance marketing raised substantial problems of international finance. By 1888 Henry Hyde was "continually worrying about our currency in foreign countries," and proposed to have investment bankers (in this case, Kidder, Peabody and Company) run the Equitable's international banking affairs: "They can let us know the best way to take Russian money to London, and could give us advice upon a thousand and one other questions respecting our foreign finances." Such problems were numerous enough to affect corporate organization. In 1893 the Mutual's finance committee reviewed the "very large and increasing money transactions of the Foreign Department." To pay foreign policy claims and to meet governmental deposit requirements more easily, the company's overseas financial transactions were consolidated in the office of its London manager. In addition, foreign securities could be purchased more advantageously at the world's financial center, where quotations were especially trustworthy. To implement this decision, a London branch of the Mutual-dominated Guaranty Trust Company was established. But at the same time, the Mutual considered it necessary to take foreign investment policymaking from the purview of the foreign department and put it under the treasurer. Thus investment abroad could be handled "more strictly in accordance with the general system of investment prevailing in the other transactions of the Company." At George W. Perkins' suggestion, the New York Life in 1901 established a foreign advisory board supervising the security purchases necessary for overseas deposit requirements. But as in the case of the Mutual, the home office kept overall control of the company's European investments.[14] Again, the dictates of bureaucratic regularization cut across the more evident demands of entrepreneurship: for the purchase of securities overseas was in fact more a part of the insurance marketing process than of the companies' investment programs.

The Big Three's overseas investments soon reached impressive size, tens of millions flowing into real estate and securities (see Table 4).

TABLE 4. The Big Three's foreign bond and stock holdings, 1890–1905 (book value)

Year	New York Life	Equitable	Mutual
1890	$2,566,125[a]	$3,010,081[b]	$313,608
1905	35,661,526	12,126,890	16,596,861

[a] Fixed deposits: $1,420,908
[b] Fixed deposits: $2,137,467
Source: Schedules in *New York Insurance Report*, 1891, 1906.

This development was part of a broader economic phenomenon: the emergence of the United States as a creditor in its international balance of payments. The life insurance companies played a signal role in the early flow of securities investment from America to Europe. In 1899 the Big Three held forty to forty-five million dollars' worth of European securities, while all other American investors had about fifteen million. For several years thereafter, the demands of growing national armaments and social expenditures, the Boer and Russo-Japanese wars, and the favorable conditions prevailing in the New York money market induced European governments to turn to the New World for funds. The great life insurance companies, with their extensive overseas business, their experience in the purchase of European securities, and their intimate relationships with the American financial community, were ideally suited to participate in this development.[15]

But the companies' investment policies went beyond considerations of placement and return. It became necessary to strive for a delicate balance on the pinpoint of self-interest among the conflicting pressures of the expected return on investments, the factor of public relations, and foreign government deposit requirements.

The goodwill factor was substantial. In 1903, as troubles with the French government mounted in intensity, the New York Life and the Equitable announced their intention to purchase $8,000,000 worth of French *rentes;* the Paris *Herald* promised that this would "only be the beginning." In Austria, Germany, and Russia, George W. Perkins used his company's investment power to enhance its marketing prospects. Public relations, rather than pure investment, predominated in the companies' real estate acquisitions abroad as at home. The desire to display their corporate strength in visual form led them to purchase or construct impressive office buildings in major cities everywhere. The New York Life bought a substantial structure in Paris' *Boulevard des Italiens* in 1884, and constructed splendid edifices in Berlin (1885), Vienna (1887), Amsterdam (1892), and Budapest (1894). During the same years the Equitable put up buildings in Berlin (where one of its tenants was the American embassy), Vienna, Madrid, Sydney, Melbourne, and Paris. The Mutual, more cautious, limited itself at first to a Berlin building, but after 1900 added properties in Paris, London, Sydney, Capetown, and Mexico City.[16]

The building program was not simply the product of inflamed ambitions in the home offices. Pressure from agents in the field contributed heavily. In 1899 the New York Life's European manager asked for a new Paris structure in time for the 1900 Exposition. "You can well imagine what a European and world-wide *réclamé* it would be for our Company," he wrote. McCall and Perkins were more than willing to respond to such an appeal, and in the year of the Exposition what McCall called "a very showy building" rose in the French capital. Mutual solicitors in Paris, smarting from the glories of the New York Life's building, induced McCurdy to match his competitor. The New York Life's Budapest representative pleaded long and eloquently for a company building in his city. He assured the home office that "with a building like those already erected by the Company in Vienna or Berlin, Hungary will soon become one of the best countries in Europe for our company's business," and warned: "if we wish to maintain our good position here, we must satisfy our policyholders, who wish to see a building here most urgently, and who will not continue their payments if we do not build." The company agreed to a Budapest building — and had its leading Hungarian policyholders participate with much publicity in selecting the plan.[17]

The bulk of the Big Three's overseas investments met reserve deposit requirements set by foreign governments. Company real estate sometimes satisfied the demand: the New York Life built in Amsterdam, and contemplated doing the same in Milan and Turin, for this purpose. A member of the firm's finance committee declared, with fine disdain for Old World economic institutions: "I would rather have the security of real estate in any City abroad than to deposit in any National Bank there, or hold any of their Government bonds." New York Life's president Beers went to London in 1891 to investigate real estate for deposit purposes, and in 1905 the Equitable acquired a new Paris building to meet the French government's requirements.[18]

But the companies most often met deposit obligations by securities purchases. Deposit investments were an exceptionally unstable category, subject as they were to the changing demands of governments and to fluctuations in the amount of insurance in force. The New York Life finance committee's minute books were filled with the details of deposit investments; in number of transactions, if not in bulk value, they rivaled the company's domestic financial activity.

The firm met steady increases in its Canadian deposit requirement with Canadian Pacific and City of Quebec bonds, finally gaining permission in 1895 to replace these securities with United States railroad bonds. But rarely could it turn to the comfort and greater earnings of American securities. The company satisfied an 1891 increase in its Russian deposit requirement by purchases of a conveniently available Interior Ministry Loan. Soon the Russians desired to exchange these securities for 4 percent *rentes* redeemable at the pleasure of the government. The New York Life agreed, but asked for written assurance from the Finance Minister that interest on the *rentes* would not go below 4 percent before 1900. In 1892 the Italian government demanded a deposit increase, and the company considered various alternatives of investment. It placed its entire deposit in 4 percent Italian *rentes* when those securities appeared in 1896, and acquiesced when the Austrians required the investment of the deposit in national securities. In June 1902 the firm replaced its United States bonds on deposit in Great Britain with British consols. Brazil required that foreign insurance companies use a special bond issue floated for that purpose alone. By 1903 the New York Life found it necessary to append a special foreign deposit schedule to its annual statements; the total of such deposits mounted from $25,000,000 in 1903 to $38,000,000 in 1905.

Deposit investments thus grew with the success of the companies' overseas business. But the Big Three often were more than ready to invest abroad. Offerings of distinction found eager takers in the great companies: the Equitable subscribed £2,000,000, the Mutual £1,000,000, and the New York Life £2,000,000 to the 1901 British Boer War loan. George W. Perkins joined the New York Life's finance committee at the beginning of 1899, and thereafter that company became a prime American investor in European securities. Purchases went beyond deposit requirements to become part of the firm's overall investment program. As Perkins put it, "we are not holding to our old hidebound theory that we must stick to the exact amount of our reserve in each country." [19] In August 1899, $1,500,000 worth of British 3 percent Exchequer bonds became part of the company's portfolio, and in September the finance committee took a 12,000,000 franc issue of 4 percent bonds from the Canton of Geneva with the intention of selling half of it in the American market. A loan of 2,500,000 francs went to Vevey, Switzerland; and the company was authorized to purchase 1,000,000 to 2,000,000 marks of a State of Bremen offering. In succeeding years the firm took $250,000 worth of a Kuhn, Loeb flotation of City of Stockholm bonds, a Deutsche Bank of Berlin offer of Mexican Consolidated 5's, 25 percent of a 20,000,000 crown Copenhagen loan, and shares in syndicates handling Imperial Japanese loans stemming from the Russo-Japanese war. Most dramatically, the New York Life smoothed the way for the first substantial German and Russian flotations in the United States. These activities attested to the truly international character of the company's investment program.

4

Henry Hyde had his doubts about the venture overseas, and Winston of the Mutual stayed within the United States as a matter of policy. But the next generation of executives — McCurdy, McCall, and Perkins, and to some extent Alexander and James Hazen Hyde — found the foreign business an exciting and promising field. In marketing challenge and response, in investment policy and performance, the foreign enterprise was an especially rich expression of the Big Three's maturity and thrust.

Practical reasons such as the desire to hedge against the possible exhaustion of the domestic market helped to justify the venture. But so extensive an overseas business was a conscious act of business ideology, not merely a logical market expansion. The identity existing by 1900 between the ideology of life insurance and the foreign business was too great to be accidental. The missionary theme so often attached to domestic marketing now took on heightened meaning. An American consul in Turkey, once an insurance man, was moved to write on "The Influence of American Life Insurance Companies Abroad." The great firms' foreign agents, he thought, were "like so many missioners educating the people on the duty they owe to the State, their dependents and humanity." [20]

Richard McCurdy was especially ready to ascribe such values to his company's foreign business. In January 1886, soon after becoming president of the Mutual, he established a foreign department and underlined his high hopes for its success by making his son Robert its superintendent. Cautious in his early years (there was board opposition to the overseas venture), McCurdy at first soothingly guaranteed that no company building would be erected in foreign cities, and that the Mutual would not leave deposits under the control of other governments. But soon he made the firm's foreign business an integral part of his grandiose plans for expansion. Returning from an inspection trip overseas in 1889, he successfully called on his board of trustees to rescind the earlier limitations on buildings and deposits, and spoke warmly of the perpetuation of the Mutual "as a cosmopolitan institution." Although he had guaranteed that the company would not go beyond countries with populations of American or European ancestry, by the early 1900's it was doing business in China and Japan, and the talk in the home office was that the sun never set on the Mutual's flag. Disingenuously, McCurdy discounted any desire for "the glory of universality" or for self-aggrandizement. Rather, the venture overseas was "a natural, necessary and scientific development of the idea in which [the Mutual] was founded: to get the greatest possible coverage of risk." But he could not suppress some headier considerations: the Mutual had "simply yielded to the spirit of the age," for "no phenomena in our civilization has been more noteworthy during the past fifty years than the rapid union of the accumulating wealth of all civilized nations into a single mass, so as to be affected together by the same influences, for good or for ill." It seemed fitting that insurance should take the lead in this work, for by its very nature — its independence of race, residence, occupation — it eventually would help to make wars impossible and turn the society of men into a peaceful and happy community.[21]

Although the New York Life's foreign business was a venerable one, it did not at first command enthusiasm like McCurdy's. Upon assuming the company presidency in 1892, John McCall commented that if the overseas branch was just beginning, he might oppose it; since it was decades old, he would give it his support. But the interest of his right-hand man, George W. Perkins, soon converted this shaky acceptance to spirited encouragement. For the ebullient vice-president, the company's foreign division was "the State Department of the life insurance business," and he gave special attention to the commercial equivalent of the political post that he most coveted. With some of McCurdy's grandiloquence he declared: "In statesmanship we stand as a link between the nations, gathering together into one great cooperative society the best, the healthiest, the most unselfish men of all nations"; sentiments which his disciple Darwin P. Kingsley would carry to heights of hyperbole.[22]

The confidence, exuberance, and success of the Big Three's overseas venture was synchronous with their spectacular expansion at home. For Europe, which bore the brunt of this turn-of-the-century American commercial imperialism, it was a striking display of the great new power emanating from the colossus of the West. Proudly the New York Life boasted on its 1899 letterhead: "The Oldest International Life Insurance Company in the World. Supervised by 82 Governments." But the boast betrayed the venture's essential instability. The very size of the business raised continuous, extensive, and in the end insurmountable obstacles to its success. The world of the late nineteenth and early twentieth centuries proved highly resistant to the outward push of American corporate enterprise, even enterprise in so palatable and sophisticated a form as the overseas venture of the life insurance companies.

VII * The Challenges of Nationalism

The companies quickly discovered that their foreign business raised a host of problems. Abroad, as at home, growth brought difficulties which were inherent and integral, not chance or casual, parts of the process. The very intensity, ingenuity, and success of the American venture overseas generated forces which in the long run helped bring it to a close.

The potential of the Big Three's foreign business had its limitations. Their deferred dividend policies, the heart of their international success, appealed only to prosperous, financially sophisticated customers — to white-collar workers, professionals, and businessmen ready to respond to a complex investment proposal.

The cost of the venture turned out to be a major attritive force. Before 1900 the common view was that the foreign business, with lower expenses and longer-lasting policies, was cheaper than its domestic counterpart. Richard McCurdy considered foreign lives as safe a risk as domestic ones, and pointed to the economies of the overseas venture: the lack of rebating, the rarity of policy lapsing, the greater, prompter adherence to contractual obligations in the Old World. At the end of 1898 the Mutual computed that of the $47,000,000 in foreign premiums collected to that time, $23,000,000 went into the company's reserve, $2,100,000 into foreign government securities, $1,500,000 into overseas office buildings, and $130,000 into cash deposits. McCurdy implied that the remainder, well over $20,000,000, more than covered business costs.[1]

Yet through the 1890's doubts were expressed about the foreign venture's profitability. An insurance journal in 1890 questioned the wisdom of an international business, and in 1894 the New York Life's European chief worriedly wrote to McCall: "It has been mentioned to me several times that the general impression prevails that the European business is a burden on the Home Office." Even McCurdy admitted that the initial cost of the Mutual's overseas marketing was especially heavy, but he considered this offset by the greater persistency of premium payments.[2] Henry Hyde became cost-conscious as the Equitable's foreign business failed to match domestic levels of success. In 1893 he noted with concern the fall or lack of advance in his company's European volume, and two years later flatly declared: "We do not desire to extend our business in foreign countries and are gradually retiring from some of them." He ended the Equitable's venture in Latin America and Asia because of currency and exchange problems, difficulties with premium collection and risk selection, and high mortality rates. Where the business remained, Hyde pushed hard for cost reduction, and happily noted substantial savings in 1896. But by 1901 mortality rates in Europe were also a source of concern, and Hyde's successor, Equitable president James Alexander, spoke of an "irrepressible conflict" between overseas volume and expense which could not be resolved because high mortality rates blocked the indefinite expansion necessary to long-run success. The Armstrong investigation of 1905 unearthed numerous examples of unsatisfactory foreign expense ratios, which were blamed on unfavorable contracts with overseas managers, business falloffs, and poor trade conditions.[3]

The Mutual and the New York Life continued to insist that the overseas business was profitable. Robert McCurdy claimed that the Mutual's 1903 foreign expense ratio equaled the domestic level — no great mark of economy in itself — and a New York Life publication in 1909 staunchly insisted that the company's foreign business was profitable, despite "certain insinuations to the contrary." [4] But whatever the truth, concern over the cost factor remained an irritant which, in combination with other, more dramatic difficulties, cast a shadow over the venture overseas.

No great expectations of profitability attached to the companies' foreign investments: clearly these were not attractive for their own sake. Buildings overseas, as in the United States, returned less than 3 percent. James W. Alexander burst out in 1900: "Just look at the trouble we have got into all over the world about buildings! How gladly we would like to be relieved of most of them! It is the low interest of our real estate that is hanging like a millstone around our necks to-day." Diverse sources contributed to this unsatisfactory performance: McCurdy complained in 1898 that anti-American feeling in France adversely affected the value of the Mutual's Paris building; the Equitable and Mutual protested against special Australian government assessments.

Foreign securities were not much more gratifying. The average interest rate of the New York Life's foreign bonds was consistently below the level of its total securities portfolio. Of course, return was not the sole criterion for buildings erected to enhance public relations and securities purchased to meet government deposit requirements. But the spotty earning record, no less than an uncertain cost structure, added to the readiness of the companies to abandon their foreign business when more concrete and substantial difficulties arose.[5]

Yet another restraining element was the attitude of state insurance commissioners in the United States. The Connecticut commissioner cautiously wondered in 1891 if the game was worth the candle: high mortality rates, difficulties in risk selection, remoteness from the home office, interference and control by foreign governments, and problems of currency protection diluted his enthusiasm. He called for legislation limiting the companies to the healthier portion of North America — or at least to countries with adequate mortality data. In the early 1890's defalcations in the New York Life's South American division and low returns on overseas real estate disturbed the New York department of insurance. The commissioners from seven states who examined McCall's company in 1894 were not impressed by the worth of its foreign business. Hyde seized upon their statement as an excuse for closing the Equitable's Asian and some of its Latin American offices. After 1900, when the New York Life alone conducted its overseas business aggressively, its foreign operations came in for special attention by a New York insurance department otherwise notably lenient.[6]

2

Constraints upon the companies' overseas venture appeared most frequently and most painfully in their dealings with the authorities of the countries in which they plied their trade. Unlike Standard Oil, whose chief overseas problem at this time was the competition of other suppliers, the life insurance companies asserted their marketing superiority over domestic firms almost everywhere. But their very success fed the inclination of foreign governments to constrain, assess, penalize, and expel the American firms.

The product that the companies offered could be duplicated everywhere — by government insurance if need be. Although they were a strong and skillful corporate group, they could not evoke power mechanisms equal to those of the meanest national state. The complexion of sovereignty in the late nineteenth and early twentieth centuries worked against the American companies. They were attempting to make their way in a world of increasingly rigid nationalism. Europe was a place of heightening suspicions, tensions, barriers; general war was not far away. Latin American goodwill toward the United States, never abundant, was especially sparse in the imperialistic aftermath of the Spanish-American War. Nor would the Far East, wracked by the rise of Japan and Western intervention in China, be responsive to a product dependent upon stability and order. In the Middle East, complained an agent, Islam's emphasis upon the joys of an afterlife made life insurance seem "superfluous."

But the companies were among America's — and the world's — most sophisticated corporations, and they fought vigorously against unfriendly supervision. The struggle involved international political, diplomatic, communications, and juridical institutions. The firms had to weigh factors as complex as the effect of American tariff policy on their European business. They had to participate in extended negotiations which at one time or another involved the President, Congress, Department of State, and state insurance departments of the United States, and premiers, foreign ministers, ministers of interior, and representative assemblies of foreign nations. Shy of the judicial process (an Equitable counsel told his company's European agents: "The Company has great horror of litigation, — its special pride being that it keeps itself out of the Courts"), the firms nevertheless had to defend themselves before tribunals everywhere. The Equitable suffered an adverse decision and a fine in the Swiss courts for advertisements declaring that its policies were "incontestable" and "free of all restrictions." The New York Life between 1898 and 1902 engaged in twelve suits in Russia, six in Hungary, two in Bulgaria, and one each in Italy, Great Britain, and Chile. Of seventeen decisions recorded, fourteen went against the company.[7]

The chief irritant was regulatory authority. Supervision ranged from Great Britain's laissez-faire reliance on publicity to the highly organized systems of Germany and Switzerland. During the 1890's and early

1900's the American firms clashed with insurance authorities everywhere. In the mid-1890's the New York insurance superintendent observed that the Equitable's difficulties with other governments had made its foreign business "less desirable than hitherto." This development did not affect the Big Three alone: British life insurance companies, too, found it necessary to withdraw from Germany, France, and even from South Africa. But the American firms were most heavily involved in regulatory battles around the turn of the century.

Almost every country came to insist that domestic securities or a cash deposit be set aside to cover the insurance companies' policy commitments and any legal judgments that might be found against them. The long-term nature of the policy contract and the alien location of the home offices made such guarantees logical and proper. John McCall considered foreign deposit and investment restrictions superior to their domestic equivalents, and Henry Hyde was ready to make a $200,000 deposit in Italy even before the government required it. But as deposit demands, often linked with restrictions on deferred dividend policies, increased, the companies came to treat the requirements as a threat to their business. They turned often to the American government for assistance. When Elihu Root became Secretary of State in 1905, he resigned as a Mutual director because "the foreign business of the Company has been to so considerable an extent in the past and may be in the future the subject of consideration by the State Department." Presidents Cleveland, Harrison, McKinley, and Roosevelt took note of the companies' foreign difficulties in annual messages to Congress, and the State Department of Richard Olney, John Sherman, and John Hay responded warmly to the entreaties of this important corporate group.[8]

But what victories the companies scored in their battles with foreign authorities were due more to their own efforts than to the intercession of their government. The overseas venture of this corporate group, substantial as it was, did not coincide in any significant way with the national interest. And even the great companies' skillful private diplomacy could not indefinitely check the wasting force of nationalism.

3

Although the Big Three entered some of the classic areas of American commercial expansion — the Far East, Canada, Latin America — local and nationalistic forces and inherent business difficulties made these unsatisfying ventures.

China and Japan were risky business environments around the turn of the century. The Equitable scored some success with wealthy citizens in Tientsin, and Perkins eagerly sought Chinese concessions. But the market was a limited one, marked by anti-Western feeling. The New York Life was one of the firms included in the Chinese boycott of American companies which foreshadowed the revolution of 1911.[9]

The Big Three felt the effects of Japan's emergence into world politics. The Equitable's activity in the Island Kingdom dated from 1867; but the company withdrew temporarily in 1894, at the time of the Sino-Japanese War. Hyde's company returned in 1895, and was joined by its two rivals in 1902. By May 1903 the New York Life looked benignly on a record of over 2700 policy applications in four months. But in the same year, because of the nationalistic ferment preceding the war with Russia, Japan sharply increased her reserve requirements for foreign insurance companies. The intent of the action was to protect "native Insurance Companies by excluding from competition the great foreign companies." The American firms were the obvious target, for they did a larger business than all the other non-Japanese firms combined. The Equitable and the Mutual vigorously resisted the new requirement, but the State Department could find no treaty violation or arrant injustice to justify a protest. And soon the New York Life broke with its fellows by accepting the regulations. The vigorous objections of the British minister and the unofficial representations of the American envoy softened the terms of the law, and the Equitable, too, soon worked out a satisfactory arrangement. Only the Mutual found the conditions insupportable and withdrew.[10]

Even the neighborly business environment of Canada presented some difficulties. As early as 1877 many American firms underwent a crisis of withdrawal and (for some) return over a Canadian deposit law. The Equitable in 1884 complained about constant attacks by the "more active Canadian companies envious of our successful competition," and a decade later the companies found it necessary to work in unison against undesirable Canadian legislation.[11]

Troubles far more extensive and exotic arose south of the border. Latin America proved to be as subject as the Old World to the dictates of nationalism. The form of resistance often was different, but the spirit was the same. Government corruption in Argentina, Brazil, and Mexico; revolution and social unrest in Uruguay and Cuba; anti-Americanism attendant upon the creation of an American territorial and commercial empire — all were as unsettling to a private corporate group as the fierce winds of chauvinism besetting pre-1914 Europe.

Problems of currency stability and value, present everywhere, took on a special urgency below the border. The New York Life and the Equitable agreed, until 1893, to do their South American business in gold only. Concern over the soundness of local banks forced the issue of whether or not to forego the convenience of local accounts for the safety of remissions to the home office. In 1896 General Valeriano Weyler, Spain's commandant in the rebellious island of Cuba, ordered the compulsory circulation of Bank of Spain notes — and the Equitable worried about the consequent effect on policy contracts stipulating premium payment in gold. Later, when Cuba was in process of becoming a republic, the Mutual had knotty problems with bond titles in that country.[12]

Fraud seemed to be an inescapable feature of the Latin American business landscape. In 1891 the director of the New York Life's Spanish American department was implicated in defalcations totaling around $500,000. The company blamed its failure to notice the deception on the department's rapid expansion, and on "the difficulty of communication with many of these countries, the lack of direct steamship lines, the necessity of communicating by way of Europe with a large portion of the territory, the disturbed condition of affairs in some of the South American Republics" — in other words, on the business environment itself.

Everywhere the companies had to cope with the special unpopularity of *Yanquis*. Sometimes this hostility took on a dramatic color and violence. An intrepid New York Life confidential agent, responsible for the breakup and conviction of a Mexican gang that was murdering people after insuring them, set out after another group of insurance swindlers in San Domingo. He secured arrests and indictments, but in so doing aroused local passions, and a mob of a thousand people surrounded his hotel. The company got word of his plight ("he managed to get the dispatch through their lines") and appealed to the State Department: "The danger, of course, is that the rioters will fire the hotel and shoot him as he comes out." [13]

In Cuba the New York Life was caught up in problems incident to rebellion, occupation, and independence. For years it wrestled with the legal aftermath of a wild and elaborate fraud involving common-law marriages, attempted murder and a fraudulent death claim, bribery and blackmail, a company agent who had been a bandit during the war with Spain and had been in jail for forgery, and unreliable witnesses (the New York Life representative at the trial reported that one woman giving testimony had a reputation "such as to absolutely discredit her as a witness. During the hearing and at other times, she continuously smoked black cigars"). One of the principals in this attempted fraud, a doctor, happened also to be a leader in the Liberal party of José Miguel Gómez, Cuba's President after the American intervention of 1907–09. The company's attorney, a member of the opposition Conservative party, soon found himself disqualified from the case. Although the manifest complicity of the defendants forced a verdict of guilty, they were amnestied as soon as American troops left in 1909, and the company thereafter engaged in a long and fruitless effort to return them to prison.[14]

The difficulties of Latin American life insurance marketing appeared in their most exotic form in Uruguay. Casimiro Castro, a native entrepreneur, took out New York Life policies on the lives of Uruguayan army officers, with himself as beneficiary. The premiums were paid by the officers. In return, Castro assumed the costs and expenses of his clients' pending bankruptcy proceedings, a situation apparently endemic in the officer corps. The New York Life representative in Uruguay discovered the scheme, and brought Castro to court on charges of fraud. The defendant promptly responded with a countersuit for defamation of character. His calculation of the damage he had suffered, based on an estimate of what he would have earned from the policies of 100 officers in fifteen years, was $1,250,000.

Castro was a man of influence in Uruguayan politics: while the company's suit languished, the courts ordered that an arbitration panel determine the precise amount of damages due him. An obviously biased board of arbitrators awarded Castro his claim of $1,250,000 — in gold. When the New York Life refused to pay such a sum, the Castro forces had the company's Uruguayan manager and many of its trial witnesses put in jail.

The firm appealed for help to the Department of Commerce's Bureau of Corporations, and then to the State Department. Intervention in the judicial process of Uruguay was difficult, but the company was not without resources. The Uruguayan Foreign Minister had been an examining physician for the firm, and the Interior Minister had served as its counsel. Although the Foreign Minister denied the right of the United States to intervene, he was anxious to avoid a situation "which must result in humiliating Uruguay." Sentiment in the nation's Senate favored the New York Life, and it became clear that the government planned to intervene in the case.

In the fall of 1903 President Batlle y Ordóñez called for reform of the Uruguayan judicial system, including a new appeals court which would act as the country's highest judicial body and would then be able to review the Castro case. The Uruguayan Congress was considering this bill when a government crisis in November precipitated civil war. By May 1904 the fortunes of war made it imprudent to try to push the bill through "the Congressional fragment in session in Montevideo. The original friends of the measure are gone. They are refugees in Buenos Aires." The attention of President Batlle was fixed on the military situation, and in September the House of Deputies rejected the judicial reorganization.

Meanwhile, the Castro group was ready to settle with the company, which had the additional worry of being represented by attorneys "some of whom are as avaricious as Castro." The American ambassador also pushed for a compromise, and finally the bad publicity attendant upon the 1905 Armstrong investigation induced the New York Life to agree to a settlement out of court.[15]

The adventures of the New York Life in Uruguay were unusually dramatic; elsewhere in Latin America, more mundane problems of taxation and deposit were the rule. The Equitable in 1890 warned that a proposed Argentinian law "would destroy the business of American Life Insurance in Buenos Aires — a business that has reached large proportions." A more substantial challenge came in 1898, when the authorities demanded that deposits be made with government bonds issued especially for this purpose. The New York Life interpreted the law to mean that it could safely stop doing business in Argentina without taking on the new securities as a deposit for its existing policies. But it soon learned otherwise, when its Buenos Aires representative was threatened with six months' imprisonment for failing to obey the act. "If an official decree, signed by the President and the Minister of Finance cannot be relied on, with what safety can any business be transacted with that country?" the company plaintively asked the State Department. But in the ensuing complex negotiations, which ended in a compromise settlement, the New York Life did not get the diplomatic help it counted on. William I. Buchanan, the American minister, coldly reported that the company "has seemingly assumed that the Department of State has taken the case in hand and that it will be made a Diplomatic question," but his own view was that the firm had made "neither a perfectly correct nor a fair presentation of the case." [16]

The New York Life contributed to the corruption of the Peixoto regime in Brazil by bribing the Minister of Agriculture to deny the Equitable a renewal of its license. Only after the Minister was removed from office could Hyde's company return. Animosities between local agents prevented united opposition to a new Brazilian deposit and tax law in 1895. The American ambassador reported that New York Life agents there supported the measure, and undersecretary of state Alvey A. Adee severely observed: "It would be most unfortunate and detrimental to . . . just and impartial advocacy of legitimate American enterprises . . . were the interests of two great companies to clash in this important regard." When it appeared that the New York Life's Brazilian agents were acting contrary to home office instructions, Adee sighed that the matter was "too confusing to admit of intelligent instructions." As if in deference to State's disinclination to intervene, both companies ceased to do new business in Brazil before the end of the year.[17]

Their withdrawal did not avoid stiffening regulations on insurance already written. The Equitable complained about such a decree in 1902. It asked the State Department, which had blocked Brazilian discrimination against American flour by threatening an impost on coffee, to give the same "energetic and emphatic support" to life insurance interests. But the department refused to be hurried into action. The New York Life complicated the situation by seeking readmission to the Brazilian market. This time it assured itself of the American minister's support. McCall and Perkins first worked to retain the friendly Thomas L. Thompson in the post, and then established good relations with his successor, Charles Page Bryan. These politically minded insurance leaders also engaged former minister to Argentina William I. Buchanan as an international diplomatic trouble shooter for the New York Life. Their fence-mending soon paid off. The Sul America, a Brazilian insurance firm, resisted the New York Life's return, and Thompson indignantly reported that the local company was using a large fund to obtain "the assistance of . . . Senators and persons influential with the Administration and the courts." Energetically and successfully he worked for the New York Life's right to do business in Brazil.[18]

The Mexico of Porfirio Diaz, no less than the Brazil of Florian

Peixoto, offered American life insurance companies both the temptations and the dangers of a corrupt, authoritarian government. As president-elect in 1884, Diaz became the handsomely remunerated head of the Equitable's Mexican advisory board — and a year later the company won a case in the country's courts involving $2,000,000 in fines. Yet in 1893 a new deposit and tax law drove the Equitable and the New York Life out of a country where in any event, as Hyde put it, "long experience leads us to think there is no money." The Mutual boldly chose to remain, and in 1897 McCurdy cosily advised the Minister of Interior on techniques of insurance regulation, laying particular stress on the evils of taxation. The other companies returned, unable to stay away from an environment so favorable to American enterprise as Diaz' Mexico seemed to be. By now, troubles were limited to the endemic problem of private fraud. The Mutual's Mexico City manager committed suicide after an audit of his books began in 1897, and the New York Life had trouble in extraditing to the United States two Americans suspected of committing murder to obtain a policy payment.[19]

The difficulties of the life insurance firms in Latin America were suggestive rather than final. The business stakes involved were small, and the prevalence of individual fraud clouded the real nature of the problem. It was in Europe — the heartland of the insurance companies' foreign business — that the dilemma of the venture overseas had its sharpest and most meaningful delineation.

4

The Europe of 1900 — settled, wealthy, sophisticated — offered business conditions very different from the fraud, violence, and revolution of Latin America. Nevertheless, underlying nationalistic forces in the Old World transformed a confident, successful American enterprise into a harried, weakening rear guard action.

England was the friendliest European market. Its regulatory system, in which the Board of Trade exercised loose supervision and publicity was the only deterrent against wrongdoing, suited American firms wise in the ways of public relations. No deposit was required; no language barriers impeded sales; no native tradition of direct salesmanship or deferred dividend policies detracted from the impact of American marketing. George Perkins surveyed the New York Life's British business in 1898 and found it booming in the industrial towns of the Midlands;

he suggested that the company establish a London office separate from the Paris branch. The Mutual and the Equitable already had English departments.

But even in this favored environment, it was not possible to escape the central difficulty of corporate foreignness. The Equitable in 1885 sought to incorporate its English branch, but the terms of its American charter and the necessity of securing a special Act of Parliament made this impractical. Domestic companies in England resisted American encroachment as fiercely as did their Continental counterparts. Incisive newspaper attacks were leveled at the expansion of the United States firms during the 1880's and the early 1890's. Other irritants were the frauds and controversies of agents far from home office control, concern over the effect of the Venezuela boundary controversy in 1896, and the impact of company scandals at home.

England was unique in not requiring company deposits (although one American firm kept $500,000 in a London bank in case of a change in the law). But difficulties counterbalanced that advantage. The Equitable protested a ruling that gave the Mutual and the New York Life, as mutual companies, a preferred tax position. Its appeal to the House of Lords was denied, and it paid its 1900 taxes under protest. By 1903, James Alexander thought that taxes in England offset the advantageous mortality rate there, and called for legislation to lessen the levy. But there was no cause for diplomatic intervention by the United States, which limited the effective action available to the company.[20]

5

On the Continent, the success of the American firms evoked the resistance of embittered domestic competitors and aroused governments. In 1893 the Equitable protested the "arbitrary action" of the Serbian authorities in passing a new insurance law, and in the following year withdrew from the country. The companies' business in Spain during the 1890's was punctuated by difficulties over mortality rates, newspaper attacks, taxation, and of course the Spanish-American War. Taxation troubled the companies in Portugal. A New York Life Turkish agent complained that the government, "acting on the instigation of the Ottoman Insurance Company to promote their own interests," used onerous licensing regulations to keep him out of many provinces. But the American minister reported that the requirements were not limited to the American firms, and were similar in spirit to those of other

European countries; hence no diplomatic intercession was feasible. It was a rare relief for the American mutual companies to learn that a Swedish law forbidding nonstock foreign insurance enterprises from doing business there was directed against assessment firms, and not against them.[21]

In the more substantial markets of the Continent, troubles developed in direct proportion to the extent of the Big Three's business. The Austro-Hungarian Empire was an area of special difficulty. Despite the intervention of the State Department, a decree prohibited deferred dividend policies and established retroactive deposit requirements. The opposition of domestic companies unable to compete successfully with the vigorous American firms, and resentment over United States tariff policy — two recurrent themes in Continental hostility to American life insurance — caused the action. The *Weekly Underwriter* had warned prophetically in 1886: "The last resort for the Austrian home protectionists is government supervision, which, probably, they think that they may be able to control." The State Department could not be more than peripherally helpful. The American ambassador reported that "as . . . the powers of intervention in behalf of the business interests of private corporations on the part of one friendly government against the administrative action of another are not clearly defined by existing rules of international law or usage," he had to limit himself to an unofficial proffer of good offices.

The companies thus were forced to depend on their own diplomatic resources. At first they tried to work in unison, but after the Austrian promulgations each responded according to the dictates of its own diplomacy. The Equitable stopped doing new business in 1897. Henry Hyde did not want to be forced to buy Austrian securities or to accept the government's assessment of his Vienna building to meet the deposit requirement. Nor did he care to have his business restricted to annual dividend policies. "With expenses as they stand to-day," he explained, "and the interest rate as it stands to-day, we cannot expect to have these policies compete satisfactorily with the foreign companies. I do not like the temper shown by the Austrian Government in forbidding tontines." The Mutual, anxious to stay, negotiated with the authorities in Vienna. But it was the New York Life's George W. Perkins who took the lead in company diplomacy. At first he was ready to withdraw his firm rather than make the additional reserve deposit required; he feared its precedent-setting effect elsewhere. But in Vienna consultations during the early summer of 1897 he worked out satisfactory arrangements on both deposits and policies, and the New York Life and the Mutual remained. The lure of the companies' investment power seems to have been a major factor: in October the New York Life sold United States Government 5's and bought Austrian 4's in order to meet its deposit requirement.[22]

On the heels of the Austrian negotiations of 1896–1897 came a challenge from Switzerland. The Equitable had withdrawn as early as 1891 under the threat of hostile legislation in this land of well-developed domestic insurance firms and a tight regulatory system. Now, in 1898, the New York Life ran into trouble. When the company applied for renewal of its license, the Swiss demanded that it lower its reserve valuation rate. The equity of deferred dividend policyholders was the ostensible reason for the change; a larger deposit would be its consequence. The State Department vigorously intervened, Secretary Hay stressing "the high standing of the Company, and the eminence of the men who administer its affairs." But again, direct negotiations between company and country settled the dispute. Perkins, fresh from his triumph the previous year in Vienna, descended on Berne with actuaries and bookkeepers. He met with the chief of the Bureau of Insurance, worked out a satisfactory arrangement, and the New York Life's license was renewed. The American ambassador reported: "The case was fairly won on its merits," and optimistically predicted that the company's victory in so severe a regulatory environment would help it elsewhere.[23]

6

It seemed ironic, but was in fact correlative, that Germany, a market particularly congenial to the American companies, produced the most substantial governmental reaction against them. With some bitterness McCurdy observed that as soon as his company began to succeed in that country, it was attacked. The same society whose thrifty burghers responded eagerly to American salesmanship in the 1880's found the Big Three's success all but insupportable by the turn of the century.

Difficulties originated with the Prussian rather than the Imperial government. In 1891 that state's authorities demanded fuller accounting procedures for deferred dividend policies. Soon after, foreign firms were required to invest half of their Prussian premium returns in local bonds as company deposits. In 1895 the Prussians made it clear that they were disturbed, too, by the increasing costs, high legal fees, and lack of details on receipts and expenditures characterizing the American companies' business methods.[24]

Rigorous only in comparison with the slack standards of American insurance regulation, the Prussian requirements nonetheless aroused the ire of companies in no mood to submit. McCurdy was especially irked by the obligation to list securities at their purchase rather than at their market price. The static condition of most European investments made this stipulation a minor burden for domestic German companies. But it hit hard at American firms investing in their own country's lusty economy. The Equitable from the first chose withdrawal rather than resistance, and left Prussia in July 1894. Henry Hyde shrugged off the departure as a "small matter," and declared that it would have come earlier "but for the danger of the company's action being misrepresented as a sign of weakness." The New York Life's John McCall, tired of Prussian officials "undoubtedly instigated by home companies and their agents . . . constantly engaged in making warfare upon the American Insurance Companies," was ready to leave in 1894 but for his firm's large investment there. The New York Life and the Mutual refused to abide by the Prussian requirements, and in 1895 the authorities expelled them.[25]

The two firms responded vigorously. The Mutual complained of the "onerous and unequal conditions" imposed by the Prussian Ministry of Interior, and asked that the State Department use its influence against the restriction of an American enterprise. McCall, a prominent Democrat, got President Grover Cleveland to refer in his 1895 annual message to the "narrowing circle of onerous and unforeseen conditions" which had forced the companies out of Prussia. McCurdy tried unsuccessfully to get the support of the Senate Foreign Relations Committee. But the American life insurance firms were in Germany only on sufferance and were subject to any regulations that the authorities chose to impose. Failing a settlement between the companies and the Prussian government, the State Department could only obtain delays in the date set for their expulsion.[26]

The companies' dependence upon state rather than national supervision heightened the problem of diplomatic representation. They turned to state insurance departments for help as freely as to the Federal government. As early as 1893 the Illinois insurance commissioner threatened retaliation against German insurance companies in his jurisdiction. After the 1895 exclusion of the New York Life and the Mutual, John McCall invited all state commissioners to discuss retaliatory measures with company representatives; those from New York, Massachusetts, Connecticut, Kentucky, Texas, Missouri, and Rhode Island responded. Letters of protest from New York's governor and insurance superintendent and from the commissioners of Missouri, Massachusetts, and Connecticut went to the Prussian government. McCurdy, supported by Hyde, put pressure on Governor Levi Morton of New York for "additional legislation to meet the present situation," and warned that failure to pass a retaliatory act would be a "declaration of acquiescence in one of the most unseemly attacks upon American interests of which arbitrary power has ever been guilty."

But the disadvantages of fragmented authority now appeared: Connecticut, Massachusetts, and Illinois decided not to exclude German companies in retaliation; and the Pennsylvania and Texas commissioners saw no reason to refuse admission to Prussian fire insurance firms since no companies from their states had suffered. Only Missouri, whose commissioner was particularly responsive to the wishes of the Equitable, and the ever pliant New York department of insurance passed retaliatory legislation.[27]

In addition, the New York department set out upon an extraordinary diplomatic venture of its own. Poultney Bigelow, a journalist and onetime classmate of Emperor William II, went to Berlin late in 1895 as a representative of insurance commissioner James F. Pierce. He conferred with Imperial and Prussian officials, pretentiously announcing that "the government of the State of New York has authorized me to deal with your Government in regard to certain points on which we appear to hold opposite views." He dramatized the seriousness of the American companies' exclusion by comparing it to the barring of German steamship lines from the port of New York, and threateningly hoped that "nothing would interfere with their continued prosperity." From then on, Bigelow labored to convey the impression that New York retaliation might work against German shipping as well as against Prussian insurance companies.

This brash performance yielded nothing. Bigelow antagonized the American ambassador by "interference in his prerogatives." The Prussian Minister of the Interior coldly asked the American envoy if it were not possible "for the central government to exercise a restraining influence on the local authorities" and expressed surprise that the insurance superintendents "considered it proper to communicate through any other than a diplomatic channel with an official of a foreign government."[28]

Bigelow's mission was impeded, too, by the Kaiser's anger over the United States' role in the Venezuelan boundary dispute. Indeed, insurance interests were thoroughly entangled in the web of German-American relations. The most exacerbating issues were American tariff barriers against German products and German agrarian sentiment against American imports. By 1898 McCurdy was convinced that United States tariff policies bred retaliation, and that the insurance companies, "as the victims nearest at hand and most conveniently reached, have played the part of a vicarious sacrifice." The Prussian insurance enactments of 1891 and 1892 followed close on the heels of the McKinley tariff of 1890, which affected German exports to the United States. The reciprocity agreement of January 30, 1892, inaugurated a period of good will between the two countries, but the 1894 Wilson-Gorman tariff's new differential duty on subsidized beet sugar touched off the sudden demand in 1895 that the American companies quit Prussia. The State Department assured the worried Mutual president that "this branch of our business interests abroad may be looked after in the pending reciprocity negotiations." But it was small comfort to leave one's fate to discussions which inevitably would concentrate on other commercial interests. The companies in the last analysis had to rely on their own diplomatic resources. To avoid "working at cross purposes," in 1892 they hired General George S. Batchellor to represent their interests in Berlin. A soldier, politician, diplomat, and judge, Batchellor crisscrossed the continent as a "tontine ambassador" of the Big Three.[29]

But collective company action was no more productive than intervention by Federal and state authorities. Differing approaches fractured the common front. Hyde, who had quickly withdrawn the Equitable, showed no interest in returning to Prussia. McCurdy fluctuated between allurements and threats. In 1894 he invited the Prussians to check the Mutual's financial standing. The Archduke Joseph, cousin of Emperor Francis Joseph of Austria-Hungary, had been helpful (for a fee) in smoothing the Mutual's entry into Hungary; McCurdy thought that financial sweetening might induce him to aid the company in Berlin. A petition asking for the Mutual's readmission, signed by 3000 German-Americans, went to the German Chancellor. In a harsher vein, McCurdy threateningly pointed to the more than 70,000,000 marks' worth of German loans held by his company, and warned that the Mutual would no longer purchase German securities. But nothing availed, and McCurdy, full of frustration, exploded to his Berlin manager: "That a corporation like this, whose magnitude in revenue and outgo exceeds that of many of the sovereign states of the Union and that of several of the kingdoms of Europe, while its transactions are carried on in nearly every civilized country of the globe, should be forced thus to disclose the details of its administration with the head of a Police Department [the Prussian Minister of the Interior] . . . trenches upon the domain of *Opera Bouffe*." [30]

Appeals to the Federal and state governments were primarily the work of McCurdy. The bulk of the State Department's domestic correspondence was with him; and Bigelow worked closely in Berlin with special Mutual counsel Charlton Lewis. But McCurdy soon realized that he was not in tune with his competitors. In June 1895 he cabled Lewis to "hold no confidential intercourse with New York Life people under any circumstances." The State Department in early 1897 warned the New York Life: "Desultory discussion, if not representing the common interests of the . . . principal companies, may not advance your purposes."

At first McCall cooperated with McCurdy in calling on the United States government for help and in working for retaliatory state legislation. But in 1898 he agreed to serve as a trustee of the Magdeburg Insurance Company, a Prussian firm seeking entry into the United States, and protested Iowa and Kansas tax discrimination against English insurance companies. The New York Life henceforth used cajolery rather than intimidation in its foreign diplomacy.

The fine hand of vice-president George W. Perkins lay behind the change. The failures of the State Department disgusted him; he described the American ambassadors in Europe as "absolutely useless . . . to any commercial enterprise that American men have wanted to develop over there." Boldly he committed the New York Life to corporate diplomacy. He hoped to "harmonize all conflicting interests" by getting the New York insurance superintendent to readmit the excluded Prussian fire insurance companies, and with the aid of the Equitable worked successfully to this end. He offered, too, concrete evidence that his company was ready to meet Prussian requirements. Several Prussian commissioners came to New York in May 1899 to examine the American companies' books, and received an especially warm welcome in the offices of the New York Life. When the commissioners objected to the firm's stock holdings, the management (which had other — investment policy — reasons for wanting to do so) quickly agreed to get rid of such securities within two years. McCall and Perkins willingly consented to the commissioners' other demands: that foreign business expenses be closely controlled, and that the surplus derived from Prussian deferred dividend policies be accounted for yearly and reported to the Ministry of the Interior.[31]

Perkins perceived that the favor of the Imperial German government was as important as that of the Prussian authorities. In the late 1890's German insurance matters passed from provincial to national jurisdiction, and the policy concerns of the nation came to weigh more heavily than the competitive interests of domestic companies. Perkins worked skillfully to win the confidence and approval of the Kaiser's ministers. At his direction the New York Life representative in Berlin wrote to President McKinley of Foreign Minister Bernhard von Bülow's interest in the United States. He told McCall: "if there were any confidential pointers that could be obtained from Washington . . . that we could . . . communicate to von Bülow, it would be of excellent use during the next five or six weeks."

Perkins' diplomacy triumphed in October 1899, when the German cabinet voted to readmit the New York Life — but not the Mutual — to Prussia. The firm's agency committee exultantly reported: "the whole situation in Europe has materially changed. The attitude of all the foreign governments towards the Company is noticeably different already." Perkins, "ever mindful of the golden rule that one should do unto his neighbor as his neighbor would do unto him, but do it first," considered keeping the Mutual out of Germany a task as important as getting the New York Life in. He doubted if McCurdy, personally involved in many company investments, would sell the Mutual's stock holdings. "There are one or two things that McCurdy . . . cares more for than getting into Prussia," he knowingly told McCall. On a higher plane, the New York Life president thought that the precedent established "will show the way to a better method of settling all commercial differences and in securing additional and valuable privileges for American business interests the world over." Perkins agreed, and expected the settlement to smooth the way of the New York Life into Germany's concession area in China. He spoke enthusiastically of a joint commission of United States and German businessmen settling issues that divided the two countries, and induced McKinley to endorse the plan in his December 1899 Message to Congress.[32]

Partly to strengthen his company's position and partly because the venture appealed to his ambitious business spirit, Perkins offered the New York Life as a major purchaser of German securities. In July 1900 he announced that the New York Life was ready to participate in a rumored Imperial German Loan to cover the costs of the Boxer expedition to China. Two months later a $20,000,000 German government issue was offered, with $12,000,000 (an unprecedented portion of a European loan) allotted to the American market. Perkins moved quickly, especially after he heard that the Mutual and the Equitable showed no immediate interest in the loan. His company's finance committee authorized a purchase of $2,500,000, with an option for as much again.

Perkins made sure that the Equitable and the Mutual would be excluded from the initial purchase list and that the New York Life would handle newspaper publicity. His company's official share (so far as the German government would know) was to be $5,000,000, without mention of the option. Solemnly he told his Berlin representative: "As soon as I learned that the German Government was in this market I felt that our duty was plain, viz., that we should leave no stone unturned to make her entrance into our financial market an instantaneous success." Since one problem was that "our people are not yet educated to placing their money in securities outside of the United States," the right sort of publicity was necessary. Items appeared in the press describing the loan and the interest in it of so reputable an institution as the New York Life. Unremittingly, Perkins exploited the competitive advantages of participation in the loan. He instructed his Berlin representative to explain to the German authorities the key role that the New York Life played in the issue's success, and to stress that the Equitable and the Mutual "have both sneered at this loan. They are apparently using all their moneys just now in local enterprises in which their officers or Trustees are interested." [33]

In the face of this whirligig of diplomacy and international finance, McCurdy continued to fluctuate between threats and inducements. But so clumsy a technique availed little against Perkins' imaginative deftness. The Mutual chieftain retreated into injured indignation: he spoke of the Prussian Minister of Interior as "surrounded by influences adverse to

* FOUNDERS AND PROPHETS *

BEGINNING in the 1870's, a generation of dynamic life insurance executives turned their firms into corporations of great wealth and size, and so laid the foundation for the turn-of-the-century society of companies.

Henry B. Hyde, the founder of the Equitable and its president from 1874 to 1899. He battled fiercely with Winston of the Mutual, and by 1880 surpassed his competitor in new business.

Joseph F. Knapp was president of the Metropolitan from 1871 to 1891, and raised it from struggling anonymity to the threshold of its twentieth century prominence.

Frederick S. Winston, president of the Mutual from 1853 to 1885 and the overseer of its rise to eminence in the years following the Civil War.

John F. Dryden, from its inception the active force in the Prudential, became its president in 1881 and held the post until his death in 1911.

William H. Beers was the least consequential of this first generation of life insurance magnates. President of the New York Life from 1885 to 1892, he was of the same genre, but not of the same stature, as Hyde and Winston.

BY THE turn of the century only John F. Dryden remained of the first generation of corporate empire-builders; a new group of men, oriented particularly to high finance, stood at the apex of their companies.

Richard McCurdy watched over the Mutual from 1885 to 1906 with a special blend of hauteur and aggressiveness.

Under the highly politic leadership of John McCall, the New York Life became the giant among the giants at the turn of the century.

John R. Hegeman presided over the Metropolitan's rise to corporate grandeur. He remained in office until his death in 1919, although Haley Fiske had effective control of company operations after 1905.

James W. Alexander, longtime associate of Henry Hyde, succeeded to the Equitable presidency in 1899. Never the strong man that his predecessor was, he succumbed to the stresses of 1905.

the claims of this country," and warned a correspondent that Germany's standing in American financial circles had been adversely affected by Prussia's treatment of the "largest moneyed institution in America, which stands here as the bulwark of credit." When the New York insurance department reversed itself and readmitted the Prussian companies to the state, McCurdy icily told a department representative that "his position in the insurance world was such that his views . . . ought not to be over-ridden." He continued also to appeal to the national government for aid; Senator Mark Hanna was sympathetic but unhelpful. The Mutual president testified vigorously on his company's Prussian difficulties before the House Interstate Commerce Committee. That body reported out a resolution favorable to the Mutual, but it failed to pass in the House because of what a McCurdy ally darkly called the "stupidity, at least" of another congressman. Grandiloquently McCurdy lashed out at "the trumpery insinuation that I have been playing with Congress for the mere purpose of getting a factitious advantage for my Company," and was sure that the obstruction to his cause had the "same insidious and malicious origin" as the combination of "Prussian mediaevalism and an un-American and unscrupulous ally in this country."

This broadside was not unfounded: George Perkins worked to block the House resolution. At the end of the year, the close relationship that McCall and Perkins had with President McKinley bore further fruit. In his annual message to Congress, the Chief Executive made it clear that he considered the New York Life's return to Prussia a satisfactory settlement of the insurance companies' troubles with Germany. After that, congressional action was out of the question. Querulously McCurdy complained to Secretary of War and Mutual counsel Elihu Root: "The treatment of the foreign insurance companies in Germany is part of the trade warfare which has been going on for a long time . . . and it would seem that *our* Government ought to side with *our* industries and not be misled into helping our opponents." [34]

Perkins' diplomatic performance had been varied, bold, original; his success seemingly complete. But in the midst of his triumph, the conditions governing the German business changed. An Imperial law in May 1901 provided for a separate department of insurance, headed by a council of forty-eight prominent citizens. It required a cash deposit of 2,000,000 marks ($476,000) from each foreign company as a guaranty against nonpayment of taxes or judgments. Almost as though the new regulatory system allowed it to save face, the Mutual applied for readmission under these vigorous new requirements, and in 1902 achieved it.

There is no record of New York Life opposition to this dramatic undoing of its vice-president's painstaking labors. The challenges of domestic investment finance now engrossed Perkins' attention, and the New York Life's experiences with Germany may have dampened its ardor. Although the company continued to buy German securities in 1901, by the end of the year it had disposed of all of them. At the same time the German government found the New York money market devoted to domestic investment, and returned to home financing. And in Germany the shift of authority to the Imperial government stiffened regulation. In 1903 McCall complained about a request for a special, additional deposit on deferred dividend policies: "if they are disposed at the instigation of the German Companies to demand impossible things, it shows a spirit that I was not quite prepared for." The Equitable, after leaving Prussia in 1894, had continued in Germany's Hanseatic District. But the 1901 law's depository requirements drove it (along with numerous other non-German insurance companies) out of the country entirely. In 1904 the Mutual, too, decided in the face of increased deposit requirements to leave the market it had just re-entered.[35]

Although the New York Life, more committed than the other companies, stayed on in Germany, the spark was gone from its venture. Perkins continued to speak grandly of collaboration between the businessmen of Germany and the United States, but perpetuation of the cordiality characteristic of the turn of the century was impossible. The chancellors of the 1890's — Caprivi and Hohenlohe — thought in terms of tariff reduction, encouragement of German overseas markets, and the acceptance of American agricultural imports. They reflected a political atmosphere in which the diplomacy of George Perkins — practical, businesslike, rooted in the *quid pro quo* — had a chance of success. But the rising force of agrarian nationalism looked on the American insurance venture as the work of a hated external capitalism. The union of the Agriculturists and the Prussian Conservative party from the mid-1890's, and after 1900 the chancellorship of Bülow (who previously as Foreign Minister had been reasonably friendly to the United States companies) gave German policy a more protectionist, nationalistic tone. Bülow extended government social insurance during the same years that the American insurance market in Germany began to go to pieces. In the face of these tendencies, the marketing and diplomatic skills of

American life insurance became all but useless, and the essential insubstantiality of the venture lay exposed.

7

The problems inherent in the overseas transposition of the American life insurance business appeared with great clarity in Russia as well. As elsewhere, the Americans faced the opposition of domestic and other foreign insurance firms. A year after the New York Life's 1885 appearance in Russia, its manager was in jail for doing business without formal authorization, and the Minister of the Interior was demanding a full reserve deposit and modifications of the company's deferred dividend policies. Nor did the Equitable find things easier. It soon complained of "considerable opposition . . . and though willing to comply with all requirements yet owing to the activity of foreign companies and their agents we cannot obtain the needed concession." Not until 1890, after the interposition of the American ambassador, did the Equitable get official authorization to do business in Russia. At that it had to accept more rigorous conditions than did the New York Life a few years before.[36]

It became apparent in the early 1890's that the companies had a formidable opponent in Minister of Finance Sergei Witte. Dedicated to the creation of a modern economy in Russia, Witte looked upon premium payments to the American firms as a drain on his country's wealth. As criticism mounted from such sources as the Society for the Support of Russian Commerce and Industry, rumors spread that the government soon would flatly prohibit the sale of deferred dividend policies. Tontine ambassador George S. Batchellor went to St. Petersburg to plead the companies' case before the Ministers of Finance, the Interior, and Foreign Affairs. Through 1893 the threat persisted, with the companies "much harrassed by this state of uncertainty." United States ambassador Andrew D. White summed up the situation: "The Companies have flourished marvellously here, and herein lies the whole difficulty." Witte, now Foreign Minister, was friendly toward the United States, but persisted in regarding the firms as unproductive and parasitical impositions on the Russian economy. Although White considered Witte's opposition "nothing more or less than a bold bid for vulgar popularity," he confessed that the Foreign Minister was "all powerful and the matter is entirely in his hands."

White was instructed to argue that the companies' success had improved business prospects for all insurance enterprises in Russia, "a result which usually follows competition in every department of business activity." But this American homily had little relevance to a government leader not so much interested in competition as in a heightened Russian national purpose. More effectively, the ambassador spoke of the "strong feeling . . . sure to be aroused among a very large and influential class in the United States" by the companies' exclusion. He warned that the sentiment would extend "in quarters and in questions where it would be a misfortune to both countries to have it appear" — a reference to pending reciprocity negotiations.

But despite the fact that the United States Legation "pushed its intervention almost to an extreme limit," the Tsar in April 1894 signed a decree requiring dividend distributions at least once every four years. The law was "pressed by many Russian Capitalists, Witte, and the Russian Insurance companies." Ninety-five percent of the New York Life's Russian policies deferred dividends for five years or longer, and the company withdrew in August.[37]

As in Germany, the American companies reacted in different ways to the challenge. The New York Life left. The Equitable devised a special modified annual dividend policy for the Russian market, and in 1900 sold insurance whose worth was more than $5,500,000. The Mutual, which previously disclaimed any intention of entering Russia, renewed its interest after the New York Life's withdrawal. In 1898 McCurdy offered to invest in the bond issues of several Russian cities as a means of gaining admission.

The departure of the New York Life by no means signified its passive acceptance of the situation. George W. Perkins, busy with his Austrian, Swiss, and German negotiations, kept a close watch on Russian developments. In 1897 the New York Life finance committee rejected an International Bank of St. Petersburg proposal to exchange the company's Russian deposit securities for state bonds, but was ready to make additional purchases of the new issue. Within a month the insurance firm participated largely in the American share of a syndicate floating Vladikavkas and Southeastern Railroad debentures.[38]

In the fall of 1899, with the perils of diplomacy in Austria, Switzerland, and Germany behind him, Perkins went to St. Petersburg. McCall smoothed his way, eliciting information from the State Department on "financiers, Bankers, and prominent people" in Russia. Perkins dealt directly with the source of Russian opposition to the American companies: Count Witte. In Witte he met a close approximation of himself. Both men were able, energetic, masterful exponents of the time's outreaching capitalism. Witte had been director of Russia's most prosperous railroad at the age of thirty-seven. As Minister of Finance, Foreign Minister, and finally Premier, he devoted himself to modernizing the nation's economy. Perkins judged Witte "a most aggressive man. He has not only come to be the financial backbone of Russia, but he has really become the first politician of that country" — a statement of the New York Life executive's ambitions for himself.

The personal compatibility of the two men supplemented a momentary identity of interests. Perkins, ready to use the New York Life's investment power to further its cause in Europe, found Witte eager to welcome foreign capital. The Russian statesman's interest in the American money market was stimulated by French and German attempts to create a bear market for Russian securities. With Russia on the gold standard since 1897, and with Witte dictating the country's financial policies, investment prospects seemed promising to the New York Life executive.[39]

At the end of October 1899 Perkins struck a contract with the International Bank of St. Petersburg. The New York Life agreed to underwrite an $8,000,000 share of the state-guaranteed bonds of the Vladikavkas and Southeastern Railroad, which Witte was developing as part of the Trans-Siberian rail network. This was the lion's share of the first Russian issue floated entirely in the New York market. In return the insurance firm got several concessions. Its affiliate, the New York Security and Trust Company, became the American financial agent of the Russian government, with the right to establish the first trust company in the tsarist nation. The Russians agreed not to allow American insurance firms other than the New York Life and the Equitable to do business in the country. Again McCurdy and the Mutual had been blocked. In 1901 the New York Life took $5,000,000 of a new $13,000,000 Vladikavkas Railroad bond issue, on the assumption that it would be readmitted to Russia and be allowed to sell deferred dividend policies. McCall smoothed the way of the transaction by asking President McKinley to retain a Russian-American reciprocal trade agreement.

But as in Germany, the triumph was vitiated almost immediately. Before the close of 1900 Perkins was interested in Russian railroad securities as a representative of J. P. Morgan and Company as well as an executive of the New York Life. Thereafter, the Russian interests of

Morgan, and of United States Steel as a supplier of railroad cars, held his attention. This new orientation did not further good relations with Witte. In 1902 the Russian leader called for an international antitrust conference to deal with the pernicious effect of American and German price markdowns on Russia's infant industry.[40]

Russian placements on the New York money market, no less than the German issues, suffered from the 1901 boom in domestic securities. The Russo-Japanese War further depressed tsarist bonds. When the New York Life found in 1902 that its Russian deposits were over the legal reserve requirements, it asked for — and got — the return of the excess. By the end of 1904 the company had rid itself of its tsarist railroad holdings. Russian equities shrank to such an extent that the Equitable in 1905 used 1904 market values in its report to avoid the increased deposit that the lessened values required. In the Armstrong investigation, McCall felt obliged to defend his company's Russian securities by arguing that they were paid for entirely by Russian policy premiums. Perkins returned to Russia in 1905 — as Morgan's representative at a bankers' conference called to deal with the depressed state of Russian issues. When a foreign loan attempt failed the following year, Witte believed that the "treachery" of Morgan was responsible. The problems of Russian industrialization and finance in the early 1900's had destroyed the concord attained by Perkins and Witte in 1899.

Nor did the insurance business itself meet expectations. Although sales continued high, and the American firms retained their dominant position, an Equitable official reported in 1901 that the New York Life's Russian expenses were three times his company's, and that it wrote policies on doubtful risks. Finally, the abortive revolution of 1905 began a period of social unrest and chaos which eventually destroyed the Russian insurance market.[41]

8

The companies' venture into France had both symbolic and quantitative importance. The New York Life's European headquarters were in Paris, and all three firms owned impressive buildings there by the end of the nineteenth century. In 1898 the Mutual's French business volume stood second to its English total, and the Equitable's sales were twice those of the previous year. By 1905 the companies had about 50,000 policyholders in France and Algeria.[42]

Even though France had well-established domestic life insurance firms, the Big Three won their usual quick success. The opposition to this triumph was substantial. Authorization to do business in 1882 had to come through the persistent efforts of the American ambassador against the combined resistance of French insurance, banking, and railroad interests. Within a year Henry Hyde was complaining that "the entanglements of the French Agency business are beyond anything I have ever experienced." As the companies prospered, newspaper attacks, court actions, and government regulations steadily harassed them.

Other forces conditioned the business environment. The Equitable's European counsel complained in 1885 that the Chamber of Deputies was "seized as by a delirium for protection." He noted the growth of agrarian protectionism in French politics, which by 1890 dominated the Chamber. The United States' tariff policies in the ensuing decade, which so damaged the companies' Prussian business, caused repercussions in France as well. The McKinley tariff of 1890 led to renewed press attacks on the American firms. A threat in 1898 by the Minister of Commerce to expel the Mutual seemed to be related to American duties on French beet sugar.[43]

In this charged atmosphere the companies defended themselves as best they could. The Equitable wined and dined the French delegates to the American Actuarial Congress of 1888–89. In 1892, new regulations directed at the Big Three were defeated because they clashed with the French companies' own interests. But so fortuitous an occurrence did not change the exposed position of the American firms. Ambassador Horace Porter, formerly an Equitable director, had a special interest in defending the American companies, and took credit for preventing hostile government action. But in 1902 a substantial group in the Chamber of Deputies sought legislation requiring deposits in French securities, annual declarations of dividends due policyholders, and more rigorous supervision. Porter ascribed this pressure to a "combined and formidable effort" by domestic companies to compel their American competitors "to conform to the French method of doing business," and noted that "in this they have followed the successful example of Austria, Germany, Japan."[44]

The Big Three reacted to this threat with their customary resourcefulness. Besides enlisting the aid of the State Department, they launched an intensive propaganda campaign in the French press. The Mutual and the Equitable split the $40,000 cost. They also brought the lure of their investment powers into play. But the Chamber of Deputies passed the hostile legislation at the end of 1904. The American companies pleaded their case before a Senate committee: their evidence was heard and ignored. The committee, under heavy pressure from French insurance firms, unanimously recommended that the Senate pass the legislation. In March 1905 it became law. The next recourse of the United States firms was to see to it that the Minister of Commerce put the law into effect "in such a way as to injure as little as possible foreign companies." But this official turned out to be friendly to domestic enterprise. The only strong pro-American influence in the government was Premier Maurice Rouvier, who as Finance Minister had warmed to the American companies because of their substantial investments in French securities.

The Big Three's divergent interests further weakened their defense. The New York Life's failure to join its peers in their French press campaign may well have been in retaliation for the Mutual's refusal to agree to its proposal that each firm buy 5,000,000 francs' worth of French *rentes*. After the passage of the 1905 law, while the companies and the American ambassador were working for a liberal interpretation by the Minister of Commerce, the Mutual toyed with the idea of unilateral withdrawal.[45]

The whole course of French political and intellectual life in the early years of the new century — the rise of Rightist "integral nationalism" after the victory of the Republic in the Dreyfus Affair; the first Moroccan Crisis and the subsequent atmosphere of diplomatic tension; the growing strength of agrarian, protectionist political elements — weakened the position of foreign corporations. Ambassador Porter spoke at the end of 1904 of "the pressure in this year of political excitement," and his successor considered the 1905 legislation a manifestation "of the spirit and underlying purpose prevailing everywhere in Europe." Among the factors at play were the United States Senate's rejection of a reciprocity treaty with France, the belief that French foodstuffs suffered overcritical inspection on arrival in America, and the ascendancy of the nationalistic Minister of Commerce Trouillot over the more amenable Premier Rouvier and Foreign Minister Théophile Delcassé. The early stages of the first Moroccan Crisis forced Delcassé out of office in June 1905; by the end of the year Rouvier's overthrow was imminent, and a New York Life spokesman feared: "In that event we should be left without a protection in the cabinet." The departure of Rouvier in 1906 and regulatory developments subsequent to the Armstrong investigation amply confirmed this doleful prediction.[46]

For a brief moment at the turn of the century a palpable rapport existed between George Perkins, the exemplar of a bold, imaginative, questing American corporatism, and a group of sympathetic European leaders. Witte in Russia, Rouvier in France, Caprivi and even, for a while, Bülow in Germany, seemed to have the same hopes for an international commercialism that animated Perkins. He, in turn, found much to admire in the purpose and order of the European states. He later commented wistfully: "In Germany . . . a captain of industry is knighted and here he is indicted." [47]

But this identity of interest and outlook was transient. The pre-1914 chauvinism that engulfed Europe's popular and high culture and its economic and foreign policy pushed Witte, Rouvier, and Caprivi out of power and made Bülow a model of Prussianism. The ties had been fragile despite Perkins' finesse. When common economic interest gave way there were no principles of power or of order that enabled a private corporation to bargain effectively with national states.

When [laws] . . . are the work of a Power which has become, with its every growth, more enervated by the strife of factions, their confusion makes them ludicrous.

Bertrand de Jouvenal, *On Power*

Part Four * The Investing Power

One consequence of the companies' growth was their emergence as a major source of capital investment. Entry into the world of high finance promised to fulfill, more satisfactorily than the venture overseas, the power ambitions of the insurance leaders. Here, refined business techniques and their drives for power and place most happily conjoined. This managerial orientation had several satisfying results. Investment policy became flexible and dynamic. The firms built up impressive structures of bank, trust company, and investment banking affiliations. And many new syndicate ventures yielded substantial profits.

But these activities clashed too strenuously with established expectations of life insurance company behavior. Even before the Armstrong investigation of 1905 formalized society's disapproval, the success of this venture in high finance was questionable. In addition, characteristics that had blunted the companies' quest for power in other spheres appeared in their investment experience. Decision and policymaking became fractionalized, beset by conflicting considerations. And once again, countering forces — this time other financial interests — kept the companies from achieving the control their leaders desired.

VIII * The Investment Environment

The growth of the great life insurance companies had momentous investment consequences. Their emergence as a major source of savings coincided with a significant institutionalization of American finance. As a result, their entry into high finance was an especially vivid expression of their evolution into a powerful and sophisticated corporate group.[1]

1

Law and custom made pre-1890 life insurance investment a model of restraint in a society and time not usually given to cautious fund placement. Mid-century legislation in New York and elsewhere limited life companies to government securities and to municipal bonds and farm mortgages within the home state. Company charters cautiously required double the face value of a loan as collateral security. Real estate mortgages, premium notes (a necessary means of stimulating early policy purchases), and government securities were the only substantial categories of investment. Property generally could be held only for business purposes; the Equitable's attorney cautioned that "very great care should be taken not to do anything which will have a semblance of speculation in real estate." When the Equitable in 1879 toyed with the idea of lending on the market value of collateral, a form of investment recently permitted by New York law, counsel frostily warned: "I think the statute would be very strictly construed against the Company." The traditional yardstick of satisfactory insurance investment — that the market value of the company's assets should equal the policy reserve — did not require highly productive fund placement.[2]

The magnates who transformed life insurance marketing did not at first challenge this conservative investment tradition. John F. Dryden proudly declared of the Prudential in 1884: "Our investments have been confined exclusively to Government bonds and first mortgages secured by improved real estate worth at least twice the amount loaned . . . We make security the first consideration, the rates of interest secondary." New York Life's President Beers declared in the 1870's: "I am in favor of leaving insurance companies to make their own investments; but I am not in favor of allowing them to make investments at random by any means." The otherwise aggressive Joseph F. Knapp prudently concentrated the Metropolitan's real estate mortgage loans in his home city of Brooklyn. When Richard McCurdy became president of the Mutual in 1885, he roundly criticized his predecessor's excessive concern with the accumulation and investment of capital. The company, he complained, "had gradually been converted into a loan and trust institution with a life insurance branch, instead of remaining a life insurance company with its loan and trust department as a part of its management." McCurdy sold substantial quantities of securities to gain the capital for the marketing expansion which came first in his business ambitions. Henry Hyde's investment practices were direct and unsophisticated. He put money in New York City bonds through the friendly offices of the city's comptroller rather than through financial intermediaries; his keen personal interest in electrical development led him to invest Equitable funds in George Westinghouse's ventures and to participate in the creation of Consolidated Edison.

Considerable caution attended the massive shift of life insurance investment to railroad securities during the 1880's. When the New York Life took West Shore 4's and New York Central 5's in 1888, its finance committee noted that prevailing low money rates and the difficulty of getting other bonds for the permanent portfolio made these purchases necessary, but that they were only temporary acquisitions. To justify the purchase of another bloc of railroad securities, the committee declared that as individuals they had made private purchases of the issue. There was reason for this wariness: discussion of a Toledo, St. Louis and Kansas City Railroad offering was enlivened by the opinion of "a prominent Wall Street gentleman" that the road "would probably have to be reorganized before the signatures are dry." [3]

Investment funds grew with the American life insurance enterprise; the ideology of fund placement, however, lagged behind marketing sophistication. But developments within the companies and the securities market worked a change. At the turn of the century, investments became the most conspicuous expression of the great companies' quest for place and power.

2

The large firms' emergence as a prime financial force came after long evolution of life insurance investment patterns. The asset distribution of twenty-nine leading companies in 1860, 1890, and 1900 (Table 5) illustrates the more distinctive trends. The most dramatic change was the rise in corporation bonds, at the expense of mortgage loans and premium notes and to a lesser extent of United States bonds. Smaller but significant gains occurred in cash on hand, stock holdings, real estate, public bonds, and policy and collateral loans. Generally, investments keyed to property and insurance business expansion gave way to negotiable securities. The decline in the attractiveness of farm mortgages during the troubled 1890's spurred the flow of capital to new investment sectors.

TABLE 5. Assets of twenty-nine life insurance companies, 1860–1900 (percentages)

Type of Asset	1860	1890	1900
Cash items	2.4	4.2	4.3
Premium notes	20.5	1.2	0.9
Real estate	2.7	10.4	9.0
Mortgage loans	59.2	41.0	28.8
Collateral loans	1.6	4.6	4.3
U.S. bonds	3.1	0.9	0.4
Public bonds (other than U.S.)	2.8	8.3	8.2
Corporation bonds	0.9	22.4	32.2
Stocks	2.3	4.0	5.5
Miscellaneous	4.5	3.0	6.4[a]
Total	100.0	100.0	100.0

[a] Policy loans, previously an insignificant item, constituted 3.7 percent of the total.

Source: Adapted from Lester W. Zartman, *The Investments of Life Insurance Companies* (New York, 1907), p. 14.

These shifts took place within a steadily more liberal regulatory atmosphere. New York in 1872 allowed its companies bond and mortgage holdings in neighboring states. By the early 1880's New York life insurance firms could make collateral loans everywhere and own real estate other than their home office buildings. The general insurance law of 1892 allowed unlimited bank deposits and policy loans up to the full reserve value. New Jersey had passed the first general insurance investment statute in 1852, but at the beginning of the twentieth century the Prudential felt constrained by legislation "adapted more to . . . local operation than to national operation." As Dryden put it: "Our laws . . . were much narrower than the laws of most of the states. We found ourselves early in the history of the company very much cramped with respect to our power to invest." The New Jersey Assembly responded in 1904 with legislation which allowed the Prudential free rein in its investment policies.[4]

The rapid transformation of the American financial system at the end of the nineteenth century galvanized this long-range liberalization of investment choices. Dramatically expanded areas of capital placement and a complex new structure of financial institutions provided the milieu in which the great companies applied their investment power. A period of feverish investment activity followed the depression of the mid-1890's. Security flotations from 1897 to 1902 had two major purposes: to launch heavily capitalized new enterprises, or to consolidate existing firms into new, corporate giants. The very names of the new ventures — American, Continental, United States, National, and International superseded Amalgamated and Standard in popularity — suggested the spirit and the trend. Increasingly sophisticated financial institutions — investment bankers, trust companies, securities exchanges — serviced the new activity. High finance was closely akin in spirit to the business ideology of life insurance. And the great companies had the resources, in Brandeis' words an unmatched pool of "quick capital," suitable for grandiose investment purposes. In 1891 the *Commercial and Financial Chronicle* spoke respectfully of the "enormous accumulations, relatively as well as absolutely unprecedented, held by the great companies."[5]

During the 1890's insurance executives examined the impact of these trends on their companies' policies. Henry Hyde in 1894 reaffirmed his traditionalist belief in the special value of municipal, state, and county bonds, but he also dwelt on the problem of the growing size of the Equitable's funds. There was an evident need for "some positive and definite rules in regard to the investment of our money." He planned to seek the advice of "the best moneyed experts in the country," and put them on the Equitable's finance committee.

Richard McCurdy also took an expansionist view of the Mutual's investment role. He came to believe that "in its investment side this Company necessarily performs the functions of a business corporation for its constituents." Winston's investment policies once bothered him because they seemed to take priority over marketing. Now, in the 1890's, McCurdy was irked by their conservatism: "the policy of the late President, who was brought up in the country and believed nothing to be of such steady value as farming lands, has loaded the company with a great quantity of foreclosed farms producing little revenue." By the end of 1898 McCurdy was selling off state and municipal bonds as unprofitable investments.

George W. Perkins and John McCall turned the New York Life away from investment in office buildings, collateral loans, and stocks. They preferred high-interest, long-term bonds which, though not "high class investment bonds," were less likely to shrink in value during depression years and had a longer prematurity life. Perkins considered the company's "going substantially to a bond basis" and the policy, after 1903, of claiming cost price rather than market value in surplus computation to be moves "in the direction of a more conservative method of investment." But his investment policy committed the New York Life to the securities handled by the great financial intermediaries of the time. And the muckraker Thomas W. Lawson declared, with a reasonable show of evidence, that it dovetailed with the appearance of large, watered bond issues based on stock collateral.[6]

The mass purchase of railroad bonds was the most important result of the new trend in life insurance investment. In the early 1880's the Metropolitan began to buy these offerings; by 1890, railroad securities accounted for 25 percent of its total assets. The Mutual, too, turned to rail bonds and stocks in the early eighties, as did the Equitable a few years later. By 1904, about one third of all life insurance assets lay in this field, and the companies' holdings added up to 10 percent of the national rail securities portfolio.[7]

Industrial stocks and bonds generally remained outside the pale of insurance investment respectability. These securities were held to be too susceptible to changes in the quality of industrial managements, or to the impact of depression. Public utilities were unduly subject to legislative influence. Dryden opposed industrials on principle; McCurdy proclaimed that the Mutual's rule against industrial stocks kept it from becoming a "storage house for the unmarketable securities sometimes manufactured." Henry Hyde too frowned on stock holdings. Perkins used the complaints of Prussian investigators in 1899 as "an opportune reason for getting the New York Life entirely out of stock investment."

There was a suspicious vehemence to this rejection. Certainly, railroad bonds had not been free of financial malpractice; and stocks and industrials, though newer and perhaps more hazardous forms of investment, had obvious potential.[8] Perhaps these protestations of caution and conservatism compensated for other insurance investment practices — syndicate participation, bank and trust company ownership — which were aggressive and venturesome. It was suggestive that Perkins committed the New York Life to a no-stock policy in 1899, when the company's performance in other investment fields was reaching its full, spectacular maturity.

3

The companies' systems of investment reflected these changes in the volume, practice, and policy of fund placement. Massive, continuous investment obligations called for centralized decisionmaking. Top company officers were formally authorized to buy and sell securities, to vote stock holdings, and to designate banks of deposit. Hegeman in the Metropolitan, Dryden in the Prudential, McCurdy in the Mutual, Perkins and McCall in the New York Life, Henry Hyde (and then James Alexander and James Hazen Hyde) in the Equitable, came to pay more attention to their roles as financial magnates than as insurance marketing men. Finance committees joined boards of directors in becoming spectators of, rather than participants in, policy formation.

McCurdy was ready in 1891 to broaden his company's treasury department; in 1893 an assistant treasurer was added. In investment policymaking, he worked most closely with Frederic Cromwell, treasurer from 1884, and with certain members of the finance committee: First National Bank president George F. Baker, George G. Haven, and Adrian Iselin, Jr. In 1895 a special subcommittee of the finance committee decided that the need for rapid action made it desirable to empower the treasurer to buy or sell up to $1,000,000 worth of securities at his discretion. Treasurer Cromwell, a member of the subcommittee, did not sign the report "from motives of personal and official delicacy." His was an understandable discretion in the face of so dramatic a movement of investment policy power from the committee to the treasury department. The size of the Mutual's holdings made necessary a refinement of the treasurer's role in 1897. Thereafter he limited his duties to representing the Mutual "in general financial operations and exterior relations with banks, railway and trust companies and cognate corporations with which it may have business."

Henry Hyde's chief investment adviser was General Louis Fitzgerald, president of the affiliated Mercantile Trust Company, J. P. Morgan's representative in numerous railroad consolidations, and from 1884 chairman of the Equitable's finance committee. After the elder Hyde's death in 1899, James Alexander and James Hazen Hyde relied heavily on finance committee member George H. Squire. A special four-man subcommittee controlled all areas of Equitable investment except mortgages. Again, the demands of a greatly expanded investment responsibility required control more centralized than the finance committee could provide.[9]

George W. Perkins, so conspicuous in the New York Life's corporate policymaking, came by the late 1890's to dominate its investment program. The company's cashier, Theodore M. Banta, steadily lost the considerable influence that was his at the beginning of the decade. The treasury department, strategically located at 5 Nassau Street in the New York financial district rather than at the home office (346 Broadway), became the center of the New York Life's financial operations. The treasurer was able to receive company funds, deposit them, and draw checks without going through the cashier's office. In 1896 treasurer Edward N. Gibbs relinquished the presidency of New London's Thames National Bank so that he might give full attention to New York Life financial affairs. He and his successor, Edmund D. Randolph, who likened the treasury department to "a bank within a corporation," faithfully implemented Perkins' investment goals.

The Drydens, Wards, and McCarters controlled Prudential investment policy from the company's executive offices, board of directors, and finance committee. As elsewhere, there was a felt need to formalize the concentration of control over fund placement: in 1898 two members of the finance committee were designated to take charge of the company's bond purchases. No significant changes occurred in the Metropolitan's investment structure during the 1890's, but none was necessary. Financial policymaking rested securely in the hands of President John Hegeman.[10]

4

Growth had made the insurance business technique a complex affair, both in performance and in purpose. Size and wealth also transformed investment policymaking. Fund placement according to simple precepts of safety, profit, and legality gave way to other considerations: the ambitions of company executives to whom high finance was a power challenge more arresting than life insurance marketing; or the effect of investment on policy sales and public relations. The result was a continuing and complex tension between security and possibility, between safety and profit.

The peculiar purposes of life insurance investment placed a greater premium on earning rate and longevity than on market value. Thus, when the rising market price of a block of securities reduced its proportionate rate of earnings, the adverse effect on the Metropolitan's investment earning performance induced the company to rid itself of an otherwise flourishing security. For the same reason, a low real estate valuation was preferred to a high one. The New York insurance department in 1899 substantially raised the valuation of the New York Life's property. In view of the company's need to earn 3½ percent on its real estate, this revaluation was the equivalent of a loss of $1,500,000 in property values. The Metropolitan exchanged coupon bonds for regular bonds of the Northern Pacific because the former were being called in for redemption while the latter remained in force. New York and New Jersey law required insurance companies to rid themselves of foreclosed real estate within five years, and at least two companies (the Prudential and the Equitable) conveyed parcels to dummy holders in order to evade this limitation.

Insurance marketing considerations strongly affected investment policy. As early as 1876, a New York Life agent complained that the company's large United States bond holdings made it difficult to write policies on wealthy foreigners. Premium notes, a substantial form of life insurance investment until 1870, declined rapidly thereafter, in great part because the institutionalization of policy marketing made this form of sales stimulation unnecessary. The relatively well-off purchasers of deferred dividend policies strongly desired policy loans, and this category of insurance investment rose significantly at the turn of the century.[11]

The impact of marketing and public relations considerations was particularly evident in the field of mortgage and collateral loans. A major problem was the relative advantage of concentration in New York as opposed to national dispersion. After legislative restrictions were lifted, widespread lending became a possibility; as the great companies developed into national institutions, it became politic as well. Overconcentration in the metropolitan area lowered interest rates, and there were greater earning prospects in the South and West. But the heavy expenses, risks, and technical difficulties of distant loans acted as a damper. Henry Hyde wrestled with the problem. In 1890 he complained: "In making our loans we are tied down by stringent State laws," and supported a "McCurdy bill" to permit investments in other states. But he admitted too that the finance committee's preference "to invest our money . . . in this locality" made loans outside of New York "exceptions to our rules."

Sometimes the deciding factor in expanded mortgage and loan investments was their impact on life insurance marketing. The Equitable hopefully made loans in the West through an affiliate, the Mercantile Trust Company, but found that neither the numerous rejected loan applicants nor the few successful ones bought the company's policies. The New York Life's mortgage lending at times reflected the pressure of local agents. Its decision in 1894 to bid for a $500,000 California state bond issue stemmed in part from criticism that it had no investments in that state. In 1904 the company, anxious to prevent policy lapses, proposed to lend $2,500,000 to policyholder victims of a Baltimore fire. After Senator Preston B. Plumb of Kansas told fellow members of the Mutual's board of directors that loans and investments in the West would please old policyholders and create new ones, they called for deposits in Western banks.[12]

The Prudential entered the loan business in California and the South in part because its agents claimed that this would encourage life insurance sales. And its farm loans increased because other firms, among them the Northwestern Mutual, Penn Mutual, and Mutual Benefit, were active in the field. Unlike its rival, the Metropolitan shunned Western and farm loans in order to concentrate on more familiar investments such as Brooklyn real estate. The New York Life, too, had qualms about investments in exotic areas far from New York City. It looked askance at Montana loans because of the state's reliance upon one industry, "and that mining"; and it rejected a Little Rock, Arkansas, fund request because "we are not at the moment prepared to act favorably upon applications for loans in that region of the country." McCurdy of the Mutual came to agree with Hyde on the doubtful efficacy of Western investments and the need to concentrate "on interests which centre or are more easily reached just here." Particularly in the uncertain mid-nineties did he approve of investments being "congested in the great money centres." [13] If marketing considerations led to Western investments, concern over the region's political instability during the Populist 1890's spurred fund withdrawals. Both conditions underscored the existence of investment policy factors which, though ultimately related to profitmaking, were far from purely financial in nature.

5

Diverse internal business factors thus shaped insurance investment. At the same time, another influence came into play: widespread recognition that the great companies were a ponderable factor in high finance. In 1892 an independent actuary, David Park Fackler, told the National Convention of Insurance Commissioners: "Our Life Companies are becoming vast financial corporations, and may become a source of danger to the commonwealth by reason of the vast money power lodged in the hands of a few men." A Chicago newspaper in 1895 saw nothing to stop the firms from using their enormous assets to depress security prices and manipulate the market. It concluded that "life insurance, if measured by money values and its effects upon the financial and commercial interests of the country, is by far the greatest question confronting the people." The Massachusetts insurance commissioner in 1903 envisaged the possibility of some "bold manipulator" gaining control of a company's assets, transferring his rights to a trust or trust company, and through it "financing large enterprise and promoting all kinds of corporate consolidations" — a prevision of the fears that arose when Thomas F. Ryan secured control of the Equitable in 1905.

By the time of the Armstrong investigation the financial power of the large life insurance companies evoked widespread concern. One commentator voiced the general sentiment: "When the great companies clash, it may well be said to be a battle of giants; when they cooperate, nothing can successfully oppose them in the money market." Another noted in 1906: "for fully a decade, life insurance funds were freely used in most of the important underwriting ventures in New York." Louis D. Brandeis placed the companies above the ups and downs of the economy: "Indeed, they derive certain benefits in time of adversity."

As "the creditors of our great industries with all the power which that implies," they were the "greatest economic menace of to-day." Equitable director Jacob H. Schiff told the Armstrong Committee that insurance companies should invest only "in securities that do not control anything. The danger to the States is in these large accumulations." Actuary Fackler, called before the 1906 New Jersey life insurance investigating committee, was unable to give a specific instance where life insurance money had a planned and improper effect upon the securities market, but he spoke for many of his contemporaries when he explained: "I have simply supposed that in some quiet, unknown way large sums of money may have been used." [14]

Life insurance executives accepted the prevailing view of the extent, if not the morality, of their investment role. The Equitable's Alexander boasted of "these great central monetary agencies." Richard McCurdy flexed his investment muscles before the railroads: he reminded the New Haven's president that it would be well to have "an associate who can buy large amounts [of securities] at *first hand*." A consciousness of power, fed by the size of the capital involved and by the ideology of the life insurance business, first found formal expression in the 1890's. Insurance company deposits played a role of some consequence in providing banks with the capital necessary to end the panic of 1893. The New York Life congratulated itself on making the largest single subscription to the government loan designed to ease the gold crisis of 1894, thus "making this Company a conspicuous assistant in sustaining the credit of the Government." As the Spanish-American War approached, the New York Life pledged a $10,000,000 loan on the government's terms. On April 19, 1898, on the eve of the war declaration, the finance committee suspended real estate loans in anticipation of a government call for funds. (But a week later real estate loans were being considered again, and within a month United States bonds were sold to buy securities of the Utah and Northern Railroad.) [15]

As substantial financial institutions, the companies interested themselves in the currency problem. John McCall of the New York Life circulated great quantities of literature attacking a bimetallic or silver-based currency. At the end of 1890 the company adopted a rule requiring loan payments in gold; in 1892 this clause was extended to municipal, county, and state bonds. The Metropolitan followed suit in 1893. The New York Life's finance committee resolved not to consider loan applications from any state legislating against the payment of debts in gold, and 1894 Denver City bonds were refused "because of the Populist and Silver sentiment prevailing in Colorado." In July 1896, after Bryan's nomination heightened Eastern financial concerns to a fever pitch, Hyde proposed that counsel from the Big Three meet and decide whether or not to require policy premium payments in gold.

But the exigencies of day-to-day investment practice vitiated this stand, just as the New York Life's April 1898 investment patriotism proved to be only a vagrant mood. A few months after McCall's company established its 1890 gold payment rule, it had to waive the clause on Wall Street temporary loan notes: for occasionally the provision could not be included in otherwise desirable loans. In 1891 the firm waived its gold clause in a purchase of Jefferson County, Alabama, bonds which were subject to a state law forbidding issues payable in gold alone.[16]

But these reminders of the constant pressure of business needs did not seriously shake the view company officers and critics alike held of life insurance investment power. The boom market of 1897–1902 afforded the opportunity for an impressive display of financial prowess. By the early 1900's the heads of the great companies had every reason to regard themselves as at the very heart of high finance. In addition to the sheer bulk of their investment potential, they could lay claim to an awesome interlocking network of affiliations with investment banking houses, trust companies, banks, and other fiduciary institutions: a structure that attested to their consequential role in the flowering of American finance capitalism.

IX * The Structure of Investment

Two developments shaped the investment environment of 1900: the rise of diverse financial institutions, and their consolidation into distinct groupings under centralized leadership. It was possible — and increasingly it was fashionable — to speak of a "Standard Oil group" or a "Morgan group" of banks, trust companies, brokerage houses, and insurance companies. Dominating these clusters, as allies or in battle, were the great financial titans: J. P. Morgan, Jacob Schiff, George F. Baker, John D. Rockefeller, James Stillman, and Thomas F. Ryan. It was in this milieu that the large life insurance companies operated as financial institutions. Their magnates drew together complexes of affiliated financial institutions, and, so bolstered, strove for place within the highest circles of high finance.

The insurance companies had special claims to primacy in the world of high finance. The muckraker Thomas W. Lawson believed that in "the tremendous correlation of financial institutions and forces that I call the 'system' . . . the most potent factor . . . is the life insurance companies." The size of their investment capital and the connections of their officers and directors put them into intimate contact with the most powerful circles of high finance. The controlling values of the great financiers — centralization, rationalization, giantism — also were those of the life insurance magnates. By 1900 the most exciting thing about the insurance business for men like McCall, Perkins, Dryden, Alexander, McCurdy, and Hegeman was its investing power. In entering the highest levels of the financial world these leaders saw great prospects for corporate and personal gain, unmatched opportunities for the expression of their sense of achievement and place. When the New York State Library's *Index to Legislation* for 1902 moved its list of insurance laws from the charities to the banking section, it reflected a substantial change in the ideology of the business, one which the great firms embraced in a special way.[1]

A web of mutual needs and expectations enmeshed the large life insurance companies with other institutions. The sheer size and availability of their investment capital — as McCurdy put it: "we have the money necessary to supply the sinews of war" — made them likely objects for the attentions of financiers. A trust company officer obviously had in mind favors readily and plentifully granted when he referred to the Mutual as his firm's "grandmother." Although the companies could not participate directly in the great stock flotations at the turn of the century, their bond purchasing capacity made their patronage desirable indeed. And affiliated financial institutions could use life insurance money to make loans and buy securities not acceptable to the companies themselves. Their investment situation, constrained though it was by regulation and tradition, nevertheless had certain advantages. Insurance companies had less need than banks for investments quickly convertible into cash. The notable laxity of state insurance department bookkeeping methods also was attractive. And the huge company surpluses were tempting pools of investment capital.[2]

Insurance executives emphasized the other side of the coin: an overriding insurance business necessity. The fundamental cause of the Mutual's financial alliances, said Richard McCurdy, was the company's marketing success. As deferred dividend premiums mounted, "we had a lot of money coming in that we did not know what to do with." Effective investment was important to a man who exhorted his colleagues to remember that "the greater the amount of new money brought in and invested . . . the greater grows the snowball of compound interest we are trying to roll up." Henry Hyde, too, hoped by 1888 that the Equitable's finance committee "will find some safe way of putting . . . out" the company's growing receipts. Chauncey Depew later recalled that he became useful to Hyde because of the "ease and facility with which I could reach where [investment] knowledge could be had."

The Mutual's management claimed to be reared on life insurance marketing, and pleaded unfamiliarity with the intricacies of large-scale investment. Furthermore, the company found that the financial milieu did not permit it to place substantial amounts of money directly. When the Mutual took on the features of a building and loan association in making loans in the Midwest, the Indiana Supreme Court declared this to be an improper function for a life insurance company. The firm's treasurer later told of trying to buy securities directly from President Stuyvesant Fish of the Illinois Central: Fish refused on the ground that it was necessary for him to handle his financing through his banking associations. There was "no question" but that banking institutions controlled the flow of investment. Affiliates such as the Mutual's Title Guaranty and Trust Company filled the need for specialized investment: "they command business, and we do not, and we cannot get the applications." It was simple logic to "get closer to the cost price of the manufacture of investments and securities" by "going into partnership with people who knew more about it than we did." [3]

From this viewpoint, the dependent partner in the relationship was the insurance company. Mutual treasurer Frederic Cromwell humbly observed that the large banks "sell more bonds in Europe in a week than we buy in a month. This is a very big world . . . and if the insurance companies undertook to control the situation they could not do it. You have to meet the situation as it is . . . You have to fall in and get as good securities at as favorable a rate as you can." The financier Edward H. Harriman, questioned about his Equitable dealings, offered the same perspective: "when a man has some sixteen thousand miles of railroad and thirty-five or forty steamships . . . he has not much time to think about life insurance, and I should not think Mr. Ryan would either."

But these disclaimers of significance, the innocence implied in McCurdy's declaration that his "own particular pet slogan is 'I am not a financier,'" do not correlate with the tough and aggressive corporate image otherwise so prevalent in the great companies. McCurdy was enough involved in the intricacies of the financial system to become a strong exponent of the expansion of branch banking at the expense of small, local firms. He and Hyde managed their banking and trust company affiliations with great vigor and skill. The Mutual head explained: "How better could the Trustees of the Mutual . . . insure the proper custody and management of this Company's funds than by arranging that a considerable number of their own body should at all times be members of the Boards of Directors of those Companies?" And George W. Perkins, as a partner in J. P. Morgan and Company, took a place in the first rank of financiers in investment banking's golden age.

The ideological values that led insurance leaders and their firms into a sophisticated marketing structure worked as well to impel them to close identification with high finance. James Alexander's ambitions for the trust companies affiliated with the Equitable were much in the spirit of Henry Hyde's life insurance salesmanship: "we *must* perform some coup and increase [the Equitable Trust Company's] . . . size and importance. Also in the case of the Mercantile Trust. I would like to buy up a couple of trust companies and double up that concern." The Equitable's reforming Frick Committee described the prevailing animus: "The ambition for bigness naturally extends to the investment of funds. There is chafing under the laws which govern the investments of a life insurance company. Alliances are made with other institutions with the idea of yielding to the Society results which are not possible under the operations permitted to insurance companies. Systematic but uninteresting plodding is neglected, while energies are directed towards 'coups.' "[4]

By 1900 the very nature of insurance investment seemed to demand these relationships. The fundamental shift from mortgages to railroad bonds stemmed from an internal business need for large-scale, long-term placements; but this choice meant also that the companies were inextricably involved in the financial structure through which these securities flowed. Significant, too, was the general decline in interest rates during the late nineteenth and early twentieth centuries. This phenomenon had a special impact on an investment group committed to stable, long-range returns. By 1891 it seemed to the *Commercial and Financial Chronicle* that policy lapses rather than investments were the chief source of surplus earnings. In 1899 John McCall organized a symposium of leading bankers, who agreed that the interest rate in the foreseeable future would hover around 3½ percent — which meant a depressed insurance earning valuation rate of 3 percent. McCurdy in 1898 glumly noted the general decline, and found no comfort in the fact that "the spirit of enterprise and speculation is rising rapidly," for this would depress long-term bond earnings still more.[5]

The paradox of falling yields in the midst of a gathering boom market was especially poignant for these aggressive life insurance magnates. As in the case of their executive earning capacity, frustrations stemmed from the peculiar constraints built into the life insurance business. Shut off from speculation in securities values, committed to a passive, nearly helpless dependence on long-term rates of yield, they turned eagerly to financial alliances that might give them greater control of, and profit from, their investment environment.

With involvement in high finance as much an expression of personal executive desires as of inescapable business requirements, it was difficult for these leaders to draw a line between private and corporate interest. Officers and directors were involved as individuals in many of the ventures to which they committed their companies' funds. Even if it was desired, a differentiation of interests would have been difficult because of a widespread intermixture of executive and directorial roles. Insurance officers sat on the boards of banks and trust companies, and financiers shared in the investment deliberations of the great life firms. All moved within the circumscribed New York financial world. Mutual treasurer Cromwell, trying to explain the overlapping investment ventures of the Mutual and the members of the finance committee, observed: "Why, we were together . . . every day." As in the companies' managerial structures, the concentration and rationalization of investment decisionmaking resulted not in cleaner and more precise direction, but in the multiplication of the pressures shaping policy choices.

2

The companies' alliances included some relatively simple, intramural arrangements. The Metropolitan required its mortgagees to place fire insurance on their properties with Dutcher and Edminster — whose senior partner was finance committee member Silas B. Dutcher. In addition to numerous safe deposit company interests, Hyde once controlled the Liberty Fire Insurance Company and parceled out shares to life insurance associates and to the governor of Massachusetts. Close ties existed also with surety companies, which by the turn of the century were bonding many life insurance agents. Several insurance executives held stock in the American and National Surety companies. The Equitable had two directors on the American Surety's board, and Hyde had to resist pleas from the firm's officers that the life insurance company purchase more American Surety stock. Comparably intimate were the relations of the New York Life with the National Surety Company.[6]

The great life firms' connections with brokerage houses were more complex financial involvements, for these conjoined personal ambitions with greater control over the insurance investment milieu. Reliance on brokers for securities grew gradually. But after 1890 the size and complexity of insurance investment, and brokerage control over the largest and most attractive flotations, led to formalized relationships between insurance companies and investment houses.

The Prudential settled down to a close connection with the venerable New York firm of Robert Winthrop and Company. One member of this house, Mark T. Cox, was also a director of the Fidelity Trust Company and the Public Service Corporation, which with the Prudential made up a tightly knit financial cluster. Besides supplying a large proportion of the Prudential's securities purchases, Winthrop had a continuous collateral loan arrangement with its customer. Demand loans to Winthrop ranging from $150,000 to $500,000 and sometimes totaling $1,500,000, secured by constantly changing sets of New Jersey utilities securities (the stuff out of which the Public Service Corporation empire was being created), stood on the Prudential's books through the 1890's and the early 1900's.[7]

The Metropolitan matched its sister firm with its ties to Vermilye and Company. William A. Read, a longtime friend of John Hegeman and a Metropolitan director, was the Vermilye partner responsible for the liaison. Around 1880 Hegeman and Knapp had come to Read's office seeking professional investment guidance; and he had furnished it ever since that day. Of $72,577,000 in bonds and stocks bought by the Metropolitan up to the end of 1904, $66,000,000 worth came through Vermilye; of $26,000,000 sold, $24,000,000 was handled by that house. Certain benefits came to the insurance company — or at least to its executives — in return. "Because of the large business interests that we had with him," the brokerage house secretly rebated to Hegeman the interest on his personal account. When the Metropolitan wished to keep collateral loans from appearing in its annual report to the New York insurance department, Vermilye obligingly took them for a few days over the turn of the year. This was, in essence, a personal rather than an institutional alliance. When Read left Vermilye at the beginning of 1905 and opened his own firm, the Metropolitan promptly began a deposit account there. Hegeman brusquely "explained" his motivation to the Armstrong inquisitors: "Because we had the money and selected them, perhaps, as against some other depository."

The Big Three were more sophisticated in their investment relationships. Brokerage alliances generally took second place to bank and trust company affiliations. The Mutual showed some preference for the offerings of Arbuckle Brothers; company director James N. Jarvie was a member of that house. But its securities purchases were too substantial, and McCurdy's ambitions were too vaulting and ramified, for the relationship to be more than peripheral.[8]

In 1888, when Henry Hyde sought an arrangement with the Boston firm of Kidder, Peabody and Company, it was for handling money transfers rather than for purchasing security offerings. Nor did Hyde plan to rely solely on the Boston house even for this limited function: "we had better peddle around and do the best we can." By the turn of the century, the Equitable, through its financial adviser George H. Squire, had close relations with the investment banking firm of Kuhn, Loeb and Company. Jacob H. Schiff, Kuhn, Loeb's head, was a member of the Equitable's finance committee. But of the $197,000,000 worth of securities bought by the Equitable between 1900 and 1905, Kuhn, Loeb provided only about $33,000,000. The Equitable's securities purchases far transcended the services of a single house.

The New York Life had ties with Harvey, Fiske and Sons, and with the broker W. S. Fanshawe, but its most significant investment understandings were with J. P. Morgan and Company. George W. Perkins acted as the liaison between the insurance company and the investment banking house; from 1901 to 1906 he was a Morgan partner as well as a New York Life vice-president. As in the case of the Equitable and Kuhn, Loeb, the New York Life by no means bought the bulk of its securities directly through Morgan.[9] But the New York Life–Morgan and Equitable–Kuhn, Loeb relationships involved more than stock brokerage. The great investment banking houses were not passive intermediaries, but positive forces creating the time's most important security flotations. Identification with them was, for the life insurance firms, evocative expression of their entry into the highest levels of investment finance.

The most substantial sector of the companies' structure of financial affiliations involved banks and trust companies. New York banking increasingly served the capital and deposit requirements of the nation's new corporate system. The proportion of the country's banking business passing through the New York Clearing House went from 57 percent in 1897 to 64 percent in 1902. In addition, trust companies came into their own at the century's end as a major factor in the development of a centralized yet flexible national financial structure. The diversity of operations permitted by their charters made them admirable agencies for the complex fiduciary needs of large corporations. In 1887, New

York law authorized trust companies to accept "any and all such trusts and powers, of whatever nature or description, as may be conferred upon or intrusted or committed to [them] . . . by any person or persons"; after that their potentialities were boundless. Between 1898 and 1901 general deposits outstripped deposits in trust in these institutions; by 1902, 727 trust companies had aggregate deposits of one and a half billion dollars.[10]

These bank and trust company developments could not fail to catch the attention of insurance leaders ambitious for financial place and power. Restrained by the ethos of life insurance conservatism from the more stimulating investment opportunities, yet driven by falling interest rates and by their own aggressiveness to freer use of their huge investment funds, insurance magnates found the ideal solution in bank and trust company affiliations. The stock of these institutions had a unique aura of soundness and substantiality. At the same time access could be gained, through the banks and trust companies thus controlled, to areas of investment closed to life insurance funds per se. As one observer put it: "The trust company is the irrigating canal of Wall Street, the insurance company the reservoir." Such alliances struck the Massachusetts insurance commissioner as one of the most challenging "of all the hard corporation problems of the day with which both Nation and State have to deal." [11]

The extent, diversity, and complexity of the life insurance bank and trust company relationships demand closer examination. For far from being helpless pawns in the hands of more sophisticated financiers, the insurance companies often shaped the terms of the relationship to their own ends. In so doing, the life insurance executives provided yet another example of the vigor and resourcefulness with which they worked to create an investment structure suitable to their vaulting business ambitions.

3

At the peak of his life insurance marketing triumph Henry Hyde turned his attention to bank and trust company control. From the first he made no clear distinction between his own and the Equitable's purchases of such stock. In the 1880's he — and his firm — gained control of the Mercantile Trust Company. The Mercantile's president, Louis Fitzgerald, in turn became Hyde's assistant in Equitable investment policymaking. In this first stage of acquisition, the life insurance firm

* RIGHT-HAND MEN *

IN SEVERAL companies men of special talents rose as indispensable aids to presidents who more and more substituted the challenges of high finance for the responsibilities of the life insurance business.

Haley Fiske was the firm, skillful vice president in charge of the Metropolitan's operations.

Gage E. Tarbell took charge of the Equitable's marketing and agency activities after Henry Hyde's death.

George W. Perkins was the greatest of the Warwicks, the force behind McCall in the New York Life's marketing, agency, investment, and political activities.

WHEN THE large life insurance companies came into their majority, their home office buildings served as physical manifestations of their wealth and corporate power.

The Metropolitan building in Madison Square was the greatest of all the home offices. Its first section was completed in 1893, and in 1909 the famous tower, then the tallest on earth, was added.

The Prudential building in Newark was designed, in president Dryden's words, to exemplify the company's "all-pervading spirit of beneficence and its ingrained love of the golden rule."

The Mutual building, in the midst of the financial district at 34 Nassau Street, was largely expanded in 1892.

The Equitable's headquarters at 120 Broadway, completed in 1887, was as solid and as massive as Henry Hyde himself.

The home of the New York Life at 346 Broadway was embellished in 1896 with an annex designed by McKim, Mead and White; the result, according to the company, was "a Temple of Humanity."

* THE SONS OF THE FATHERS *

AS THE companies waxed fat, nepotism flourished — and so did the well-placed sons of well-placed fathers.

Robert McCurdy had, among other plums, the well-rewarded post of general manager of the Mutual's foreign agencies.

James Hazen Hyde was the most spectacular of the prodigals and an immediate cause of the crisis of 1905.

Forrest F. Dryden was secretary of the Prudential and, after his father's death, the president of the company.

John C. McCall was secretary of the New York Life and an active figure in the company's lobbying activities.

also took over the Mercantile Safe Deposit Company, and fostered safe deposit firms in Equitable buildings in Boston and St. Louis. In 1893 Hyde and several associates, along with the Equitable, bought control of the Western National Bank of New York. Brayton Ives, the bank's president, was an Equitable director and president of the Northern Pacific Railroad. Fitzgerald and the Mercantile Trust, and Ives and the Western, became intermediaries between Hyde and the world of high finance, and prime supplicants for the depository bounty that was at Hyde's disposal. Before his death in 1899, Hyde developed close relations with the Commercial Trust Company of Philadelphia as well.

In the new century president James W. Alexander and vice-president James Hazen Hyde expanded the Equitable's alliances to include the Franklin National Bank and the Lawyers' Title and Lawyers' Mortgage Insurance companies. In 1902 the American Deposit and Loan Company was reorganized as the Equitable Trust Company. The insurance firm and its officers and directors shared the requisite stock purchases. In the same year the Morton Trust Company bought control of the National Bank of the United States, which already had merged with the Equitable's Western National Bank. By the end of 1903 the National Bank of Commerce also had become part of this merger. The process brought the banking interests of the Equitable, the Mutual, and the Prudential within the spheres of such giants of the financial world as J. P. Morgan and Thomas F. Ryan.[12]

As the Equitable's circle of financial affiliates grew, so did the intensity of its involvement in their activities. Hyde's relations with the Western National Bank exemplify this process of identification and involvement. Brayton Ives, the president of the Western, appealed for assistance in building up his bank's deposits, and Hyde was more than ready to grant it. He applied to the problem the quality of concentrated inventiveness which had served the Equitable so well in life insurance marketing. He planned to find out which New York banks offered a 1½ percent interest rate, obtain their out-of-town bank deposit lists, and entice those depositors with the Western's 2 percent rate. Western board members who did not bring in large accounts were superfluous, and should be replaced by directors who had access to big depositors: "We have all got to get out of the old-fashioned ideas to accomplish anything now at the end of the nineteenth century." The Equitable would induce its out-of-town depository banks and large securities sellers such as the Pennsylvania Railroad to use the Western for their

New York City banking needs. He guaranteed that the Equitable and the Mercantile Trust would back the Western in difficult times. "You want to keep your money in the strongest place, as no man knows what favors he might want to ask," he reminded the president of the New Orleans National Bank.

Nor did Hyde forget the Equitable's political connections. He knew that Chauncey Depew was closely connected with the Lincoln National Bank, which controlled accounts throughout New York State, and he saw no reason why this Equitable director and legal adviser could not turn over half a dozen or so of these accounts to the Western. And could Mark Hanna, as president of the National Bank of Cleveland, induce that institution to use the Western in New York? His animus was simple, intense: "I do not think it is respectable to have the deposits at less than twenty millions." Intervention so personal stirred jealousy and rivalries between Fitzgerald of the Mercantile Trust and Ives of the Western. Later, the two combined in their resentment of the favoritism shown by Alexander and the younger Hyde toward the Equitable Trust. Hyde and his successors played the role of grands seigneurs without reluctance; the structure of affiliations satisfied psychological as well as investment needs.[13]

4

In the extent of their bank and trust company affiliations, in their collateral loans to favored financiers, and in their intertwining of personal and company interests, McCurdy and the Mutual were outstanding. There was a special intensity about McCurdy's financial empire building: his grandiose sense of self must have suffered particularly from the limited remuneration of a mutual company. He did not even have the joys, however vicarious, of company stock ownership which belonged to Hyde.

The Mutual's financial relationships were justified on grounds of business necessity. A director from California pressed for a company deposit in the Bank of California until Treasurer Cromwell sighed that it had to be done "if we are going to have any peace." McCurdy credited his affiliates with "affording a larger field for investment and profit." He tried not to glory in the resulting web of influence, speaking of the Mutual's "freedom from entangling alliances," and declaring that his own stock holdings in the National Safe Deposit Company stemmed "from a sense of duty." In 1900 he piously warned his board: "we should not feel that we are simply here to build up a great financial system including the organization of trust companies, the management of banks and participation in the various enterprises with which at the present time our Country at large and the moneyed centres in particular are teeming." But he could not hide his real feelings. When he recalled that "my life had been devoted to learning the business of life insurance, but of banking except in its theory I knew nothing," his satisfaction over his new-found skill in banking practice was patent. He took a personal as well as a business satisfaction in the fact that the Mutual's treasury department "is at present a power in Wall Street." [14]

The best evidence of his true commitment was the network of affiliations itself. The Mutual's financial empire began in the early 1890's, and by the middle of the decade it was official company policy to buy into "financial corporations." The first acquisition was the stock of the New York Guaranty and Indemnity Company, an inactive institution but one that held a broad trust company charter. Soon the Mutual's holdings, combined with the private purchases of its officers and directors, gave it control. In 1896 it turned the Guaranty and Indemnity into the Guaranty Trust Company, with half of the new firm's stock held by the Mutual and half distributed "to secure the best business connections and the highest financial support."

McCurdy deeply interested himself in the activities of the Guaranty Trust. When it sought to become the Pennsylvania Railroad's New York City registrar of stock transfers, he threw the Mutual's weight as the leading Pennsylvania bondholder behind the Guaranty Trust's application. In the wake of the 1893 panic he decided to allow policy loans, and let the Guaranty Trust handle a form of investment that was distasteful to him as a life insurance man.[15]

McCurdy's boldest step was to act as "the founder of the Guaranty's policy of foreign expansion." The Guaranty and Indemnity, the parent of the Guaranty Trust, had been the United States fiscal agent in Manila. But it found that Oriental banking did not pay, and transferred its interest to the International Banking Company. McCurdy had connections with the International; his secretary spoke of it as "to a certain extent . . . the outcome of some of his own suggestions." The International made a specialty of overseas banking, and sought a charter from Congress. After that, McCurdy expected, its administration would "pass into entirely congenial hands."

But the International never met the hopes reposed in it, and Mc-

Curdy's overseas banking ambitions centered on the Guaranty Trust. From its establishment in 1896 he had the "definite design" to establish a London branch of the Guaranty. Although he and his Mutual associates were ignorant of foreign banking procedures, the novelty of the venture excited him; it was something that "no American corporation as yet has seen its way to do. We shall be first in the field and we ought to be able, with all the alliances and associations at our hand, to create in a . . . short time a very powerful European concern through the 'British branch,' for the transaction of a general international banking." [16]

The London office of the Guaranty Trust had a British board of directors to add to its attractiveness. But as a foreign company the firm could not obtain the participation of leading English businessmen and financiers; nor could the Bank of England be used for discount by a non-British bank. Clearly, the venture needed a British charter. The opportunity came in 1899. Levi P. Morton, head of the American brokerage house of Morton, Bliss and Company, also controlled the English firm of Morton, Chaplin. With five unmarried daughters and no sons, he sought a way to ensure family control of his partnership interest in the houses after his death. His plan was to incorporate the business, make the Mutual trustee of his daughters' stock, and allow the Guaranty Trust's London branch to merge with Morton, Chaplin and thus take advantage of the latter's British identification. In June 1899, Morton, Bliss was dissolved and reorganized as the Morton Trust Company. Both the Mutual and the Mutual's officers were substantial stockholders. The board of the new firm included McCurdy, Cromwell, Haven, Jarvie, and Juilliard of the Mutual, James Alexander of the Equitable, Henry M. Flagler of Standard Oil, and a representative of Kuhn, Loeb. Within a year, by grace of a special bill hurried through the New York legislature, the Morton Trust merged with the State Trust. The Morton Trust flourished and prospered, but the business of the Guaranty Trust's London branch remained limited and, from McCurdy's point of view, unsatisfactory.[17]

In less grandiose domestic ventures, McCurdy's aggressive ingenuity had freer play. After securing stock control of the United States Mortgage and Trust Company (USMT) in 1893, the Mutual made the firm one of its depositories. Stock ownership was dispersed, in order to bring experienced men into the operation of the USMT. It quickly came to act as a feeder of Mutual investments on a national scale. Substantial men from cities like St. Paul, San Francisco, and Seattle were invited to be stockholders, and were assured that the company would favor investments in their areas. Life insurance marketing considerations also figured: McCurdy hoped to capitalize on the feeling that the New York Life and the Equitable put Western premium payments into Eastern investments.

McCurdy treated the United States Mortgage and Trust with the same benevolent paternalism that Henry Hyde applied to the Western National Bank. He complimented USMT president George W. Young for pushing his own banking policies "with praiseworthy ambition," and told the director of the Guaranty Trust's London branch not to expect the Mortgage and Trust to use it for its foreign exchange transactions, for Young might feel that he was "being put out to nurse." It was best to avoid any relation between the two Mutual affiliates "which has the appearance of guardianship or tutelage." He put pressure on Pennsylvania Railroad president A. J. Cassatt to use the USMT as registrar of a new stock issue, pointing out: "the Mutual . . . is the largest stockholder in the United States Mortgage and Trust Company and also the largest stockholder in the Pennsylvania Railroad Company and I respectfully ask that these two facts should be weighed carefully." [18]

The end of the boom market in 1903 dampened McCurdy's enthusiasm for new bank or trust company affiliations. But until then he, his associates, and his company actively participated in banking amalgamations and consolidations. The Mutual president was a stockholder in the Hide and Leather Bank, which joined with the Equitable's Western National to become the National Bank of the United States. The combination came through a capital increase substantially financed by the Mutual. Both McCurdy and his company had stock in the National Bank of Commerce, which profitably absorbed the National Union Bank — in which both McCurdy and his company had stock. To assure the prosperity of the heavily capitalized Bank of Commerce, Mutual directors joined its board and it became the insurance company's "leading bank." Mutual deposits ranged up to $10,000,000. By 1900 this alliance seemed so satisfactory that the Bank of Commerce was reorganized with double its former capitalization, and with J. P. Morgan as its vice-president. As a large stockholder the Mutual stood to benefit from the bank's profits; as a life insurance company it could see its deposits used for such profitable, if unconservative, investments as collateral loans and industrial bond purchases. The life insurance company contributed more than deposits to the bank's success: it put pressure on its out-of-town banks of deposit to use the Bank of Commerce as their New York agent.[19]

For all the business justification of such alliances, McCurdy's commitment was essentially personal. Like Hyde, he made little distinction between his own interests and those of his company; the financial activities of the Mutual and Equitable leaders were governed by a highly individualistic outlook rather than by an overriding sense of corporate purpose. This quality characterized McCurdy's strong interest in certain New Jersey financial institutions, chiefly the Morristown Trust Company. Contiguous to his country estate, the Morristown Trust numbered himself, his family, and his friends among its stockholders. In 1893 McCurdy told the institution's president that he might have a share in the Broadway and Seventh Avenue Railway syndicate. In return the trust company was expected to sell some of the bonds, and to help maintain their general marketability. "I can't force you into these things unless you do your share," McCurdy adjured with parental sternness. His severity was not unalloyed; in 1899 he was concerned lest the Morristown Trust feel inferior to the Guaranty Trust in his affections. And, like any parent, he took on certain prerogatives as his due. When a new Morristown Trust stock issue appeared, and promised to be worth considerably more than its initial cost, he had the United States Mortgage and Trust put up the money for his share — with his share the collateral for the loan. Grandly he distributed portions of this windfall to favored Mutual directors.[20]

Extensive as the Mutual's financial structure was, it often seemed to be in essence a highly personalized instrument of McCurdy's desires and ambitions. The resulting tension between institutionalized purpose and personalized performance, as in the Equitable, made for a profound structural instability.

5

The New York Life's early financial affiliations closely resembled those of its peers. It had a hand in charter amendments to the Merchants' and American Exchange National banks in the mid-1880's. The company dealt in a free-wheeling manner with its banks of deposit. It refused its Baltimore outlet's request for eased deposit terms, and shifted to another bank there; it made William H. Seward and Co. of Auburn, New York, a place of agency deposit because "they are a very important factor in business and financial circles in all Central New York, and it would be greatly to our advantage to have a deposit account with the firm." The New York Life's Chicago inspector of agencies put pressure on the home office to place a deposit in the Central Trust Company of Illinois in order to encourage a Central officer to take a $50,000 insurance policy.[21]

As the company's corporate stature and investment power increased, it entered more rarified financial levels. William L. Strong, a member of the finance committee, was president of the Central National Bank of New York, and offered his institution's securities to the life insurance firm in 1891. Within a year the New York Life had $2,500,000 worth of Central stock, and mutual accommodation on deposits and interest rates was the rule. In step with the Equitable and the Metropolitan, the New York Life took control of a tenant safe deposit company, the Manhattan. And with the New York Security and Trust Company it developed the same sort of fecund and varied relationship that characterized the Equitable and the Mercantile Trust, or the Mutual and the Guaranty Trust.

In the late 1880's the New York Life took over the charters of the Commercial and Manhattan Trust companies, and out of them created the New York Security and Trust (NYST). The insurance company held the major share of NYST stock. Its officers, with holdings of their own, were conspicuous in the trust company's directorate, and controlled its stock distribution. At the end of 1892, the New York Life bought fifty shares and directed the trust company to place it so as to bolster its business. In a week the shares went at cost to Blair and Company, stock brokers who presumably would be helpful in the NYST's investments.[22]

As elsewhere, stock ownership prefigured the creation of numerous functional ties. The NYST became the depository of New York Life special purpose accounts (some paying only a nominal interest rate), and handled covert payments to political lobbyist Andrew Hamilton. When the governor of Alabama appeared before the insurance company's finance committee in quest of an emergency short-term loan to his state, the NYST acted as the lending agency in a transaction that did not comport with accepted standards of life insurance investment. By the early 1900's the bulk of the New York Life's deposits in the NYST were used for stock collateral loans and other investments in which the company could not participate directly.

The New York Life's no-stock agreement with the Prussian government in 1899 affected its NYST holdings. McCall, Perkins, and NYST president Charles S. Fairchild became the stock's trustees in order to get it off the New York Life's books, and eventually arranged for its sale. But "the close relationship and interest" between insurance and trust company continued; the NYST remained "a *friendly* office." The patterns of mutual accommodation which developed during the years of stock control persisted long after outright ownership ceased.[23]

6

The great industrial companies, with assets considerably smaller than the Big Three, wielded proportionately less influence in the world of high finance. But their investment structures had the same characteristics as those of the straight life firms, a suggestion of the animus common to the society of insurance companies.

Parochial considerations were paramount in the Metropolitan's first financial affiliations. Its initial acquisition was the stock of the Hamilton Trust Company, in president Joseph Knapp's home city of Brooklyn. The president of the Hamilton was Silas B. Dutcher, a member of the Metropolitan's finance committee and head of its favorite brokerage house. But the Metropolitan Bank became the closest financial affiliate. The insurance company's new building at Fourth Avenue and Twenty-third Street had space for banking facilities. A Wall Street bank thought to open a branch office there, but the plan fell through. The insurance company, conscious of the need for banking facilities close at hand and desirous of reaping some of the profits from such an enterprise, thereupon established the Metropolitan Bank. When the new venture proved shaky, the Metropolitan made substantial deposits which helped it along.

The Metropolitan's managers were personally involved in their company's financial affiliates. Knapp, Hegeman, and Fiske, as well as their company, held stock in the National Shoe and Leather Bank, and considerable amounts of Metropolitan money were deposited there. The officers' holdings extended as well to the Mutual's Guaranty Trust and United States Mortgage and Trust. And they toyed with a plan to develop the International Banking Corporation as a central bank of control over the 1800 to 2000 Metropolitan banks of deposit in the United States — a scheme worthy of the boldest aspirations of the Big Three.[24]

The Prudential's Newark location, as well as its smaller size, deterred alliances with New York financial institutions. But its fiscal operations were extensive enough to require deposits in 268 banks in 1902, and it became the focal point of a well-developed financial structure within its own state. Its coadjutors were the Fidelity Trust Company, the Public Service Corporation (PSC) of New Jersey, and to a lesser degree the Union National Bank of Newark. The Prudential played a substantial role in the development of the Public Service network of utilities and transit firms. The Fidelity Trust Company, whose offices were in the Prudential building, acted as the investment banking intermediary. This tripartite arrangement rested on tightly interlocked managerial and directorial personnel. The leading Prudential stockholders — the Drydens, the Wards, the McCarters — were conspicuous also in the Fidelity and the PSC. Thomas McCarter best represented the interconnection. Once state attorney general, he resigned to become general counsel for the Fidelity, and finally rose to be president of the Public Service Corporation. As an attorney he represented the Prudential in the Robotham case, which involved Dryden's Prudential-Fidelity merger. It is not surprising that the president of Public Service described the relationship of the three firms as "very intimate" and "most harmonious; we have no friction at all." [25]

7

Complex financial affiliations, like sophisticated corporate structures and business techniques, stimulated intercompany cooperation. As individual investors, and as corporate fiscal managers, insurance magnates shared increasingly in each other's bank and trust company stocks. Thus, McCurdy instructed his Union Trust Company of New Jersey to reserve some of its securities for officers in the Equitable and the Prudential. The Prudential's officers were interested in the Equitable Trust as stockholders and directors; and Dryden held 100 shares in the Equitable's Western National Bank. The Prudential head placed a large company deposit in the Mercantile Trust, also in the Equitable orbit. The Equitable in turn built up its deposits in the Prudential's Fidelity Trust Company, and bought Fidelity stock.[26]

Both the Mutual and the New York Life opened accounts in Hyde's Western National Bank. But the increasing community of financial interest between the Mutual and the Equitable was particularly noticeable. Hyde shared in the stock of the Mutual-dominated Fifth Avenue Trust Company, and placed a $500,000 Equitable deposit in the Mutual's National Union Bank. He promised to make this an active account, and hoped that "it is but the beginning of more intimate relations between the two Companies." In 1903 the Equitable and the Mutual created the National Bank of Commerce, on the ground that their interests would be better served by one powerful bank than by two or three lesser ones. The Equitable reduced its interest in other institutions — the North American, the Park Bank, the Knickerbocker Trust — in order to concentrate on those which it and the Mutual jointly controlled. Even the Metropolitan, less involved than the others, shared in this trend. It found in 1903 that its International Banking Corporation was better designed to handle a Far Eastern exchange business than the domestic central banking that the Metropolitan wanted. Thereupon it tried to interest the New York Life, which had a growing Far Eastern insurance business, in the stock of the International.[27]

By the early 1900's the insurance companies' structure of financial affiliations stood as a dramatic manifestation of their corporate sophistication and power. Their bold, extensive, and complex relationships with the highest reaches of the world of finance were as evocative of their corporate nature as their great venture overseas. But the operation of their investment structure revealed the same enervating qualities that trammeled the foreign business.

X * The Investment Performance

The contour of the companies' investment performance appears in an analysis of their fund placement from 1890 to 1905 (Table 6). Distinctive investment profiles emerge. The bulk of Metropolitan and Prudential assets went steadily into real estate, mortgage loans, and bonds, with only moderate expansion of collateral loans, premium notes and policy loans, bank deposits, and stock holdings. The Big Three displayed during this period a marked and growing preference for negotiable securities over real estate and mortgages. By 1905 the Equitable had 54 percent of its ledger assets in this sector, the Mutual had 55 percent, and the New York Life had 73 percent. It is suggestive that the Big Three were less inclined than the industrial firms to invest in farm mortgages.

All companies had substantial surpluses, thus providing pools of capital freed from the demands of policyholder accountability and available for flexible, long-range placement. The Mutual and the Equitable steadily expanded their collateral loans, expressions of the personalized investment policymaking that flourished under Richard McCurdy, Henry Hyde, and James Alexander. The fund placements of the New York Life reflected George Perkins' purposes: a subtle, institutionalized role in domestic investment which preferred substantial bond purchases to comparatively ephemeral collateral loans or stock ventures; an aggressive, expansionist marketing technique which used premium notes, policy loans, and foreign bond purchases to increase the company's business volume at home and abroad.

The years around 1900 were a time of generally declining interest

TABLE 6. The Big Five's investments, 1890–1905 (millions of dollars)

Investment	1890 Amount	1890 Percent of total	1895 Amount	1895 Percent of total	1900 Amount	1900 Percent of total	1904[a] Amount	1904[a] Percent of total	1905 Amount	1905 Percent of total
Equitable										
Real estate	27.2	23	40.9	21	38.2	13			28.5	6
Mortgage loans	24.4	21	27.2	14	45.4	16			86.6	19
Collateral loans	3.7	3	2.6	1	25.4	9	10.8	3	0.2	
Policy loans, premium notes					7.4	2			29.3	6
Deposits	12.0	10	10.0	5	17.6	6	22.7	7	13.8	3
Stocks and bonds	46.3	40	110.4	57	147.6	52			243.7	54
Railroads	33.8	30	89.8	47	131.4	46			180.0	40
Bank and trust company holdings	4.2	4	3.3	2	14.6	5	23.0	7	13.8	3
All stocks (railroad, bank, and trust company)	12.5	11	19.6	10	17.7	6			48.8	12
Foreign securities	3.0	3	4.0	2	7.7	3			11.6	3
Ledger assets	115.5	100	194.0	100	282.1	100			410.0	100
Surplus	21.5	18	39.4	20	65.9	23	80.4	23	62.1	14
Mutual										
Real estate	13.5	10	22.1	11	23.6	7			31.0	7
Mortgage loans	63.0	43	67.7	33	77.2	24			109.8	25
Collateral loans	8.6	6	10.3	5	12.2	4			18.2	4

Policy loans, premium notes					8.6	3			28.2	6
Deposits	3.6	2	12.0	6	13.3	4	18.0	4	8.9	2
Stocks and bonds	51.3	35	95.8	46	162.6	51			240.0	55
Railroads	41.1	28	55.6	27	125.3	39			195.1	45
Banks and trust company holdings			3.2	1	25.4	8			22.1	5
All stocks (railroad, bank, and trust company)	4.5	3	12.9	6	32.7	10			51.8	12
Foreign securities	0.3		1.5		7.7	2			16.4	4
Ledger assets	146.5	100	209.0	100	325.8	100			437.4	100
Surplus	9.9	7	26.9	13	56.5	18	74.4	19	78.3	18
					New York Life					
Real estate	14.3	13	16.0	10	17.0	7			14.0	3
Mortgage loans	19.4	17	32.7	20	34.8	14			25.6	6
Collateral loans	4.2	4	1.8	1	2.9	1			3.2	1
Policy loans, premium notes	0.4		4.8	3	16.5	7			49.1	11
Deposits	6.3	6	6.1	4	14.1	6	17.7	4	11.1	3
Stocks and bonds	63.9	58	102.1	62	160.2	64			318.0	73
Railroads	52.3	47	63.1	38	114.0	46			234.3	54
Bank and trust company holdings	1.3	1	1.6	1	2.6	1				
All stocks (railroad, bank, and trust company)	3.5	3	3.5	3	3.0	1				
Foreign securities	2.6	2	4.5	3	26.3	10			34.4	8
Ledger assets	108.8	100	164.1	100	246.9	100			424.7	100
Surplus	15.1	14	25.2	15	46.0	18	47.5	12	45.8	11

TABLE 6 (*continued*).

Investment	1890		1895		1900		1904[a]		1905	
	Amount	Percent of total	Amount	Percent of total	Amount	Percent of total	Amount	Percent of total	Amount	Percent of total
				Metropolitan						
Real estate	1.3	12	7.3	30	10.8	19			17.5	12
Mortgage loans	6.1	57	10.6	44	19.7	34			38.1	26
Collateral loans									3.7	3
Policy loans, premium notes			0.6	2	1.0	2			3.7	3
Deposits	0.2	2	0.4	2	2.2	4	7.3	6	3.7	3
Stocks and bonds	3.0	28	6.5	26	25.3	43			79.3	54
Railroads	2.3	21	5.8	23	18.1	31			52.8	44
Bank and trust company holdings			0.2	1	0.7	1			4.1	3
All stock (railroad, bank, and trust company)			0.6	2	3.2	5			11.4	8
Foreign securities										
Ledger assets	10.7	100	24.9	100	59.1	100			146.5	100
Surplus	2.1	20	4.5	18	9.3	16	14.0	11	15.4	10

				Prudential						
Real estate	0.6	12	2.6	17	7.2	18			12.4	12
Mortgage loans	3.6	72	7.2	48	11.3	29			18.9	19
Collateral loans					0.8	2			4.7	5
Policy loans, premium notes			0.1		0.5	1			3.6	4
Deposits	0.3	6	0.8	1	2.2	6	6.8	8	7.4	7
Stocks and bonds	0.4	8	4.7	3	16.2	42			54.7	55
Railroads	0.2	4	2.6	2	12.0	31			38.6	39
Bank and trust company holdings					1.0	3			2.9	3
All stocks (railroad, bank, and trust company)					0.6	2			2.9	3
Foreign securities										
Ledger assets	5.0	100	15.3	100	38.6	100			102.4	100
Surplus	1.3	26	3.3	22	9.2	23	15.0	18	17.9	18

[a] When significant, 1904 (pre-Armstrong investigation) figures are added.
Source: New York Insurance Report, 1891, 1896, 1901, 1906.

rates, especially so in the types of bonds that caught the companies' attention. A comparative analysis of insurance investment earnings (Table 7) is suggestive. The great firms generally did not match the industry-wide experience, but they excelled in the more speculative areas of profit from securities sales and gains in market value.

Contemporary critics did not think that abuses of the investment structure deeply affected the companies' earnings. Charles Evans Hughes declared in the midst of the Armstrong investigation: "I don't mean to suggest . . . that the business of the companies . . . has not been conducted very profitably and that their assets are not growing at a tremendous rate." An Equitable directors' investigation committee, not inclined to be generous in its evaluation of the company's investment activities, concluded that "few losses have been incurred in the ordinary investment of the Society, and . . . even in investments in the affiliated [financial] companies large profits have on the whole been realized." A similar group reviewing the New York Life's more speculative investment ventures found that profits easily outweighed losses.[1]

There could not be any question of the general profitability of the firms' bank and trust company stock. The Mutual invested $19,000,000 in such securities between 1893 and 1895. At the end of June 1905, these holdings were worth over $33,000,000 and returned annual dividends of 8 to 20 percent. Dividends of 30 percent on the Prudential's Fidelity Trust Company stock were common.[2] Nor were the companies helpless pawns in the hands of scheming investment brokers, banks, or trust companies. If nothing else, the size of the assets involved made such a relationship difficult and unlikely. Even Hughes later discounted the significance of Kuhn, Loeb and Morgan providing securities to the Equitable and the New York Life while Jacob Schiff and George W. Perkins were on the companies' boards.

Nevertheless, the structure and ideology of investment that prevailed around 1900 did not long survive the Armstrong investigation of 1905. The public and regulatory opinion of the time held that this *was* an unsatisfactory investment experience; that the companies *were* victimized by their financial associates; that this was, in the last analysis, an insupportable investment milieu.

The performance that caused so violent a reaction was an organic outgrowth of the structure itself. Its most striking characteristic was an extensive fractionalization of the interests concerned with insurance investment. To the initial consideration of safe, long-term, reasonably

TABLE 7. Comparative investment earnings of selected companies, 1895–1904 (percentages)

Company	Interest, rent and dividends		Profits from investment sales		Gain in market value		Total	
	1895–1899	1900–1904	1895–1899	1900–1904	1895–1899	1900–1904	1895–1899	1900–1904
Equitable	3.79	3.69	0.29	0.18	0.94	0.37	4.44	4.24
New York Life	4.51	4.19	0.24	0.29	0.41	0.09	4.68	4.39
Mutual	4.25	3.92	0.33	0.16	0.75	0.40	5.33	4.48
Four lesser American companies	4.85	4.44	0.11	0.06	0.25	0.03	4.99	4.41
Twelve British companies	3.81	3.68	—	—	0.07	0.04	3.88	3.64

	1891–1895	1896–1900	1901–1905
Number of companies with earning rates higher than highest of Big Five	18	18	15
Number of companies with earning rates lower than lowest of Big Five	—	1	1

Sources: Equitable, *Supplemental Report in the Investigation of the Equitable . . . March 15, 1906*, p. 63; Lester W. Zartman, *The Investments of Life Insurance Companies* (New York, 1907), pp. 97–99, 102.

productive investments were added other, tangential, ultimately debilitating concerns. Now there was a group of institutions — rather than one alone — making calls on the managers' loyalty and their sense of purpose. The stock of affiliated banks and trust companies often brought profit, but sometimes also brought loss; and insurance magnates had to respond not only as officers of the life companies but as officers or directors of the affiliates. The responsibility of the insurance companies for their affiliates' fund management became, as the Equitable's counsel pointed out, more than a narrowly legal one: "The Trust Companies did not act independently, but under the controlling influence of the Society, of which their officers undoubtedly considered their companies to be almost a part." [3]

For most of the insurance managers there was another dimension to investment decisionmaking: their responsibility to themselves. When a man was an officer in an insurance company and in an affiliated trust company, and was an individual investor as well, his primary commitment was not easily discernible. Often his ability properly and precisely to divide responsibility was strained beyond its limits. Treasurer Frederic Cromwell explained: "The Mutual Life did exactly what I did, and I did exactly what the Mutual Life did." New York Life director John Claflin declared: "We invest in things every one of which every member of the Finance Committee believes is good, and . . . would be willing to make a purchase for himself on the same terms." But outsiders not unnaturally judged these to be less than satisfactory methods of determining the investments of a great life insurance company.

The company managers themselves sometimes recognized the friction that resulted from multiple allegiances. The Mutual's finance committee decided in 1897 that an officer in the treasurer's department, who was also second vice-president of the affiliated U.S. Mortgage and Trust, should leave the trust company and devote himself to the investments of the life insurance firm. Equitable president James W. Alexander noted in 1902: "I have already experienced the embarrassment of hearing matters discussed in the Executive Committee of the International [Banking Corporation], which I am presumed to favor for the benefit of that institution, but which I ought to favor for the benefit of the Western National." The Equitable resolved the difficulty by getting rid of its International stock. A similar conflict of roles involving the Morton and Mercantile Trust companies led Alexander to resign from the

Morton's board. But the problem was not always so easily and ethically handled.[4]

As purpose and responsibility fractionalized, the dictates of life insurance business necessity were blurred and weakened. At worst, the consequence was insurance investment policy shaped by the personal greed of the controlling managers. Otherwise, simple concern for the insurance company's profit or loss gave way to decisions conditioned by the diverse and often conflicting demands of the investment structure. Indeed, the continuation and well-being of that structure and its relationships, rather than the return accruing to the insurance company, often became the determinant factor in investment decisionmaking. And because that structure, and those relationships, often were at odds with commonly accepted standards of life insurance investment, actions increasingly involved a degree of subterfuge and evasion. An example of this development was the treatment of surplus funds in company reports. The surpluses' great size could be justified only by the companies' investment structures and ambitions, and in consequence a terminology of evasion appeared. From the mid-1890's, with Perkins' New York Life blazing the trail, the bulk of company surpluses came to bear such labels as "extra reserve voluntarily set aside," "additional reserves," "other funds," "special reserves," and "reserve for contingent guarantee fund."

During the Armstrong investigation, the insurance managers were closely questioned on their companies' investment performance. Their answers were vague, sometimes defiant, usually unsatisfying. The Metropolitan's John Hegeman limply explained the sale of railroad bonds in May 1905 and their repurchase at a higher price in August: "We probably sold them because we believed it was a wise thing to do at the price we were offered . . . We evidently bought them back because we thought it was wise to take them back." [5] Investment policies rooted to something other than the direct self-interest of the life insurance companies were difficult indeed to justify.

2

In the areas of insurance investment most closely identified with the structure of financial affiliations — bank deposits and collateral loans — the effects of fractionalized decisionmaking appeared with particular clarity. Traditionally, bank deposits had direct and uncomplicated insurance purposes: to provide the cash on hand necessary for premium payments and other business expenses; or to serve as a temporary resting place for funds when market conditions made other investments unpromising. Thus, at the end of 1893 the Mutual, "owing to the plethora of money in the market," sharply increased its bank and trust company deposits to $10,000,000. A quarter of the total went to the Guaranty and Indemnity, which as a useful affiliate paid 3 percent interest (compared to the 1.94 percent average of the eleven other places of deposit.)

But as both the investment structure and the managers' ambitions flowered, the role of deposits changed. They became a ponderable investment element of their own, growing out of proportion to the rise in company assets. Obviously an unprofitable mode of investment (deposit earnings in the early 1900's averaged 2 percent or less), these accounts were justified as props to affiliated banks and trust companies. Thus even the Metropolitan, which "kept invested up pretty close," increased its deposits in the Metropolitan Bank "to give the Bank a chance to get started"; and Hegeman explained his company's non–interest bearing account in the Hamilton Trust by pointing out that "we were largely interested in their prosperity." The Mutual had substantial, stable deposits in its affiliates "because we have a large interest in these companies." [6]

This paternalism was personal as well as institutional. McCurdy's company put $250,000 at 2 percent in the floundering Mutual Alliance Trust Company because, as treasurer Cromwell cosily put it, "it became a pet of two or three of us to make it succeed." Similarly, the Mutual deposited funds without interest in the American Exchange Bank because president George S. Coe was a trustee of the insurance company, as was "old Mr. Coe . . . before him . . . and we haven't felt it would be gracious in us to close the account." President Uzal McCarter of the Fidelity Trust admitted that when his company needed funds, he asked the Prudential to increase its deposits temporarily, and the insurance company usually did so. Henry Hyde made a policy of pegging the Equitable's deposits to the Mercantile Trust's ability to put the money out. He instructed Mercantile president Fitzgerald to inform him whenever the trust company's balances were larger than could be readily invested, and then "I will instantly relieve you of such excessive amount." The New York Life was as helpful to the New York Security and Trust. In 1902 it ostensibly turned over more than $5,000,000 in time loans to its affiliate. Treasurer Randolph explained that most of this was in fact "a mere bookkeeping offset-entry, involving neither money nor loans, and without other effect than to merely swell by that much the volume of your apparent deposits, which I understand at the time would be quite agreeable." [7]

Large bank and especially trust company deposits were also a means of getting insurance funds placed in ventures not readily accessible to the life firms. The Mutual's treasurer explained that his company's deposits were "to keep us on large securities," and that "a trust company can engage in a business which would be profitable and on which you can make money through your stock interest that your company could not directly engage in." McCurdy's firm made special deposits when its trust company affiliates had particularly promising investment opportunities. It supplied $1,000,000 for a Guaranty Trust loan to the New York Central which included a "gentlemen's agreement" not to withdraw the sum for several months. As Treasurer Cromwell described the procedure, "we conceived it wise for them to go into an undertaking which required more money than they could comfortably use."

Bank deposit earnings, even when unencumbered by special arrangements, were limited. But deposits of such size, and for such purposes, raised serious questions of investment efficacy. During the "rich men's panic" of August 1903 investment opportunities were particularly good. But although the Equitable had $36,400,000 on deposit at the time, President Alexander spoke of the company as "strapped for money." Pettishly he remarked: "All this is very annoying, because if we had five or ten millions of dollars to invest now, we would make a great deal of money"; but prior commitments bound tight the company's capital. Less than a year later he contemplated reducing the Equitable deposit in the Commercial Trust Company of Philadelphia. But, he concluded, this would adversely affect the insurance company's Commercial Trust stock holdings, and would make a bad impression on the "Philadelphia contingent just at this juncture when we are desirous of having their co-operation in other directions." Sums so enmeshed were difficult to justify. When the Prudential, under the pressure of the Wisconsin and Massachusetts insurance commissioners, reduced its Fidelity Trust deposits from nearly $5,000,000 to $1,500,000, it tacitly conceded the questionable propriety of the large deposits.[8]

If bank and trust company deposits traced the institutional lineaments of the insurance investment structure, collateral loans denoted its interpersonal relationships. Among the Big Three, loans rapidly assumed a ponderable place in the investment list. Let out at proper rates or in special circumstances, collateral loans were a reasonable investment. The Metropolitan entrusted almost $1,000,000 to William A. Read and Company for this purpose while a high money rate prevailed; and Read placed the funds without charge to the insurance company. The Mutual had extensive brokerage loans out at a productive 6 percent. Theoretically temporary, they were in fact long-standing, with the collateral changed occasionally. But when rates were low, these loans were not much more productive than bank accounts: the Mutual often earned only 2 percent. And personal factors, rather than company investment policy, frequently governed the loans. Such purposes had to be clandestine. When Hegeman took an $80,000 loan for himself from his own company at a rate of 1½ percent he had it transferred to Vermilye and Company so that it would not appear on the Metropolitan's books. His justification for the action — that it was to keep away "a horde of applications for call loans from the Wall Street district" — only underlined its irregular nature. The Equitable, burdened by embarrassingly large amounts of cash on hand at year's end from 1897 on, set up dummy loans with minor employees. These came to total a substantial $10,000,000. Before 1902, Kuhn, Loeb helped this arrangement along by supplying the necessary covering securities. After that year, the investment house gave certificates of deposit only, another questionable step in an already doubtful procedure.[9]

The managers often used their companies' lending power to reward their friends and associates. The Metropolitan made substantial demand loans at 1½ to 2 percent to its favorite stockbroker, William A. Read; the Prudential did the same at more serviceable rates for Robert Winthrop. Read himself demurred at the low cost, but was told that the Metropolitan considered itself under a special obligation to him for his services, and chose to reward him in this fashion. Silas Dutcher of the Metropolitan's finance committee borrowed $200,000 at 2 percent; again, his manifold contributions to the company made it "simply decent" to provide this service. Like the Metropolitan's Hegeman, Henry Hyde and Chauncey Depew of the Equitable and the Prudential's Leslie D. Ward, Thomas N. McCarter, and Anthony R. Kuser (John Dryden's son-in-law) borrowed from their companies. Hegeman and McCall had their firms lend each other substantial sums at a rate of 1½ percent. The Metropolitan advanced $30,000 to George W. Perkins on his Westchester property, although the company did not as a rule make investments of this type.

As the scope and ambitions of the managers broadened, so did the use of their lending power. McCurdy approved a Guaranty and Indemnity loan to former Secretary of the Treasury Charles Foster as an "expedient" service to an "influential public man." Under Perkins' influence, the New York Life finance committee approved loans to the wife of Navy Secretary William C. Whitney and to Representative Theodore Burton. The logical conclusion of this tendency was substantial credits to leading financiers. This was not completely new: in 1890 the New York Life counted the railroad magnate Collis P. Huntington among its debtors. But the extensive loans, sometimes on extremely favorable terms, advanced to E. H. Harriman during the early 1900's by the Equitable and the New York Life involved something more than the functioning of normal insurance investment policy.[10]

Useful though they were, collateral loans could only be a minor part of the complex investment performance of the early 1900's. After the turn of the century only the Mutual, under the exceptionally individuated McCurdy, increased its stake in this investment area. The New York Life and the Equitable reduced their collateral loans and concentrated on more institutionalized forms of high finance.

3

The great bulk of investment decisionmaking dealt with negotiable securities. The weight of law and custom, and the necessity of continuous, large-scale fund placement, restricted most securities investment to parochial business judgments of probable profit or loss. But this gave ambitious insurance magnates all the more reason to concentrate on areas where more venturesome considerations could have play.

Investment syndicates provided one great outlet. These were arrangements whereby bankers or brokers paid commissions to institutions or individuals who guaranteed the sale of a securities offering. The life insurance companies initially entered syndicates for the straightforward purpose of obtaining securities at a wholesale price. But by the turn of the century bolder, more speculative purposes prevailed: syndicate participation, even when the insurance firm did not actually buy the security offered, was justified because the companies had "outgrown the investment field." [11]

Unquestionably, profits — although rarely substantial ones — were more common than losses in the companies' syndicate ventures. But a corruption of investment technique accompanied these practices, and extended to many large-scale securities purchases as well. Deviousness and uncertain legality joined fractionalization of interest as all-too-frequent factors in the companies' investment performance.

The details and rate of this corrupting process differed from firm to firm. But the development was sufficiently widespread to suggest that it was an inherent and inescapable accompaniment of the great companies' investment policies.

4

The industrial companies were keyed to a lower investment pitch than the Big Three. But with them, as elsewhere, deviations from acceptable, routinized procedure stemmed from the interplay of personal and structural arrangements and from the press of investment ambition.

The Metropolitan's closeness to brokers Vermilye and Read brought the company into numerous syndicates. More than half of its purchases from Read came out of such participations; between 1895 and 1905 the company entered thirty-nine syndicates with participations totaling $21,126,000, and earned a modest net profit of $644,919, about 3 percent on its investment. The Metropolitan usually purchased its syndicates' securities. But these included risky and uncertain ventures: the Western Pacific Railroad, a cloudy project of Jay Gould; and an Allis Chalmers flotation in which the insurance company lost over $800,000.

The insurance firm made a multitude of other arrangements with its favored brokers. It split the commission on a purchase of Northern Pacific Receivers' Certificates with Vermilye and Company; it sold $250,000 worth of Minnesota, St. Paul and Sault St. Marie Railroad bonds to W. A. Read and Company on the assumption that the price would drop and the bonds could be bought back at the lower price. This intimacy did not always work to the benefit of the Metropolitan. Read bought 500 shares of Lake Shore Railroad stock at 320, sold it the same day to another broker for 340, and induced the Metropolitan to purchase the stock for 350. An arbiter in December 1906 decided that over $13,000 earned by Read in commissions on this deal should properly be returned to the insurance company.[12]

The Metropolitan's officers, as well as its brokers, became personally entangled in its investment performance. In their desire to sustain the Minnesota Car Company, whose bonds were owned by the Metropolitan,

President Hegeman and Vice-President Fiske personally discounted the firm's notes. When these notes finally shrank in size to $11,000, the insurance company's finance committee recommended that Hegeman and Fiske be reimbursed for their payments and relieved of further responsibility. Less justifiable was the fact that Hegeman participated in twenty-four of the Metropolitan's thirty-nine syndicates, and netted personal profits of about $65,000. In early 1905, on the eve of the Armstrong investigation, he gave $16,000 to the company as syndicate earnings derived from his Metropolitan affiliation. For Hegeman the problem was not so much a conflict of investment interests as it was the gap between what was proffered and what was proper in insurance executive compensation: "I have never been able to see . . . why . . . a man who was fortunate or unfortunate enough to be a life insurance company president should be shut out of those profits, which an ordinary man should be permitted to participate in." But it was precisely the unusual nature of the enterprise that created the restraints — and made necessary the evasions.[13]

The Prudential, alone among the great firms, avoided direct syndicate participation. Its identification with New Jersey securities kept it out of the great New York market ventures; and a court decision in 1903 held that the company could purchase stocks and bonds only on the open market. But the Prudential's intimate affiliation with the Fidelity Trust strongly shaped its securities investment pattern. Large blocs of Jersey utilities bonds, elements in the expansion of the Public Service Corporation, came to the insurance company through the brokerage auspices of the Fidelity. Indeed, the Prudential was under contract to take substantial amounts of Public Service securities. In several cases, stock bonuses on bonds purchased by the Prudential were kept by the trust company. Dryden explained that the Fidelity, not the Prudential, had been a member of the syndicates handling these issues, and was entitled to the bonuses. But since the insurance company was a sure recipient of these securities, the Fidelity ran no real risk as a syndicate member. In any event, the difficulty in keeping separate the interests of the Prudential and the Fidelity was clear.

As elsewhere, the personal interests of the managers often coincided with Prudential investments. Dryden and other Prudential managers and directors participated in Fidelity syndicates in which the insurance company was a major securities purchaser. Like Hegeman, Dryden insisted that he was able to make unbiased judgments on these purchases; but the problem of his multiple commitments — to the Prudential, to the Fidelity, to the Public Service, to himself — could not be so easily resolved.[14]

5

The Mutual's investment performance, no less than its structure of financial affiliations, reflected the force and ambition of Richard McCurdy. His intensely personal interpretation of investment policy shaped many of the company's substantial dealings. Too often, the private interests of McCurdy and several of the Mutual's officers and directors were intermixed with the Mutual's participations. Too often, the Mutual seemed to be only a front for these personal ventures, putting up the money demanded by the syndicate and bolstering the syndicate's success by large purchases on the market, but sharing only fractionally in syndicate profits.

McCurdy's dealings in the securities of the Lawyers' Title and Lawyers' Mortgage Insurance companies suggests the prevailing investment animus. These firms substantially increased their stock in 1901 without including the Mutual, and thus roused McCurdy's ire. Henry Morgenthau, the broker handling these issues, excluded the Mutual ostensibly because of its interest in the Title Guaranty and Trust, a competitor of the Lawyers' Title. Morgenthau had reason to be disturbed by McCurdy's anger, for his firm depended on mortgage loans from the Mutual. Yet he could not assuage McCurdy with Lawyers' Title stock, for none was available. The Mutual head suggested a merger of the Lawyers' Title and the Title Guaranty as an alternative, but this proved infeasible. Finally, McCurdy agreed to accept Morgenthau's own allotment of 1000 shares of Lawyers' Mortgage stock. Supposedly destined for the Mutual itself, the stock in fact was distributed among McCurdy and his associates. Bought at 125, it soon was worth over 200, and the holders were garnering a profit that properly belonged to the Mutual.[15]

Mutual investment practices progressed from relatively simple techniques based on direct, immediate views of the company's self-interest to arrangements of more complex and diffused purpose. Thus in the mid-1890's the Mutual sponsored the Brooklyn Wharf and Warehouse Company, an attempt to consolidate Brooklyn warehouse and dock properties in which the insurance firm had extensive holdings. The Wharf and Warehouse Company's bonds misfired, and the Mutual took a substantial loss. But for all its unsuccess, the venture at least was rooted in the general investment interests of the life insurance company.

The Mutual's relations with the Washington Traction and Electric Company a few years later involved more remote investment considerations. Washington Traction was an effort to consolidate the District of Columbia's streetcar companies. The Mutual had a $2,000,000 share in the enterprise, and president McCurdy had a substantial personal participation. McCurdy pressured Chauncey Depew to try to push enabling legislation through the Senate's District of Columbia Committee. But the Traction Company was unsuccessful, and in 1900 was reorganized as the Washington Railway and Electric Company. Despite the record of past failure, and its lack of direct investment interest in Washington traction lines, the Mutual took another $1,000,000 worth of stock. The two holdings were combined so that the $3,000,000 total had an average purchase price more acceptable than the by now profitable cost level of the initial holding. When a public offering of Washington Railway securities failed, McCurdy, but not the Mutual, got a special price from the managers to ease his disappointment. Eventually the Mutual emerged with a profit, but it proved difficult to justify the venture in terms of standard insurance investment policymaking.[16]

Unlike its two peers, the Mutual did not ally with a particular investment banking house — a suggestion of McCurdy's personal impress on his company's investment policy. The leading supplier of securities to the Mutual was Kuhn, Loeb, but substantial amounts came too from Speyer and Company, J. P. Morgan, Strong, Sturgis and Company, and Harvey, Fisk and Sons. This did not, however, prevent substantial syndicate participations. From modest beginnings with a "guaranty syndicate" in 1893, the Mutual moved into many of the great flotations of the era: the International Mercantile Marine, Western Union, the Louisville and Nashville Railroad, the Long Island Railroad, and, especially attractive to the wide-ranging McCurdy, bond issues by Japan, Cuba, and Mexico. Though generally profitable (treasurer Cromwell claimed profits of $10,000,000 between 1895 and 1905), these ventures also included losses: $400,000 in the Mercantile Marine flotation alone.

In these operations, interests often were thoroughly confused. Mutual officers and directors shared heavily in many of the company's purchases. Some of the Mutual's Imperial Japanese bond holdings were allotted to the affiliated United States Mortgage and Trust to enable that company to share in the profits. Similarly, Mutual earnings in a Missouri Pacific syndicate went to the USMT and the Guaranty Trust. As treasurer Cromwell righteously explained, "we did not propose to make anything out of a security of a road in which we never invested. I presume any high-toned man would feel the same thing." Yet lack of direct investment characterized the arrangements by which the insurance company, as a depositor and a stockholder, benefited from the investments of its affiliated banks and trust companies. And though the Mutual chose not to buy into a new Pennsylvania Railroad issue because of its already large holdings in that road, it had no compunction about entering the syndicate underwriting the issue. Clearly, the traditional standards of insurance investment did not explain these special arrangements; and what did explain them was not accepted practice.[17]

6

Like the Mutual, the Equitable's management and directorate invested extensively in the same securities that the company took; like the New York Life, the company was closely identified with a great investment banking house and consequently with the highest levels of high finance. This combination of managerial cupidity and financial entanglement made for an especially unsatisfactory investment record: between 1899 and 1903 the Equitable had next to the lowest rate of interest on invested assets of a group of thirty life companies, and in 1903 it had the lowest.[18]

Henry Hyde's successors in the Equitable leadership continued his practice of intermixing his own and his company's investment interests. President James W. Alexander and vice-president James Hazen Hyde sought out contacts and arrangements with the highest reaches of the financial world. In February 1902 the younger Hyde wrote to Kuhn, Loeb and Company asking that syndicate allotments henceforth be sent to a group including the Equitable, most of its affiliated banks and trust companies, "and such personalities as I and my associates may designate." Formalizing an already existing collectivity of investors into "James Hazen Hyde and Associates," this document was a high watermark in the fractionalization of the great life insurance companies' investment interests. Hyde and his associates played several, closely interlocking roles: as directors and stockholders of the Equitable's financial affiliates they channeled flotations to the insurance company; as Equitable officers and directors they shaped that company's investment policy; as individual investors they participated in the same securities flotations. Yet this was not an organic response to the specific investment needs of the life insurance business. Hyde and his associates conjoined because "that particular lot of men happened to be thrown together in their relation to bankers."

Profuse risks attended this diffusion of investment policymaking and responsibility: the primacy of the insurance company's interest declined in proportion to the complexity of investment arrangements and the number and pressure of other claimants. Speyer and Company, handling Southern Pacific bonds in 1900, apologetically noted to Hyde, "the best we can do is to offer $250,000 to your company and $100,000 to yourself and associates." Jacob Schiff, the head of Kuhn, Loeb and an Equitable director, gave to the Equitable securities his own house did not keep because "it would not have been business prudence" for "conservative bankers." Special, masked accounts in Squire's and Alexander's names testified to the constant need for subterfuge and disingenuousness generated by the system.[19]

Clearly, insurance executives enmeshed in this complex investment structure required special reserves of managerial skill and corporate responsibility. The younger Hyde had neither. He did try to assert his control over the distribution of securities to his associates, but his general performance was flaccid. As Edward H. Harriman delicately put it, "he was a young man with a great deal of power . . . surrounded by people who were catering to his particular desires . . . without any special reference to what influence it might have on the Equitable's affairs." In 1905 Hyde confessed ignorance of the fact that the Equitable was meeting all calls made on a syndicate in which he and his associates also participated: both the fact and his not knowing it betrayed the impropriety of the system.[20]

These defects were particularly evident in the Equitable's syndicate participations. In several — the International Mercantile Marine, the Long Island Railroad, the Santa Fe, the Imperial Japanese loan, the Metropolitan Street Railway — allotments destined for the Equitable were shared by Hyde and Associates. The syndicate as a speculative venture often took precedence over the Equitable as a securities purchaser. The company shared in a Railroad Securities Company flotation and agreed to yield up its syndicate share as Kuhn, Loeb sold the securities. It would then make its own portfolio purchases on the open market. It kept only one third of its $1,500,000 participation in a Chicago, Burlington, and Quincy syndicate, distributing the rest among Alexander, Hyde, Fitzgerald, Depew, and others. When Squire got a call from J. P. Morgan, the syndicate manager, to take up his share, he contacted Alexander. The latter, now the Equitable's president, responded: "We have got more money than we need, why not pay for it ourselves, and when it is closed out charge each individual so much interest and divide the profit up." Thus, the Equitable got 4 percent on the money it advanced, while the individual participants earned, without any capital risk, the profits of the syndicate. Yet in 1903 Alexander complained to Hyde that its fund commitments kept the Equitable from investing in a rising market.[21]

The Equitable's experience with Union Pacific securities demonstrated to what extent its investment self-interest could be vitiated. Contesting Morgan for control of America's transcontinental rail lines, Harriman in 1902 issued $50,000,000 worth of Union Pacific stock. Syndicate subscribers had to agree not to sell their holdings for five years, during which time Harriman, Schiff, and James Stillman controlled the securities' voting power. Kuhn, Loeb distributed shares in the syndicate to a "circle of friends," including James Hazen Hyde and his associates. Hyde at first took a $2,500,000 participation, but then decided that this was too great a commitment and transferred it to the Equitable, complete with the five-year proviso. The interfusion of interests was overwhelming. Harriman and Schiff were Equitable directors; Hyde was swayed as a personal investor by Harriman's blandishments. Squire acted as a syndicate manager in asking for an Equitable syndicate payment; then, as the Equitable's chief financial officer, he signed the voucher meeting the call.[22]

This mixture of managerial greed and intimate involvement in high finance soon proved insupportable. The Mutual was to some extent shielded by the strong-willed McCurdy; the New York Life, more than the others, was given over to institutionalized rather than personal financial arrangements. But the Equitable, torn between the old cupidity and the new sophistication, inevitably became a battleground and not just a mélange of interests. The ensuing tension and intramural strife evoked in 1905 the first substantial exposure of the great companies' peculiar investment performance.

7

When George W. Perkins declared in 1899 that the New York Life's investment policy was to buy the "underlying bonds of leading railway systems," he described a program already well under way. For almost a decade the company had been investing selectively in major railroad bonds, meanwhile refusing to take more traditional offerings such as New York City debt refunding certificates. Early, too, the firm interested itself in syndicatelike arrangements. In 1894 it bid for Jersey City bonds with the idea of reselling them immediately in collaboration with an interested brokerage house. Three years later it considered a Kuhn, Loeb offer of Santa Fe securities accompanied by a "plan of making a market for these bonds of 84 to 85 before selling." Nor did the attraction of Morgan-sponsored securities date from Perkins' association with that investment banking house. In 1895 and 1896 the company bought heavily in United States bonds in part because Morgan headed the bankers' syndicate handling the flotation.[23]

But after Perkins became chairman of the New York Life's finance committee in 1900, and a Morgan partner in 1901, the firm's investment performance took on a new complexity; it became, indeed, the crown of the great companies' investment experience at the turn of the century. Perkins himself concentrated on placements "of special moment, because I was in a position in the financial community where I knew perhaps quite as much as any member of the [Finance Committee] as to what was going on." His dual role as the New York Life's chief investment policymaker and a Morgan partner was the most dramatic example of the diffusion of insurance investment responsibility. The arrangement was novel enough to meet with the initial disapproval both of John McCall and of J. P. Morgan. Morgan never more than grudgingly accepted Perkins' dual role, but McCall soon became "a very thorough believer" in it.[24]

The arrangement was a logical extension of Perkins' dynamic, grandiose corporate ideology. He later recalled that when Morgan's invitation came to him, the New York Life's officers were grappling with the problem of how "to connect the man who insured away off in some part of the world with the original issue price of the security we were going to put his money into." A relationship with Morgan was particularly desirable because of that house's world-wide banking business; the New York Life "had . . . to come in touch with . . . international banking affairs, as we were doing business all over the world and handling all sorts of securities." But the essence of the arrangement lay in the flotation of domestic securities, and in the New York Life's role as a prime purchaser of those offerings.

In April 1905, stirred by revelations of malfeasance in the Equitable, the New York Life's board of directors evaluated the Perkins-Morgan tie. "Our needs for reserve and other investment purposes were growing greater almost hourly," it recalled, and the Morgan relationship seemed to be "an opportunity for our Company, absolutely safe and promising substantial benefits, which had not come to us before." The prime advantage lay not so much with the securities offered by Morgan as in the knowledge gained "of contemporary movements in the business world; in timely information as to the properties and earnings of corporations offering bonds in the market; in knowing the rock-bottom prices for offered securities; in the freedom of purchase, and in the knowledge that the interests of our Company were paramount to every other interest of individual or firm." Granting the other claims, it was precisely this last contention that proved difficult to sustain.

Perkins had recognized the danger. In 1902 he suggested to the New York Life finance committee that the company's deposit account with Morgan be ended, a suggestion that evoked the amused inquiry if he thought the banking house was weaker since his entry as a partner. His New York Life salary went down from $75,000 to $25,000, and he turned over to the insurance firm the profits he received as a Morgan partner for issues in which the company participated. The degree of interfusion between the New York Life's officers and directors and the company's major investment ventures was considerably lower than in the Mutual or the Equitable. Perkins declared that "the people's interests" was his sole guideline: "my greatest pride at my time of life is that I represent a great many people." But this evaded the central, inescapable point: that in lieu of a specific prime obligation, his ultimate responsibility lay nowhere.[25]

Under the Perkins-Morgan aegis, New York Life syndicate participations climbed steeply to eleven in 1901 and 1902 and to thirteen in 1904. All told, the insurance firm entered thirteen syndicates organized by Morgan, earning a respectable (though not spectacular) profit of $1,773,715 on ventures totaling $31,013,500.[26] But this was not the whole of the connection. Many New York Life syndicates were entered in joint accounts with the stockbroker W. S. Fanshawe, who, despite Perkins' disclaimer of "any underground manner by which things go from Fanshawe to Morgan . . . and the New York Life," had close ties with the great investment banking house. Perkins was "very proud of this joint account business; it was of my own origin and we have gotten securities very cheap under it, and have made a great deal of

* THE CRISIS OF 1905 *

THE EQUITABLE scandal of 1905, and the Armstrong investigation that followed, marked the formal end of the large companies' thrust for power.

Thomas Fortune Ryan was the Wall Street operator whose purchase of the Equitable lay at the heart of the interplay of interests that culminated in the Armstrong investigation.

Charles Evans Hughes was the austere and devastating inquisitor at the climactic New York inquiry.

James Hazen Hyde faces the Armstrong committee. Senator Armstrong is at the far right.

* THE FACE OF REFORM *

IN MOST of the companies, substantial managerial changes came on the heels of the Armstrong investigation. New men, committed to retrenchment and a more narrow definition of their companies' activities, assumed the leadership of the life insurance enterprise. Haley Fiske's control of Metropolitan policy grew — but he took the company in directions very different from those characteristic of the pre-1905 business ambience. Only Darwin P. Kingsley of the New York Life tried — unsuccessfully — to retain the spirit of the turn of the century.

Paul Morton, Ryan's choice to head the Equitable, weathered the storms of 1905 and lasted in office until his death in 1911.

Alexander E. Orr supervised the post-Armstrong house cleaning of the New York Life as president in 1906 and 1907.

Charles A. Peabody, Jr., steered the Mutual in the direction of restrained corporate practices from 1905 to 1927.

Richard Lindabury, corporation lawyer and man of influence in the affairs of United States Steel, kept a close eye on the affairs of the Prudential after 1905.

money out of it." He recalled with relish that a non–New York City life insurance company "which looked upon Wall Street with holy horror" bought an issue at a price 10 percent higher than the New York Life had paid in joint account with a group of stockbrokers. But Charles Evans Hughes asked, apropos of the Armstrong investigation's disclosures, "Its horror is still probably undiminished?" And the fact of the matter was that for all the joint accounts' advantages (price reductions through large purchases, the security marketing talents of participating brokers) the insurance company generally made the advances and did the purchasing. Its partners thus earned riskless commissions. In addition, as Hughes noted, joint accounts injected another participant — the broker-partner — into an already overcrowded investment process.

The New York Life's investment performance became deeply colored by Perkins' ingenious financial guidance. The other officers were airily indifferent to the details of the company's placements. "That is the modern syndicate method," treasurer Randolph explained, adding that too much inquisitiveness might lead syndicate managers to exclude the firm from their participations. (The danger seemed remote: the New York Life was entered in one syndicate without its financial officers' knowledge.) As the Armstrong investigation illuminated the complex investment activities of the insurance company, it appeared that fractionalized interest and devious technique had gone far indeed:[27]

1) The New York Life took a $2,000,000 participation in a Morgan Atlantic Coast Line flotation, and agreed to buy $1,000,000 worth of the bonds to bolster their public sale. It consented, too, not to sell its acquisition for a year, in return getting a price concession and the "reasonable assurance" of the syndicate managers that they would "create a market which will enable us . . . to sell our securities at a profit, if we wish to."

2) As a Morgan partner, Perkins brought to the insurance company's attention an offering of St. Louis Terminal bonds. Then, as the New York Life's financial representative, he took it up. (Hughes incredulously summed up the transaction: "You were dealing with yourself.") He secured the finance committee's authorization for a purchase of $4,000,000 worth but was unable to get delivery on the bonds before the end of the year. Meanwhile he invested the $4,000,000 in other Morgan-sponsored bonds, earning 3½ percent as against the St. Louis Terminal issue's 4 percent. Morgan made up the difference. When the original

bonds finally became available, Perkins decided on his own to keep some of the securities which had been held in their place.

3) In 1902, during a time of "great financial stress," the Secretary of the Treasury agreed to accept high-grade nongovernment bonds as collateral for the deposit of Federal funds in national banks. The banks themselves did not have large amounts of this type of security, but the life insurance companies did. Perkins snapped at the opportunity. The New York Life lent Massachusetts 3's and New York City bonds to the First National Bank of Boston. In return it received its interest on the bonds lent, plus 2 percent on the currency procured by the bank from the government. Thus the New York Life's earnings on these bonds was increased — not illegally, but circuitously.

4) Perkins moved with equal facility when Kidder, Peabody and Company offered Mexican Central Railway bonds for immediate purchase. First he proposed a joint account with Morgan and Peabody; but Morgan was unable to participate. He then decided to take the bonds for Nylic, the New York Life agents' association whose investment fund he managed, but allowed Kidder, Peabody to think that it was selling the bonds to the life insurance company. The necessary quick capital he borrowed from the New York Life, using the bonds to be purchased as collateral for the loan.[28]

5) The New York Life's most spectacular syndicate failure was its participation in Morgan's International Mercantile Marine (IMM). The purpose of the IMM was to secure a dominant place for American interests in the steamship traffic of the North Atlantic. The four largest British and American shipping lines were to be combined into one giant corporation. Both corporate and political expansionists were excited by the scheme, and Perkins was closely identified with it.

The New York Life took a $4,000,000 participation in the first IMM syndicate. But the expected market response failed to materialize. In 1902, $3,200,000 of the insurance company's share was called by the syndicate managers at a price that made probable a substantial loss. When in 1903 the remaining $800,000 was called, the New York Life cast about for a purchaser. On December 31, to remove the embarrassing acquisition from the company's books, Perkins sold the $800,000 worth of IMM bonds to J. P. Morgan and Company. These came back to the New York Life on January 2, 1904, and at the end of the year were sold to J. S. Morgan, Ltd., J. P. Morgan's London affiliate, at a loss of $160,000. Perkins made up half the loss himself. He later claimed that there had been a real sale to Morgan; that "it was my intention, if we were not able to sell it during that very brief time . . . [to] buy it back and go on trying to sell"; that he was "chagrined" to learn that it was not Morgan's custom to buy the shares of participants in its syndicates. But these evasions did not justify the subterfuge. Perkins' ultimate explanation — "I used my judgment" — in effect heightened the underlying point: that incisive judgment was difficult when responsibility and purpose were fractionalized.[29]

6) The same uncertain propriety characterized the New York Life's contact with the greatest of Morgan's enterprises, United States Steel. Although it was logical for Perkins' insurance company to participate in so primary a Morgan undertaking, the New York Life's no-stock bylaw was a hindrance. The solution to the problem was to use the New York Security and Trust as the ostensible purchaser. McCall tortuously justified the arrangement: "We were not prohibited from taking the profits. We were from taking the stock." Perkins' multiform financial role smoothed the way: "I was Chairman of the Finance Committee of the New York Life and I was a trustee of the Trust Company, and my duty was to both corporations in a fair way." (To this might also be added his responsibilities to Morgan and to United States Steel, whose finance committee he would head.) He gave most of a $3,000,000 Steel syndicate participation under his control to the New York Security and Trust, and had that firm made the registrar of United States Steel preferred stock. In return, the trust company had to turn over 75 percent of its profits to the New York Life. Its risk, however, was minimal, for the insurance company deposited $2,325,000 to be used for the participation. The arrangement was carefully kept off the New York Life's books, which thus failed to record the transaction's unhappy conclusion: a loss of $82,303. Nor was this the end of the New York Life's *sub rosa* connection with United States Steel. McCall had been using accounts in the Central National Bank and the New York Security and Trust to advance money to legislative agents from 1896 to 1901. At his request, Morgan arranged to have these lobbyists' debts paid from Steel Company earnings lodged in the Security and Trust.[30]

7) Less prominent ventures sometimes involved even more complex and questionable arrangements. In 1902 the New Orleans Railway Company set out to combine the city's utilities. The New York Security and Trust had substantial bond and syndicate holdings in the firm. But in 1904 the trust company was on the verge of consolidation with the

Continental Trust, and one of the conditions of merger was that the NYST reduce its security holdings and increase its cash on hand. In March 1904, the New York Life stepped in to relieve the NYST of its New Orleans stock and syndicate participation, although strikes and other troubles had plagued the utilities venture in 1902 and 1903. Less than three weeks later, the Louisiana attorney general began action against the New Orleans Railway Company to stop it from absorbing street railway and lighting companies. Eventually a corporate reorganization was agreed upon, but meanwhile the New York Life decided to rid itself of its suddenly unattractive holdings. Most of the bonds went to its broker affiliate J. S. Fanshawe at 75 percent of their cost. Fanshawe was to market them and pay any profit, less 5 percent, to the insurance company; the New York Life would absorb any loss. What was more, the broker paid for the bonds with money borrowed from the insurance firm — with the bonds as collateral. The New York Life's final loss in the transaction was over $320,000; but the unwanted securities were removed from their awkward place in the company's portfolio.[31]

8) Similar problems beset the New York Life's participation in a United Collieries syndicate. The securities involved were industrials, which the company supposedly avoided. The transaction was covered up by "lending" the necessary funds to two minor company employees, who gave notes based on United Collieries collateral. When the syndicate was unsuccessful, the insurance firm had to accept the securities, and the finance committee was "very anxious that the bonds shall be closed out so as not by any possibility to appear among our holdings at the close of the year." J. S. Morgan came to the rescue: the banking firm lent money to the New York Life (which hardly needed it) and took the Collieries bonds as collateral. As the bonds were sold, with J. S. Morgan having full discretion as to price, the loan would be decreased. The arrangement was convenient, and the J. S. Morgan services welcome, but the difficulty could not be accounted one natural to life insurance investment.[32]

9) The tensions inherent in the relationship between accepted life insurance investment patterns and Perkins' policies appeared in the company's stock holdings as well. The vice-president's agreement with the Prussian insurance authorities, and his rejection of stocks as a proper insurance investment, committed the New York Life to rid itself of such holdings by the beginning of 1902. This pledge "caused no end

of trouble." John McCall reasoned that the Prussian agreement required only that stock not be listed, not that it be sold. Stock bonuses accruing from bond holdings and syndicate operations were regarded as "surplusage," and were treated as unrecorded nonledger assets. Treasurer Randolph picturesquely justified this nest egg: "The institution that has a conservative management the world over has something over in the way of assets which they do not count, and which they can fall back upon in case of need." [33]

10) Perkins himself took over the disposition of 10,000 shares of Chicago and Northwestern and 5300 shares of Chicago, Milwaukee, and St. Paul railroad stock. He understood that William Vanderbilt and a Pittsburgh group flush with funds from the United States Steel consolidation would bid against each other for these securities. But "a sort of holdup," based on the knowledge that the New York Life had to rid itself of its stock holdings by the end of 1901, seemed in the offing. To circumvent this, the railroad stock appeared on the insurance company's books as sold to the Central National Bank in late 1901, when in reality the New York Life retained ownership. With maneuvering time thus gained, Perkins profitably sold 5000 shares of Chicago and Northwestern to one group, and "with great impartiality" an equal amount to the opposing interest. The money from the sale went to the New York Security and Trust to enable that institution to buy the stock from the New York Life and pass it on to its ultimate purchasers. The St. Paul stock did not fare so well, and the loss sustained in that issue was covered in part by charging to it commissions earned in other syndicate participations.[34]

11) An increasingly complex investment structure and technique demanded equal complexity in accounting and bookkeeping procedure. Subterfuge and circumvention became common; at its extreme it would bring an indictment of Perkins for forgery of the New York Life's books. The company's profits in syndicate participations were used to reduce the reported cost of the same securities bought for the investment portfolio. In 1901, agents' balances were deducted from market earnings, because state insurance departments did not accept the balances as assets. Stock holdings and deferred dividend earnings were obscured or misrepresented to satisfy the requirements of the Prussian insurance authorities. Even securities handling procedures succumbed to the pressure for ambiguity. In 1900 and 1901 New York Central stock was removed from the New York Life's vaults for a few days, and a check from the affili-

ated Central National Bank substituted. The nontaxable New York Central stock was lent by the Central Bank to a client, the Merchants' Trust Company, for its own accounting purposes. This arrangement, in which the New York Life enabled a banking affiliate to help a customer, symbolized the diffusion of self-interest increasingly afflicting the insurance company's investment policymaking.[35]

The complex investment experiences of the New York Life were only the most dramatic expressions of a dilemma common to the great companies: as their investment structures and power expanded, so did the need for practices at odds with the accepted standards of the insurance business. For an industry ideologically committed to a quasi-public role, the result was an increasing tension between corporate ambition and public accountability. And there were signs that the increasing fractionalization of managerial purpose and interest was adversely affecting the investment well-being of the insurance companies.

The investment performance thus was closely akin to the development of the firms' corporate structure and their marketing experience. All gave evidence of the special drives animating the great companies: all engendered organically similar tensions, dangers, diffusion of company purpose and being. But the ultimate test of the companies came in the area furthest removed from their basic entrepreneurial purpose. Their sophistication and power met its greatest challenge in their diverse relationships with the state.

In our world everything is political, the state is everywhere, and public responsibility is interwoven in the whole fabric of society.

Karl Mannheim, *Freedom, Power, and Democratic Planning*

Part Five * The Companies and the Commonwealth

The business of insurance, by nature and tradition, came under the close attention of the commonwealth. Government supervision posed a special challenge to corporate power; and the great life firms addressed themselves to the problem with considerable imagination and vigor.

Their contacts with public authority were numerous and diverse. State and Federal courts were constant battlegrounds of regulatory, contract, and agency litigation. Widespread state supervision led the companies to create an equally extensive system of political influence. And as they became national — and international — corporations of the highest rank, their contacts with and demands upon the national government increased accordingly.

Certain uniform experiences characterized this interplay of companies with commonwealth. For a time they approached their litigation aggressively; but the courts gave them little encouragement, and they soon turned away from legal action as an instrument of corporate policy. Despite a highly organized structure of state lobbying, they found no great security as the system of regulation steadily expanded. Seeking to avoid the stresses of state supervision in a drive for Federal control of the life insurance business, the firms met their ultimate rebuff.

Thus the experience of the companies with the several levels of the commonwealth paralleled that of their internal organization, their domestic and foreign marketing, and their investment policies. They found, in their relations with the state as in the other sectors of their corporate experience, that complex and profound obstacles kept them from attaining the degree of power and control that they desired.

XI * An Experience at Law

Few corporate groups matched the great life insurance companies in the richness and diversity of their legal experience. Their product, the policy contract, was a cornucopia of litigation. And as their corporate being became more complex, so grew the necessity for adjudication by the courts.

At first, peripheral, part-time consultants satisfied the companies' needs for counsel. But their spectacular increase in size and complexity demanded greater legal specialization. The Prudential in 1885 began to require the exclusive attention of its attorneys; the Mutual and the New York Life established their first full-time solicitors in 1893; the Metropolitan had a claim and law division by 1897. During the early 1900's counsel such as Bainbridge Colby, Elihu Root, and William D. Guthrie for the Equitable, James M. Beck for the Mutual, and Richard Lindabury for the Prudential gave important legal advice and participated in company decisionmaking.

Life insurance litigation traditionally was scant; one authority counted only about 100 cases down to 1870. Nor were the large companies strongly inclined toward court action during the ensuing years; Hyde complained in 1877, "I don't think we have contested as many [policy claims] as we should." [1] But in the 1890's, appellate decisions affecting the Big Three and the Metropolitan increased out of proportion to the rate of their business growth. The imbalance suggests that the companies were more inclined than before to contest suits to a judicial conclusion, a legal philosophy that correlates with their aggressive marketing and investment performance.

Conversely, between 1900 and 1905 the companies' litigation leveled off or declined, although their rapid business growth continued. This signified the development of a conviction that no great profit lay in court battles: it is noteworthy that the New York Life's out-of-court settlements doubled during these years. The firms could have observed that as the number of judicial decisions mounted in the mid-1890's, so did the likelihood that the company would be the loser. When the rate of litigation eased in the early 1900's, the proportion of procompany decisions rose.

There seems to have been a highly complex, but nonetheless effective, judicial pattern of constraint which ultimately dissuaded the companies from looking to the courts as a promising arena for the exercise of power.[2]

2

In decisions dealing with regulation, the courts set down substantial caveats to the great companies. On the surface, regulatory decisions may have seemed to be governed only by the spirit of case-by-case equity. The same Kansas court in one year found twice for the state insurance commissioner's right to withhold licenses from several of the large companies — and twice against it. The United States Supreme Court handed down seemingly contradictory decisions on a New Orleans tax, distinguishing between actions on highly subtle grounds. And when the Massachusetts Supreme Court approved of the state commissioner's authority to pass on New York Life policy forms, it reserved the right to review such administrative decisions. But a fundamental commitment to the principles and practices of state supervision underlay the judiciary's flexibility. The majority of the large firms' regulatory cases went against them. In a period not marked by judicial approval of business regulation, jurists frequently dwelt on its necessity in the insurance field. Between 1890 and 1908 the courts found only about 1 percent of some 2000 insurance laws unconstitutional. And in *Cravens v. New York Life* (1900) the Supreme Court strongly upheld state supervision of life insurance.[3]

As American business firms became national organizations, the courts began to limit the traditional control that states could impose on foreign (out-of-state) corporations. The large life insurance companies benefited to the extent that they won a slight majority of their litigation in this area. Their victories might be described as a "coalition of exceptions" to the traditionally strict containment of the foreign corporation: points of jurisdiction, technical details of service and judgment, and, less often, the invalidity of the regulation itself were the means by which the courts implemented their policy of liberalization.

The technique here at play — a mass of legal exceptions adding up to a substantial deviation from established legal tradition — appeared in other areas of the companies' litigation as well. And given the general disposition to regard life insurance as a quasi-public enterprise, more often than not the trend of decisions worked against the firms.

The judiciary also concerned itself with the organizational crises that periodically wracked the society of great companies. The New Jersey Court of Chancery granted an injunction to dissatisfied Prudential stockholders contesting John F. Dryden's exchange-of-stock arrangement with the Fidelity Trust Company. After 1905 the Prudential, Metropolitan, and Equitable managements undertook to mutualize their firms, and court decisions generally assisted what was commonly judged to be a desirable organizational change. Exposures of managerial deficiencies led often to resignations, and to litigation between the outgoing officers and their firms. Here, too, the courts usually supported the interests of the companies in situations where they were held to be the parties with the greater sense of public responsibility.[4]

In sum, during a period of particular reverence for the letter of the law and the sanctity of private interest, the judicial system acted out of a strongly rooted belief in the overriding public worth of a responsibly constructed life insurance enterprise.

3

The policy contract was the source of the great majority of life insurance litigation. The judicial system long had looked favorably on contracts as a device eminently suited to the release and fostering of American enterprise. But revolutionary changes in life underwriting in the nineteenth century created an immense gulf between insurers and insured, and the courts took heed of the resulting imbalance. The New York Court of Appeals in 1891 voiced the sentiment of a juridical generation:

> Life insurance companies perform very important functions in modern society . . . A very large number of people are interested in them. They are resorted to for the purpose of making provisions for families and dependents after the death of the insured, and for that purpose many persons invest in

them the accumulations of their labor and their thrift. The nature of insurance contracts is such that each person effecting insurance cannot thoroughly protect himself.[5]

The first stage of the policy contract was the application. The governing legal principle was the venerable rule of warranty: that the applicant's declarations, if false, voided the policy regardless of their import or relevance. Yet this model of legal clarity afforded the most dramatic example of judicial contract interpretation in favor of the insured.

Nineteenth century company counsel had insisted on the strict enforcement of the warranty rule. Thomas I. Parkinson, professor of law at Columbia and later president of the Equitable, ironically recalled "the extraordinary service which insurance lawyers rendered in years gone by, in exaggerating warranties to the point where they were almost one hundred percent protection against claims, only to develop a public atmosphere and judicial decisions and legislation which puts the insurer under his contract in a worse position . . . than is any other contracting party. That is overservice by the profession." [6]

This development occurred around the turn of the century. In 1891 the warranty still was of obvious consequence in life insurance law; by 1911 it seemed to one expert to be of little importance. The courts used numerous legal devices in their ameliorative work: the concept that an application statement was a representation, not a warranty; findings that waivers of application requirements had been allowed by company or agent; and, "an American innovation in the law of insurance," the rule that parol (oral) waivers were admissible evidence of a modified contract. Legislatures, too, enacted laws deeming the applicant's statements, in the absence of fraud, to be representations rather than warranties, and in other ways lightened the burden of the ancient rule.[7]

The courts struck a close balance for and against the companies in the sum of application cases. Procompany decisions almost always were based on straightforward findings that the warranty (or, occasionally, the representation) required was real and valid, and that the applicant clearly had failed to meet its requirements. It was necessary to follow a more torturous route in many of the decisions that found for the applicant. The misleading role of the agent, unintentional company waivers, and technical points of pleading and action were among the devices used by the courts to protect the applicant even when he made a false declaration. That applicants won as often as the companies becomes, then, a significant measure of the extent to which the courts mitigated a traditional rule of insurance law.

A lapse in premium payments was in theory as substantial a breach of contract as false warranty, for it struck at the heart of the policyholder's contractual obligation. Few would have quarreled with the 1887 dictum of the New York Court of Appeals: "Punctuality in the payment of premiums in the case of a life insurance company is of the very essence of the contract; and, when payment is not made at the time, the company has the right to forfeit." [8]

Nevertheless, the courts found ways to avoid the rule almost as often as they upheld it. Proinsured findings demanded rather subtle justification: that the company or its agents had waived premium payments; that the company had not specifically provided for policy forfeiture on nonpayment; even that the lapse in payment was too minor to void the policy. Once again exceptions became an instrument of judicial purpose: this time, to preserve the equity of lapsing policyholders.

The final phase of contract litigation dealt with questions of settlement and causes of death. Rigid proof of death requirements, and numerous disavowals of company responsibility in particular causes of death, characterized nineteenth century life insurance policies. But by the end of the century the great firms were under competitive pressure to liberalize these provisions, and the courts adapted to the trend.[9]

The treatment of suicide as a cause of death typified this liberalizing process, in which courts and companies worked together. The judiciary had shared an optimistic society's repulsion from such an act, and readily accepted the companies' traditional disinclination to pay for so horrendous a breach of contract. The Supreme Court in 1898 voided a Mutual policy on this ground even though the contract did not specify suicide as an excepted cause of death. The decision argued: "A contract, the tendency of which is to endanger the public interests or injuriously affect the public good, or which is subversive of sound morality, ought never to receive the sanction of a court of justice." [10] But several companies came to accept suicide as a valid risk. This fact, and the difficulty of determining whether or not suicide actually had occurred, encouraged the courts to find alternatives to policy avoidance. In cases of reasonable doubt they found that death was accidental; or they decided that insanity and a consequent inability to understand the moral obloquy of the act saved the policy.

The companies' settlement litigation often involved several beneficiary claimants, or beneficiaries and assignees, or beneficiaries and estate executors. To escape involvement in such litigation, the Metropolitan and the Prudential put "facility of payment" clauses in their contracts which set up classes of beneficiaries (relatives or creditors, for example), denied the vested rights of individual beneficiaries, and specified that payment of the policy benefits discharged the company's obligation. But the courts did not often allow the companies to escape settlement litigation.[11]

Strikingly, a heavy proportion of the firms' settlement cases went against them. The judicial system was especially ready to decide against the insurer at the end of the policy contract cycle, when the equity of the insured was at its peak. Only in one area of settlement litigation, that involving deferred dividend policies, were the companies generally victorious.

The Big Three's tontine policies matured in large numbers around the turn of the century. The disparity between the glittering prospects originally held out to purchasers, and the payments actually made, led to considerable litigation. The prevailing judicial attitude was *caveat emptor;* holders of such speculative policies could not engage the courts' favor. But this view only heightened by contrast the judicial inclination in other areas of settlement litigation to stress the social values of life insurance.[12]

4

Agency problems were second only to the contract itself as a source of litigation for the great firms. Like any corporate agent, the insurance solicitor was essentially the spokesman of his company and subject to its control. In consequence, many firms filled their application and policy forms with provisions designed to place the burden of the agent's actions on the policyholder. The result was a web of contract stipulations that resembled the application warranty in their threat to insurance purchasers.

But the pressures of competition and the drive for bigness led the companies' agents to make on-the-spot contract modifications: informal waivers of application requirements, rebates on premium payments, the acceptance of premium notes. Litigation frequently raised the question of the companies' responsibility for these arrangements.

The juridical response was much the same as in the case of the warranty: to hold the companies to "a more than ordinarily stringent rule of responsibility." The sum of agency opinions seemed to be a mass of "hopelessly conflicting decisions which can not be reconciled on any theory other than the desire of the courts to do justice in the particular case." But, as elsewhere, a manifest social purpose — the protection of the policyholder — underlay the surface chaos. A heavy majority of the companies' agency cases went for the insured.[13]

The same pressures of expansion and competition that so often made the agent's acts a source of litigation generated justiciable issues between the solicitor and the employing company. The courts were not yet ready to look upon the engagements of an employee with his employer in the same light that they regarded the contractual situation of the insured or the beneficiary. When faced with actions involving the conditions of agent employment and control, the relationship of the companies with their general agents and subagents, and questions of commissions, renewals, and advances, the courts found for the companies in a two-to-one ratio. As in the case of the courts' response to deferred dividend litigation, this pattern heightens by contrast the distinctive thrust of judicial policymaking in the central areas of regulation and the policy contract.

No doubt the life insurance decisions of this period, as critics said, made for confused and mistaken law. But out of the seeming chaos emerged social sense and purpose; the order of equity, if not the equity of order. By clearly stating certain value judgments on the social role of life insurance, the judicial system eliminated itself as an instrument of the great companies' quest for power. Here, certainly, commonwealth and corporation stood apart. But greater opportunities for influence existed in the structure of state administrative and legislative supervision.

XII * The Structure of Supervision

The same forces that shaped insurance law governed insurance regulation. The antiquity of the enterprise, and its quasi-public nature, ensured continuing legislative and administrative concern. Insurance supervision evolved from statutes of incorporation and enactments of specific, limited scope to general laws enforced by special departments and officials. The reformer Elizur Wright induced mid-nineteenth century Massachusetts to accept nonforfeiture and valuation laws, and in 1865 engineered the first formal regulatory authority, a three-member commission. By 1873 twelve states had some form of institutionalized insurance regulation; in 1890 the total was seventeen. A National Convention of Insurance Commissioners dated from 1871. New York superintendent George W. Miller, who was most responsible for the National Convention's formation, set down its regulatory ideal: "to afford the fullest possible protection to the public, with the least possible annoyance or expense to, or interference with, the companies." [1]

The conflict of purposes implicit in this statement long remained unresolved. The structure of regulation grew in an age committed to laissez-faire in theory and fact. After a decade of scandals and business difficulties, Governor Lucius Robinson of New York called in 1879 for the end of the department of insurance and the transfer of "its few necessary powers" to the comptroller's office. Governor Grover Cleveland wanted the state's insurance law "reduced to a plain and simple enactment." Superintendents, too, often denigrated their function, declaring that the least supervision consistent with safety was best.[2]

From the first, insurance companies bent the supervisory structure to their purposes. Elizur Wright left Massachusetts' pioneering regulatory commission because of their pressure. The California insurance superintendent failed in an 1876 attempt to secure nonforfeiture legislation, and glumly reported to Wright: "The foreign Life Companies, with their vast means . . . were too much for me . . . and did not hesitate to say to our Legislature, that you and your reforms, had been kicked out of . . . Massachusetts." The actuary of the St. Louis Mutual Life sought to be Missouri's first insurance commissioner "for the purpose of keeping the office out of the hands of those who know nothing of the importance of the interests involved." In Connecticut, the identification of regulator and regulated was complete. Benjamin Noyes, the state's insurance commissioner in 1868, also was president of the American Mutual Life Insurance Company of New Haven, the only firm excluded from New York and Massachusetts as insolvent and unsound. With nicely controlled sarcasm, the New York superintendent pointed out that the company "is, therefore, in especial need of home supervision more critical and incisive than will probably ever be exercised by the present Commissioner over himself as President." [3]

But the plain facts of the matter — the growth of the enterprise, and its quasi-public nature — could not be ignored. The Connecticut superintendent observed in 1890: "The good name of the State is involved in the successful management of our life insurance companies. They are creatures of the State's creation, over which she rightfully assumes a supervision, and for whose management and failure it is impossible to escape censure." Missouri's commissioner dwelt on the uniqueness of the insurance policy, and concluded that "only the state can be the disinterested authority seeing that the contract is met." [4] Haltingly a widespread structure of supervision emerged in the late nineteenth century.

2

By 1890, insurance legislation "may fairly be said to have reached its majority." [5] Thereafter, steadily growing codification and detail made this a most substantial body of regulatory law, baroque in its diversity. These statutes were part of a general increase in state legislative activity around the turn of the century. But in number they held their own with far more extensive areas of enterprise (see Table 8).

The emergence of the insurance enterprise as a major economic institution spurred this legislative efflux. But the bulk of legislation was

TABLE 8. State legislation in selected areas of enterprise, 1890–1905

Year	Insurance			Banks, trust companies and other financial institutions	Transportation	Corporations, trusts, and manufacturing
	Life[a]	Taxation	Total			
1890	21	1	35	33	81	44
1891	36	—	77	63	130	85
1892	15	—	25	12	45	24
1893	28	—	74	75	136	65
1894	25	—	43	35	30	27
1895	46	18	130	83	103	119
1896	18	3	49	25	43	29
1897	47	13	135	128	110	62
1898	14	—	51	59	47	32
1899	56	10	162	75	153	100
1900	28	4	52	28	52	22
1901	59	11	168	86	125	112
1902	26	6	52	34	63	48
1903	74	18	109	89	111	113
1904	38	2	65	40	45	52
1905	73	11	169	111	156	106

[a] Includes legislation affecting industrial as well as straight life companies.
Source: New York State Library Bulletin, *Index to Legislation*, 1890–1905.

no guarantee of regulatory vigor. One estimate held that fewer than 20 of the 168 insurance enactments of 1901 were of any import. An examination of the 1905 legislation, on the eve of the post-Armstrong flood, concluded that it "is not exceptional in any important respect, and . . . it contains little that is of real wide-reaching importance as regards the organization and conduct of the insurance business." New York's Insurance Law of 1892, the state's first codification since 1853 and the period's most important legislation, suggests how the tension between supervision and permissiveness went unresolved. The statute extended the powers of the insurance department — but that department was particularly subject to the great companies. Numerous accounting and reporting requirements were set down — but solvency was no longer a primary concern. And the law failed to require data on the essentials of company expenditure, investment, and managerial control.[6]

New insurance departments and the expansion of existing ones followed hard on the development of insurance as a major American enterprise. Between 1884 and 1905 nine states created insurance departments; the seventeen departments in 1890 increased to twenty-two in 1905. Other enactments gave insurance commissioners, secretaries of state, and state auditors responsibility for insurance matters. In Kansas, Wisconsin, and Delaware, the commissioner became an elected official. Frequent extensions of original authority, salaries that replaced fee compensation, and increases in departmental staffs contributed to the rapid institutionalization of the supervisory system.

There was a widespread belief in regulation through publicity. The prevailing supervisory theme was that "restrictions on the right of contract have proved detrimental while regulations to secure publicity have been of inestimable value." The commissioners' powers of examination, and company report and statement requirements, received considerable legislative attention. Although it still was easy for companies to hide many business details, there was substantial improvement. In 1902 the National Convention of Insurance Commissioners adopted a uniform reporting blank which subdivided company income under twenty-seven items, disbursements under twenty-nine, assets under twenty-seven, and liabilities under twenty-four.[7]

Numerous state deposit requirements assured the financial stability of insurance companies. But the wording of some laws — that companies *might,* if they chose, make securities deposits in the state treasury, or register securities at the commissioner's office — suggested that deposits had a public relations as well as a protective function. Similarly, company statements and annual reports served publicity purposes as much as regulatory responsibilities.

The right of the states to license companies and to impose fees was unquestioned; and by 1900 these powers were in widespread use. Fees for changing securities on deposit, for approving company charters and their revision, for securities valuation, or for licensing itself became so substantial that some states passed legislation redirecting the flow of revenue from the insurance commissioner's office to the treasurer.

Taxation was another matter. Here lay the most hotly contested ground of dispute between the companies and the regulatory structure. State authorities and legislatures, no matter how responsive to company interests, were tempted by the revenue that insurance taxation offered; and it was difficult for the firms to reject taxation in principle. The New York Life in 1876 deducted state tax payments from its policyholders' dividends, but the popular reaction soon forced the company to absorb the levy. When the Equitable questioned its counsel on the propriety of a Pennsylvania tax law in 1873, he warned: "The law is strictly and ably drawn, and undoubtedly requires your Society to pay the tax." Insurance levies were prominent in the late nineteenth century development of corporate taxation (see Table 9). In 1862 Massachusetts stopped ex-

TABLE 9. State corporate taxation, 1890 and 1895

Type of enterprise	1890	1895
Insurance companies	$3,076,173	$4,361,984
Banking	3,245,640	4,142,412
Railroads	7,081,473	11,966,983
Other corporations	5,273,391	4,941,129

empting most insurance from taxation; life insurance, the last to escape, succumbed in 1880. General insurance taxation came to Illinois in 1883, and soon constituted a substantial source of state revenue. By 1905 life insurance companies provided over $9,000,000 in revenue to the states; in Illinois insurance taxes brought in $623,000, general corporation fees $555,000. The Prudential was New Jersey's leading taxpayer in 1903, and insurance levies furnished the largest single increment to Kansas' revenue.[8]

Taxes fell on policies, on gross premium receipts, and on insurance agents. The prevalence of interstate retaliatory laws made the system national in scope, although state-administered. For the time, it seemed rigorous; even the courts contributed by refusing to allow states to exempt insurance companies from taxation. The president of one firm asked: "Why should insurance companies be singled out in state after state as specially doomed to bear extortionate taxes?" An expert in insurance law concluded, "No other business is taxed as is the insurance business, and of no other tax can so little be said in its favor."

Yet rates of 1½ or 2 percent on gross premium receipts were anything but onerous. And the companies had defenses. When Pennsylvania planned in 1895 to collect a levy directly from policyholders, the Equitable's attorneys advised that "by proper agitation an Act could be passed through the next Legislature, which would prohibit such taxation." Indiana ventured a policy tax which the State Supreme Court struck down, arguing that the weight of custom and tradition bore against such a levy. The courts likewise voided a Kansas tax on policies bought by its citizens from companies not authorized to do business in the state. New York's 1 percent tax on gross premium receipts could not be applied to policies issued before it took effect. In this sensitive area, as elsewhere in the structure of insurance supervision, corporate sanctity vigorously contested a still nascent control.[9]

Life insurance was substantially involved in a traditional area of corporation regulation, the status of foreign companies. A flow of legislation, especially in the West and South from 1895 to 1903, subjected foreign insurance corporations to taxation, licensing, agents' residence, deposit, and liability requirements. A closely allied group of statutes dwelt on company responsibility for legal service, process, and judgment. Statutes dealt with the location, time limit, and type of litigation — generally to the advantage of the insured. Insurance commissioners were able to revoke the license of a company that failed to satisfy execution of a judgment or applied for a case's removal from state to Federal jurisdiction. But the practice of state control did not necessarily put these instruments to effective use.

Legislation dealing with the structure of insurance companies concentrated on matters of concern to new or lesser firms. Minimum capitalization, insolvency, stock companies, and the state's power of incorporation were the most common subjects. Assessment firms received considerable statutory attention. In part this was protective, since fraternals had considerable popular support. But more stringent regulations also appeared because many fraternals were unsound, or because the fixed premium companies asked for action.

In dramatic contrast, few statutes dealt with industrial or standard life insurance companies as such. The problems of deferred dividend policies, policyholder representation in mutuals, and cash surpluses were all but ignored. Industrial companies faced intermittent efforts to limit child insurance, but only Colorado actually passed such a statute. New York helpfully made minors over fifteen legally competent to contract for insurance. The normal protectiveness of insurance commissioners (the New Hampshire superintendent criticized "the periodical agitation waged against industrial insurance") was in this case heightened by the lack of an established tradition of industrial insurance supervision.[10]

In general, company management was not a concern of the regulatory system; substantial action in this field came after 1905. Investment, however, long had been considered a proper matter for state regulation. The turn of the century saw considerable legislation prescribing the types of securities that companies might purchase, often expanding the permissible range. In the same sympathetic spirit, legislatures continued to deal in notable detail with questions of reinsurance and reserve valuation.

Thus the structure of supervision was at its friendliest when dealing with the technical details of the business. The policy contract itself, however, was a subject of fruitful and alert legislative concern. Among the achievements of the period were the mitigation of the warranty rule, nonforfeiture legislation, and increased protection of the beneficiary. This anxiety for the insured spilled over into legislation, unusual for the time, treating marketing methods. Laws supported by the large companies condemned premium rebating. Agents themselves, held to be something more than salesmen, were subject to licensing, state residence, and legal service requirements. Perhaps most suggestive of the way in which the needs of the insured roused legislative sensibilities was the series of statutes in the industrial states forbidding rate discrimination against Negro policyholders.

By their very existence, these enactments reflected significant positive assumptions about the place of insurance in the society, and about government's watchdog role. But their effect depended in great part on the vigor with which state insurance departments enforced them.

3

At the core of the supervisory structure stood the New York department of insurance. Most directly charged with regulating the industry's giants, it set the pace and tone of the national system of surveillance. The department dated from 1859, but did not have the rigor that Elizur Wright bequeathed to Massachusetts supervision. (One account credited its origin to the state's leading fire insurance companies.) Its first commissioner, William Barnes, was a son-in-law of New York Republican boss Thurlow Weed: the first of the particularly close ties with state politics that characterized — and plagued — the department.

Barnes' annual reports revealed the flaccid and unformed state of the regulatory art in the 1860's. Protectively, he took his companies through the perils of the Civil War. In 1862 he proposed to revoke the charter of any firms allowing Confederates to pay lapsed premiums — and thus encouraged forfeitures profitable to the companies. Cupidity and patriotism were easy bedfellows:

> Many of our Life Insurance Companies . . . have nobly offered to carry the policies of the citizen soldiers . . . An extra rate has been charged in

such cases, which has thus far proved amply sufficient to cover the increased risk. If in the future . . . this rate should be found inadequate . . . the loss to the companies will be one of those contingencies, for which it is the obvious duty of all patriotic corporations to provide, and will afford a claim hereafter for governmental aid and protection to the interests of Life Insurance.

Barnes gave thanks to the "Supreme Ruler" for improved business in 1863, and expressed his "particular gratitude [to] that generous American public which has so notably aided and supported these vast business interests." [11]

George Miller, Barnes's successor in 1870, was a Democrat close to boss William Marcy Tweed. He used his annual reports as a weapon with which to belabor his predecessor. Noting Barnes' obscurity and relative poverty on entering the department, he frostily remarked: "still, his honesty has been so great and his frugality so marked, that at the end of the ten years he had erected . . . a costly and spacious mansion in Albany." The return of the Republicans to legislative dominance in 1872 led to an investigation of Miller's performance in office, and it developed that he himself had received substantial sums from insurance companies, particularly from the Mutual. Miller claimed that Barnes, "this Mephistopheles of insurance," inspired the investigation, that he himself hoped to "make supervision mean something." But as superintendent he assured the companies that he was "not in favor of legislative interference with the mere details of business," and hoped that "the good sense" of company managers would "lead to the correction of existing evils, and the production of those results which will secure public confidence and obviate special legislation." [12]

Miller resigned in the face of legislative hostility, to be followed by the Republican Orlow W. Chapman. But the department's regulatory spirit remained unchanged. Chapman generously declared: "I believe it to be the duty of every superintendent to protect against oppressive and adverse legislation, not only his own companies, but the companies from other states." He saw no reason why the commissioner should interest himself in legislation, and suggested that a strong, honest company would be able to "exhibit its financial standing by means of state supervision."

In 1876, William Smyth succeeded Chapman as acting superintendent — and within a year was the subject of a legislative investigation. The inquiry of 1877 proved so illuminating on company-department relations that the Big Three had the official record bowdlerized. A political adventurer named William S. Manning obtained the full testimony and printed it in book form, but the printing was bought up by the large firms, who further restrained the author by an annual retainer for years thereafter.[13]

Effective regulation could not develop in this atmosphere. Superficially the state was active enough: the powers of the commissioner were expanded, and legislative insurance investigations occurred in 1870, 1872, 1877, 1882, and 1885. But the large companies themselves supported the strengthening of a department notably friendly to them; and the inquiries were not so much signs of regulatory vigor as they were expressions of interparty strife. A contemporary journal noted with disgust "the utter worthlessness of state supervision to protect the people against the impositions and deceit of dishonest insurance officers and rotten insurance companies."

Instances of governmental impotence abounded. In the wake of the 1877 disclosures the legislature required that company examination fees be audited and paid out by the state Treasury, which would then be reimbursed by the insurance firms. Superintendent Smyth refused to obey. The governor recommended his removal, but a small Assembly majority sustained the department head. With characteristic guile, the companies vitiated the effect of an 1879 nonforfeiture act. They secured an amendment allowing a clause waiving nonforfeiture to appear in red ink on the policy's margin. Thereupon the New York Life issued a contract printed entirely in red, in which the punitive clause lurked unseen. The legislature passed a premium tax law in 1880, but not until 1887 were legal impediments to its implementation removed. Thereupon the law was repealed, amid rumors — but nothing more — that bribery from the companies had played a part. In the mid-eighties policyholder dissatisfaction with tontine dividend returns led to investigations in several states. New York's inquiry was a model of restraint: hearings lasted but four days; the investigation committee had no counsel; and no legislation resulted. The committee's report plaintively asked: "Was ever a greater effort made to prevent inquiry and smother an investigation?"

An 1890 New York law specified that suits which might circumscribe the life insurance business be handled by the attorney general, thus making it much more difficult for an individual policyholder to bring an action against his company. This and an antirebate bill in 1889 (also supported by the great firms), along with the mild limitation of forfeiture in the 1870's, were the major achievements in New York insurance legislation between the Civil War and the beginning of the 1890's: evidence of the halting uncertainty of the regulatory system.[14]

The New York department remained the plaything of politics and sycophantic regulation past the turn of the century. In 1904 the president of a non–New York insurance firm resignedly observed: "It is taken for granted that the Insurance interest[s] in New York manage to have the Insurance Department under their control." Commissioners John McCall (1881–1885) and Robert A. Maxwell (1885–1890) were prominent members of the state Democratic organization; and McCall later became one of the magnates of the life insurance business. Maxwell quarreled with his appointer, Governor David Hill, and left the department muttering darkly of being "solicited to do things which no honest man could do." Yet his supervisory ideal was a familiar one. Proudly he declared that "harpies were never permitted to fasten on the insurance interests of the state while I was superintendent." [15]

Governor Hill replaced Maxwell in 1890 with James F. Pierce, who made his five years in office a model of regulatory laissez-faire. It was not for his department, "benignant in its conception and . . . protective in its operation . . . to erect over the lawfully appointed custodians of the people's funds another custodian who should intermeddle in their corporation administration." Before taking office he received an attorney's retainer from the Mutual, and rumor had it that he was lobbied into the commissionership by that company. Hyde, too, interested himself in the vacancy that Pierce filled. He instructed James Alexander, "we want to take some action with regard to a new Superintendent. Have Chauncey [Depew] keep it in mind, and I think McCall had better do what we talked about the other day, so as to make himself 'solid.' "

Pierce was amiably receptive to the great companies' desires. He actively helped the Big Three in their Prussian negotiations. Full of fraternal sentiment, McCurdy called on the superintendent to accept certain questionable items in the Equitable's report for 1893. The Mutual head asked his aid, too, against proposed taxation of life insurance companies. When other states were reluctant to accept New York's reserve valuation rate, McCurdy prepared letters to the Illinois and Missouri commissioners for Pierce to send as his own.[16]

No less than his predecessors, Pierce came to his office with a political rather than an insurance background; and in 1895, when both the governor and legislature were Republican, there was talk of his impeachment. His G.O.P. successor, Louis F. Payn, represented a still greater mixture of politics and insurance regulation. A professional lobbyist who had served the interests of Jay Gould, Payn in the 1890's was New York boss Tom Platt's closest lieutenant. His appointment touched off widespread criticism as an overdirect infusion of bossism into the state administration. And indeed Payn seemed to initiate a more regularized boodling. The commissioner later said of political levies on the companies: "I am of the belief that all great corporations . . . are subject to just such taxes . . . and that they pay them all right." By calling these exactions "taxes," Payn suggested how systematic they had become. But if Payn was more expensive than his predecessors, he was no less amenable to company interests. He worked closely with McCurdy on a bill "intended to secure . . . great protection to the interests of New York corporations."

The fact that Platt's lieutenant took the insurance commissionership suggests how tempting to political machines were the succulently rich insurance companies. But the large, sophisticated firms became restive with this political exploitation, and the special qualities of the enterprise that excited the bosses' cupidity also made for a widespread sentiment against bossism in insurance regulation. Payn worked against Theodore Roosevelt's 1898 gubernatorial nomination, and, once elected, T.R. turned his wrath on the commissioner. In 1900 he refused to reappoint Payn on grounds of malfeasance in office. Speaking of the superintendent's "professional immorality," Roosevelt sarcastically noted that "being a frugal man, out of his seven thousand dollars a year salary he has saved enough to enable him to borrow nearly half a million dollars from a trust company, the directors of which are also the directors of an insurance company under his supervision."

Roosevelt replaced Payn with Francis Hendricks, a Syracuse political power acceptable to Platt but also a banker of considerable respectability. Of, but not in, the machine, Hendricks represented the more restrained, less venal type of supervision that had first appeared in the person of John McCall. But honesty did not necessarily bring with it greater vigor. Hendricks' regulatory views differed not at all from those of his predecessors. He devoted little time or attention to his duties as superintendent, and proudly declared: "I have never attempted to manage the companies. That must be left to the directors." Hendricks represented a fusion of politics and regulatory policy especially satisfactory to the companies; and in this sense he was a product of their power and sophistication.[17]

Suggestive, too, were evolving company attitudes toward departmental examinations. Something less than zeal traditionally characterized these inquiries. Superintendent Pierce saw no need for "subjecting" the companies to an examination every three to five years unless a special situation demanded it, and the New York and Albany offices of the department worked in "harmonious inactivity." When examinations did occur, they were cumbersome affairs lasting for nine or even eighteen months, and they failed to come upon the evils later uncovered by the Armstrong investigation. The New York Life underwent two examinations between 1895 and 1905; the Mutual, three; the Equitable, four. Ecstatic praise for the managers' wisdom and honesty was the prevailing result.

Nevertheless, the Mutual's McCurdy judged examinations "a necessary evil *to be minimized and alleviated by all proper means.*" In 1898 he faced surveys by Wisconsin, Minnesota, Michigan, Illinois, Missouri, and Ohio. Hurriedly he called on Texas commissioner Hollingsworth, who was on the Mutual's payroll, to come and make a favorable analysis of the company's condition. In addition he asked Superintendent Payn of New York to begin his own examination; once under way, this would block other inquiries. Payn complied, and came up with the finding that the Mutual was a solvent corporation — hardly a matter in question. Asked later why he did not conduct a more thorough inquiry, the superintendent explained that the companies had been complaining about examination costs.[18]

But the officers of the New York Life, especially alert to such nuances, came to look upon examinations as a positive good. President John McCall requested such a survey in 1894, noting that three years had passed since the last one — and that this was the company's golden anniversary. When it developed that the New York examiners would be busy elsewhere, he extended the invitation to the insurance departments of seven other states and all accepted. Low comedy enlivened this parody of supervision: the Massachusetts commissioner at first was reluctant to participate, but after New York's superintendent spoke out against mass examination by other state departments the Bay Stater truculently declared that he would indeed join the others. In 1903 the New York Life again sought out investigations that could not fail to provide usable copy on the company's efficiency and strength: this time it invited the New York department and, still more ambitiously, the United States Department of Commerce and Labor.[19] By the early

1900's, then, New York supervision had settled down to a quiet accommodation of the great companies; and what was on the surface an impressive regulatory structure had become yet another area in which the great firms could expect to exert their corporate power.

The Prudential enjoyed a similar relationship with the insurance department of its home state of New Jersey. Before the department was established in 1891, New Jersey insurance matters were in the lax, friendly hands of Secretary of State A. C. Kelsey. Substantial insurance legislation followed hard on the creation of the department, but it was no source of anxiety to the Prudential. On March 25, 1892, new statutes established a light rate of taxation, and affirmed the right of boards of directors to set officers' salaries and protect stock dividends. New Jersey's insurance laws were codified in 1902, with Prudential representatives close at hand. Two years later the firm secured legislation substantially broadening its powers of investment.

The department of insurance was as acquiescent as the state legislature. It examined the Prudential in 1893, 1899, and 1903, and found all well. As in New York, regulation stopped with these examinations and the company's annual statements. It was the sense of the department that financial soundness was its proper concern, not business methods or expenses. The examiner later admitted that he did not discuss the Prudential's stock expansion plans in his report because "I hated to say anything that might seem to reflect upon the company."

David O. Watkins, New Jersey's insurance superintendent during the early 1900's, served the Prudential in a more positive manner. When the proposed Prudential-Fidelity Trust Company merger aroused concern, he refused to provide the Massachusetts and Wisconsin commissioners with information on the trust company; he could not, he said, divulge the "sacred and strictly confidential" affairs of a banking institution. The department's only response to the Prudential-Fidelity relationship was to propose that the two companies' securities be examined simultaneously, to obviate any switching.[20]

In other states as well, friendly commissioners and complacent departments testified to the companies' lobbying strength and skill. Horace S. Merrill of Massachusetts had intimate connections with Henry Hyde. When Merrill warned Hyde of a coming examination by a group of Western insurance superintendents, the Equitable head thought it would be well for the Massachusetts commissioner "to have a general engagement with me to examine the Equitable, at such time as will suit your convenience, so that if I am approached, I will be able to say that an examination of the Company is being made by you, and thereby stop any examination by the western superintendents." In 1895 he called on Merrill to attend the National Conference of Insurance Commissioners (NCIC) convention in order to obstruct a plan to investigate the companies' mortality tables and to support a change in the reserve valuation rate.

Hyde had much the same kind of relationship with Missouri superintendent James R. Waddill, advising him on the role he was to play in the NCIC gathering in 1896. Sycophantically, Waddill entreated Hyde to speak before the convention, but the Equitable president demurred, saying that his presence might "cause the Superintendents greater embarrassment, in carrying out what we all desire." At the same time he asked Rhode Island's "blind Boss," Senator Charles R. Brayton, to have that state's insurance commissioner take the free-lance actuary Sheppard Homans to the NCIC convention as a special assistant: "There are many things in connection with the business of life insurance that are hardly understood by the Superintendents and we are very much embarrassed at times that we are not represented by actuaries who have full knowledge of the situation." [21]

Pennsylvania was more difficult, not because of its regulatory zeal, but because of the excessive venality of the Quay-Penrose machine, which was inclined to extract what revenue it could from an enterprise based primarily in other states. Israel ("Is") Durham, boss Matt Quay's closest assistant and Pennsylvania's insurance commissioner, played the role of a friendly critic in his reports. At the end of 1893 he supported a law fixing a standard valuation on insurance assets, and judiciously observed: "Life companies have no right to invest their assets in doubtful securities, at low figures, in the hope that large profits will be realized; neither can they be expected to invest and keep invested the large sums in their keeping except at a very conservative rate" — a position the great firms heartily endorsed. Piously he spoke out against undue regulation: "Life insurance companies are great trusts . . . and while it is proper to enact such laws as will assure a faithful administration of the trust, certainly no one can desire that any burden shall be put upon policy holders unnecessarily by legislation."

But Durham also put pressure on the companies. In 1894 he menacingly declared: "The Pennsylvania statutes bearing upon insurance, and presumably made for the protection of the public, are ridiculously weak and insufficient in many particulars." A year later he refused to go along with other state commissioners in supporting retaliatory legislation against Prussian fire insurance companies. During his superintendency he personally accumulated $141,000 from company license fees, and regularly sent friends to New York for expensive "examinations" of the great companies. The rapacity of the Quay-Penrose machine extended beyond the department of insurance. In 1897 state senators approached Metropolitan agents with the offer to kill proposed legislation against child insurance for a cash consideration. Quay was reported to be for higher taxes on out-of-state insurance companies, and the *Weekly Underwriter* acidly observed: "No doubt Sen. Quay knows from past experience how easy it is to bleed insurance companies for political purposes." Durham finally was ousted in 1905 by Governor Samuel W. Pennypacker, a political move similar to Roosevelt's removal of Payn. The new commissioner, David Martin, was Boies Penrose's choice for the job, and the regulatory tone of the department did not noticeably change.[22]

Problems of a similar kind existed across the country in California. In 1897 Superintendent Andrew F. Clunie held that the Equitable, as a stock company, must double its capital in order to do business in California. The state attorney general did not uphold him, and Clunie then questioned the Big Three's policy returns, threatening a major examination. To forestall this the companies gave substantial sums to the Mutual's San Francisco counsel, who made liberal payments to Superintendent Clunie's brother.[23]

4

McCurdy often voiced his contempt for the regulatory system. When the Ohio and Kentucky commissioners submitted a detailed questionnaire on salaries, political expenses, and other sensitive matters, he exploded: "Can't you fellows — the whole forty-four of you — agree once and for all what you want, and then let us alone about extra requirements?" Gratefully he noted that the 1902 Arkansas insurance report was limited to statistical tables, and "did not indulge in any accompanying wearisome remarks." When Arkansas governor James P. Clarke wrote to complain about his policy's dividend earnings, McCurdy commented pointedly on the governor's inexperience in insurance matters: "Probably I would make a very poor hand at being Governor of any state. I carry the comparison no further from motives of courtesy." Noting that the

Chief Executive had tried to shoot a member of the Arkansas legislature, he delicately warned that though "an attempt to shoot another gentleman is not specified among the specially hazardous occupations or employments which are prohibited by the policy . . . such an occupation is liable to be extremely dangerous to the gentleman who engages in it." Seven Western examiners, properly treated, produced a report complimenting the Mutual's management. McCurdy presented it to his trustees with easy cynicism: "You can take it for what it is worth, although I doubt if you would take it for what it cost."

But beneath the contempt was the shortened temper of an insurance executive dealing with an expanding regulatory structure. By the turn of the century the flow of legislation had increased so that company concerns became generic rather than specific. A leading insurance journal spoke of "the avalanche of hostile legislation which is year after year burying the freedom of action which is so essential to the conduct of any business"; another noted that the enterprise was "engaging more and more closely the attention of those whom we have elected to take care of our legislation." McCurdy listed 27 undesirable laws from 16 states in 1897; the Prudential computed that over 700 bills affecting life insurance companies were introduced between 1901 and 1905; over 750 proposed enactments threatened the New York Life's interests between 1898 and 1905. The *Weekly Underwriter,* the *Insurance Monitor,* and the *Chronicle* made regular surveys of impending legislation.[24]

Legislation and supervision took on a new, more vigorous tone. When nine of thirty insurance bills introduced in New York in 1891 became law, the great companies probably objected to none of them. But Western and Southern legislation in the Populist decade was something else again. At first, anticompany bills in turbulent states like Kansas were consistently blocked, and the *Weekly Underwriter* confidently predicted that "the result of the past can safely presage the future." However, this did not prove to be the case. The accretion of anticorporation, anti-Eastern sentiment, a major theme of the Populist movement, led to widespread regulatory and legislative action against the great companies.

Petty annoyances were constant. In 1895 North Carolina and Alabama considered legislation forcing companies to make payment on forfeited or contested policies; when the law passed in Alabama the Metropolitan stopped taking new business there. McCurdy angrily reported that the Equitable's state manager had helped in the creation of an Alabama department of insurance in 1897. Alexander of the Equitable, threatened with an examination by the hitherto friendly state of Missouri, truculently declared: "We do not propose to have it done and have a variety of methods to avoid it." Yet the examinations continued. George Perkins' description of one conducted by Nebraska officials in 1900 was wry as well as amused: "Yesterday two gentlemen blew in the front door. It remains to be seen whether or not they will blow up the building." He expected the inquiry to last for five days; "While the cool weather continues the New York hotels and the Roof Garden performances are not so bad." There was, he supposed, "some political game in it somewhere," and he had the New York Life's Chicago lobbyist "tap the Lincoln end of the wire" to be sure that nothing untoward occurred. On the eve of the Armstrong investigation, a New York Life official complained of "obnoxious" deposit bills before the Missouri and Arizona legislatures, and cautioned the company's chief lobbyist: "You say there is no hurry about Wisconsin. You doubtless know more than we do but there would seem to be two or three bills of such magnitude as to ruin life insurance if they pass." At the same time Perkins reported to McCall: "We propose to fight South Dakota tax bill through our agents and policyholders . . . If we get beaten then [I] think we ought to withdraw." [25]

This perpetual, anxious sense of conflict was not eased by the appearance, around the turn of the century, of a new breed of insurance commissioners. Men like Frederick L. Cutting of Massachusetts, E. L. Schofield of Connecticut, Zeno M. Host of Wisconsin, Thomas D. O'Brien of Minnesota, Reau E. Folk of Tennessee, Webster McNall of Kansas, Henry R. Prewitt of Kentucky, and Willard Vandiver of Missouri had diverse motives and techniques, but they shared a common determination to instill vigor and effectiveness into the system of state insurance supervision.

Supervisory challenges from Texas, Kansas, and Wisconsin most keenly tested the companies' political prowess. Under the influence of Texas' Populist governor James S. Hogg, insurance commissioner John E. Hollingsworth attacked "the present craze for volume" in 1893 and declared that "the trend of insurance legislation of late years has been in the interest of the premium receiver rather than the premium payer." Charles A. Culberson, Hogg's successor and no Populist, nevertheless inherited his predecessor's hostility toward the Eastern insurance firms. In 1896, in the wake of Bryan's defeat, he sent off a questionnaire asking companies for data on their officers' salaries, their political contributions, and their dinner and wine costs. The Mutual refused to answer — "This is insult. It is tyranny," McCurdy blustered — and, in harness with the Equitable, engaged former Governor Hogg himself as counsel. When former insurance commissioner John E. Hollingsworth (who later also came on the big companies' payroll, a destiny not uncommon for anticorporation Populists) tried to interest the Mutual in Texas county bonds, McCurdy's secretary frigidly declared: "this Company has no use for Texas securities at the present time." He instructed Hogg to tell the governor that he was willing to forgive and forget; that he would be glad to give him expert advice on revision of the state's insurance laws; that he would even visit him if invited.

Soon, McCurdy could report to Hyde that he was getting results. Insurance commissioner Jefferson Johnson was accommodating, and McCurdy worked for his reappointment in 1898. Governor Culberson looked forward to a seat in the Senate; and a Mutual representative offered help in attaining that objective. Yet the trouble would not down. In 1899 the unwanted questionnaire was revived; the Mutual refused to answer; its Texas license was threatened; and finally it responded — but without reporting any campaign contributions.[26]

The impact of Populism on Kansas had even more unsettling consequences for the great companies. The danger of hostile legislation and supervision persisted there through the 1890's. Growing opposition to the Eastern companies finally erupted over the Hillmon case, in which the Mutual, New York Life, and Connecticut Mutual refused to pay the proceeds of a policy to a widow because of the strong suspicion that she had murdered her husband. Insurance commissioner Webster McNall revoked the three companies' Kansas licenses. Leader of the state's silver Republicans, he was a formidable adversary in the bitter time following the 1896 election. The companies fought back: contempt proceedings were instituted against McNall, and a Circuit Court judge charged a grand jury to look into the matter. The panel indicted the commissioner for acting illegally, and the court put an injunction on his activities. But McNall ignored both jury and bench.

As in Germany, the Mutual and the New York Life had to deal with exclusion and with a difficult authority; and once again McCall's company soon was handling the problem in its own way. Its lobbyists came to terms with McNall, and in November 1897 the company withdrew its suit against the commissioner on the ground that he now was treating it "very fairly." McNall began issuing licenses to individual

New York Life agents, explaining that the firm "had promised to be good"; and in February 1898 he restored its full power to sell insurance in the state. The Kansas Supreme Court, meanwhile, upheld McNall's right to exclude the Mutual from the state: a tribute to the New York Life's political shrewdness.

McNall and his party were beaten in the November 1898 elections, after which the irrepressible commissioner declared that he had refused a $50,000 bribe offered by the insurance companies. His successor readmitted the Mutual, but the New York Life's influence in the department remained strong. The commissionership was made elective in 1900 — which, if anything, eased the course of company control. The incumbent candidate in 1904 reported to a New York Life lobbyist that "after paying my [political party] assessment I am entirely out of funds," and got the few hundred dollars he wanted for his own campaign.[27]

La Follette's Wisconsin raised the most substantial and serious challenge to the great companies. William A. Fricke, the state's insurance commissioner during the late 1890's, became a New York Life lobbyist on his retirement; but his successor, Zeno M. Host, was of another stripe. Coldly noting: "Life insurance companies have had little to complain of as to adverse legislation, and that little, has been solely due to their methods of doing business," Host set out to make vigorous supervision an important part of La Follette's progressive program.

His major targets were the Equitable and the Prudential. He ruled that the Equitable had violated a Wisconsin statute in failing to distribute its surplus at least once every five years, and threatened to revoke the company's license. The lower courts found Host's ruling valid, but the Wisconsin Supreme Court decided otherwise, and the Equitable's license remained untouched. In the heat of the battle, the New York insurance department was ready to "go to the limit" in defense of the company, and the Big Three, seeing Host's ruling as a challenge to them all, shared the Equitable's legal expenses. Another weapon in the Equitable's arsenal was the mollifying offer of a $2000 contribution to La Follette's re-election campaign in 1904.

The Prudential's troubles with Host derived from its proposed merger with the Fidelity Trust Company. Unable to get information on the Fidelity Trust's financial condition from the New Jersey commissioner, Host refused to grant the Prudential a license to do business in his state. But the insurance company obtained a court order enjoining Host to grant the license, and after some further negotiating induced the commissioner to yield.[28]

Meaningful supervision appeared in the non-Populist East as well as in the excited South and West, suggesting the growing appeal of effective insurance regulation. Commissioner Schofield of Connecticut fought the Mutual and Equitable custom of listing deferred dividend funds as liabilities rather than as surplus; he attacked the Big Three's foreign business in 1891 and their giant size in 1892. And Frederick L. Cutting restored to Massachusetts regulation something of Elizur Wright's dedication, moving vigorously in 1903 against the proposed Prudential-Fidelity Trust merger.[29]

At the century's turn, then, the large firms had some reason for discontent with the regulatory system. Powerful political machines in New York and Pennsylvania made the control of supervision expensive. Unfriendly regulation was increasingly common, particularly in the South and West. Not surprisingly, the companies turned their considerable powers to the task of systematically controlling the structure of supervision.

XIII * The Response to Regulation

Companies so substantial, yet so caught up in an expanding, sometimes hostile, supervisory structure, moved to safeguard their position. The technique that they adopted — a sophisticated, highly organized application of corporate power — was an expression of the euphoria that characterized them at the turn of the century.

The masterful Henry Hyde kept close watch over the Equitable's political influence. His lieutenants were John McCall, an influential Democrat who left the Equitable's comptrollership for the New York Life presidency in 1892, and Chauncey Depew, long a fixture in Republican state politics. Hyde used McCall chiefly to counter taxation. He called on him to see to reductions in the Equitable's real estate levies: "With our influence in various directions" considerable savings were possible. In 1890 the comptroller was assigned to "look after the appointment of a tax Commissioner. It is of vital importance that the man who occupies that position should do the fair thing by us." Always Hyde sought tax reductions: "it seems to me that with our political influence, we ought to get them cut down." As a substantial stockholder in the United States Illuminating Company, Hyde kept a close watch on legislation affecting the burgeoning electric light industry. Opposing one measure, he told McCall to "use every ounce of your strength and influence in inducing the Governor to veto the bill." Depew was equally useful when Republican politicians needed cajoling. Concerned about the taxation of trust companies, Hyde hoped that the statesman "will be able to conquer it." [1]

The Equitable president's network of political influence was direct and uncomplicated. His contacts ran the gamut from Thomas Coman, laden with Tammany connections, who looked after matters such as health violations in Equitable-owned property and the officers' property assessments, to Tom Platt, the Republican state boss. Yearly Equitable contributions of $10,000 — delivered in cash to Platt's office by special messenger — sweetened this relationship. Other Equitable retainers were liberally dispensed. One recipient was Thomas B. Husted, brother of the longtime chairman of the legislature's Insurance Committee; another was the former Democratic governor of the state, David B. Hill. In 1895 lobbyist Hill wrote to Equitable vice-president Alexander: "I feel pretty well now that Congress has adjourned and the Country is safe. When legislature adjourns the State will be safe."

But this system had its dangers. Limited to New York State, it was not suited to deal with the political problems of a national enterprise. Associate auditor A. W. Mayne handled out-of-state matters, but his influence was limited. And by dealing directly with the state machine, the Equitable left itself open to equally direct levies. In 1904 Governor Benjamin Odell, Platt's successor as head of the Republican organization, initiated legislation to repeal the charter of the Equitable-controlled Mercantile Trust Company. It developed that Odell had lost considerable money on the stock of the New York Shipbuilding Company, a venture handled by the Mercantile Trust. The governor told Equitable counsel Bainbridge Colby that in his estimation the trust company had not properly protected his interests. After some negotiation, the Equitable paid Odell $75,000 to mend his injured fortunes, and he promised that there would be no legislative action against the Mercantile — a promise based on "my knowledge and experience in the Legislature," as the governor delicately put it.[2]

The Mutual had a long lobbying tradition; its sophisticated, scholarly special counsel, Charlton Lewis, was a familiar Albany figure during the 1870's and 1880's. Like the Equitable, McCurdy's firm contributed $10,000 a year to Boss Platt, and engaged such useful men as William Barnes, Jr., son of the first commissioner, and former insurance superintendent James F. Pierce to serve its political interests.

The Mutual's banking and trust company affiliations also made special demands on its political prowess. As United States senator, David Hill helped McCurdy convert the Guaranty and Indemnity into the Guaranty Trust. The Mutual president concerned himself with a bill affecting savings bank investments. And with the help of New Jersey's Senator

William Sewell he labored for a revised Morristown Trust Company charter which would be "less likely to attract attention and comparison and therefore arouse discussion." [3]

But the Mutual went beyond the Equitable in systematizing its Albany relationships. Andrew C. Fields, a power in the Westchester County Democracy, was its full-time lobbyist. Fields maintained a house in Albany where legislators and insurance department employees were entertained. The building attracted much attention in the Armstrong investigation, and the press promptly labeled it the "House of Mirth." In addition to this frothy establishment there was a substantial network of liaisons with members of the legislature's insurance committees and the insurance department. A typical contact was Charles P. McClelland, a close friend and neighbor of Fields's. He lived in the Mutual's Albany house, in what he disparagingly described as "a little bit of a room with a bed and bureau and one chair in it." Although his own ambitions ran toward the Finance Committee, McClelland was made chairman of the Insurance Committee in 1892, "and it seemed as though I could not get off it after that." Out of office, McClelland received a Mutual retainer from 1899 to 1902, and steadily consulted Fields and Mutual general solicitor Edward L. Short on proposed insurance legislation. McClelland's function was to advise on the desirability of an act, not on how to defeat it: "I am not an artist in that line." In 1903 he was back in the Senate and, of course, back on the Insurance Committee. There he rendered "considerable services" against franchise, trust company, and savings bank taxes pushed by Governor Odell.[4]

This was a specialized lobbying system, far more systematized than Henry Hyde's direct contacts. Robert A. Granniss, McCurdy's chief assistant, got a daily report from the *Weekly Underwriter* on insurance bills introduced in the legislature, consulted with attorney Short, and then turned the matter over to Fields and his associates for proper disposal. The system belonged to the Mutual, but the Equitable, recognizing its worth, contributed to its costs. Fields, Short, McClelland, and others in the network received Equitable retainers. The Equitable's comptroller, Thomas D. Jordan, kept up a steady flow of instructions to Fields during legislative sessions from 1898 to 1905. A note to Fields from Jordan in 1903 suggests the scope of the system:

> Referring to Albany matters during the present session please note that we will be interested in all banking and insurance measures, taxation fees, and bills affecting particularly the following interests:

Safe deposit companies, banks, trust companies, street railways, and all measures affecting Suffolk County, New York, Franchises, Water Rights, Land under Water, Transportation, etc.[5]

An organized lobbying system presumably made for greater efficiency and effectiveness. But it also had consequences difficult to justify. The Mutual's Albany establishment was expensive. The firm's legal expenses climbed relatively slowly from $249,000 in 1895 to $305,000 in 1900, and to $364,000 in 1904; but this was only a fraction of the costs of political representation. Fields's expenses were covered by funds credited to advertising, printing, stationery, and postage, an item totaling $484,000 in 1895, $591,000 in 1900, and $1,135,000 in 1904. Much of this went to a dummy corporation, the Globe Printing Company, which passed it on to Fields for "legal expenses." Another confidential fund was maintained for those "many cases where counsel are employed that do not appear, and money is used to pay them, and they prefer not to give receipts for it." Mutual vice-president Walter R. Gillette justified the arrangement: "in all corporate interests there are certain transactions that are done in a confidential way, and these moneys were used in this way."[6]

The New York Life rarely gave money to Platt's organization, but this did not signify political indifference on the part of an otherwise dynamic corporation. The company most committed to a sophisticated business technique and investment structure developed the most complex system of political representation.

Numerous influential lobbyists served the New York Life. Edward McCall, John's brother, represented the firm in Albany, and then with the aid of a healthy gift of company money to Tammany ascended to the State Supreme Court. William H. Buckley, formerly of the New York insurance department, also was active in Albany. William C. Beer, close to President William McKinley, handled the company's Washington matters. Perkins described Chicago attorney Edward O'Bryan as "our confidential representative . . . a lawyer who knows most everything . . . and keeps in touch with all the politics of the town." To circumvent an Indiana tax law "one of our special men . . . who does errands of this and a kindred nature" rushed to the scene.

But the dominant figure in the New York Life's structure of political influence was Andrew Hamilton, a lawyer and an old friend of John McCall. He first acted for the company as special counsel in its successful attempt to rescind the pension granted outgoing President William H.

Beers in 1892. Hamilton's personal gifts and his wide political acquaintanceship made him useful to the New York Life in other ways, and he stayed on as an adviser and attorney until 1895. Then, as McCall put it, "he was given charge of the entire United States" in "the matter of legislation and taxation." The company created a special bureau of taxation and legislation with Hamilton at its head, on the assumption that "if a secret service was a permissible governmental agency, a confidential service would be the only effective and . . . proper plan to guard the welfare of the most extensive commercial interests in the world — the life insurance business of . . . New York."

Hamilton vividly described the lobbying system that grew out of the bureau of taxation and legislation: "At the capital of every State we have either retained representatives for the companies, or are in cooperation with some one who has retained representatives duly influential." Working secretly, these men learned of and suppressed legislation at its inception. Useful too were "pledges in advance [not to bother the companies] obtained through influential persons," which left the New York Life representatives "free to parry attacks from quarters not so well protected." Speed of operation was essential to this sensitive and widespread network: a threat could develop overnight, and "my representatives . . . must be people who are in touch with every movement and who can learn of every change in time to advise me and to receive instructions." No armchair strategist, Hamilton was constantly in the field. The cumulative effect of political power was overwhelming. Former insurance superintendent Payn recalled: "He went to Texas — that was the rumor — 'Hamilton has gone to Texas,' and then you would hear of him in Kansas and then in Illinois, all over the country." [7]

Just as the Equitable participated in Fields's Mutual organization at Albany, so did all of the great companies support Hamilton's interstate structure of political influence. Fields and the Mutual had primary charge of New York State matters; otherwise the United States was divided into three groups of states, each the special responsibility of one of the Big Three. Warren F. Thummel handled many Mutual matters outside of New York, often working closely with Hamilton. Fields, too, occasionally tackled the hinterland, with McCurdy instructing his general agents to honor any drafts that the lobbyist made on the Mutual.

The cooperation in Hamilton's organization was as organic an expression of the society of great companies as their growing collaboration in business and financial matters. From the mid-1890's, examples of joint political action multiplied. When the Equitable sought the Mutual's aid on a bill regulating building heights, McCurdy was ready to "help along in a good natured way." Hyde helped the Metropolitan's Hegeman to secure some desired legislation. Bluntly he instructed an assemblyman: "I very much hope that you can carry out my wishes in the matter, and by so doing you will confer a very great favor upon me." The great insurance firms joined with trust companies, banks, and real estate brokers to oppose a mortgage tax bill pushed by the avaricious Platt.[8]

These joint efforts made Hamilton's structure a sophisticated, rationalized response to the problems of a complex supervisory milieu. McCall recollected:

> In 1892, 1893, and 1894 there were constant clashings as to the bills in the various States. This agent would write in and say, from Texas, that the best man in connection with a bill was John Doe, and another agent would suggest Richard Roe, and there was a constant suggesting and iteration and reiteration of names until the accounts could not be handled at all to anybody's satisfaction. The details were tremendous and for that reason the Bureau was organized in 1895, giving Judge Hamilton absolute and entire control of all legislation introduced in the United States and Canada.

By 1895 existing methods of company influence could not cope with the increasingly unfriendly flow of legislation. The use of agents "as guardians of insurance in legislative affairs" was unsatisfactory; political lobbying was too big and too specialized a job. In theory, policyholders were a useful force. The Equitable's Gage Tarbell, who "always maintained that . . . it should be a very easy matter for [life insurance companies] . . . to defeat any improper legislation through their policyholders," met with Mutual and New York Life officials to discuss ways and means of doing this. But attempts at mobilizing the insured had not been successful, and McCurdy considered Tarbell's plans "impracticable." Formal legal counsel were no more effective. Hamilton observed, "the very fact that the great life insurance interests of New York favored or opposed pending legislative propositions, would of itself concentrate the opposition." Demands would arise that political favorites be taken on as counsel; but this would put the companies "at the mercy of those who did not possess our confidence." Smooth, secretive, national organization seemed to be the only alternative.[9]

Hamilton recognized that the resulting structure of political influence reflected the growth of the companies into national institutions: "A savings bank is subject to control and taxes by a single State. The great railroad systems may extend into a dozen states, but the great life insurance companies . . . have more than fifty bosses in the United States." For all his rodomontade and his natural tendency to exaggerate the scope of his work, he voiced the outlook that gave the society of companies its special tone. If Perkins best represented that ambience in the areas of corporate management, business and investment technique, and national political power, Hamilton and his structure of influence embodied it on the level of the states.

But the very size of Hamilton's political operations generated substantial problems. His lobbying expenditures were considerable. Before 1895, the New York Life's yearly legal costs were about $10,000. But then legislative disbursements rapidly mounted. Hamilton's stated expenses went from $41,417 in 1896 and $65,674 in 1897 to over $100,000 in 1898 and 1901, and to more than $140,000 in 1904. Actually, lobbying absorbed far greater sums: between December 1903 and March 1904 alone, Hamilton got New York Life checks totaling $235,000. The best estimate was that he spent about $1,300,000 between 1895 and 1905.[10]

So substantial an operation, yet one so questionably related to the accepted means and ends of a life insurance company, induced subterfuge and *sub rosa* arrangements. Hamilton's very appointment set the tone. The company's Minutes stated only that he was taken on for the "examination of real estate titles, and such other business as may come before the Real Estate Department." This position served Hamilton as a cover, just as Fields hid behind the Mutual's division of printing and supplies. Payments to Hamilton usually were made by home or branch offices on President McCall's written authorization. Originally a matter of convenience, the system became a means of avoiding the dangerous paraphernalia of receipts, vouchers, checks, and a company record. The loose and casual nature of Hamilton's accountability (and, he claimed, the unevenness of his operating costs) encouraged him to run up substantial personal notes discounted by McCall. A hastily scribbled memo from the New York Life president to Perkins suggests the tone of the arrangement: "The Judge [Hamilton] wants $10,000. Can you help him?" [11]

Not surprisingly, Hamilton's own relationship to the funds he handled became suspect. He received a retainer of $10,000 a year, 5 percent of his disbursements up to $100,000, and 50 percent of any unexpended portion of the initial $100,000. McCall had "a perfect understanding" with Hamilton "that there should be no request from me in relation to his work, that I should have no vouchers." His compensation arrangements could be flexible indeed. In 1902 he argued before the New York Supreme Court that a new premium tax did not apply to policies written before the law went into effect. As a stimulus to his legal effort the New York Life offered him one third of all that the company recovered if the decision went in its favor. Ultimately the companies won their case. Hamilton's reward, around $10,000, perforce came to him secretly.

As Hamilton's lobbying system expanded, the underground flow of money to him increased in complexity and bulk. New York Life syndicate profits were secretly funneled to him, and the New York Security and Trust and J. P. Morgan and Company either lent or advanced funds. Just as the scope and sophistication of the New York Life's investment policy led to more and more dangerous practices, so did its lobbying structure increasingly depend on arrangements which, if exposed, were sure to alienate the very public and regulatory opinion that the company was trying to placate.[12]

2

The great industrial companies developed a political apparatus strikingly similar to and tightly interwoven with that of the Big Three. The Metropolitan and Prudential found the 1890's a time of rising supervisory and legislative challenges, as did their straight life peers. "The increasing dangers of hostile legislation" bothered the Metropolitan in 1891. It approved of the treatment of industrial companies in the 1892 New York Insurance Law, but had to work for the defeat of adverse bills in New Jersey and Massachusetts. President Hegeman and Vice-President Fiske personally attended to the threat in the Bay State "with the result, as is hoped, that if any laws are passed they will be in accord with the wishes of this Company." A law restricting child insurance threatened in Canada, but the Prudential was looking into it. The year 1893 saw "almost unprecedented trouble with the various Legislatures"; the Metropolitan's interests "had to be looked after in Connecticut, Pennsylvania, Massachusetts, Illinois, Mississippi, Kentucky, and Ohio." But practically all of these threats were fended off. Of a series of attempts at child insurance limitation which ran into the early 1900's, only Colorado's was successful.[13]

This record was the result of a distinctive system of political representation. Dryden shied from paid lobbyists or legislators: "We want to stay just as far away from State Capitols as we possibly can." As a result, Haley Fiske, the Metropolitan's omnicompetent vice-president, took on the same role as Fields and Hamilton. When Pennsylvania considered child insurance legislation in 1897, Fiske had "full charge" of the joint resistance of the Metropolitan, the Prudential, and the John Hancock. On the scene for a month, his special brand of suasion blocked the legislation.

Admirably adapted to the industrial companies' more limited legislative needs, this arrangement proved to be economical as well. The Prudential's legal expenses in 1899 were under $16,000; they climbed to $49,000 in 1904 chiefly because of the proposed merger with the Fidelity Trust. The Metropolitan's legislative costs between 1896 and 1905 were about $48,000 — plus an occasional special retainer to Hamilton. The John Hancock's expenses stayed under $6000 a year. Nevertheless, this was a highly ordered lobbying system. The companies contributed to Fiske's costs according to their size: two fifths each from the Metropolitan and the Prudential, one fifth from the John Hancock. Dryden complacently said of the arrangement, "we have found it more economical and often more efficient; instead of working at cross purposes there is a concentration and uniformity of effort."

The companies liked to think that this was a corruptionless form of political representation. The Metropolitan's board of directors declared in 1901 that its new policy of distributing some of its surplus to its industrial policyholders "has made the Company a powerful factor in political economy. It has repeatedly enabled us to defeat threatened hostile legislation without the corrupt use of money." But in Massachusetts, where "we had the fight of our lives" in early 1905, it was necessary to pay the newspapers a dollar a line to get the Metropolitan's case before the public. The company's finance committee in 1897 rewarded Fiske with a $15,000 bonus for his fight against the "bitter legislative attacks upon the business of the Company during the last 5 years, all of which attacks have, thus far, been defeated." It is difficult to imagine that this record was a tribute only to his eloquence.[14]

3

For all the complexity, sophistication, and apparent success of their political structures, the great firms were not satisfied with their relationship to state supervision. A sense of constant danger, of unending legislative imposition upon their prerogatives, oppressed company leaders. "With the beginning of every year," declared John McCall, "I daresay it is the feeling of every executive officer . . . that . . . we shall be badgered and harassed to death in every state of the Union by the introduction of bad bills of every kind." He estimated that three quarters of all insurance bills were introduced with a blackmailing intent. James Alexander asked, "Do Governments and Law Makers Regard Life Insurance from the Right Point of View?" and regretfully concluded that they did not. McCurdy found insurance supervision unique: "There is no other important branch of business in which the people would submit to such a sacrifice of the principles of free government, and such extreme paternalism, as is practiced by the States towards citizens who desire to enjoy the benefits of scientific methods of Insurance."

The dialogue of the industry echoed this view. One journal called most insurance legislation "the decrepit spawn of congenital idiocy"; another observed that since *Paul v. Virginia,* the 1868 Supreme Court decision upholding state insurance regulation, the business had been "delivered over, bound hand and foot, to the mercies of the various states." A Penn Mutual executive thought that insurance legislation was based on the theory that the enterprise "is among the necessary evils, and tolerable only when in bonds; that company managers would abuse their trust and oppress the public, in order to enrich themselves, were they not closely followed and watched." [15]

The climactic complaint was that the system of state regulation was expensively corrupt. One estimate had it that the large companies paid up to $250,000 a year to state examiners alone. A spokesman called for "the abolition of a system of state supervision of insurance under which blackmail has become a science and high crime and dishonesty flourishes." Hamilton declared that his chief concern was with "the outrageous bills introduced to tax the policyholders . . . for the purpose of adding to the revenue of the State, defended for no other reason than because the State needed the money." Here, perhaps, was the essence of the problem. The turn of the century saw the states increasingly committed to positive government — sometimes venal, sometimes in the public interest — and it was particularly easy to perform this role through the taxation and regulation of an enterprise both wealthy and quasi-public. Indeed, company spokesmen themselves found it impossible to oppose state regulation in principle. McCall admitted that "the evils of supervision are such as inhere in all governments, the evils of non-supervision are the evils of anarchy"; and even McCurdy declared that he was no opponent of state supervision as such.

Chauncey Depew expressed the companies' dilemma at the Armstrong inquiry. Pressed to defend a procompany New York law which allowed the attorney general to intercede for what Hughes called a purely private interest, Depew asked: "Well, is it purely private interest?" Just so; but the principle had at least as many possibilities for meaningful regulation as for legislative favoritism. For all their skill in containing the resulting pressures, there was no certainty that the great companies would be able to succeed indefinitely. The problem became acute in the early months of 1905: with the Equitable immobilized because of its managerial troubles, "a great many more states than usual had to be taken care of" by the two remaining members of the Big Three. The Armstrong investigation of that year hit companies already uncertain in their relationship to state supervision.[16]

More than burgeoning state regulation impaired the great firms' control over the political environment. In the state capital battlegrounds of lobbying and influence, they learned the bitter truth that corporate interests were far from monolithic; that noninsurance enterprises, and insurance companies themselves, were swayed by diverse and divisive purposes.

Hamilton had a sharp sense of the danger of legislation pushed "by other corporate interests endeavoring to remove the burden from their shoulders and place it on the life insurance policyholder." Mutual lobbyist Warren Thummel offered a case in point. The Nebraska legislature in 1902 had before it a general revenue bill with "very disastrous" implications for the great life companies. Rushing to the scene, Thummel found "a combination of other corporations" in control. "Every class of corporation was fighting . . . to get its own taxes as low as possible. The railroads were entirely too much for us. They had an organization complete before we even knew of the situation." This was not an isolated instance. "There are efforts being made all along the line for increased revenue, and the subject of those attacks . . . are corporations generally. We have nothing in common with any class of corporation, not even the fire insurance corporations, because they are usually against us . . . We make our own fight always."[17]

The unease engendered by this situation was even greater when the competing corporations were other life insurance firms. Hamilton told of persistent state efforts to tax the surrender value of life contracts, and ascribed it in part to the pressure of insurance companies offering no such advantage in their policies. Even in its home state, the New York Life in the early 1890's had reason to suspect the intentions of superintendent Pierce, once on the Mutual's payroll. Perkins thought that the New York *Times*' attacks on the company in 1891 were inspired by the Mutual, Pierce, and Tammany. The company's counsel labeled the ensuing insurance department examination one-sided and unfair. The obvious counter to this situation was an opposing circle of political influence. Hegeman invited McCurdy to participate in a luncheon to be attended by Alexander, McCall, New York superintendent Pierce, Massachusetts commissioner Merrill, and Massachusetts Legislative Insurance Committee chairman Morse. The Mutual president "did not care to walk into that combination without knowing what was going on." Except for Pierce "these parties always hunt together and against us," and he preferred "to have them come at him in some other way than through his stomach." [18]

These divisive tendencies culminated in a major contest between the New York Life and the Mutual. By 1900 the rise of the New York Life to industry-wide supremacy was so pronounced that McCurdy's firm backed a bill in the New York legislature limiting a company's business to insurance worth $1,500,000,000. It was difficult for the New York Life to oppose such a bill publicly: the Equitable did not object to it, and Governor Theodore Roosevelt seemed to favor it as a reasonable restraint.

Perkins responded to the challenge with all of the ingenuity that he applied to his fight with the Mutual in Prussia and Russia. Lobbyists Hamilton and Edward McCall assured him that "much can be done in [a] quiet way to hold [the] matter up." Although the Mutual was "willing to pay" to secure the limitation bill, Perkins and Hamilton were "laying all the pipes that can be laid at Albany." Benjamin Odell, soon to be governor, received a $2500 retainer. With typical subtlety Perkins thought it wise to induce another state's commissioner to support the bill — and a limitation of investments that "would scare the liver and lights out of [the Mutual]."

Most effectively of all, Perkins exerted direct pressure at the highest political levels. He planned to speak to Mark Hanna: "I am going to lock him up in a room and paint him a story in regard to this Limitation Bill that will make the few hairs on his head stand up straight. I am going to tell him that if Platt lets this bill go through now he can count us entirely out of any support next Fall, and he can figure that all the insurance agents of New York State will be up in arms against the Republican Party." Perkins also met privately with Theodore Roosevelt for the first time, the beginning of one of the more significant associations of the period. Quickly he eased the governor's distrust of McCall and of the New York Life; deftly he ended Roosevelt's support of the Limitation Bill. By early March of 1900 McCurdy conceded defeat, and the threat was over. A New York Life Albany lobbyist jubilantly reported: "We had our machinery so working that there was not a chance to get the bill out of committee." [19]

A few days after their meeting, Perkins noted, Roosevelt in speeches on the trusts declared "that we should try to regulate them before we tried to strangle them." He traced this line of argument to his talk with the governor, "in which I said that it seemed to me the State ought to try to regulate before it tried to strangulate its great life insurance companies." [20] Perkins overstated his influence, but his was a trend of thought common to the executives of the great companies. Frustrated by the problems of state regulation, yet flushed with the sense of their corporate power, insurance leaders looked for new possibilities in the relationship between the corporation and the commonwealth. Increasingly they acted on the assumption that these lay within the purview of the national government.

XIV * The Companies and National Power

The tumultuous developments of the 1890's, which suddenly made state insurance supervision unreliable and even menacing, also thrust the great companies into national politics. Yet Bryan and free silver, the generative issue, was an immediate rather than a fundamental cause. By their very growth into a substantial corporate group with widespread economic influence, the great insurance companies came into contact with politicians of prominence. At the turn of the century, Supreme Court Justice Rufus W. Peckham, Senators William J. Sewell and Preston B. Plumb, Navy Secretary William C. Whitney, and Elihu Root served on the Mutual's board of trustees. Former Secretary of Agriculture J. Sterling Morton suggested himself, without success, as a candidate for board membership. Hyde and McCurdy, men of large affairs, dealt closely and easily with United States senators. Aldrich of Rhode Island responded to the requests of the Equitable head; Sewell of New Jersey was something more than responsive to the dicta of McCurdy. John McCall, an active Democrat high in the New York business world, commanded President Grover Cleveland's attention.

Insurance executives at first used their political connections in a pragmatic and fragmented way. They defined their corporate self-interest in simple, straightforward terms, and called upon their friends in power accordingly. McCurdy, for example, concerned himself with such constricted matters as his brother-in-law's desire to rent a house to the government, or with a congressional bill allowing the Post Office Department to purchase Mutual property in Asbury Park. As yet he had no broader political vistas. He declared in May 1895, "The Company sedulously refrains from any intervention in the politics of the State or the country at large. Its membership and its directory are composed of men of both parties, and no questions are ever asked as to which party a member of either may belong." The companies' indifference to larger issues appeared, too, in the lack of campaign contributions before 1896, and in George Perkins' outburst of laissez-faire in 1894: "when our friends at Washington become weary of well-doing, and go home to their loved ones, there is no telling how the business situation may brighten." [1]

But the economic dislocations of the 1890's increasingly intruded on the executives' consciousness. The Wilson-Gorman tariff first caught their attention. Perkins declared in 1893: "it is the Tariff more than the Silver that is scaring people." McCurdy was more concerned over the bill's income tax provision, and in unusual cooperation with the New York Life had company agents collect antitax petitions from policyholders.

For institutions that were substantial creditors in the national economy, led by men who increasingly thought of themselves as financiers, the silver controversy was the most fearsome of the time's developments. McCurdy, surveying the situation in early 1894, feared that conditions "presage a further storm of free silver and cheap money legislation." In 1895 each of the Big Three subscribed $2500 to the New York Chamber of Commerce's "sound money agitation fund." [2]

The election of 1896 transformed the companies' political participation from an occasional and casual indulgence into a positive, organized expression of managerial policy. Political influence, once negligently accepted, now was actively sought. The business community widely believed that Bryan's victory meant far more than a change of power from one party to another; that radicalism, repudiation, even revolution, were the likely consequences. For the great insurance companies, the contest was particularly meaningful. And their special sense of corporate power heightened their readiness to influence the election's outcome.

The consequent result was the first massive infusion of insurance company money into presidential politics. The New York Life contributed $50,000 to the cause of McKinley; the Mutual, $15,000; the Equitable, an unspecified but substantial amount. The industrial firms, too, acted out of a sense of crisis: the Prudential contributed $6000 to the Republicans; the Metropolitan gave $7500 to the G.O.P. and $1000 to the Palmer-Buckner Gold Democratic ticket. A few lesser firms — the Aetna and the Penn Mutual — also gave; but more of them — the John Hancock, the Security Mutual, the Northwestern Mutual, the New England Mutual — did not.[3]

Insurance men defended this break with tradition as a necessary response to a special crisis. The Penn Mutual noted that its only similar action had been a $5000 contribution to Philadelphia's Committee of Public Safety in 1861, at the outbreak of the Civil War. McCall, until 1896 a loyal Democrat, declared passionately: "I made up my mind I would do all in my power to defeat that candidate and that platform, and I did it with my heart and soul . . . I consented to a payment to defeat Free Silver, not to defeat the Democratic Party, [but] to defeat the Free Silver heresy, and I thank God that I did it." The Metropolitan's directors considered their company's contribution "more a matter of morals than it was of policy"; they were fearful of "the disturbance of values and the impairment of those things which we had which made for security of the policyholders." [4]

The companies' participation went beyond contributions. Even McCurdy, cautious enough to refuse a donation to the Honest Money League less than a month before the election, did his part. He told Hanna that he would not ordinarily let a Mutual agent in Arkansas run for governor, "but the maintenance of the gold standard for our National currency and the payment in gold or its equivalent of all obligations, is vital to this Company, and I therefore consent — it being understood that he is to devote himself chiefly to the discussion of the supreme issue." Hyde was swept by the fevers of the campaign, lunching with Hanna and Cornelius Bliss, treasurer of the Republican National Committee.[5]

For McCall and especially for Perkins, 1896 meant still more. The New York Life vice-president was a horrified observer at the Democratic convention, and feared that the New York business community failed to recognize the strength of silver sentiment in the South and West. The company actively distributed progold literature — to the extent that Colorado officials threatened to throw it out of the state. Perkins' ingenuity found other ways to help the cause. He got up small pamphlets listing the 1892 electoral vote and inviting the recipient to predict the 1896 results. The ostensible purpose was to get names of prospective policyholders for New York Life agents; but the pamphlets served also as a rough sort of poll on the course of the campaign. Fully

750,000 were distributed by mid-October. Returns came in at a rate of 1000 a day, and Perkins hurried the results to Republican leaders.[6]

2

After 1896 every great company, except the Metropolitan, remained enmeshed to some extent in national political affairs. Not surprisingly the New York Life, which most thoroughly played the role of the puissant company in other areas of the life insurance enterprise, assumed a place of special prominence in the field of national politics.

McCall the old Albany politico and Perkins the ebullient, questing man of big business affairs were ideally suited by background and inclination for political activism. Perkins' role was particularly illuminating. The ideology which made him the spokesman of the most dynamic aspects of the life insurance business enabled him to identify with equally aggressive politicos. His closest political friendships were with the young and ambitious senator from Indiana, Albert J. Beveridge, and with Theodore Roosevelt. Common values and beliefs bound these men together: the strenuous life in politics, the mystique of a dynamic new generation rising to political dominance, the righteousness and desirability of American imperialism. Unabashedly they reveled in energy and power. Perkins exuberantly wrote to Beveridge of "this country where there is life and vigor in the air, — where we are doing things, accomplishing things, seeing and making the 'wheels go 'round.' " The Indiana senator told his New York Life friend of his response when Roosevelt mentioned dining with McCall and J. P. Morgan. " 'What!' said I, 'the President of the greatest government in the world, the President of the greatest insurance company in the world and the greatest constructive financier yet developed among mankind — well, that is a triumvirate that might well rule the world!' "[7]

This exhilaration found an outlet in American imperialism. Perkins, like many other businessmen, at first opposed entanglement in Cuba: "A few of us have believed that we ought to be able to get out of our Spanish difficulty without a war." The *Maine* explosion did not unduly excite him. He proposed to leave for Europe in the midst of the crisis, and jauntily wired a friend: "Will sail next week. Congressional library closed for fear magazines will blow up. Ta-ta." The great companies went out of their way to support the conciliatory policies of President McKinley and his ambassador to Spain, onetime Metropolitan counsel Stewart L. Woodford.[8]

But once the war began, Perkins moved steadily toward an aggressive expansionism. His initial ironic pique with the upset of war — "This thing of any nation being allowed to interfere with the great philanthropic work I am engaged in is a dispensation of Providence that I myself cannot understand" — did not last. The Philippines and Cuba interested him: "I cannot help feeling that there is only one thing for us to do and this is keep them all." American expansionism, he now saw, dovetailed neatly with the growing overseas business of the New York Life: "I cannot see how it is possible for a nation of our size and commercial magnitude to any longer hope to keep out of international questions. How perfectly absurd for a country harboring the Home Office of the Oldest International Life Insurance Company in the world to disclaim any idea of mixing up in the greatest international questions of the world!" Perkins and Beveridge stimulated each other: "You and I and other men of our ages are going to see to it that America does not stand still in our day!" Perkins participated in Beveridge's successful 1899 senatorial campaign; and soon thereafter the New York Life executive was in Washington talking to Hanna and Dawes about the new senator's committee assignments.[9]

The election of 1900 was another opportunity for the New York Life to show its political prowess. At least $35,000 went to the Republican campaign fund, but McCall and Perkins again did more than contribute money. The New York Life president emotionally told McKinley: "Everything I am and everything I have and can control shall be devoted to the work of making your triumph in 1900 greater than the victory of 1896." Perkins, identifying himself with the "younger element in the party," worked closely with Beveridge. He reassured Roosevelt about the vice-presidential nomination; he placed his company's Chicago counsel at the service of G.O.P. factotum Charles G. Dawes; he stayed in close touch with Hanna and Bliss.

Perkins resurrected his 1896 method of determining public opinion by a pamphlet questionnaire. By mid-October 700,000 copies had been distributed, particularly in doubtful states and in workingmen's areas such as New York's East Side. In addition to eliciting opinion, the pamphlets contained a subtly worded defense of imperialism — "a pretty strong campaign document," Perkins observed.

He reacted to McKinley's decisive victory with the manner of someone who had played a major role in securing it. Solemnly he wrote to the Chief Executive: "All hail to the first President of the Twentieth

Century"; slyly to Roosevelt: "What are we coming to when a man having so much influence with Van Wyck, Croker and Devery [Tammany leaders with whom T.R. warred while governor] can be elected Vice President on the Republican ticket?"; archly to Hanna: "You naughty wicked man, how could you be so greedy." With McKinley's death in September 1901 and Roosevelt's accession to the presidency, Perkins — and the New York Life — had an entrée to national political power matched by few other corporations.[10]

In this effulgent atmosphere, the New York Life's political influence waxed mightily. Its contacts were nation-wide, as widespread as its state lobbying system. James H. Millard got his Nebraska Senate seat through New York Life Washington lobbyist William C. Beer's connections with Hanna and McKinley, and through Perkins' influence with the Burlington Railroad. When a vacancy appeared in the Senate Finance Committee, Millard asked the New York Life to support him for the seat. "You can well understand that it would be no detriment," he wrote to Beer, "to the interests of our good friends in New York." Chester I. Long, sent to the Senate by the Kansas legislature in 1903, was grateful for Perkins' assistance. Kansas politicos Joseph L. Bristow and Charles Curtis were in touch with agent Beer, as was Senator Joseph B. Foraker of Ohio. Beer asked Foraker to support a prospective state attorney general acceptable both to the New York Life and to Standard Oil because he "will be favorably disposed on almost any reasonable question which may be presented to him."

Perkins and McCall took a special interest in the Department of Commerce and Labor, an example of the friendly partnership between big government and big business that appealed both to Roosevelt and to the New York Life officers. At the President's request, Perkins put his considerable influence behind the bill establishing the department. He kept in close touch with George B. Cortelyou, the first Secretary of Commerce, and with typical business ingenuity proposed that Cortelyou certify the New York Life's assets.[11] From the defensive anti-Bryanism of 1896 Perkins had moved to positive calls upon the national government.

This growing activity in the arena of national politics, most notable in the New York Life, appeared elsewhere in the society of great companies. Equitable president Alexander nervously reacted to the New York Life's preferred position, warning James Hazen Hyde that they had better get close to Roosevelt or "Perkins will try and poison his mind." Alexander at first was disinclined to contribute to the Republican campaign in 1900, but he found it expedient to change his mind before election day. The Equitable's $25,000 donation to the Republican Congressional Campaign Committee in 1902 bespoke its leaders' eagerness to establish closer rapport with the administration.

McCurdy's interest in politics developed slowly. In 1898 he still was cautious: "It is not . . . the province of a company like this to enter the political field, or to take any part in the conflict of parties; or even in the public discussion of public questions." Unwilling to serve on the National Civic Federation, where Perkins was active, he continued to treat politics primarily in terms of his company's most direct and parochial self-interest. Thus he utilized his contacts with leading Republicans for business matters such as his Prussian difficulties or the end of the Spanish-American War stamp tax on life insurance policies. He exhorted New Jersey's Senator Sewell to secure the deepening of Buttermilk Channel in New York harbor, which would benefit the Mutual's Brooklyn Wharf and Warehouse interests. When he worked against immigration restriction, it was because he feared its effects on steamship and dock company securities held by his firm. But the Mutual's continuing — and expanding — Republican campaign contributions, and McCurdy's support of Cortelyou for the post of Secretary of Commerce, suggested that he, too, felt the lure of national politics. By 1905 the Mutual had a "gray ghost" of a lobbyist in Washington who was "doing all kinds of stunts" for the company.[12]

Evidence abounded that the great firms were a palpable political force. Prudential president John F. Dryden entered the United States Senate in 1902. A complaisant New Jersey legislature appointed him to the seat left by the death of William J. Sewell, who had faithfully served the interests of the Prudential and the Mutual. The New York Life's Perkins also had a hand in Dryden's selection. In the Senate Dryden was, in the words of Lincoln Steffens, "the chief visible representative of the system," a spokesman for the Prudential, the Equitable, and the Pennsylvania Railroad.

The election of 1904 demonstrated how settled and substantial the firms' political participation had become. The Democrats offered not the fearsome Bryan but the impeccably conservative Judge Alton B. Parker; yet life insurance company contributions to the G.O.P. were greater than ever. The Mutual gave $40,000, $5000 more than in 1900, and an additional $2500 to the Republican Congressional Campaign

Committee; the Equitable and the New York Life gave the most substantial of all donations, $50,000 each; and the Prudential contributed $10,000. Later explanations of these contributions varied: "we were menaced by the St. Louis [Democratic] platform and we rather feared that snake, no matter whether it bore the head of Bryan or Parker, and we thought it our duty to scotch it"; it was "to the best interests of the Equitable . . . that the Republican party should be re-elected and kept in power"; a Democratic victory "would probably result in Tariff agitation and other legislation attempted that would be of such a character as to upset business." But it was difficult to read danger and tension into the placid contest of 1904. Hughes delicately asked a Mutual officer: "The size of your contribution I suppose indicates the remoteness of the danger?" [13] The truth of the matter was that large-scale campaign contributions had become yet another expression of the drive to power and place that animated the great firms.

But as in their other forms of power-oriented corporate expression, the companies' involvement in national politics led to ultimately embarrassing subterfuge and stealth. Every effort was made to conceal the New York Life's 1896, 1900, and 1904 presidential campaign contributions. Both McCall's company and the Mutual ignored their 1896 contributions when reporting their political expenditures to Western state officials. McCall explained this disingenuousness: "I was not in the frame of mind to trace through our books with this man [Governor Culberson of Texas] to help him find this thing, because I understood that he was inimical." In 1904 Perkins paid the Republican National Committee by personal check, and was then reimbursed by J. P. Morgan and Company with funds belonging to the New York Life. To do these things, and then to justify them, as McCall did, by reference to the prerogatives of executive authority, was to be dangerously at odds with prevalent public expectations of life insurance company performance.[14]

National political activity proved to be unsatisfying as well as unsafe. A sizable gap separated the firms' expectations of the national political system from what that system was able to do for them. Limited successes were within their scope: the government placed a stamp tax on insurance policies during the Spanish-American War, and the Metropolitan managed to lessen the burden to a fifth of what had been expected; in 1901 the companies successfully ended the levy. But generally their awesome affiliations produced miniscule returns: the courtesies of the New York port for a company executive returning from Europe ("You know of course the connections between the New York Life and J. P. Morgan and Company"); a request that the New York Life be made a woman's agent in the adjudication of her Federal pension claim ("relying upon your memory of what we have endeavored to do to uphold President McKinley and all that he stands for, I am sure we can depend on you to grant us this additional favor"). When the government was asked for more substantial service — dramatically so in the case of the Big Three's requests for aid in their overseas difficulties — the response was scant. The central issue of the great firms' relationship with the national government was not so much what Washington might do *to* life insurance as what it might do *for* it. McCall sadly gave the apparent answer in 1905: "Insurance has been held not to be commerce, and how a Republican Government at Washington could help the New York Life is past finding out." [15]

This, however, was disillusionment after the fact. It came at the tag end of the companies' boldest bid for aid from national authority: their drive for Federal regulation of the life insurance business.

3

Insurance company restlessness with the structure of state supervision was as old as the structure itself. As early as the 1850's insurance lawyers argued before the Supreme Court that the due process clause in state constitutions protected their clients from legislation. The first substantial proposal for an alternative to state control came after 1865. Federal authority had a passing popularity in the aftermath of a war fought and won for the sanctity of the Union. It was to this concept that a portion of the insurance business turned. Congress was bombarded with company petitions calling for national legislation to supplant or modify state regulations. Insurance leaders unburdened themselves to Elizur Wright, the grand old man of insurance supervision: "State lines appear to me perfectly absurd, if raised as barriers against free commerce . . . The diverse . . . laws, taxes, returns etc. of the different States are becoming intolerable . . . One return — one tax — one supervisory control for all companies." In 1866 the firms most interested in national supervision organized the Chamber of Life Insurance as a mouthpiece for their interests. Congress considered a bill to establish a National Chamber of Insurance in 1865, but the measure was buried in the House Judiciary Committee. President Winston of the mighty Mutual opposed the plan ("We should . . . be placed between the upper and nether millstones of United States and State [Sovereignty] taxation and control") and the countervailing pressures—for state control, for laissez-faire—were too great. The New York insurance commissioner contemptuously dismissed this "abortive attempt . . . to wrest from the several States their legitimate and constitutional functions of supervision and control." [16]

State regulation was attacked also in the courts, but with no greater success. A group of New York fire insurance companies challenged a Virginia law that required deposits and licenses from out-of-state firms. In its *Paul v. Virginia* decision (1868) the Supreme Court specifically upheld the state's regulatory power. It dealt a heavy blow to the movement for national insurance regulation when it said: "Issuing a policy of insurance is not a transaction of commerce." Elizur Wright worriedly wrote of the decision: "This loss of nationality is a very serious matter. If there is any possibility of . . . securing to life insurance the supervision and protection of national law . . . the guardians of life insurance should now bestir themselves." But the wartime respectability of central authority was rapidly ebbing, and the *Paul* decision remained a massive judicial obstacle to Federal insurance regulation.

As competitive chaos and the structure of state regulation grew conjointly in the 1870's, the large firms warmed to the idea of Federal control. Mutual actuary Sheppard Homans told Wright in 1870: "I begin to have hope of the *nationalization* of life insurance"; he was "now in a position to second your efforts in that direction." Charlton Lewis, the company's chief attorney, opposed national regulation in the 1860's, but by 1873 was ready to agree with Wright on "the evils and dangers of state supervision." Suggestively, the acquiescent New York insurance commissioners of the 1870's spoke out in favor of supervision by the Federal government.[17]

This change of heart had no immediate consequences. In the 1870's and 1880's the energies and skills of insurance managers were devoted solely to the expansion of their enterprise; they had neither the will nor the means to initiate national legislation. But in the 1890's the industry attained its maturity, and renewed its efforts to better the regulatory environment. John M. Pattison, the politically minded president of Cincinnati's Union Central Life Insurance Company, took the lead. A member of Congress (later he would be governor of Ohio), Pattison introduced a bill in 1892 providing for a National Bureau of Insurance within the Treasury Department. He sought—but did not get—the assistance of the industry's giants in his cause. McCurdy saw no benefits from a National Bureau "unless it should in effect abolish the forty independent State Departments, and that, in view of the pertinacity with which the doctrine of State Sovereignty is held by most of our States, is more than problematical." Bereft of support, Pattison's bill died a quiet death in committee.[18]

As more vigorous, and occasionally hostile, insurance supervision appeared in the 1890's, business leaders came to look on Federal regulation with new sympathy and understanding. McCurdy was particularly influenced by the Mutual's Prussian troubles and the consequent need to call on the United States government for aid. In 1895 he wanted Cleveland to speak of Federal supervision (defined by McCurdy as "strictly . . . statistical in its character") in the President's annual message to Congress, and to stress the magnitude and the interstate character of the life insurance business. The insurance press and commissioners' reports took a new interest in the matter. George Perkins, with McCall's encouragement, advocated Federal regulation by 1898. As in the late 1860's, the Hartford insurance companies were particularly committed: Senator Orville H. Platt of Connecticut introduced a national supervision bill in 1897. McCurdy supported it, but the powerful Henry Hyde was no friend to the idea. "I am so driven with the cares and important business interests of the Equitable, that I do not desire to enter into any campaign [for Federal regulation]," he told one advocate, adding that "in the abstract I do not approve of your views." [19]

Yet by the early 1900's even the Equitable's opposition weakened. Alexander shared some of Hyde's disinterest in the subject — he was willing to have actuary Charlton Lewis write an article on Federal control, for "it doesn't make any difference to us which side of the question he takes." But "hampering legislation and unwise official supervision" helped him to understand why "many who have the interests of widows and orphans at heart look longingly to . . . a National Department at Washington."

No uncertainties impeded the more politically attuned McCurdy, McCall, Perkins, and Dryden. The Mutual president solicited Alexander's support for Federal regulation in 1901, and fitted the movement into the prevalent neo-Hamiltonianism of the time: "The extraordinary industrial development of the American people . . . working through the great natural agencies of steam and electricity coupled with the wide diffusion of commercial credits, has . . . practically obliterated State lines." Obstructive state insurance legislation was "injurious to that 'general welfare' to which the Federal Government . . . is solemnly dedicated." Perkins too felt constrained by established institutions — "I think this country has moved so far since the Spanish-American War that our laws are entirely inadequate to the general business of the country" — and supported the drive for a National Bureau of Insurance. But the most dedicated partisan of Federal regulation was Prudential president John F. Dryden. Convinced that insurance, as "the first business of the land" and "in its very nature . . . different from . . . the ordinary corporation," needed special supervision, Dryden argued that national control of necessity would benefit the great companies. As a United States senator from New Jersey he spearheaded the movement for congressional insurance legislation.[20]

More than an elevated sense of national and entrepreneurial destiny animated the movement for Federal regulation. The irritations cropping up ever more frequently in the system of state supervision heightened interest in a single, presumably malleable, authority. As Dryden frankly phrased it: "Every company would naturally prefer just one set of regulations, for that would make it so much easier to shape policy." New York Life lobbyist Andrew Hamilton declared: "I am such a great believer . . . in national supervision . . . that I have incurred considerable expenditure . . . in attempting to create a sentiment in favor of [it]." Much was made of the need for "protection from the inharmonious, exacting, and often conflicting laws of fifty different States [and territories]," of "the inconveniences, hardships, impositions and scandals that too often spring out of State Supervision." Lighter taxation was one commonly expected boon. An enthusiast pointed out that in 1903 Federal supervision cost national banks only $325,000, while Wisconsin alone extracted $500,000 from insurance companies doing business within the state. A Mutual lobbyist assumed that Federal regulation "would decrease the costs of doing business . . . very much." Substantial support for the companies' proposals came from the industry at large, from the law and the other professions, and from the universities. The agitation was a tribute to the great firms' puissance, and to the widespread readiness of influential circles to respond to sophisticated concepts of an entente between big business and big government.[21]

No place was more receptive than the Federal government itself. Roosevelt's new Department of Commerce and Labor in particular sought insurance supervision. Perkins and McCall supported the creation of the department in 1903, hoping for the inclusion of a Bureau of Insurance headed by the amenable District of Columbia insurance superintendent, Thomas E. Drake. No such unit materialized, but the department's Bureau of Corporations was granted an information-gathering power which embraced "corporations engaged in insurance." The first commissioner of corporations, James R. Garfield, responded by collecting material on the state regulatory structure, clearly with the intent of suggesting how that structure might be supplanted. In March 1904 Garfield conferred with New York Life president McCall and general counsel George Hubbell "for the purpose of considering the work of the Bureau of Corporations in relation to insurance." He asked their aid in selecting the Bureau's insurance expert, and they suggested William A. Fricke, former Wisconsin commissioner — and current New York Life lobbyist. Although Fricke's ignorance of fire and marine insurance matters scotched his appointment, Hubbell and McCall continued to look for the right man for the bureau. Not surprisingly, Commissioner Garfield endorsed Federal insurance regulation. In 1905 the bureau supported Senator Dryden's efforts for a Federal supervision act and influenced the American Bar Association Insurance Law Committee's favorable report on national control.

The Bureau of Corporations' position reflected the view of the administration. Friendly with George Perkins, aware of the great companies' substantial Republican campaign contributions, President Theodore Roosevelt could be accounted a special friend of the enterprise. In 1902 he spoke approvingly of life insurance companies as "practically mutual benefit societies — especially helpful to men of moderate means." He strongly backed the idea of Federal regulation. In his December 1904 message to Congress he proposed that the Bureau of Corporations be given powers over interstate insurance, and in his 1905 message, after close consultation with company representatives, he made a substantial appeal for Federal control. His statement, appearing as it did in the midst of the Armstrong investigation, spoke of the need for stricter supervision of an errant enterprise. But its source clearly was the confidence and verve of the great companies. Perkins told Roosevelt: "It is the one thing which in my judgment, is absolutely necessary if the commercial leaders of this country are to go on in their development of our interests, at home and abroad, on a foundation sufficiently strong to endure and bring to us the commanding position to which our people are entitled in the commerce of the world, during the next quarter of a century." [22]

The movement for national supervision was an especially evocative expression of the great companies' quest for power and place in early twentieth century America. Yet it came to an untoward end. One difficulty was the widespread opposition to the plan. Within the insurance business, men of substance such as Morgan J. Bulkeley, president of the Aetna and like Dryden a United States senator, vigorously rejected Federal regulation. Lesser firms, particularly in the South and West, frowned on the plan as a device of the great Eastern companies. Congress in 1905 began to pass the railroad rate-fixing legislation that culminated in the Hepburn Act; and this "effectively killed the enthusiasm of the fire officers for national supervision." The general manager of the Phoenix Mutual of Hartford spoke for many of his peers when he declared that he would rather rely on "the almost automatic operation of natural forces — the laws of progress and the effect of competition — which are always to be preferred to arbitrary restriction." Finally, many state insurance commissioners opposed a plan calculated to end their power.[23]

Outside of the industry, both conservatives and reformers opposed Federal regulation. Attorney Moorfield Storey gravely warned: "If the door is once opened, it is opened wide to federal supervision of another class of business . . . What we want to do is to set our faces against the first step." The president of the Chase National Bank feared a corrupt government insurance department, and the stalwart New York *Sun* spoke of the movement as a "symptom of the general . . . mania for . . . increasing the power of the government, Federal, state, or municipal." The *Commercial and Financial Chronicle* argued that insurance was essentially private enterprise, "a Business which offers the least conceivable occasion or excuse for anything which savors of . . . Government control." Louis Brandeis rejected the plan as the creature of the companies: "Federal supervision would serve only to centralize still further the power of our Government and to increase still further the powers of the corporations." Even Roosevelt had to admit: "I am by no means sure that . . . Federal Supervision will be up to the Massachusetts standard." [24]

Especially potent was the legal view, dating back to *Paul v. Virginia* in 1868, that the insurance contract was not an article in interstate commerce, and that the Federal government thus had no power to supervise the industry. A prominent attorney engaged by several large companies to prepare an opinion on the issue found the *Paul* decision binding, and saw no reason to expect its overturn. The legal literature of the time generally upheld this view.[25]

But the final test was political: the fate of Federal insurance regulation in the congressional arena. Abortive attempts were made to raise the issue in Congress in 1901 and 1903. A bill in December 1904 tried to attach insurance regulation to the National Banking Act; but the most serious efforts came in 1905 and 1906. In the wake of Roosevelt's December 1904 appeal for national control, Dryden again submitted his plan for a National Bureau of Insurance within the Department of Commerce and Labor. Perkins considered this an especially "opportune" time for the bill; as indeed it was, with the Equitable's management troubles coming into public view. However, the measure never got beyond the Senate's Judiciary Committee. In December Senator Dryden tried again, sententiously announcing: "By this bill the business of insurance is made a national business interest." In the House, Butler Ames of Massachusetts proposed that the District of Columbia insurance department be transferred to Commerce, there to act as the nucleus of a system of national regulation; and Roosevelt seized upon this as a practical alternative. But all efforts failed. In the spring of 1906, the Judiciary committees of the House and Senate unanimously concluded that Congress was without authority to regulate the life insurance business. The Ames Bill became so burdened with amendments while in committee that it never appeared before the House.[26]

Ostensibly, the drive for federal regulation foundered on the rock of doubtful constitutionality. Even its most committed government supporters questioned its legality. Bureau of Corporations commissioner Garfield concluded in November 1905: "in view of the decisions of the Supreme Court, I was not justified in attempting to exercise any jurisdiction over the insurance companies." His successor in the bureau, Herbert Knox Smith, observed, "The present condition of statutory law and court decisions is very much against any theory that this Government has a right to exercise supervision over insurance." While preparing his December 1905 plea for national control, Roosevelt thought it "doubtful whether Congress will assert its power over the insurance business, and it is even doubtful whether it has the power to assert."

Other supporters flagged too. The American Bar Association in 1906 had serious second thoughts about the constitutionality of Federal regulation, and an insurance column in the *Independent,* traditionally friendly to the large firms, sharply warned that "the net result of increasing the power of the Federal Government . . . would probably be to render impregnable the position and power of a comparatively small number of men in the insurance business who would co-operate in controlling the Federal Bureau, just as they have controlled . . . the insurance commissioners and legislatures of certain states." Equitable counsel Paul Cravath advised president Paul Morton in February 1906 not to support the Dryden bill. He argued that if it should pass, and then be declared unconstitutional by the Supreme Court, "the result would be to unnecessarily emphasize the extent to which the States are independent of Congress, so far as the control of the insurance business is concerned." Even McCurdy, hitherto strong for Federal regulation, thought by November 1905 that "these questions are rather academic at present." [27]

The obvious source of these doubts and second thoughts was the Armstrong insurance investigation. The year 1905 turned out to be not a year filled with the triumphs of a proud corporate group, but rather a time of troubles: of scandals, of exposés, of the climactic New York inquiry. The damaging consequences of the companies' quest for power now came in for their full accounting.

Big business is an amiable monster, far kindlier and more innocent than anything Machiavelli could have anticipated.

George Santayana, *The Genteel Tradition at Bay*

Part Six * The Limits of Power

We have seen how the very process of corporate growth evoked conditions that checked, or put in jeopardy, the companies' quest for power. New York's Armstrong investigation of 1905, and the governmental restraints that emerged from it, thus supplemented limiting factors already at work. By focusing public and political attention on the nature of the society of companies, the inquiry added bite to the constraining process.

As a result, the companies' managerial leadership, corporate goals, foreign business, investment activities, and political relationships rapidly changed after 1905. Their disengagement from power was substantially complete by 1910. The consequence was a new corporate visage, less power-oriented but more consistently viable, which has stood the life insurance enterprise in good stead during the ensuing half century.

XV * 1905

The legislative investigation is the morality play of American society. Like any well-wrought drama, the successful investigation produces a great catharsis — of the presumed social ill, of an aroused public indignation. The Armstrong life insurance investigation of 1905 was one of the most spectacular of its genre. Never before had a legislative committee subjected a group of major corporations to such thorough and searching scrutiny. Never before had so vigorous and disinterested an investigator as Charles Evans Hughes worked with such freedom and to such effect. Never before, and scarcely since, has an inquiry produced such substantial corrective legislation. There is a more than casual correlation between the lustiness of the society of companies and the vigor of the investigation that finally contained them.

At first glance, the Armstrong inquiry was not a particularly appropriate expression of early twentieth century reform. Monopoly and the trust — the consolidated threat to free competition — was the bogy of the time. The large life insurance companies, however, constituted a broadly based, indeed expanding, oligopoly which, whatever its other sins, did not drive competing firms to the wall. Nor could a society that freely judged enterprises in moral terms (Roosevelt's "good" and "bad" trusts) say that the great life companies were more conspicuously sinful than their peers, for the firms committed themselves to at least the ideology of public responsibility and a quasi-public function.

But it was precisely these entrepreneurial qualities that gave the Armstrong investigation its special bite, and made the great life insurance companies the chief corporate object of progressive reform. Attorney

General William H. Moody observed that "this tremendous insurance power" was "pulled down like a house of straw — not by any prosecutions, but by public opinion." The same urbanizing, rootless Americans who responded to the marketing appeals of the great companies looked askance at the firms' assumption of corporate power. Here in essence was the paradox of progressive America, dependent upon, yet fearing, the corporate devices of a matured, urban-industrial society. The strongly procorporation *Commercial and Financial Chronicle* found "so much that is unsavory, so much that offends the moral sense" in the Equitable disclosures. John G. Johnson, an attorney of the old school whose moral sense allowed him to serve Standard Oil, nevertheless told his colleague Paul Cravath, "there is such a damned scandal about everything connected with the Equitable, that I would prefer not to appear as the recipient of any moneys connected with it." As the New York Life's actuary perceptively noted, those setting out to reform the companies were interested primarily in purifying the existing, middle class oriented insurance structure, not in extending it to the other, poorer segments of the population. He concluded that this was essentially a consumers' revolt against the cost of the product.[1]

Other elements in the companies' success contributed to their downfall. Their oligopolistic rather than monopolistic nature, their advanced political practices, public relations, marketing methods, and investment structure, made them in some ways the most formidable of all corporate groups. Theirs was the power not of monopoly, not only of bigness, but of maturity and sophistication. Because they were thus in a special way at odds with the accepted business values of the time, they were the object of a special effort to bring them back to a socially acceptable corporate role.

2

The origins of the Armstrong investigation did not foreshadow its destructive impact on the pre-1905 society of great companies. The first substantial criticism of the companies came in a series of articles in *Everybody's* by a reformed stock manipulator, Thomas W. Lawson. During the summer of 1904 Lawson spelled out the iniquities of Wall Street freebooters, generally men and interests with whom he himself had tangled. The Big Three's relationships with investment bankers was one of his targets, and he clashed sharply with a Mutual attorney in the press. But Lawson's questionable reputation and motives — he may have been part of a speculative group seeking control of the Equitable's stock — vitiated the force of his attack.[2]

In early 1905, however, the Equitable's difficulties became public knowledge and set off the sequence of events leading to the Armstrong investigation. The time was nearing when James Hazen Hyde would have complete control of his Equitable stock. Company officials motivated by internal corporate rather than external financial reasons blew the struggle wide open. On January 31, 1905, Hyde gave a lavish party at Sherry's, an ill-advised affair (though in the flamboyant manner of the society of great companies) which the press magnified into a "French ball" of Lucullan proportions. On this pretext, a group of Equitable officers headed by President Alexander petitioned the board of directors to permit policyholder voting for Equitable directors, and protested Vice-President Hyde's continuation in office. Other considerations aside, Hyde's behavior was unacceptable to deeply involved "company men" like Alexander and Gage Tarbell.

But from the first, this was more than a struggle between a wayward, irresponsible youth and a concerned corporate management. Substantial financial interests were fighting for the tempting prize of Equitable stock control. The power of the financiers involved — George Gould, Thomas F. Ryan, E. H. Harriman — focused public attention on the situation. Thus the very strengths of the Equitable — its wealth, its influence, its investment prowess and sophistication — evoked the crisis that eventually brought down the whole pre-1905 life insurance order.[3]

In the glare of newspaper and magazine publicity, the battle of words between the Hyde and Alexander factions mounted in intensity. There were two formal attempts at a peaceful settlement: an examination and report by a directors' committee headed by Henry C. Frick, and a departmental investigation by New York insurance superintendent Francis Hendricks. The Frick report, which was strongly influenced by Edward H. Harriman, condemned both Hyde and Alexander and added fuel to the growing public conviction that things were badly awry in the Equitable. Superintendent Hendricks frankly admitted: "It was . . . a great surprise to me . . . when internal dissension arose in this institution," and he subjected the company to an examination. He called for "elimination of stock control, and . . . the elimination of Wall Street control." But the details of the Hendricks report dwelt on past affairs such as the late Henry Hyde's stock holdings in Equitable affiliates. The superintendent did not examine more recent matters like the company's Union Pacific stock syndicate participations because, he said, it turned a profit in the transaction; and he admitted that his examination was only "a little more thorough than former ones." In the course of his work, Hendricks consulted George W. Perkins; and the New York Life official expected the report to be "satisfactory." The departmental action, then, was as much an expression of the prevailing Big Three influence over the New York regulatory system as it was a stroke for reform. Similarly, the Frick report did not represent an external reform impulse so much as the financiering purposes of E. H. Harriman and Standard Oil.[4]

But whatever their limitations, these events heightened an already considerable public preoccupation with the condition of the life insurance business. One journal welcomed the furor as free publicity for the Equitable, but this was an unusual reaction. Prevailing opinion held that the gathering crisis was "pregnant with the possibilities of great danger to the cause of American life insurance." The *Nation* somberly warned, "No greater calamity to the insurance business can be conceived than the invasion of its field by the snatching and grasping methods which marked our railway and industrial company finance of 1901 and 1902." New York, Boston, Colorado, and South Carolina policyholder committees sprang into existence, demanding the right to vote for Equitable directors. The Tennessee and Kentucky insurance commissioners made special inquiry into the company's political contributions and financial investments.[5]

Yet it is conceivable that there would have been no legislative investigation without the heightening struggle over the Equitable's stock. James Hazen Hyde apparently was induced by Harriman to agree to the Frick investigation, and to accept the report sight unseen. Frick and Harriman also made efforts to get him appointed ambassador to France. Hyde soon became aware of the underlying purpose, to induce him to sell his Equitable stock. At the Armstrong hearings he bitterly commented: "I think their reasons for taking this extraordinary interest in my absence from this country became rather obvious since then." Perhaps out of pique, Hyde sold his stock to Thomas Fortune Ryan in June, thwarting Harriman's quest for control. Ryan apparently gulled Harriman into thinking that he would share control of the Equitable with the railroad financier. To restore the Equitable's rapidly unraveling reputation, Ryan immediately placed the stock's voting and administrative power in the hands of trustees Grover Cleveland, Morgan J.

O'Brien, and George Westinghouse, and made former Secretary of the Navy Paul Morton president of the company.

But the groups involved were too numerous and too committed to be so easily appeased. Alexander and his followers had joined Hyde in denouncing the Frick report; before the year was out attorney Elihu Root, representing Harriman, was fighting legislation introduced by "the Alexander faction." Nor would Harriman passively acquiesce in Ryan's stock victory.

Root played a suggestive role in the frenzied maneuvering of 1905. At one time or another he represented Alexander, Harriman, Ryan, and the Mutual's McCurdy, but above all he was the peacemaker. Convinced that "the interests at stake are too great to be imperilled," he sought to end the wrangle, to restore the sophisticated alliance of insurance and high finance so dangerously disrupted. He worked on the plan to allow policyholders to vote for a portion of the Equitable's board of directors. Though in favor of an impartial and rigorous examination by the insurance department, he reminded Governor Frank Higgins and Superintendent Hendricks that "the least sensational treatment is the best." It would be well, he counseled, to invite the views of minority stockholders on policyholder voting; this might be an effective bar to subsequent legal action, or at least "put the Company in a much stronger position to defeat litigation." In March he got the Hyde, Alexander, and Frick-Harriman factions to agree to an amended Equitable charter. He asked McCurdy to work for its implementation: "I hope you will do anything you can to promote favorable action . . . in [the] interests of peace and general business." Under Root's tutelage, Ryan set up his trustee system, and brought Morton in as the Equitable's chief executive. The attorney induced Theodore Roosevelt publicly to welcome Morton as a reform president, and thus bolster the Equitable. "The loss of confidence affects the whole insurance business of the country," he warned, "and weakens that great agency for the promotion of thrift and providence." [6]

But Root ran serious risks in his sophisticated mediation. The New York State administration whose examination he welcomed was by no means uncommitted in the swirling Equitable controversy. Commissioner Hendricks was responsive to G.O.P. state boss Benjamin Odell — and Odell served the interests of E. H. Harriman and Standard Oil. During the Armstrong investigation Hughes remarked to Harriman, "it has been openly charged that through your relations with Mr. Odell you have political influence." The financier replied: "Well, I should think that Mr. Odell had political influence because of his relations with me."

Some of the impetus to the Armstrong investigation came from Harriman after Ryan corralled the Equitable's stock. Odell, too, may have looked on the inquiry as a means of embarrassing Governor Frank Higgins, who was showing signs of political independence and did not welcome an investigation out of his control. William W. Armstrong, the Rochester senator who headed the examination, was a follower of that city's Republican leader, George W. Aldridge, a cog in the Odell machine. A New York Life lobbyist tersely summed up the set of relationships: "Odell owns Aldridge . . . who bosses Armstrong absolutely." [7]

Indeed, almost everyone found cause to support the forthcoming inquiry. Thomas Fortune Ryan welcomed it as an opportunity to display the superior virtue of the reformed Equitable. Company counsel Paul Cravath thought "that the committee is as likely to conduct an honest and effective investigation as any which could have been chosen." He and his associates would facilitate the inquiry — and would "see to it that there is also a thorough and impartial investigation of the other companies." New York Life president McCall, on the other hand, looked forward to further revelations of wrongdoing within the Equitable. Just before the investigation he told Armstrong: "There has long been need of some intelligent revision of the insurance business of this state." A New York Life lobbyist may have fed information on the other companies to Hughes. The *Insurance Monitor,* friendly to the large firms, concluded that the investigation was "the wisest course"; if properly conducted, it was "likely to be of benefit to the life insurance interests, not because any great reforms are to be brought about . . . but because it will help to satisfy a popular demand, and possibly prevent mischievous laws." For crusading newspapers such as the *Evening Post* and especially the *World,* whose apostasy made McCall "feel that our patronage is wasted," an inquiry was a necessity.

Only the suspicious McCurdy, who at first confidently expected the Mutual to avoid "the dreadful controversies and the frightful disclosures that are occurring very near to us," looked on the forthcoming investigation with alarm. In vintage style he asked:

> Is it not time to hold up this efflux of promiscuous criticism and suggestion, and consider whether natural causes do not inevitably produce natural re-

> sults; and whether it were not well to wait awhile and see how sweet are the uses of adversity and how ready are the men in charge of these gigantic interests to profit by the teachings of the hour . . . The panacea for all imagined evils in this great country seems to be Legislation — more Legislation — Restriction — Limitation, Restraint . . . Why not trust sometimes to the operation of natural laws?

But his peers, confident in their sense of power and place, faced the oncoming investigation without qualms.[8]

Out of this interplay of interests emerged one of the most meaningful of American legislative investigations. In great part, the unexpected result could be attributed to the chief counsel, Charles Evans Hughes. A corporation lawyer who avoided too close an identification with his clients, Hughes already had done a striking job as counsel for New York City in an investigation of gas rates. He was not the initial choice of the Armstrong committee. Chairman Armstrong himself unsuccessfully approached Joseph H. Choate, who had great prestige — and great conservatism. But Joseph Pulitzer of the New York *World* strongly supported Hughes, and William T. Jerome, in the midst of a campaign for New York district attorney, also called for his appointment.

Hughes and his staff were by no means prejudiced against the great companies. The chief counsel had represented Alexander in the early days of the Equitable controversy, and he took his post on the condition that criminal charges would not come out of the investigation. The committee's actuary, Miles M. Dawson, had advised several of the large firms. Associate counsel James McKeen was appointed as a sop to the insurance companies. During the hearings McKeen treated the Mutual's officers with marked solicitude — and later joined that company as its general counsel. Assemblyman Robert Lynn Cox, a member of the Armstrong committee, became secretary and general counsel of the Association of Life Insurance Presidents, and later an officer of the Metropolitan, after the investigation. Senator William J. Tully of the committee also joined the Metropolitan, and became the company's general solicitor.[9]

Not surprisingly, the great companies faced their moment of truth with confidence and verve. Though warned by Armstrong that company counsel would "have no rights," James M. Beck of the Mutual stressed that they welcomed the inquiry. The imposing battery of company counsel — Beck for the Mutual, Richard J. Lindabury for the Metropolitan and Prudential, Samuel Untermyer, the Cravath firm, and former

Governor Frank S. Black for the Equitable — was in itself a manifestation of the firms' power.

But as the investigation proceeded from its September 6 beginning date it turned into something unexpected and unsettling. Daily until December 30, reporters and spectators crowded into the Aldermanic chamber of New York's City Hall to watch the players in the center: the committee, impassive, usually silent, seated behind its long, bare, spindly table; the succession of witnesses giving testimony from a plain wooden platform and chair; the restless chief counsel, occasionally perched on a high stool. Hughes turned the inquiry into a broad-ranging, meaningful examination of the society of great companies. His technique was complex, probing, patient yet relentless; he showed himself to be exceedingly well informed on the complexities of the business; he faced his witnesses with great poise, calmness, and good-natured patience — giving way occasionally to biting sarcasm when he met with particular obstinacy or pomposity. He took up companies and witnesses in no apparent order; but underneath, purpose prevailed. Before the inquiry began, Hughes told Equitable attorney Paul Cravath of his intention "not to investigate the insurance companies one at a time, but to subdivide the investigation into subjects, examining each of the important companies in connection with each subject." He seems consciously to have spaced the more sensational disclosures over the course of the investigation to keep public interest high. From the beginning, he made it clear that his primary concern was with the organization and government of the companies, with their structure and nature as corporate institutions. He recognized that this, rather than individual acts of wrongdoing, was the source of the public's unease.[10]

His dissection exposed to public view the nature of the pre-1905 society of great life insurance companies. Counsel's complaints grew accordingly. Witnesses proved balky — or unavailable. Thomas D. Jordan, the Equitable comptroller, departed for places unknown; Mutual lobbyist Andrew C. Fields pleaded illness. Andrew Hamilton, the New York Life lobbyist in charge of the national system of political influence, fled to the sanctuary of Paris. There, "away from his family, away from his country," he took to drink and sat out the investigation. So effective was Hughes that worried Republican leaders strove to have him leave the inquiry and run for mayor of New York in the November 1905 election. They chose him as their candidate despite his disclaimers, and finally he refused outright to accept.

The great men of the business filed to the witness stand — and all, to some degree, wrestled with embarrassments and inconsistencies. Richard McCurdy, not surprisingly, came off worst. Elderly, his voice often falling to a barely heard whisper, he threw up an infuriating curtain of platitudes and complacency. Stubbornly, arrogantly, he portrayed himself as a titan woefully ignorant of the details of life insurance or of his own company.

George Perkins, the nonpareil of the pre-1905 society of great companies, put on the most spectacular performance at the Armstrong investigation. Confident, aggressive, he treated the inquiry as an opportunity rather than a danger. He told a friend: "I am just as impatient as I can be to get on the witness stand before that Legislative Committee. My only fear is that they won't give us a chance for fear it will be too big an ad for Nylic." Senator Beveridge spurred him on: "You are rapidly approaching the point where Senator Hanna was when he captured the country by going directly before the people." Perkins began his testimony by producing his "original contract" with the New York Life: a letter from his father telling the sixteen-year-old that he had a job as a clerk. Later he made the dramatic revelation that Hughes had a written contract for a percentage of the New York Life's profits: an insurance policy. The chief counsel's reply — "Well, I am going to inquire more particularly what you do with the profits a little later, because I am vitally interested in that matter" — was the cold quietus to Perkins' ebullience.[11]

Thomas W. Lawson, the financier turned muckraker, was disappointed with the results of the Armstrong investigation, claiming that "26 Broadway" — Standard Oil — had kept things under control. Hughes, Lawson declared, was constrained by Armstrong to the extent that he almost resigned. But the chief counsel's extensive Report was a substantial and detailed indictment of the pre-1905 society of great companies. The Armstrong inquiry systematically examined the firms' management, marketing, investment, and political performance. Devastatingly it revealed the results: nepotism and high salaries; directorial and executive self-perpetuation through proxy votes; executives who thought of themselves more as financiers than as insurance men; increasingly costly marketing methods; declining dividend returns; investment and political activities of doubtful propriety. Hughes' Report summed up the fears produced by these disclosures: The Big Three's "membership is so large and their resources are so vast as to make the question of responsible control and conservative management one of extreme difficulty, and their management, if permitted to grow unrestrained, will soon become a serious menace to the community." [12]

3

Even Lawson could not deny the investigation's impact on the reputation of the great companies. Before the inquiry, he said, the firms "loomed before the American people as the greatest, most respected, and most venerable institutions in our broad land. To-day they stand for all that is tricky, fraudulent, and oppressive." Popular interest in the investigation was intense, and its revelations stirred a massive and widespread indignation. One observer concluded that the Armstrong inquiry did "more to break down confidence . . . in the conduct of all corporations in this country, than anything that has occurred since we reached any considerable commercial importance." Writing on "Insurance in Ancient America" the satirist Ambrose Bierce forecast that the scandal would in retrospect appear to be a chief cause of the downfall of the American Republic. The companies' ideology of public service now seemed a mockery. One organ advised: "Let us hoist the black flag and stop sailing as a missionary ship."

But the investigation, like any morality play, had its purgative effect: "A new era has begun; a better day has dawned; the air has perceptibly cleared." Hughes himself, speaking on "The Moral Lesson of the Insurance Investigation," saw the inquiry as a triumph of the moral sense of the American people. The evils unearthed clearly belonged to a pre-Armstrong past: "What a fool's paradise they lived in — feeding a monster whose appetite could not be sated, constantly increasing the occasions for the expenditures which they profess to lament, making it necessary that year after year the totals should larger grow." [13]

In this ceremony of purgation, of starting afresh, the government played a substantial role. As the supervisory authority, it had unveiled the nature of the pre-1905 system; and now it would have to establish the guidelines for rejuvenation. Few doubts remained about the propriety of vigorous regulation; the *Commercial and Financial Chronicle*'s argument that the companies "have no grant from the State. They are not utilities; they own no public duty, and perform no public service," was a brand of special pleading that found few supporters. The prevailing tone appeared in state insurance reports: "The lack of practical control by policy holders inspires the demand for regulation . . . and the fear that such control cannot be so effectuated . . . creates the demand that the state also undertake control of the management" (Ohio); "If it inures to the public benefit . . . to have State supervision of insurance companies, then such supervision is a proper function of government, regardless of its effects upon private interests" (Massachusetts); "Life Insurance is something that affects us socially as well as in a business way and there should be thrown around it every possible safeguard that the law can establish" (Alabama).[14] The great New York hearing set off a chain reaction of other examinations and commissions: in New Jersey, Wisconsin, Iowa, Ohio, Massachusetts, Tennessee, and Great Britain, as well as a multistate conference.

New Jersey, like New York once conspicuously friendly to the great companies, examined its own firms shortly after the end of the Armstrong investigation. Insurance commissioner David O. Watkins still was protective: he called the Armstrong revelations "most unfortunate and regrettable," doing "vast harm to the interests of American life insurance." The New Jersey inquiry did not have the bite of the New York investigation; no figure of Hughes' stature dominated the proceedings. But the Prudential and its leaders once again were examined, and the hearings contributed to the state's important insurance legislation of 1907, which closely followed New York's Armstrong laws.

Massachusetts responded in 1906 with a committee to recodify its insurance statutes. And in the post-Armstrong atmosphere, Louis Brandeis was able to win his fight for savings bank life insurance. He offered the plan as a low-cost alternative to the expensive policies of the industrial companies, arguing: "The only way to meet the socialistic and restless spirit of the times is to meet and remove each individual case of injustice." The industrial firms, weakened by the New York revelations, could not block Brandeis.

Ohio conducted a relatively mild and restricted investigation, but Missouri and Wisconsin vigorously reacted to the Armstrong revelations. During the New York inquiry, Missouri superintendent W. D. Vandiver temporarily suspended the New York Life's license because of its officers' political contributions. The Wisconsin legislature conducted an insurance investigation that concentrated on the Northwestern Mutual. It too had a vigorous personality directing the proceedings: Herman L. Ekern, speaker of the Assembly and later insurance commissioner. Ekern successfully proposed a state insurance fund, the country's first, and in 1907 the legislature passed rigorous new insurance laws.[15]

The New York revelations induced the Tennessee, Kentucky, Wisconsin, Minnesota, and Nebraska insurance commissioners to come to New York and subject the companies to a joint examination; the Tennessee and Texas superintendents lent their support to policyholder movements directed against the great firms' managements. The companies' Republican party contributions were particularly provocative. Kentucky's lieutenant governor caustically observed: "We people 'way down in Kentucky and in the Southwest" have to "pay our premiums on our insurance policies, or make our annual contributions to the campaign fund"; and he assured policyholders that their insurance was "good as the bank; there is no election for four years." A Texas Democrat spilled out his indignation: "I have been paying premiums to the New York Life for ten years, and now find that it has been using my money to fight my people and my country." The Southern and Western reaction seemed to the Louisiana commissioner to be the beginning of "a popular movement to invoke the supreme power of the State to check the unequal and constantly increasing advantage of concentrated corporate power over individual effort."

For the companies, this stirring in the hinterland threatened the sanctity of home office control; for Theodore Roosevelt, it smacked of Democratic-oriented decentralization distasteful politically and on grounds of public policy. The President vigorously interceded. He invited the Southern and Western commissioners examining the companies to come down from New York and visit him. When Minnesota's governor and insurance commissioner suggested in November 1905 that state officials gather to discuss uniform legislation, T.R. and the procompany insurance commissioner of the District of Columbia strongly supported the idea. In February 1906 about a hundred governors, attorneys general, and insurance commissioners met at Chicago for this purpose. Attempts were made to get agreement on a new District of Columbia code as a model for all states, and a Committee of Fifteen met to prepare a Federal insurance law. But the forces of Southern and Western dissatisfaction were not to be denied. Under their influence, the committee produced a bill providing for standard policy forms, preliminary-term reserve valuation, annual dividend payments on previously issued deferred dividend policies, a more detailed annual statement, and a $50,000 limit on executive salaries — all of which District of Columbia commissioner Drake opposed. Not too enthusiastically, Roosevelt transmitted these rigorous recommendations to Congress, and he showed no public regret when they died in committee.[16]

While the clash of interests continued to check Federal insurance legislation, a great new surge of state lawmaking followed on the heels of the Armstrong investigation. In some respects an extension of the pre-1905 rise of meaningful regulation, the post-Armstrong legislation had also a quantity and impact all its own. As before, the West and the South were active, but the traditionally more acquiescent Eastern states now also paid attention to the insurance enterprise. In 1907, forty-two state legislatures met; thirty considered life insurance legislation; twenty-nine passed laws. The states enacting substantial new sets of laws, or codifying old ones, were New York, New Jersey, Massachusetts, Delaware, Maryland, New Hampshire, North Carolina, West Virginia, Louisiana, Missouri, Texas, Ohio, Indiana, Illinois, Michigan, Minnesota, Montana, North Dakota, Colorado, and California.[17]

New York's 1906 enactments were the touchstone of this nation-wide legislative response. In the spring of 1905 the companies still had close control over the Albany legislative situation: of scores of bills introduced, only twelve innocuous ones reached the governor. But a year later, after the Armstrong investigation, the pressure for reform could not be resisted. In a couple of months the legislature passed, and the governor signed, bills limiting the cost and amount of new insurance that a company could write ($150,000,000 a year); controlling investments (companies must rid themselves of industrial, bank, and trust company stock, collateral loans, and syndicate participations, and could not go beyond a maximum surplus); regulating lobbying and forbidding campaign contributions; requiring a standard policy form and limiting agents' activities (rebating was made a misdemeanor); and democratizing management (all companies had to hold new directorial elections, and file policyholder lists with the insurance commissioner for opposition groups to use). This was uniquely substantial and incisive legislation. Contemporaries, with justification, spoke of it as "the most revolutionary and drastic provisions for the regulation of life insurance corporations ever passed in this country." Burton J. Hendrick, a leading critic of the pre-1905 companies, declared that the Armstrong laws have "largely redeemed one of the most useful institutions of modern life." [18]

The New York legislation had a ponderable impact on regulation everywhere. The Massachusetts insurance commissioner noted: "In a certain sense its supervision will be a national supervision, as its companies do business in all the states." Legislative efforts elsewhere drew upon it for sustenance. The Louisiana superintendent declared of his state's new insurance laws: "If it were not for the fact that the principles of many of these laws were already on the statute books of . . . New York, and that the large life insurance companies doing business in this state were forced to submit to like requirements in New York, I do not believe that we would have been so successful against the insurance lobby."

The already burgeoning system of state insurance regulation gained strength from the events of 1905. New departments of insurance were recommended or created in Colorado, Indiana, Washington, Georgia, and South Carolina; North Carolina thenceforth chose its commissioner by popular election. Considerable legislation expanded the powers, duties, salaries, and staffs of the state insurance officers. Deposit and report requirements and agent or company responsibility for legal service and process grew apace, as did laws forbidding the removal of litigation to Federal courts. Only taxation, perhaps further developed than regulation itself before 1905, did not noticeably expand after the Armstrong investigation. But a Texas premium tax, previously enjoined on grounds of doubtful constitutionality, now was enforced.

Most spectacularly, legislatures turned their attention to corporate political activity, company control, and marketing matters. Everywhere, campaign contributions were forbidden and lobbying was regulated. Considerable legislation dwelt on the problems of corporate democracy in such matters as the selection of directors and proxy voting. Fraternals, too, felt the force of the new concern for the purity of insurance firms.

Agents and policies came under new and more stringent control. There was an increase in the number of laws subjecting agents to licensing, certifying, and residence requirements; making the solicitor the agent not of the insured but of the company; and forbidding rebating and rate discrimination. Before 1905, occasional legislation specifically allowed corporations to be licensed as insurance agents or brokers; after that date, laws just as specifically forbade companies from so doing. Limits on, or prohibition of, deferred dividend policies were frequent, as were more traditional forms of policy regulation — of advertising and misrepresentation, of lapsing and forfeiture. Some states copied New York's standard policy law.[19]

Investment, like taxation, long had a substantial place in insurance laws, and legislation on this subject after 1905 had a qualitative rather than a quantitative importance. The Armstrong revelations vitalized attempts to force the companies to invest more funds in Southern and Western states. The most important, and most successful, of these efforts was Texas' Robertson Act of 1907. The law had the backing of influential local insurance companies. It required life insurance enterprises to invest 75 percent of their Texas policy reserves in the state's public or corporate securities. After its passage twenty-one companies left the state, including all of the large Eastern firms. Their efforts to induce the governor to veto the bill were unavailing; nor could the Metropolitan successfully challenge its constitutionality.[20]

4

By 1908 the wave of legislative reform had lost its force. The lines of twentieth century life insurance supervision were set, and thereafter only minor adjustments occurred. The companies quickly restored, or perhaps never lost, their easy relations with the New York insurance department. State comptroller Otto H. Kelsey, who replaced Francis Hendricks as insurance superintendent in 1906, once had dealings with Andrew Hamilton, and had helped the insurance companies to a substantial tax refund. In his 1908 report he criticized the expense and investment provisions of the Armstrong laws, and lavishly praised the Mutual, Metropolitan, and New York Life for their reforms. His performance in the insurance department was lackluster, and Hughes, elected governor in 1907, asked for his resignation. Kelsey refused, and was sustained by an anti-Hughes coalition in the Senate. Finally, in January 1909, the superintendent resigned. His replacement, William H. Hotchkiss, was more rigorous, but assured an insurance audience in 1911 that his hostility toward the large companies had declined substantially during his tenure of office. When Hotchkiss in turn was to be replaced, Chairman James J. Hoey of the Assembly Insurance Committee asked the Association of Life Insurance Presidents to support him for the post, reminding the group of his services to the companies.[21]

New York's Armstrong laws gradually lost some of their rigor. In 1909 and 1910 several of their major provisions were eased. The standard policy form gave way to a more flexible set of standard policy provisions. The law allowed larger renewal commissions, and the legislature eased its limitations on business expenses and on the amount of insurance that a company might sell. These were "substantial concessions to the convenience of companies and agents," and by the end of 1910 it was possible to conclude that "the last serious hardships of the Armstrong legislation" had been removed. New York Life president Darwin P. Kingsley thought that the degree of modification was "not appreciated even by life insurance men."

Elsewhere, too, the legislative storm was over. Of an estimated 1650 insurance bills introduced in 1911, only 160 became law. By 1909, the president of the John Hancock observed, "the states had very generally revised their laws." After 1907 most state insurance reports dropped the verbal analysis characteristic of the Armstrong days, and returned to unopinionated statistical presentations. These years saw much codification; New York's insurance code was revised in 1909, and counsel Robert Lynn Cox welcomed the 1911 Pennsylvania code as "fair and reasonable," with no "harsh or burdensome restrictions." [22]

But there was no return to the pre-1905 state of things. The bulk of the new legislation remained, modified but still potent. Superintendent Hotchkiss of New York was a vigorous regulator, playing a role in company affairs which would have been inconceivable before 1905. His successor, William T. Emmet, had no less positive ideas on "The Attitude of Present Day Supervision." As governor of New York Hughes remained a force for effective regulation. Besides demanding the removal of Superintendent Kelsey, he fought to preserve the Armstrong laws. In 1908 the companies agreed upon a liberalization of the expense limitation, and pushed it through the legislature with only one dissenting vote. But Hughes vetoed the measure; and the Assembly did not dare to override him.[23]

Most suggestive of all was the story of the companies' attempts to meet the post-Armstrong flood of legislation with the weapons of the past: systematic analyses of pending legislation, joint company action, aggressive assertions of corporate independence. It soon became clear that the *élan* which once had made the companies so formidable a corporate group existed no more.

In December 1906 President Paul Morton of the Equitable rallied the large companies to mutual protection against hostile legislation. He inspired the organization of the Association of Life Insurance Presidents, which according to its first head, Grover Cleveland, would defend insurance interests "by methods entirely open and frank . . . by honorable and manly argument." Robert Lynn Cox, formerly a member of the Armstrong committee, was the association's general counsel and then its secretary. The large companies supported the organization's antilegislative work with contributions of $40 or $50 per $1,000,000 of assets. But in 1909 the New York Life dropped out on the ground that membership was not worth its cost. And from the first the association was criticized by lesser firms. The actuary of the Phoenix Mutual of Hartford reacted with suspicion to Morton's organizational summons: "Most of the companies have vivid recollections of previous meetings called by the 'three giants' in which they have induced the smaller companies to pull chestnuts out of the fire for them and to burn their fingers in the process." The Southern and Western companies organized their own association, the American Life Convention, in 1906. Thereafter the two groups coexisted, unsteadily cooperating on legislative and regulatory matters of interest to the enterprise at large.[24]

The great challenge to the companies, of course, was the Armstrong legislation in New York. As the Assembly prepared to hold hearings on the measures proposed by Hughes, the firms applied pressure with accustomed skill. George Perkins of the New York Life sought an audience with Armstrong, and Equitable attorney Paul Cravath proposed to the Rochester senator that his committee and a group of company representatives meet "around a table" to consider details of the legislation before public hearings were held.

The New York Life, kingpin of the pre-1905 system, took the lead in the fight against the Armstrong legislation. One of its lobbyists boasted as the investigation drew to a close, "our people still control a few railroads." Vice-President Thomas A. Buckner met for four hours with assemblyman Alfred E. Smith, who was slated to direct the legislation through the chamber. He reported that Smith will help "in loosening up" the measures enough "to make them workable." Lobbyist William C. Beer approached Assembly speaker Wadsworth as a fellow Yale man, and reported that Armstrong committee members Roger, Cox, and Wemple favored the companies "on the quiet." He blustered, "I may let Armstrong hear from *his* constituents in a quiet way that may surprise *him*." Reporters were taken care of. The New York Life men did not work alone: a lobbyist for the assessment companies cooperated with Beer. Indeed, "The woods are full of insurance men." In the spirit of former days, the Big Three agreed to take on specific areas of responsibility. The New York Life concentrated on opposing standard policy forms, the Mutual dealt with expense limitations, the Equitable watched over proposed investment legislation.[25]

But the old efficacy was gone. External pressures and internal divisions sapped the companies' resistance. Politicians responded to the public mood of indignation. Armstrong saw no reason for talking privately with New York Life lobbyist John C. McCall, and his committee, mourned lobbyist Beer, "seems to have a mind of its own." The press — especially the *World* — kept public attention fastened on the proceedings, and the International Policyholders' Committee, with Samuel Untermyer as counsel, argued for effective legislation. The March 1906 hearings on the new insurance legislation were enlivened by the sudden, dramatic appearance of New York Life lobbyist Andrew Hamilton. Defending himself and President McCall, attacking Perkins and the company's directors, Hamilton kept alive the awareness of corporate malfeasance stimulated by the Armstrong revelations.

The companies themselves were disastrously divided. From the first, the Equitable adopted a policy of acquiescence in the proceedings. Counsel Paul Cravath told Hughes of the Armstrong committee's legislative proposals: "While some . . . seem rather drastic, I am disposed to assume they must be sound because of the thoroughness and fairness of the investigation on which they are based." Cravath distinguished the Equitable from its peers, who "have not yet gone through the process of regeneration." So different was "the moral position" of his firm that he thought it best to "avoid so far as possible uniting . . . in any public way which would tend to place the Equitable on the same plane with the other companies in the public mind." The Mutual, too, was an uncertain ally. It had once supported a limit on annual business as a check on the New York Life's growth, and it was readier than its rival to give up its deferred dividend business. The Metropolitan was not represented at the hearings, and did not oppose the legislation that emerged from them.

Not surprisingly, then, the New York legislature unanimously passed the Armstrong legislation. Perkins' bitter reaction to the news — "The Armstrong recommendations have now all become laws and a nice mess they are going to make of the New York State life insurance companies . . . What do you think of the first State in the American Union leading off at the beginning of a new century with the doctrine that a legitimate business should be limited in its volume?" — suggests how dramatically the companies' regulatory milieu had changed.[26]

The firms' political prowess not only failed to meet external challenges; it also eroded from within. Even before the Armstrong laws forbade campaign contributions and regulated lobbying, the companies began to dismantle their political structure. Both McCurdy and McCall forswore future party contributions. The Mutual president declared: "for the future my view is that to a great extent the defeat of proposed legislation hostile to the interests of the policyholders should be left to them." Other forms of political expenditure were hemmed in by requirements for vouchers, detailed lists of bills opposed, and the names of counsel engaged. The New York Life's declared legal expenses of $112,459 in 1905 dropped to $77,601 in 1906 and $61,587 in 1907, despite the fact that these were the peak years of post-Armstrong legislative activity.[27]

The network of national political influence similarly fractured. New York Life Washington lobbyist Beer feared that with the resignation of Perkins and McCall "my power and influence will be gone." Elihu Root refused to become an Equitable stock trustee in 1909 on the ground that "the connection between National Legislation and the great corporations of the country" was so close that he could not sustain such "an intimate relation" while he was in the Senate.

Especially suggestive was the final unraveling of the movement for Federal regulation. Perkins' New York Life protégé Darwin P. Kingsley, who became president of the firm in 1909, continued to espouse the principle. His company brought suit against a Montana premium tax in the hope of weakening the argument for state regulation, but the Supreme Court's *New York Life v. Deer Lodge County* decision, which "was regarded as a final settlement of the status of insurance," resoundingly affirmed the authority of the states. No more successful was an attempt in 1908 and 1909 to place the District of Columbia insurance department within the Treasury Department, as a first step to a national insurance agency. By 1910 the Bureau of Corporations disclaimed any jurisdiction over an enterprise clearly not in interstate commerce. Interest faded within the business as well. Mutual president Peabody, McCurdy's successor, made no effort to support Senator Dryden's fight for Federal regulation.[28]

A similar development, already well under way before 1905, characterized the companies' post-Armstrong legal experience. The New York investigation stimulated considerable litigation. In treating the cases that emerged from the managerial upheavals of the time, the courts like the legislatures opted for reform and change. Increasingly the companies avoided legal actions. Despite rising busines volume, their litigation began to fall off: they were involved in fifty-one appellate decisions in 1910, fifty-six in 1915, thirty-eight in 1920, and forty-one in 1925. The Metropolitan, which had the heaviest pre-Armstrong docket, took on "a new point of view" around 1912: thereafter it was extremely reluctant to contest policy claims. The theme of a discussion of legal procedures in the same year was that "a bad compromise is better than a good law suit." [29]

As the companies' political power ebbed, their political objectives became more limited. The firms were entering a relationship to the commonwealth more typical of the time's corporations, and their range of political sensitivity narrowed correspondingly.

Tax matters now took on special weight. By 1910 there was an established and uniform system of state taxation of financial institutions. Taxation became the chief concern of the Association of Life Insurance Presidents. The Prudential withdrew from Texas and Arkansas because of the levies imposed by those states; and it complained recurrently of the undue tax burden that it claimed to bear. The New York Life protested a Montana premiums tax which took $13,000 of the state's $370,000 in insurance payments. Although the company's national tax burden totaled only 1.24 percent of its premium income, the board of trustees recommended that the president be strengthened "in his efforts to secure more reasonable legislation on this subject."

The prospect of a Federal corporate income tax heightened insurance sensitivities. The Corporation Tax Act of 1909 placed a 1 percent levy on insurance income, excluding stock dividends. Company pressure managed to get reserves protected from the impost. But the Prudential's directors estimated that the tax would cost their firm about $320,000 a year, and pledged themselves "to influence public opinion and action rightly." And the Revenue Act of 1913 permitted life insurance companies to exclude premiums refunded or credited to their policyholders from gross income, which substantially reduced taxable revenue.[30]

But the result was more a tribute to the special nature of the life insurance business, and to the pressure of the industry as a whole, than to the power of the great firms. The old sense of aggressive, unified political purpose was gone. This was not an isolated phenomenon: the companies underwent a change in business as well as political attributes. The disengagement from power touched off by the events of 1905 affected every aspect of the insurance enterprise.

XVI * Disengagement

The post-1905 metamorphosis embraced the managerial, corporate, marketing and investment as well as the political functions of the great companies. By 1910, when the excitement of the Armstrong years had died away, the firms had a new visage indeed. The Massachusetts insurance commissioner caught the mood of afterstorm serenity: life insurance, he thought, had attained "a higher plane, where it can . . . take its place among the other great business enterprises of the country . . . It is the sunshine and calm following the tempest and devastation, the debris of which has been cleared away." For the great firms, to "take their place among the other great business enterprises of the country" meant not growth but contraction (temporarily in size, permanently in spirit); not the acquisition of new influence but disengagement from old power.[1]

The morality play that was the Armstrong investigation profoundly affected the companies' management. In harmony with the public ceremony of condemnation and exorcism, the firms themselves turned to the cleansing ritual of reorganization. This process was not altogether voluntary: the threat of indictment spurred internal reform. George W. Perkins was assured by his attorney in March 1906 that "there is no intention to molest anyone who acted honestly, even though in a mistaken view of the law, and without making a personal profit." But district attorney William Travers Jerome, whose political ambitions led him to react to the insurance scandals with an unstable intermixture of rigor and leniency, charged Perkins with grand larceny in contributing company funds to the Republican party. Perkins circumvented a civil suit by returning some $54,000 to the New York Life. He had also to face a Jerome-induced grand jury indictment for forgery of book entries about fictitious sales of New York Life railroad stock; but the New York Supreme Court in 1907 threw out this finding. Other indictments were attempted: of Mutual vice-presidents Granniss and Gillette; of Equitable comptroller Jordan; of Metropolitan president Hegeman. Save for the president of the smallish Mutual Reserve, none led to convictions or to jail sentences. The act of indictment itself, however, was sufficient evidence of community disapproval.[2]

Closely allied in spirit to these official actions were company attempts to extract monetary restitution from their errant officers. Perkins found it expedient to cover the New York Life's 1904 campaign contribution; John McCall partially repaid his advances to Andrew Hamilton with a check for $85,000 and a real estate deed to secure an additional $50,000. Eventually the company settled too with Hamilton's estate. Under President Morton's prodding, the Equitable's Alexander and Hyde repaid a $685,000 loan made by the affiliated Mercantile Trust, and Chauncey Depew and his associates returned $250,000 borrowed from the insurance company. The new administration also canceled the generous pension voted Annie F. Hyde, widow of Henry Hyde. A special Mutual trustees' committee, guided by attorney Joseph H. Choate, brought suit against the company's pre-Armstrong officers. Seven actions were begun against McCurdy and his associates, and five more involved trustees who were on the committee of expenditures. In 1909 a settlement brought $750,000 in cash ($250,000 from the McCurdy estate) for claims of $6,000,000. The suit against the trustees was discontinued in 1910. The New York insurance department frowned on so gentle a compromise, but, no less than in the realm of indictments, the action itself seemed more important than its result.[3]

The most dramatic rejection of the managerial past was the departure of former officers from their company positions. As unusual corporate ideologues, they reacted to criticism and disavowal with a more than customary emotion. They had "enjoyed a degree of public respect and confidence accorded no other class of men in the realm of modern business affairs"; and under the strain of disclosure and rejection their confidence and health broke. The time following the Armstrong investigation saw a melancholy procession of company magnates resigning, sickening, dying.

The Equitable's James W. Alexander left the company in July 1905;

but a month before, the insurance press reported that he "has broken down under the weight of his troubles." He found surcease in flight, staying abroad until 1909. James Hazen Hyde, young and more resilient, jauntily removed himself to Paris for a "rest" that lasted thirty-five years. Gage Tarbell, enough of a management man to pass through the trials of 1905 relatively unscathed, nevertheless left the Equitable in 1907 for a career in real estate promotion. Comptroller William D. Jordan died in 1908, supposedly a victim of the Armstrong disclosures.

Richard McCurdy left the Mutual during the investigation, claiming ill health. His son and son-in-law, and several other officers, joined the exodus soon after. The Mutual chieftain lingered on until 1916, an isolated figure, detached from the company whose fortunes he so long guided. Dryden of the Prudential pleaded illness in 1907 to escape the presumably hopeless task of standing for the Senate again. His closest friend and business associate, Dr. Leslie D. Ward, died in 1910, and in November 1911 Dryden too passed away. The actual operation of the Prudential had for years been in other hands. Although the Metropolitan's Hegeman fared reasonably well at the Armstrong inquiry, he keenly felt his indictment for forgery and perjury. He kept the presidency until his death in 1919, but his was only a ceremonial post. Haley Fiske was the Metropolitan's real leader.

By early 1906, both John McCall and George Perkins had departed from the New York Life. Again, for the younger man there was escape — to the challenges of high finance in J. P. Morgan and Company and of high politics in the Progressive party campaign of 1912. Attorney William Nelson Cromwell caught Perkins' mood on his departure from the life insurance enterprise: "It must have lost its charm and only been an irritation." But for McCall, the swift collapse of power and place could not easily be borne. By the beginning of 1906 he was "lying . . . at the point of death"; his son ascribed the collapse to "the worry of the past four months." On February 18, 1906, McCall died. New York Life treasurer Randolph reported his chief's deathbed words: "I am innocent of wrong to anyone by any intention of mind. I feel no ill will to anyone. I go to a higher court there to render my account." Others in the firm also suffered: lobbyist Beer reported, "I am in such a nervous condition and like all the rest of our company, have been under the doctors care." With a certain propriety, the men of the company most committed to the pre-1905 spirit felt the impact of the Armstrong investigation with special keenness.[4]

A new crop of executives, no less unified in type than their predecessors, came into power after 1905. The Equitable led the way before the Armstrong investigation. Alexander's successor, Paul Morton, came to the company with the prestige of the Secretaryship of the Navy. Alexander E. Orr, a prominent New York merchant and president of the Board of Rapid Transit Commissioners, replaced John McCall in the New York Life. He, too, had a welcome record of public service, having been prominent in the city reform movement headed by Seth Low. McCurdy's successor in the Mutual, the New York lawyer Charles A. Peabody, Jr., stood for the same values of integrity and caution rather than ambitious aggressiveness.

These men were by no means free from connections with high finance. Morton was very much the man of Equitable owner Thomas Fortune Ryan. Peabody unconvincingly denied any ties with Standard Oil, John D. Rockefeller, or E. H. Harriman. Henry H. Rogers of Standard Oil, a member of the Mutual board, found it necessary to resign and to deny that he had been instrumental in Peabody's selection.[5]

But the *mésalliance* between life insurance and high finance was perpetuated more in appearance than in reality. And the new presidents differed markedly from their predecessors in their views of the insurance business. Peabody announced that it was his ambition to make the Mutual "the soundest Company" rather than "to build up the largest Company." Until 1927 he worked doggedly and conservatively to this end, stressing economy and business restraint. President Morton of the Equitable had similar, if somewhat more aggressive, plans for his firm: "I want it to be not only the greatest and the best, but the safest and most conservative life insurance institution . . . I want it to be known, not only as the strongest financially but the strongest morally." Although Vice-President Tarbell left the company in 1907, his outlook — "I think life insurance companies should be conducted as life insurance companies and they should let management of other kinds of business go to other people" — set the tone for the Equitable after 1905.

The New York Life, the embodiment of the pre-1905 spirit, seemed most reluctant to give up the old business ideology. Orr served as president only until June 1907, when he was replaced by Darwin P. Kingsley, a protégé, associate, and admirer of George Perkins. Others of the pre-1905 managerial core — treasurer Edmund D. Randolph, vice-president Thomas A. Buckner — remained as well. Kingsley shared much of Perkins' aggressive, ebullient business mystique. He quoted Herbert

Spencer's *Social Statics* against New York State's limit on new business, and called himself a member of "the militant school of life insurance." He equated the desire to expand with "that moral ecstasy which . . . cheerfully undertakes any burden in order to advance a religious conviction." But Kingsley was primarily a management man; he did not share the political and financial ambitions of Perkins and McCall. Nor could he fail to recognize that 1905 was a turning point in the business. He claimed that since "the tempest of popular criticism which swept over all corporate forms of business in 1905 and 1906, this company has sought, by correct methods, by open dealing and by frankness, to create a right relation between society at large and corporate work."

Presidents Dryden of the Prudential and Hegeman of the Metropolitan remained in office, but the tone and leadership of their companies changed. Attorney Richard Lindabury emerged as the dominant power in the Newark firm. He read the eulogy at Dryden's funeral in 1911, and continued to dominate the company after Forrest Dryden assumed his father's office. Principled, strong in personality, in some ways a business generalist like George Perkins — he is supposed to have played a major role in United States Steel policymaking — Lindabury kept the Prudential out of politics and high finance, and concentrated on internal business development. Haley Fiske took unquestioned control of Metropolitan affairs after 1905. One of the pre-1905 breed of Warwicks that included Perkins and Tarbell, he adapted most successfully of all to the demands of the life insurance enterprise after the Armstrong investigation.[6]

2

The society of great companies changed also in corporate organization and structure. The New York Life and the Mutual faced major crises of executive control, and the stock firms — the Equitable, Prudential, and Metropolitan — became mutualized.

New York's 1906 Armstrong legislation required the mutuals' policyholders to elect wholly new boards of trustees. The incumbent managements found themselves challenged by a strong, well-organized opposition group, the International Policyholders Committee (I.P.C.). The I.P.C. criticized the Orr and Peabody administrations for insufficient reform, and labeled the New York Life's Truesdale report "farcical and insincere." Potential supporters were told: "We believe the success of this movement will inaugurate a new era in corporate management."

The committee was directed by Samuel Untermyer, who had represented the Equitable at the Armstrong investigation and would later be committee counsel at the Pujo hearings. Prominent on the I.P.C. executive committee were political and business leaders whose common quality, perhaps, was a strain of traditionalism, of conservative unreadiness to see big business go too far too fast. They included former Secretary of the Navy Benjamin F. Tracy, 1904 Democratic presidential candidate Alton B. Parker, Cleveland's Secretary of State Richard Olney, Pennsylvania governor Samuel W. Pennypacker, and the merchant Thomas B. Wanamaker. But more than reform was involved. The *Commercial and Financial Chronicle* termed the struggle "a fight for control of approximately a billion of dollars." A New York Life lobbyist thought that Untermyer was an agent for E. H. Harriman; and James G. Colgate, the head of the Mutual Policyholders' Committee which worked with the I.P.C., supposedly had ties with Thomas W. Lawson.[7]

The incumbent managements moved vigorously in the face of this imposing threat. The New York Life retained William Nelson Cromwell to manage its campaign. Cromwell adopted a restrained, statesmanlike approach, in keeping with the companies' policy of self-purgation. He recommended that the New York Life comply with the requirement that it post policyholder lists with the New York insurance department, to be made available to the opposition. He judiciously pointed out that this would make a favorable impression on the press and on the insurance superintendent. Vice-President Buckner recognized that many new trustees would have to be offered on the administration ticket: "A 'change' is one of the things that will be demanded and if the opposition can raise the cry of 'the same old Board' etc., we would be absolutely lost at the start."

Not all administration activities were so genteel. New York Life lobbyist Beer told Postmaster General Cortelyou that Untermyer's group had influence within the New York Post Office "to such an extent that . . . we have had to buy our stamps in surrounding towns in order to cover up our trail." He hoped to approach Cortelyou for an unspecified "little favor." Mutual agents worked for the administration slate; and the company's general agent in Kentucky was dismissed because he ran as an opposition trustee. Because of this action the Mutual's Kentucky license was temporarily revoked, and there was talk of similar action in Tennessee, Michigan, Minnesota, and Missouri. The I.P.C. complained that the lists of Mutual policyholders supplied to it were defective, impeding its efforts to reach the voters; it claimed also that ballots went to New York Life policyholders with a line drawn through the I.P.C. ticket.[8]

The campaigns ended in the spring of 1907, with well over 500,000 of the two companies' total of 1,300,000 policyholders voting. The administration slates in both the New York Life and the Mutual won overwhelmingly; in the Mutual only two I.P.C. candidates gained election to the board, and the margin for administration candidates ran three to one or better. Substantial opposition arose no more; in 1908 all incumbent trustees were re-elected with the automatic ease of pre-1905 selections.[9] The process of purification did not embrace policyholder revolt any more than it included jailed officials. But even this ineffectual outburst of corporate democracy suggests the changed tone of the post-1905 insurance milieu. To win such a battle was no great achievement for the management of a large corporation; to have had to fight it at all was a measure of the anticompany pressure of the time.

The final act in the ceremony of corporate purification affected the ownership structure of the three great stock firms: the Equitable, the Metropolitan, and the Prudential. The same view which held that business practices acceptable elsewhere could not be condoned in the large life insurance companies insisted that stock ownership, and the consequent division of profits between policyholder-customers and stockholder-owners, was insupportable in quasi-public firms.

Gestures toward mutualization by managements anxious to avoid the vagaries of stockholder control occurred before the Armstrong investigation. Thus the Metropolitan leadership decided in 1902 to give voting rights to policyholders while assuring that real control would remain in its own hands. In the 1905 Equitable controversy, Alexander proposed that the company's insured vote for one third of the trustees. After 1905, full mutualization, the retirement of all company stock, seemed logical, proper, and inevitable. But just as the fact of stock ownership did not determine the nature of the pre-Armstrong companies — the mutuals had the same corporate characteristics as the stock firms — so did complete mutualization come at the end of, rather than determine, the post-1905 disengagement of the great companies.[10]

The Equitable remained after 1905 the company most enmeshed in the world of high finance, and hence most in need of full mutualization.

Yet no obvious scandal or loss occurred. Thomas Fortune Ryan gained little from his control of the stock, and in December 1909 he sold it to J. P. Morgan for $3,000,000 — his purchase price plus interest. Both Ryan and Morgan were punctiliously careful to see that the trusteeship arrangement for voting the stock continued undisturbed. Morgan J. O'Brien, Lewis Cass Ledyard, and George Perkins acted as Morgan's trustees. But this strained, ceremonial attempt to avoid the implications of stock ownership soothed no one. There did not seem to be much hope of disentangling the Equitable's stock from investment banking circles: James Stillman of the National City Bank and George F. Baker of the First National Bank offered to take half of Morgan's Equitable stock off his hands if he called on them to do it. New York insurance superintendent Hotchkiss insisted that the Morgan trusteeship arrangement be cancellable on thirty days' notice, in case a mutualization arrangement should be worked out. He pressed the Equitable to mutualize, arguing that its business decline stemmed from its Wall Street ownership.

The company, anxious to do "everything within reason to avoid further newspaper notoriety or public criticism," accepted the logic of the situation. In January 1911 a Committee on Mutualization began its work. Morgan was willing to sell in 1912, but Hotchkiss boggled at the $6,000,000 it would cost the Equitable to buy up all outstanding stock at the inflated price that Ryan and Morgan had paid. In 1915 T. Coleman Du Pont bought Morgan's holding for almost $4,400,000 and promptly announced that he intended to cooperate with the Equitable management on mutualization plans. It was increasingly clear that substantial profits stood to be made or lost in the final agreement. Finally, in 1917, a compromise gave the Equitable the controlling stock at $5400 a share (fifty-four times its par value), and the right to buy the remaining shares at $1700 each. Some minority stockholders objected, but mutualization began in 1918 and the last of the Equitable's stock was retired in 1925.[11]

The Prudential, too, found the burden of its outstanding stock insupportable after 1905. Several crises heightened the sense of need. In 1908 and each year thereafter, 10 percent of the surplus was set aside for stockholders, the rest for policyholders; but the company retained the stockholders' portion as a contingency surplus. The Prudential management thought this both wise and proper in the post-Armstrong milieu, but a group of minority stockholders disagreed. They brought suit for a larger share of the company's earnings, and for the distribution of $2,500,000 from the surplus. The Prudential resisted in the courts, and finally won the legal battle in 1912. But the incident underlined the fundamental division of interest between stockholder-owners and policy-holder-customers.

In 1911 the dangers of stock ownership appeared with even greater clarity. Under the terms of the 1902 Prudential-Fidelity Trust agreement, a near majority of the insurance company's stock rested in the Fidelity Trust Company. After Dryden's death, the Fidelity's directors sought to use their voting power to oust the existing management and to put in their own representatives. Richard Lindabury countered by threatening to appeal to public opinion and to the regulatory system. After intricate negotiations, he extracted an agreement whereby the Prudential officials voted their Fidelity holdings in favor of the trust company's management, and the latter reciprocated with their Prudential stock.

But this was at best a tenuous arrangement, and Lindabury pressed for mutualization. Former New York superintendent Hotchkiss, who had done so much to prod the Equitable toward mutualization, was brought in to help. The New Jersey legislature passed a bill in 1913 that allowed the Prudential to buy up its own stock and hold it in trust for its policyholders. Appraisers in 1914 valued the insurance company's stock at $455 a share — over nine times its original $50 par value — making a total worth of $18,200,000. Fidelity Trust officials, tempted with the additional prospect of receiving the Prudential's Fidelity stock at a price below its market value, accepted these generous terms. Mutualization began in 1915, and the Prudential quickly obtained over 90 percent of its outstanding securities. But minority stockholders resisted in the courts, and not until 1943 was the long process of mutualization completed.[12]

The Metropolitan underwent the same change with less difficulty. Most of the stock was held by Hegeman and by the heirs of founder Joseph F. Knapp. Spurred by the examples of the Prudential and the Equitable, Haley Fiske and treasurer Frederick H. Ecker induced the major stockholders to sell at $75 a share. By 1914 the remaining shareholders had followed suit, and the Metropolitan's mutualization was complete — at a cost of $6,000,000.[13]

In all three companies, the mutualization process had been complex and (to varying degrees) expensive. Major business values — the sanctity of ownership, the right to profits on investment, the special nature of the life insurance business — stood in delicate equipoise. That courts, commissioners, and company managements worked in harness to sanction these shifts in ownership was yet another measure of how far the society of great companies had come from its aggressive pre-1905 days.

3

Disengagement from the values prevalent before 1905 occurred in managerial practices and business techniques as well. Post-Armstrong legislation, and internal policy changes, transformed the life insurance enterprise.

One step in the cleansing of the Big Three was the directorial investigation committee. The Equitable's Frick committee set the pattern in April 1905; and before the year was out the New York Life's Fowler and the Mutual's Truesdale committees were preparing recommendations for tighter, more efficient management. Personnel changes, cost-cutting, new bylaws, and adjustments in administrative organization were the common pattern during the frenzied months of the Armstrong period. Salaries came down from their pre-1905 heights: New York Life president Orr "stated positively that in view of his unfamiliarity with life insurance details, he would not accept a larger salary" than $50,000; and after the Prudential's John Dryden died in 1911, his son Forrest accepted a presidential stipend of $45,000. To dramatize its break with the past, the new Mutual management sold the ornate, expensive furniture of the pre-1905 executives; and John Singer Sargent's portrait of Richard McCurdy disappeared from the Mutual offices as though it were an oppressive reminder of a past best forgotten.[14]

The forces of contraction affected insurance policies. Even before the 1906 New York legislation forbade them, deferred dividend contracts came into disfavor with lesser firms such as the Northwestern, the Phoenix Mutual, and the John Hancock. Afterward, the great companies too had to drop the tontines which had been so central to their growth. Dividend allocation remained essentially a political decision — indeed, a controversy raged over whether courts, actuaries, or accountants should set their amount — but now they would have to go out yearly, and no longer would be available for long-range company investment.

The agency structure likewise bowed before the gale of 1905, as the large companies' business fell off and smaller firms gained. The Mutual lost nearly half of its underwriting force, the Equitable between a third and a half. In December 1905 the New York Life gained 158 new agents — and lost 662. George Perkins' cherished agents' organization, Nylic, went under, and by early 1907 the company was obliged to reduce the number of its agency branches in order to keep within the business limit prescribed by law.[15]

Perhaps the most meaningful measure of the change in the business milieu was the post-1905 decline in the business of the large firms (see Table 10). The end of deferred dividends, the business limit set by

TABLE 10. Insurance in force and new business of the Big Five, 1904–1910 (tens of millions of dollars)

Company	1904	1905	1906	1907	1908	1909	1910
			Insurance in force				
Equitable	1495.5	1465.1	1376.7	1340.1	1326.5	1335.3	1347.2
Mutual	1547.6	1589.5	1517.3	1452.8	1438.4	1441.3	1464.0
New York Life	1928.6	2061.6	2029.6	2005.3	1993.6	2002.9	2039.9
Metropolitan	1470.4	1596.5	1692.9	1804.9	1861.9	2041.9	2215.9
Prudential	1056.7	1170.3	1253.1	1337.4	1434.6	1684.8	1851.3
			New business				
Equitable	306.8	215.5	88.1	73.4	91.3	110.9	111.4
Mutual	231.5	183.3	90.6	50.2	95.5	104.7	120.7
New York Life	345.7	314.9	185.1	154.6	157.8	163.2	171.0
Metropolitan	436.6	458.2	401.4	376.8	365.5	445.0	432.9
Prudential	312.0	305.4	280.1	271.4	309.7	500.1	462.0

Source: Spectator Company, *Insurance Year Book*, 1911.

New York's laws, the less aggressive ideology of the new managements, and especially the stigma of the Armstrong revelations caused this ordeal of corporate sackcloth and ashes. The Big Three were the greatest sufferers, taking a loss of half to two thirds of their pre-1905 new business at the nadir in 1907. Non–New York firms benefited commensurately. By 1908, the Northwestern of Milwaukee was writing more insurance than the Mutual or the Equitable. The number of life insurance companies (especially in the South and West) had been rising steadily since the early 1890's; with the impetus of the Armstrong revelations it leaped forward from 112 in 1905 to 214 in 1910 and a peak of 250 in 1912. Growth — rapid, untrammeled — had underlain the pre-1905 society of great companies. For these firms, contraction was as traumatic a penance as the business system afforded.[16]

4

The Armstrong revelations dealt a massive blow to the Big Three's already shaky foreign business. The year 1905, in retrospect, marked the height of the venture overseas. Insurance in force abroad reached its peak of $1,142,000,000 in that year and declined thereafter: to $980,000,000 in 1915, to $663,000,000 in 1920. The months and years following the Armstrong investigation were unpropitious ones for the foreign venture. George Perkins later recalled that to stay within the volume limit set by New York, the Big Three "naturally went abroad and cut that business off first." Samuel Untermyer was in England and France during 1906, seeking support for his International Policyholders' Committee by attacking the Mutual and the New York Life as pawns of Wall Street. Mutual president Peabody's cautious style left no room for a vigorous foreign enterprise: he announced in June 1906 that his company no longer would make deposits in other countries, and that he planned to eliminate unprofitable overseas departments. Paul Morton of the Equitable shared these sentiments. In 1909 the Equitable's European agencies were restricted to $25,000,000 worth of new business; other foreign agencies to $15,000,000; United States agencies were allowed $110,000,000. Strongly (if newly) cost-conscious, the company compared the ratio of first year expenses to premiums at home and abroad, and found foreign costs running two to five times as high as domestic expenses. In 1912 a special committee of Equitable directors recommended that the company cease entering foreign countries, and end its business in those places where costs and mortality were high.[17]

Only the New York Life sought to maintain its foreign business at the pre-1905 intensity. The Fowler committee strongly recommended that the venture be continued. Though it expected withdrawals from particular places "due to unsettled conditions, arbitrary exactions, excessive expenses, or unsatisfactory mortality," the committee considered the overseas business a source of company strength because "as a matter of policy the widest possible distribution of risks under favorable conditions is the most desirable." And President Darwin P. Kingsley shared George Perkins' belief in the worth of an international insurance business.

But the firm could not escape from the problems plaguing the insurance business overseas. It expanded into China and Japan with indifferent results; the proportion of its foreign insurance to its total in force declined to about 20 percent by the end of 1913. In 1907 the New York Life decided to quit Central America as an area not worth the cost of securing new business. More than 23,000 policies were written in Europe in 1905; the total fell to 9,039 in 1907, to 8,817 in 1910. The company suffered from the Armstrong revelations; Guido von Nimptsch, Perkins' devoted ally in the Prussian negotiations of 1899, was embittered by the disclosures. Moreover, the New York Life's new investment caution led it to sell its German and Japanese securities — and thus to lose a major prop of its overseas business.[18]

Everywhere, for all of the companies, the post-Armstrong years were a time of difficulty with foreign governments. Hostile regulatory activity took on new or renewed life from the 1905 revelations. In Latin America, the Armstrong investigation fed an already prevalent anti-Yankeeism. Rio newspapers, stoked by the leading domestic firm, the Sul America, criticized the New York Life during the inquiry. "The discussion of life-insurance and the rights of policyholders" broke out in Chile in 1908; again, rival firms were involved. Uruguay's President Batlle successfully sought new taxes on foreign insurance companies. In 1911 he secured a state monopoly of insurance, using the 1905 scandals as an object lesson. Mexico, like Uruguay in the throes of social change, turned to more rigorous regulation. The law of May 25, 1910, an early product of the Mexican revolution, required insurance companies to deposit an amount equal to the legal reserves of their Mexican policies. The Equitable and the Mutual left the country in 1911; the New York Life remained and tried to circumvent the law, but finally had to make the requisite deposit as the price of staying.[19]

Similar reactions occurred throughout Europe. Bulgaria in 1906 raised the New York Life's annual license fee, "obviously the direct result of the so-called insurance scandals in New York." The company faced a Serbian tax law in 1908, but in line with its new restraint chose to resist in the courts rather than through bribery. The Equitable and the New York Life fled Greece in the face of a drastic 1910 law; the Equitable and the Mutual left Portugal after 1907 legislation in that country. Italy in 1911 excluded foreign companies and made life insurance a government monopoly. The State Department and a bloc of European nations whose firms had Italian offices protested, but to no avail. In a flurry of diplomatic and legal negotiations, the New York Life and the Equitable departed. The companies managed to get the domestic securities requirement of a 1908 Spanish deposit law reduced from 50 percent to 25 percent. But in 1909 the government insisted that deferred dividend policyholders receive an annual accounting on their policies. The Equitable at first suspected that the New York Life's people in Spain were behind the measure. But continuing tax and regulatory difficulties, caused "not so much by hostile legislation as by hostile executive interpretations of the law," clearly stemmed from the desire to assist domestic life insurance companies by driving out the American firms. In 1916 the Equitable left the country.[20]

Even traditionally passive British insurance supervision became more rigorous after 1905. The Armstrong investigation was deeply shocking; a London newspaper thought that "nothing ever happened in this country so to damage the standing of American financial projects abroad." D. C. Haldeman, for nineteen years the Mutual's general manager in Great Britain, set up a British policyholders' protest committee, resigned from the Mutual to join the North British and Mercantile Insurance Company, and invited Mutual policyholders to switch with him. In 1906 a Select Committee of the House of Lords looked into the condition of foreign life insurance companies in Great Britain. The committee recommended that a £20,000 deposit be required of all companies, reversing a long tradition of regulatory laissez-faire. The deposit proposal became law in 1909 — as did requirements for annual statements and quinquennial examinations.[21]

Former centers of difficulty — Austria-Hungary, Russia, and France — continued to plague the companies. The Equitable, which had stopped doing business in Austria, now was forced to make deposits covering existing policies. Company property and non-Austrian security deposits were taxed more heavily. A stringent new insurance law in 1909 forced the Mutual's departure from Vienna in 1913, and, for all practical purposes, ended new business by the other companies.

Russian deposit requirements climbed in 1905, and in 1906 the New York Life complained about the "apparently unreasonable conditions exacted by the Russian Government where a Russian Nobility Bond is redeemed and the Company desires to reinvest in some other bond." An always difficult business environment became more so as Russian newspapers made much of the Armstrong revelations. The revolution of 1905 weakened the Equitable's interest in Russian business, and the company's counsel general for Europe noted in 1911: "We have machinery in Russia which is not justified by the business . . . we have been getting." The New York Life felt the weight of a new tax on profits in 1910. When it tried to avoid payment, the firm was told that the police would close its Moscow office.[22]

The Armstrong investigation had its most dramatic overseas impact in France. French interest in the scandals — an interest encouraged by the domestic firms — was keen. As early as May, the Equitable's "present trouble" led the authorities to demand proof that the company would be able to comply with new deposit requirements established in March. While French indignation waxed, State Department readiness to help waned. Undersecretary of State Adee coldly told an Equitable official: "The recent unpleasantness . . . is taken advantage of, and it is contended that if the American Companies were sound, they would not object to the legal reserve belonging to the French insured being deposited . . . The good will of the French Government cannot be doubted, but its difficulties are great." Out of the turmoil of the Armstrong months came a new demand: that the deposit law of March 1905 be interpreted to cover old as well as new policies. Premier Rouvier, the Foreign Ministry, and the Department of Commerce supported the companies' argument that the law was not retroactive. But protectionist sentiment made itself felt in the 1906 election to the Chamber of Deputies. The French government, though it wanted to help, could find no way "to do so safely." On June 9, 1906, an ordinance established the retroactivity requirement, and specified that 75 percent of the deposits be in French securities.[23]

As in 1904 and 1905, the companies reacted in discrete ways. The Mutual strongly protested, and ended its French business soon after, not so much from necessity as in accord with president Peabody's constrained view of proper marketing. Wistfully, Mutual actuary Emory McClintock declared that his firm had had in France "a satisfactory and profitable business, an excellent business in point of mortality and persistence, and our agency has been built up there at considerable expense in the past and has done very successful work." The New York Life decided to accept the ruling, reasoning that its $81,000,000 worth of French insurance in force, its substantial 1905 volume of over $13,000,000 worth of new policies, the underaverage cost of new business, and the existence of deposit requirements elsewhere justified continuation. The Equitable also decided to stay — and to fight the retroactivity provision. It appealed its case to the Council of State. In 1910 — perhaps in part because of the splendor of its new Paris office building — the company won its appeal. But in France, as elsewhere, the American life insurance business never regained its pre-Armstrong volume.[24]

The First World War devastated an already wounded venture. The untrammeled nationalism, the destruction of social stability and personal safety, the inflated currencies, the collapsed international monetary exchange of the war years made the foreign business an unworkable anachronism. Darwin P. Kingsley optimistically declared in 1915: "The New York Life is so worldwide in its operations that nothing can happen anywhere in the civilized world . . . that does not become a matter of concern to us"; but it was far beyond the capacity of the companies to cope with the environment of war.

Early in the conflict, the firms stopped taking business in Germany and Austria-Hungary. Kingsley feared that the German government might not allow the New York Life to sell deposit securities there to meet expenses which could not be covered in any other way. The Mutual complained to the Department of State that policies sent from the Central Powers to New York were delayed or lost, and assumed that the British blockade was responsible. The New York Life left Turkey in the face of new regulations in 1915, and had to cope with heavy new premium taxes in Russia. An attempt to levy payment from Germany in settlement of insurance claims arising from submarine sinkings suggested the dimensions — and the difficulties — of the wartime business milieu. No less complicated were problems of inflation. At the beginning of the war the French government legalized contract payments in legal tender. But by November 1917 the authorities were putting pressure on the New York Life to increase its securities deposit to compensate for the depreciation of its gold value.[25]

Peace in 1918 brought no surcease but rather the chaos of inflation, the collapse of old governments, and the establishment of new ones. Even the New York Life by now had given up its overseas venture; by 1919 no United States life insurance company actively sought business abroad. But when the New York Life tried to settle with its French policyholders in 1920, a French court held that the policies would have to be paid in all but unobtainable gold francs. In less stable areas the disarray was even worse; the New York Life called on the State Department to protect its interests in Austria, Russia, Bulgaria, Turkey, and Germany. The company sought to transfer to local firms its remaining policies in the new states carved out of the Austro-Hungarian empire, but was bedeviled by problems incident to these changes of sovereignty.

Through the 1920's the process of disengagement continued. Between 1921 and 1926 the New York Life reinsured or retired all of its foreign business save that in Canada, Mexico, and the Soviet Union. The problems of settlement with Communist Russia were in a class by themselves, and not until the 1930's did the Equitable resolve the last of them and so finally close the life insurance venture overseas.[26]

5

Participation in high finance had been an important expression of the large companies' pre-1905 drive to corporate power and place. Properly enough, their investment experience after the Armstrong inquiry underscored the extent of their disengagement from earlier values. The aggressive approach that prevailed before 1905 now was replaced by a more neutral, or defensive, technique: the response to a new regulatory milieu and to new investment purposes.

The Armstrong laws thrust directly at the prevailing life insurance–investment finance partnership. By demanding that the companies rid themselves of their stock holdings (including bank and trust company securities), bonds secured by stock, collateral loans, and syndicate participations, the New York law of 1906 tried to eliminate most of the ties of common interest that bound the companies to the world of high finance.

To some extent, regulatory authority responded to the spirit of this legislation. Superintendent Hotchkiss sternly demanded in 1911 that the Equitable rapidly reduce its bank and trust company stock holdings to a maximum of 5 percent of each institution's issue, and have no more than one representative on the boards of directors of corporations in which the Equitable was interested. The department in 1908 forced the companies to stop their practice of lending bonds to national banks to be used as collateral for increased bank note circulation. In 1909 the firms were pressured to rid themselves of their real estate, outside of their home office buildings, within five years. This heightened supervision was not always constraining; for example, Governor Hughes signed a bill allowing life insurance companies to participate in reorganization arrangements for bankrupt companies in which they held securities. But the dominant pattern clearly implemented the Armstrong legislation's intention of destroying the pre-1905 structure of investment affiliations.[27]

The new investment tendencies prevailed during the panic of 1907. The companies claimed to be greatly concerned over the panic's impact on their financial position. The shrinkage in security values was particularly unsettling because it came toward the end of the year, and thus adversely affected market value listings in the annual report schedules. The New York Life decided in October that "on account of the existing depreciation in market values, it will be the part of conservatism to take something off book value before declaring the dividend for the year 1909," and struck $5,000,000 off by reducing its computed interest rate from 4 percent to 3.1 percent. The New York superintendent was willing to accept computations based on an average valuation month rather than a valuation resting on the December totals alone, but he did not approve of the New York Life's action and sharply pointed out that the company could well have fallen back on its huge deferred dividend surplus. Suggestive was the protective and retrenching, rather than aggressive and expansive, quality of the New York Life's reaction to the fall in securities prices; suggestive too was the insurance department's quick disapproval of even so mild a response.[28]

The companies' disengagement from high finance had internal as well as external impulsion. Even before the Armstrong investigation, there were signs that the firms' aggressive financial policies had passed their peak: the New York Life divested itself of its stock control over the New York Security and Trust and the Mutual decided in 1903 to seek no further trust company connections. The revelations of 1905 sped up the process. The Mutual sold its Guaranty Trust and United States Mortgage and Trust stock to James Stillman and to Edward H. Harriman; soon these institutions passed directly into the hands of J. P. Morgan and Company. The Equitable's Mercantile Safe Deposit, National Bank of Commerce, and Equitable Trust holdings similarly came under the control of that greatest of investment banking houses. In January 1906 John Dryden set down the principles henceforth governing Prudential investment policy: high quality at low prices; securities purchases from diverse brokers; no Public Service Corporation bonds after the Prudential's existing obligations were fulfilled. In 1908 the Public Service Corporation made the break physical by moving its offices to a separate building. The Fidelity Trust remained on the Prudential's premises, and continued to satisfy most of its banking needs, but in the course of its mutualization the insurance company sold its FTC stock.

The New York Life's relations with the house of Morgan became more remote. President McCall told George Perkins in December 1905, while closing out his firm's Morgan account, "Please assure him [J. P. Morgan] that there is no possibility for his firm being in any way bothered in this way again as there is nothing that could by any possibility come up that would in any way involve any transaction with his house." The New York Life's finance committee Minutes testified to the disengagement of the firm once most committed of all to the world of high finance: syndicate participations disappeared; bond issues were taken from a more diversified listing of brokers; a personal call loan to the Metropolitan's Hegeman was taken up; the company's International Mercantile Marine holdings were sold.[29]

Thereafter, the New York Life, in common with its peers, concentrated on more traditional modes of investment activity. The direct, uncomplicated purchase of railroad bonds, municipals, real estate mortgages, premium notes, and policy loans became the norm. Securities investment, at a peak of 51.2 percent of the companies' assets in 1905, declined to 41.9 percent in 1915. The Mutual's President Peabody concentrated on the relatively innocuous field of urban mortgage financing; the Mutual, the Equitable, and particularly the Prudential moved more substantially into the field of farm mortgaging. Life insurance investment so directed became more of a national, and less of a Wall Street, operation. Under the aegis of the Association of Life Insurance Presidents, formulas would be worked out governing the proper distribution of investments to all of the states.[30]

In 1910 the Pujo Committee of the House subjected the interlocking directorates of high finance to examination. It revealed that the investment bankers — particularly J. P. Morgan and Company — had unchallenged control over the apparatus of high finance. Contacts still existed between the great insurance companies and the great investment houses, but they were peripheral: the life firms had a minor place in the Pujo Committee's picture of interlocking financial leadership. The Pujo report spoke of the bankers' influence in insurance companies, and their control "over other people's money and property in the determination of questions and policies," but no evidence comparable to that produced by the Armstrong investigation substantiated these accusations. At most a degree of dependence had replaced the pre-Armstrong partnership with investment banking. When Brandeis later recalled of 1905, "The fundamental and greatest danger of the insurance situation was the steady accumulation of the quick capital of the country under the control of a few individuals in or near Wall Street," he implied that this was a past phenomenon.[31]

The years immediately after the Armstrong investigation saw a profound transformation of the large firms. Their political, managerial, corporate, marketing, and investment functions shared a common disengagement from power. The pre-Armstrong society of great life companies — aggressive, self-confident, power-oriented — existed no more. And in the ensuing decades a fundamentally different business style characterized the giants of the life insurance enterprise.

XVII * The End of Power

Numerous indicators recorded the end of the pre-1905 society of great life insurance companies. The firms had been stripped of their foreign business, their investment affiliations, their structure of political influence; they were dominated by a new breed of cautious executives. During the next half century the companies found that, paradoxically, the end of power led to new heights of business success.

In the long run, the life insurance corporations showed great capacity for growth. After the immediate post-Armstrong years, the large firms — and the business in general — rose to undreamed-of volume and size. The Prudential's $500,000,000 worth of new insurance in 1909, the largest annual business volume for one company to that time, set the pace for the vast scale of life insurance marketing to come. The industrial firms, with greatly expanded straight life departments, led the way. The Metropolitan had the largest amount of insurance in force in 1910; it and the Prudential were first and second in 1915; by 1920 they had forged far ahead of their nearest Big Three competitor, the New York Life.

Although the Great Depression temporarily stopped the industry's expansion, its assets never actually diminished; annual outlays fell less than 5 percent below predepression levels, and company failure or default was extremely rare. Since the mid-1930's, in the face of the competition of Social Security, World War II government insurance, and increasingly numerous pension plans and mutual and trust funds, the life insurance enterprise has steadily expanded, to remain one of the great instruments of American saving (see Table 11).[1]

TABLE 11. Life insurance in force in the United States, 1900–1960 (millions of dollars)

Year	Ordinary	Group	Industrial	Credit	Total	Percent of increase over preceding decade
1900	6,124	—	1,449	—	7,573	115
1910	11,783	—	3,125	—	14,908	95
1920	32,018	1,570	6,948	4	40,540	175
1930	78,576	9,801	17,963	73	106,413	165
1940	79,346	14,938	20,866	380	115,530	10
1950	149,071	47,793	33,415	3,899	234,168	105
1960	340,268	175,434	39,563	31,183	586,448	150

Source: Institute of Life Insurance, *Life Insurance Fact Book*, 1961.

This substantial growth evoked little of the concern that accompanied the rise of the pre-1905 society of great companies. The delegates to the twentieth anniversary convention of the Association of Life Insurance Presidents must have derived a special pleasure from the words of speaker Charles Evans Hughes: "I am not here to review the past save as I am permitted to congratulate you upon the unparalleled growth and soundness of the life insurance enterprise. [The expansion of the last twenty years] . . . has been achieved with wise conservation in management, without undue expenditures in obtaining business, and with the returns to policy holders that are consistent with safety. I believe there is no safer or better-managed business in our country than yours." Antitrust activity has not touched life insurance; and the companies have not had a central place in the concerns of those disturbed by the phenomenon of big business.[2]

After 1905, fears were expressed that the Armstrong investment restrictions would force life insurance companies to engage in debilitating competition with savings banks for the same classes of investments, and would mean "the dropping out of our life-insurance capital from among the agencies acting as propelling forces in business." These fears were not ill-founded. The Temporary National Economic Committee's report on life insurance in the late 1930's made much of the point that the companies, bound to the safest sort of bond investments, had not been a source of venture capital. But this was the very antithesis of the pre-1905 alarm over insurance investment. The concern in the thirties was with the inertia of bureaucratized fund placement, not with the machinations of purposeful leaders. This was criticism of institutionalized flaccidity, not of institutionalized power.[3]

Just as the burgeoning companies avoided imputations of monopoly, so did their vast fund placements proceed without manifest entanglement in the higher circles of investment finance. Law and custom kept the insurance firms out of the stock market boom of the 1920's; New York's 1928 legislation allowing them to invest up to 2 percent of their assets in certain types of stocks had little immediate effect on their portfolios. During the depression years of the 1930's and the war years of the 1940's life insurance investments poured into government issues, until by the mid-1940's almost half of their assets were so placed. But even more rapidly, in the latter years of the decade, government issues were sold or replaced, and soon amounted to only 6 percent of total assets. Substantial fund placements went into urban housing and office projects, permitted by New York law after 1938, and into wide holdings of industrial bonds. Investment policy now was shaped by large, systematized departments, the companies' own; direct negotiation replaced the use of investment banker intermediaries. Growth and size now meant systematized bureaucratization, not systematized power; investment policies perhaps were unimaginative, but they were not reckless or irresponsible.[4]

The same pattern characterized the companies' dealings with the body politic. Taxation remained, of course, a primary concern. But though the principle of heavy Federal and state corporate taxation gained wide acceptance during the 1930's, life insurance companies escaped substantial levies. From 1921 to 1950, the valuation rate necessary to maintain reserves generally determined the taxable income of the industry; and that rate was established by insurance commissioners and the companies. This system made it possible for them to avoid taxation entirely during some of the depression years of the 1930's, and to enjoy low rates in the 1940's.

Although the great companies contributed to industry-wide legislative lobbying, their favorable tax experience could not be attributed to special political power. Rather, their image of quasi-public service, fostered by the very fact of their disengagement from areas of overt power, gave them protection. Thus, Supreme Court Justice Benjamin Cardozo could favor tax exemption because the purchase of life insurance was "a pressing social duty"; and taxation law expert Roswell Magill argued that since life insurance was so widely held "this tax leakage does not really derange the equity of the tax system." [5]

After 1950, Federal taxes — and Congress' interest in the insurance tax formula — grew substantially. This was due not so much to the fading of the companies' eleemosynary image as to the fact that it no longer was unique. If many corporate groups now claimed a more than private role, none could expect other than normal tax treatment. But enough of the special image of the insurance enterprise has remained to keep its tax rate moderate.

The course of insurance supervision strikingly paralleled that of taxation. After the Armstrong period, state regulation settled down as a quiet, matured institution. Numerous life insurance bills were proposed — 1,300 in 1909; 3,300 in 1923; 2,300 in 1925 — but the number enacted stayed below 150 a year. Less than ten percent of 1909's proposed legislation became law; for 1925 the figure was 4.44 percent. Sentiment persisted for systematized regulation, but the New Deal ended scattered industry interest in Federal supervision. When in the 1940's national government control became a possibility at last, the great companies were in the forefront in the successful fight to preserve the state system.

The Supreme Court's *South Eastern Underwriters* decision of 1944 reversed the judicial inclinations of three quarters of a century, and put insurance companies with a substantial interstate business under the sway of the commerce clause. The logical corollary was Federal regulation, with numerous commissions and statutes — the Sherman and Clayton Antitrust acts, the Federal Trade Commission, the National Labor Relations Board, the Fair Labor Standards Act — exerting authority over the insurance enterprise.

But no one — not President Franklin Roosevelt, nor the Justice Department, nor, of course, the industry — wanted state regulation scrapped in favor of a Federal system. Justice Robert Jackson, in his *South Eastern Underwriters* dissent, voiced the prevalent view: "To use my office, at a time like this, and with so little justification in necessity, to dislocate the functions and revenues of the state and to catapult Congress into immediate and undivided responsibility for supervision of the nation's insurance business is more than I can reconcile with my view of the function of this Court in our society." Some forty states petitioned for a Supreme Court rehearing, and the House quickly passed a bill exempting insurance companies from the Sherman and Clayton acts.

Public Law 15 — the McCarran-Ferguson Act of 1945 — was Congress' answer to the challenge posed by the *South Eastern Underwriters* decision. It was a unique enactment, telling much about the special place of the insurance enterprise. It gave the stamp of congressional approval to state regulation and taxation, and declared that the Federal regulation in question would apply only "to the extent that such business is not regulated by state law." The states had until 1948 (later extended) to pass appropriate legislation. The Supreme Court upheld what seemed very like a delegation of congressional powers to the states; it was the common consensus that state regulation was too firmly entrenched to be seriously threatened. This was a major victory for the industry. Once again, the special status of life insurance had worked to its interests. The substantiality of the post-1905 structure of insurance supervision had enabled the companies to escape the trend toward Federal regulation so central to the 1930's and the 1940's.[6]

The business technique of the companies changed no less than their investment and political relationships. Out of the post-1905 turmoil there emerged a new order of marketing. The aggressive commercialism of the pre-Armstrong days gave way to more restrained techniques. The National Association of Life Underwriters, established in 1907, worked for the professionalization of the agency corps. The Nylic agents' organization returned to the New York Life in 1910, but without the crusading flavor given it by George Perkins. The Big Three agreed in 1907 on uniform commission schedules; but they were impelled by the requirements of new regulation, not by an internal dynamic to aggrandizement. The Prudential found it necessary under the New Jersey laws to add a system of fixed salaries to its agency and superintendency contracts.

Advertising now had a defensive as well as an aggressive role. The Mutual called on N. W. Ayer for pioneering advertising agency work in public relations. The Metropolitan widely disseminated public health precepts. There developed a special brand of life insurance publicity: oblique, heavily laden with the image of public service, enhancing the eleemosynary aspect of the industry.[7]

Most notably, the companies reached out to broad, hitherto untouched masses of potential policyholders — to middle-income groups not attracted by the business-professional appeal of the deferred dividend policy or by the minimal burial-insurance offerings of the pre-1905 industrial firms. The rising interest in alternative modes of insurance — Massachusetts' savings bank plan, Wisconsin's state insurance, systems of government-sponsored workmen's compensation in Europe — stimulated the companies to widen the appeal of life insurance. The industrial firms helped to defeat attempts to spread savings bank insurance and paid close attention to European developments. The Prudential sent statistician Frederick L. Hoffman to study the impact of government insurance on European firms, and the Metropolitan drew heavily on the work of Lee Frankel and Miles M. Dawson on workingmen's insurance in the Old World. Henry L. Rosenfeld, assistant to President Paul Morton of the Equitable, went to England in 1908 to study group insurance plans there.[8]

Everywhere, signs of the new orientation appeared. The Equitable, under the lead of Rosenfeld, pioneered in American group insurance. Darwin P. Kingsley found it expedient to intersperse talks to the National Civic Federation on Federal insurance regulation with a discourse on employers' responsibilities for workingmen's insurance. The most active practitioner of the new approach was the Metropolitan. At a 1909 meeting of the National Civic Federation (symbolically enough, the favored platform of power-oriented exponents of Federal regulation like Perkins and Kingsley), Vice-President Haley Fiske heard Lee Frankel, a sociologist for the Russell Sage Foundation, report on government insurance in Europe. Within a few weeks, Frankel had become the manager of the Metropolitan's industrial department, charged with broadening the effectiveness and scope of that branch of the company's business. Frankel took the lead in developing the principle of life conservation: that it was sound business, and moral business, to lengthen the life expectancy of the common man. The Metropolitan established a welfare division in 1910, and under Frankel's guidance pioneered in health education and a visiting nurse service. The Equitable too, in 1910, created a life conservation department.[9]

In 1909 the Metropolitan completed its distinctive landmark, the tower of its Madison Square home office; in 1912 fire destroyed the ornate Equitable home office building erected by Henry Hyde. The two events symbolize a fundamental change of business style. If Hyde's Equitable was typical of the pre-1905 insurance enterprise, then the Metropolitan — gigantic, highly bureaucratized, yet projecting an image of corporate beneficence — typified the post-Armstrong face of life insurance. The New York insurance commissioner took note of the evolution in 1914. He accounted private low-cost insurance an exception to the growing tendency to look to government "for the accomplishment of quasi-public purposes." Companies like the Metropolitan, he thought, had "recognized that organized wealth under private management must if it is going to be allowed to exist at all, assume certain public responsibilities which were not dreamed of under any of the old philosophies." [10]

Manifestly the great companies remained private corporations, not social service institutions. But whatever indictments might be leveled against them, they could no longer be accused of a virile, unalloyed drive to corporate power. It is suggestive that a large sampling of corporate executives in 1959 revealed that insurance men were the best educated, the most active in community affairs — and the lowest paid. In 1956 C. Wright Mills posited an American power elite, but tangentially mentioned only one insurance leader, and dealt with the large companies not at all. In this sense the firms have continued to play a prototypal role. If before 1905 they showed the way (in the end, abortively) in a sophisticated quest for corporate power, since then they have led in the development of a business style that has allayed the suspicions of the society at large.[11]

Through decades filled with new challenges to private underwriting, the life insurance enterprise grew steadily. This was not necessarily a tribute to its efficiency and economy; government insurance might well have been more widespread and less costly. Nevertheless, the vitality of private insurance companies in the middle of the twentieth century was as striking a fact as their relative immunity from Federal taxation or regulation.

Once the great companies took on a reassuring corporate face, they were able to persist virtually unchallenged. This development has relevance to the query posed by Adolf A. Berle and John K. Galbraith: if competition and the judgment of the market place no longer check the actions of corporations, does anything serve as a brake? For Berle and for Galbraith, the answer is a complex of external, countervailing powers: the state, organized labor, public opinion.[12] But the turn of the century was not notable for the balance of social forces: especially then a powerful, committed group of corporations might have expected to make its way without serious hindrance.

Yet in seemingly unrelated spheres of activity, the companies' drive to power had similar, unsatisfactory consequences. Both the political and the investment structures fostered questionable practices which in the long run proved troublesome, expensive, self-defeating. Sophisticated marketing (both domestic and foreign) and sophisticated investment alike bore unwanted fruit: fractionalized, diffused decisionmaking which lessened the firms' effectiveness. The assumption of a quasi-public status had complex — and constraining — corporate, juridical, and political consequences. Finally, the Armstrong investigation focused the concern of an aroused community, exposed the already shaky structure of the society of companies to public view, and stimulated a profound evolution of their corporate being.

The marketing, investment, and public policy experiences of the great companies in the past half century suggest that they found success in their very weakness: outside the millrace of corporate power, they avoided the countervailing forces that have been so consequential in modern America.

The lesson is plain. To the traditional sum of external checks on power in a free society should be added the complex but significant factor of internal restraints: the problems and consequences inherent in the processes of institutional growth and maturity. Together, these internal and external limitations were sufficient to contain and transform even so puissant a group of American corporations as the large life insurance companies.

BIBLIOGRAPHICAL NOTE

NOTES : INDEX

A.A.P.S.S.	American Academy of Political and Social Science
A.B.A.	American Bar Association
A.L.I.P.	Association of Life Insurance Presidents
Arch.	Archives (if unspecified, National Archives)
B.C.	Bureau of Corporations, Department of Commerce
C.F.C.	*Commercial and Financial Chronicle*
C.R.	*Congressional Record*
Dec. File	Decimal File
Dip. Des.	Diplomatic Despatches
Dip. Ins.	Diplomatic Instructions
Dom. Let.	Domestic Letters
Equit.	Equitable Life Assurance Society of the United States
G.J.M.	*Grand Jury Minutes,* New York Life, December 1906
H.P.	History Project
Ins. Rep.	*Insurance Report*
J.H.	John Hancock Mutual Life Insurance Company
Lbs.	President's Letterbooks
M.B.D.	*Minutes of the Board of Directors*
M.B.T.	*Minutes of the Board of Trustees*
M.E.C.	*Minutes of the Executive Committee*
Met.	Metropolitan Life Insurance Company of New York
M.F.C.	*Minutes of the Finance Committee*
Misc. Let.	Miscellaneous Letters
Mut.	Mutual Life Insurance Company of New York
N.C.I.C.	National Convention [Association] of Insurance Commissioners
N.J., *Test.*	New Jersey, *Testimony Taken before the Select Committee of the Senate . . . to Inquire into the Business of Life Insurance Companies Doing Business in New Jersey* (4 v., Paterson, N.J., 1906)
Numer. File	Numerical File
N.Y.S.L.B.	New York State Library Bulletin
N.Y., *Test.*	New York, *Testimony Taken Before the Joint Committee of the Senate and Assembly of the State of New York to Investigate and Examine into the Business and Affairs of Life Insurance Companies Doing Business in the State of New York* (10 v., Albany, N.Y., 1905)
N.Y.L.	New York Life Insurance Company
Pru.	Prudential Insurance Company of America
State	Department of State
W.U.	*Weekly Underwriter*

BIBLIOGRAPHICAL NOTE

The lineaments of the life insurance enterprise may be traced through a multitude of sources. The notes specify the data for the component parts of this study. But it may be helpful to present an overview of these materials as an example of what may be used in the institutional analysis of an American business enterprise.

THE COMPANIES

The companies themselves were rich sources of material. The Equitable lost many of its records, including its minute books, in a 1912 fire, but its History Project has gathered together an impressive body of material from the home and branch offices. The secretary's office has data on the mutualization of the Equitable; and the law department has a collection of old legal opinions. In addition, the voluminous Papers of Henry B. and James Hazen Hyde are at the Baker Library of Harvard University.

The files of the secretary's office at the John Hancock are relatively sparse before 1912, but proved revealing on intercompany and regulatory matters.

The Metropolitan has the Minutes of its board of directors and finance committee and, in its Archives, newspaper scrapbooks and sundry correspondence.

The Minutes of the finance committee and board of trustees were available at the Mutual. In addition, a search uncovered the all-but-forgotten letterbooks of its presidents, dating back to the early 1880's.

The New York Life's records include its finance committee and board of trustees Minutes; some miscellaneous executive correspondence; material relating to its business overseas; microfilms of the portion of the George W. Perkins Papers that pertains to his life insurance career; and the company's early Docket Books.

Finally, the Prudential made available the Minutes of its board of directors, executive committee, and finance committee; a fairly substantial collection of clippings and correspondence; and a typescript history of the company. The papers of John F. Dryden were, alas, destroyed by his family several years ago.

Several deposits in the National Archives proved to be treasure troves of material. The records of the State Department provided enlightening data on the vicissitudes of the companies overseas; and the Bureau of Corporations files in the Department of Commerce records told much about the firms' drive for federal regulation.

The Papers of William C. Beer, New York Life lobbyist and father of the writer Thomas Beer, are at Yale University, and the Papers of pioneer actuary and insurance reformer Elizur Wright are at Harvard's Baker Library. The Library of Congress has the material pertaining to Wright's career as an abolitionist. The New York State Library has some interesting correspondence from the journalist Poultney Bigelow to the New York insurance commissioner, written when Bigelow was that official's personal ambassador to the Prussian government, charged to intercede for the American companies there.

Intermittently helpful were the collections of Albert J. Beveridge, Joseph H. Choate, Charles Evans Hughes, William McKinley, Theodore Roosevelt, and Elihu Root (Library of Congress).

The ten volumes of testimony, exhibits, and analysis produced by the 1905 Armstrong investigation in New York constitutes one of the most complete dissections of an American enterprise. This study often drew upon the great mass of testimony and data obtained by chief investigator Charles Evans Hughes and his staff.

Company histories abound, but they vary considerably in quality. The best of them for the purposes of this study were R. Carlyle Buley, *The Equitable Life Assurance Society of the United States* (New York, 1959); Shepard B. Clough, *A Century of American Life Insurance: A History of the Mutual Life Insurance Company of New York, 1843–1943* (New York, 1946); and Marquis James, *The Metropolitan Life* (New York, 1947). A lesser breed, but useful, were James M. Hudnut, *Semi-Centennial History of the New York Life Insurance Company, 1845–1895* (New York, 1895) and *History of the New York Life Insurance Company, 1895–1905* (New York, 1906); Lawrence F. Abbott, *The Story of NYLIC* (New York, 1930); Frederick L. Hoffman, *History of the Prudential Insurance Company of America* (Newark, N.J., 1900); Earl C. May and Will Oursler, *The Prudential* (Garden City, N.Y., 1950); Louis I. Dublin, *A Family of Thirty Million* [Metropolitan] (New York, 1943); and Emil Schwab, *The John Hancock: An Historical Sketch* (Boston, 1912).

Much useful material appeared in the periodical literature of the time. Most valuable were Henry S. Beardsley, "The Despotism of Combined Millions," *Era,* XIV–XV (November, 1904–February, 1905); William J. Graham, "The Romance of Life Insurance," *World To-Day,* XIV–XVI (June, 1908–May, 1909) (also published in book form as *The Romance of Life Insurance* (Chicago, 1908); Burton J. Hendrick, *The Story of Life*

Insurance (New York, 1907), based on a series of articles in *McClure's*; Thomas W. Lawson, *Frenzied Finance* (New York, 1905), drawn from an *Everybody's* series; and the articles by 'Q.P.' in *World's Work* during 1905 and 1906. The *Commercial and Financial Chronicle,* the "Insurance" column of the *Independent,* and numerous articles in the *North American Review, Nation, Arena,* and the journals mentioned above were extremely useful.

At many points my interpretation is similar to the pioneering work of Douglass C. North: "The Large Life Insurance Companies Before 1906" (unpubl. diss., University of California, 1952); "Capital Accumulation in Life Insurance Between the Civil War and the Investigation of 1905," in William Miller, ed., *Men in Business* (Cambridge, Mass., 1952); "Entrepreneurial Policy and Internal Organization in Large Life Insurance Companies at the Time of the Armstrong Investigation of Life Insurance," *Explorations in Entrepreneurial History,* V (1952–1953), 139–161; and "Life Insurance and Investment Banking at the Time of the Armstrong Investigation, 1905–06," *Journal of Economic History,* XIV (Summer 1954), 209–228.

THE ENTERPRISE

A rich source of insights into patterns of regulatory thinking, and of statistical and descriptive data on the evolution of the life insurance enterprise, are the reports of the state insurance departments. The New York Insurance Society Library has a complete set. The Legislative Bulletins of the New York State Library Bulletin indexed and analyzed insurance legislation from 1890 to 1909.

The life insurance business has had a flourishing trade press, an endless source of information on the details of the enterprise. The *Weekly Underwriter* proved most useful in this study. Also consulted were the *Chronicle; Best's Insurance News; Insurance Monitor; Insurance Times; Spectator;* and *Standard.* Few complete runs of these journals have survived; the best collection by far is in the New York Insurance Society Library.

A network of more specialized publications testifies to the scope and complexity of the life insurance enterprise. The *Insurance Law Journal*; the *Proceedings* of the National Convention of Insurance Commissioners, the National Association of Life Underwriters, and the Association of Life Insurance Presidents; the publications of the Spectator Company, especially its *Insurance Year Book*; and the *Life Insurance Fact Book* of the Institute of Life Insurance are among these sources. Guilford A. Deitch, comp., *Digest of Insurance Cases* (Indianapolis, Ind., 1889f) is a convenient summary of insurance litigation. A. J. Flitcraft, comp., *Charters and By-Laws* (Oak Park, Ill., 1905) is a useful work. Compilations of statistical material are Walter C. Wright, "Life Insurance in the United States," *Publications of the American Statistical Association,* I (1888), 127–156; Frederick L. Hoffman, "Fifty Years of American Life Insurance Progress," *Publications of the American Statistical Association,* XII (1911), 667–760; and U.S. Department of the Interior, Census Office, *Report on Insurance Business in the*

United States at the 11th Census: 1890. Part II. Life Insurance (Washington, 1895). Raymond W. Goldsmith, *Financial Intermediaries in the American Economy since 1900* (Princeton, N.J., 1958) and Goldsmith, *A Study of Saving in the United States* (3 v., Princeton, N.J., 1955) are analyses that contain a great deal of data on life insurance investment.

Contemporary writings of value include the articles on insurance that appeared periodically in the *Annals* of the American Academy of Political and Social Science; William A. Fricke, comp., *Insurance: A Text-Book: A Compilation of the Addresses Delivered before the 29th Session of the National Convention of Insurance Commissioners . . . 1898* [n.p., n.d.]; William Alexander's memoir, *My Half-Century in Life Insurance* (New York, 1935); Lester W. Zartman, ed., *Yale Readings in Insurance. Life Insurance* (New Haven, Conn., 1909); and Howard P. Dunham, comp., *The Business of Insurance* (3 v., New York, 1912).

Bibliographies of works on insurance may be found in Henrietta M. Larson, *Guide to Business History* (Cambridge, Mass., 1948), pp. 194–201; J. Owen Stalson, *Marketing Life Insurance* (Cambridge, Mass., 1942), pp. 654–656; and Terence O'Donnell, comp., *History of Life Insurance in its Formative Years* (Chicago, 1936), pp. 819–833. Works of special importance for this study include Stalson's massive study of life insurance marketing; R. Carlyle Buley's detailed history of the industry's trade association, *The American Life Convention, 1906–1952* (2 vols., New York, 1953); George L. Amrhein, *The Liberalization of the Life Insurance Contract* (Philadelphia, 1933); Charles K. Knight, *The History of Life Insurance in the United States to 1870* (Philadelphia, 1920); Edwin W. Patterson, *The Insurance Commissioner in the United States* (Cambridge, Mass., 1929); Spencer L. Kimball, *Insurance and Public Policy: A Study in the Legal Implementation of Social and Economic Public Policy, Based on Wisconsin Records, 1835–1959* (Madison, Wis., 1960); and Lester W. Zartman, *The Investment of the Life Insurance Companies* (New York, 1907). The best of the numerous histories of other American companies is Harold F. Williamson and Orange A. Smalley, *Northwestern Mutual Life: A Century of Trusteeship* (Evanston, Ill., 1957).

NOTES

CHAPTER I. THE LIFE INSURANCE ENTERPRISE

1. Alfred Manes, "Outlines of a General Economic History of Insurance," *The Journal of Business of the University of Chicago,* XV (1942), 30–48.

2. Charles Wright and C. Ernest Fayle, *A History of Lloyd's* (London, 1928), pp. 44, 80, 91–92. See William R. Scott, *The Constitution and Finance of English, Scottish and Irish Joint-Stock Companies to 1720* (Cambridge, 1912), I, 383–384, III, 363–411, on these and more respectable insurance enterprises, 1706–1710.

3. Harold E. Raynes, *A History of British Insurance* (2nd ed., London, 1950), p. 137, chap. 8; 14 Geo. 3, c. 48.

4. Willis H. Hazard, *The Fathers of Level-Premium Mutual Life Insurance* (Boston, 1924); D. E. W. Gibb, *Lloyd's of London: A Study in Individualism* (New York, 1957), chaps. 2–3; Ralph Straus, *The Gentlemen at the Coffee-House* (New York, 1938), Book One.

5. This interpretation of the insurance company in eighteenth and nineteenth century England is drawn from Armand B. DuBois, *The English Business Company after the Bubble Act, 1720–1800* (New York, 1938); Bishop C. Hunt, *The Development of the Business Corporation in England, 1800–1867* (Cambridge, Mass., 1936); and Colin A. Cooke, *Corporation, Trust and Company: An Essay in Legal History* (Manchester, Eng., 1950). See also Raynes, *British Insurance,* chaps. 13–14, and Hartley Withers, *Pioneers of British Life Assurance* (London, 1951).

6. For treatments of early American insurance, see: Charles K. Knight, *The History of Life Insurance in the United States to 1870* (Philadelphia, 1920), chap. 2; John A. Fowler, *History of Insurance in Philadelphia for Two Centuries* (Philadelphia, 1888); J. Owen Stalson, *Marketing Life Insurance* (Cambridge, Mass., 1942), chap. 3; R. Carlyle Buley, *The American Life Convention, 1906–1952* (New York, 1953), vol. I, chap. 2. See Marquis James, *Biography of a Business, 1792–1942* (Indianapolis, Ind., 1942) on the Insurance Company of North America; Alexander Mackie, *Facile Princeps: The Story of the Beginning of Life Insurance in America* (Lancaster, Penna., 1956) on the Presbyterian Ministers' Fund; and Samuel Williston, "The History of the Law of Business Corporations before 1800," *Selected Essays in Anglo-American Legal History* (Boston, 1909), III, 234, on the Philadelphia Contributionship.

7. Guy S. Callender, "The Early Transportation and Banking Enterprises of the States in Relation to the Growth of Corporations," *Quarterly Journal of*

Economics, LII (1902), 138n; Louis Hartz, *Economic Policy and Democratic Thought: Pennsylvania, 1776–1860* (Cambridge, Mass., 1948), pp. 40–41, 68; George H. Evans, *Business Incorporations in the United States, 1800–1943* (New York, 1948), pp. 26–28; Gerald T. White, *A History of the Massachusetts Hospital Life Insurance Company* (Cambridge, Mass., 1955), pp. 3, 8, 19; Stalson, *Marketing Life Insurance,* chap. 5.

8. Gerard C. Henderson, *The Position of Foreign Corporations in American Constitutional Law* (Cambridge, Mass., 1918), pp. 55, 64–66, 84, 101–108.

9. Stalson, *Marketing Life Insurance,* has the best description of the nineteenth century development of American life insurance.

10. *New York Ins. Rep.,* IX (1868), lxxxii; XI (1870), v. See also Sheppard Homans, "Life Insurance in the United States," *Banker's Magazine,* XXIV (1869), 447–453.

11. Sheppard Homans, "The Insurance Crisis," *North American Review,* CXXIV (1877), 254–264; Philip G. Wright and Elizabeth Q. Wright, *Elizur Wright* (Chicago, 1937).

12. *New York Ins. Rep.,* X (1869), lxxvii-lxxviii; Dana to Wright, Nov. 7, 1873, Sheppard Homans to Wright, Oct. 17, 1875, Wright Mss.

13. Harris Proschansky, "The Origins of the National Association of Life Underwriters," *Business History Review,* XXIX (1955), 238–262; Edward C. Howatt, "The National Association of Insurance Agents" (unpubl. thesis, University of Pennsylvania, 1945), pp. 2–3; Reinhard A. Hohans, "The Origin of the Society of Actuaries," *Transactions of the Society of Actuaries,* I (1949), 10–41. For the degree of professionalization attained by the turn of the century, see Fourth International Congress of Actuaries, 1903, *Proceedings* (New York, 1904).

14. Scott Greer, "Individual Participation in Mass Society," in Roland A. Young, ed., *Approaches to the Study of Politics* (Evanston, Ill., 1958), pp. 331, 338.

15. "Life and Fire Insurance as Related to Modern Business Economy," *Banker's Magazine,* LXII (1901), 398; *W.U.,* XLVI (1892), 391.

16. Willis D. Morgan, "The History and Economics of Suretyship (II)," *Cornell Law Quarterly,* XII (1927), 487–499.

17. Stalson, *Marketing Life Insurance,* chap. 19; Richard de R. Kip, "Fraternal Life Insurance" (unpubl. diss., University of Pennsylvania, 1951); National Industrial Conference Board, *Experience with Natural Benefit Associations in the United States,* Research Report no. 65 (New York, 1923).

18. Stalson, *Marketing Life Insurance,* chap. 20; Charles R. Henderson, "Industrial Insurance," *American Journal of Sociology,* XIII (1908), 350; Spectator Company, *Industrial Life Insurance. Its History, Statistics and Plans* (New York, 1955). On the English background, see Dermot Morrah, *A History of Industrial Life Assurance* (London, 1955).

19. *Massachusetts Ins. Rep.,* 42nd (1897), vi-vii.

CHAPTER II. A SOCIETY OF COMPANIES

1. *C.F.C.,* L (1890), 685–686, 786–787; *Chronicle,* XLV (1890), 102; *Missouri Ins. Rep.,* XX (1889), XXI (1900), x-xi; *Tennessee Ins. Rep.* (1893); quotation in *Insurance Times,* XXIII (1890), 555.

2. *C.F.C.,* LXVI (1898), 1025–1026; Mut., *M.B.T.,* Nov. 22, 1893; *Monthly Journal of Insurance Economics,* I (1899), 42; N.Y.L., *M.B.T.,* May 10, 1905.

3. L. A. Anderson, "Insurance Investment," A.A.P.S.S. *Annals,* XXIV (1904), 433; "Insurance," *Independent,* LVI (1904), 519; 'Q.P.,' "Irresponsible Insurance Millions," *World's Work,* XI (1906), 7100; "Comment," *Harper's Weekly,* XLVI (1902), 2019; McCall statement in N.Y., *Test.,* II, 1512.

4. The Prudential's Newark location was something of an accident. Founder John F. Dryden first secured a special charter from the New York legislature, but it was vetoed by the governor on the ground that the state's general in-

corporation law rendered it unnecessary. Then Dryden went to New Jersey. N.J., *Test., Report,* 170.

5. Dodd to Wright, April 11, 1867, Wright Mss.; *Insurance Times,* XXXI (1898), 119; McCall statement in N.Y., *Test.,* II, 1438.

6. Burton J. Hendrick, *The Story of Life Insurance* (New York, 1907), p. 6; Sydney A. Clark, *The First Hundred Years of the New England Mutual Life Insurance Company, 1835–1935* (Concord, N.H., 1935), p. 54; Harold F. Williamson and Orange A. Smalley, *Northwestern Mutual Life: A Century of Trusteeship* (Evanston, Ill., 1957), pp. 102–103, 108, 112; on Penn Mutual, N.Y., *Test.,* I, 232; Richard Hooker, *Aetna Life Insurance Company. Its First Hundred Years* (Hartford, 1956), p. 137. See Greene statement in "Modern Insurance and Its Possibilities," *North American Review,* CLVI (1893), 309. Other works giving the business tone of the small companies are: Richard Hooker, *A Century of Service. The Massachusetts Mutual Story* (Springfield, Mass., 1951); William S. Ashbrook, *Fifty Years: The Provident Life and Trust Company of Philadelphia, 1865–1915* (Philadelphia, 1915); Durlea Hurley, *Panorama of a Century, 1847–1947* (Penn Mutual) (Philadelphia, 1947); Albert W. Atwood, *The Great Stewardship* (Mutual Benefit Life of New Jersey) (New York, 1945).

7. N.Y., *Test.,* V, 4319. For collective profiles, see I. S. Grim, "The Masters of Insurance Finance," *World's Work,* X (1905), 6207–6214; "Men Who Control Millions. I. Group of Life-Assurance Presidents," *Harper's Weekly,* XXXIII (1889), 691–692; "Insurance Men Past and Present," *The International Insurance Encyclopedia* (New York and London, 1910), vol. I.

8. Hendrick, *Life Insurance,* pp. 107–117; R. Carlyle Buley, *The Equitable Life Assurance Society of the United States* (New York, 1959), pp. 1–2; William Alexander, *My Half-Century in Life Insurance* (New York, 1935), pp. 34–35.

9. Shepard B. Clough, *A Century of American Life Insurance: A History of the Mutual Life Insurance Company of New York, 1843–1943* (New York, 1946), p. 197; Hendrick, *Life Insurance,* pp. 124, 179–185, 188–189; Stephen English to Elizur Wright, Jan. 12, 1874, *et seq.,* Wright Mss.

10. Hendrick, *Life Insurance,* p. 193; Hyde to Wright, March 20, 1874, Wright Mss.: N.Y., *Test.,* III, 2268–2270; Clough, *Mutual,* pp. 142–145; Buley, *Equitable,* p. 59.

11. Mut., *M.B.T.,* July 25, Jan. 25, Nov. 25, 1888.

12. N.Y.L., *M.B.T.,* Feb. 18, 1890; Hendrick, *Life Insurance,* pp. 173–174.

13. N.Y.L., *M.B.T.,* Oct. 12, 1887, Feb. 2, 1888; July 8, Aug. 31, 1891; James M. Hudnut, *Semi-Centennial History of the New York Life Insurance Company, 1895–1905* (New York, 1906), pp. 245–247, 276; 'Q.P.,' "Insurance Millions," p. 7103; Perkins to Banta, July 11, 1891, Perkins Mss.

14. N.Y.L., *M.B.T.,* Dec. 1891–Dec. 1892, *passim,* April 12, 1905.

15. Earl C. May and Will Oursler, *The Prudential* (Garden City, N.Y., 1950), pp. 86–87, 99; Pru., *M.B.D.,* Dec. 31, 1878. See also "The Man — John F. Dryden," John F. Dryden file, Pru. Arch.; N.Y., *Test.,* VI, 4944–4949.

16. John R. Hegeman to various insurance companies, March 1881, Met. Arch.; Marquis James, *The Metropolitan Life* (New York, 1947), pp. 66–72, 84–85; May and Oursler, *Prudential,* pp. 90–93.

17. Emil Schwab, *The John Hancock: An Historical Sketch* (Boston, 1912), pp. 38, 42–43.

18. Hyde quoted in 'Q.P.,' "Insurance Millions," p. 7103; Mut., *M.B.T.,* Jan. 28, 1891.

19. N.Y., *Test.,* II, 1806, 1816, III, 2531.

20. McCurdy statement in "Modern Insurance," pp. 307, 309; Hyde statement in N.Y., *Test.,* IV, 2893.

21. On Perkins, N.Y.L., *M.B.T.,* Feb. 12, 1892; on Fiske, N.Y., *Test.,* I, 111. E. H. Harriman said of Bainbridge Colby: "he is the whole Equitable, and Mr. Hyde is nothing, he was the man [who] stated what they would or would not do."

N.Y., *Test.,* IV, 3092. Presidential secretaries — Hyde's William H. McIntyre, McCurdy's John K. Duer — also played important roles.

22. McCurdy statement in "Modern Insurance," p. 307; Dryden anecdote in Great Falls (Mont.) *Tribune,* June 27, 1904, Pru. Arch.

23. Richard McCurdy, "Possibly Misdirected Energy," *Independent,* LII (1900), 1385–1386.

24. Charles R. Flint, "Centralization and Natural Law," *Independent,* LIV (1902), 1027; James H. Hyde, "The Charm of the Road," *Harper's Magazine,* CIV (1902), 916–917.

25. John A. Garraty, *Right-Hand Man: The Life of George W. Perkins* (New York, 1960); David Bazelon, "Portrait of a Business Generalist," *Commentary,* XXIX (1960), 277–286.

CHAPTER III. AN IDEOLOGY OF POWER

1. Homans, "Life Insurance in the United States," p. 447; James W. Alexander, "Some Prejudices about Life Insurance," *Atlantic Monthly,* LXXXVI (1900), 23; Edward A. Woods, "Life Insurance and Social Progress," *World To-Day,* XVII (1909), 1199. See also Woods, *The Sociology of Life Insurance* (New York, 1928).

2. Hendrick, *Life Insurance,* p. 195; N.Y., *Test.,* I, 732, IV, 3569; McCurdy to Stuyvesant Fish, July 31, 1905, XXIII, Mut. Lbs.; Holmes quotation in Atwood, *Great Stewardship,* p. 7; Hegeman to Julius L. Clarke, Oct. 11, 1882, Met. Arch.; Met., *M.B.D.,* June 8, 1903; Pru., *M.E.C.,* Nov. 23, 1893.

3. William J. Graham, "The Romance of Life Insurance," *World To-Day,* XVI (1909), 388; *C.F.C.,* LIII, 385–387; N.J., *Test.,* p. 237. See also James H. Bridge, "John Fairfield Dryden," in "Captains of Industry," *Cosmopolitan,* XXXIV (1902), 167–168; and Dryden testimony in N.Y., *Test.,* VI, 4969.

4. John A. McCall, "Free Coinage and Life Insurance Companies," *Forum,* XXII (1896), 136; McCurdy to Stuyvesant Fish, July 31, 1905, XXIII, Mut. Lbs.; Hegeman to Julius L. Clarke, Oct. 11, 1882, Met. Arch.; McCurdy statement in N.Y., *Test.,* II, 1845–1847.

5. N.Y.L., *M.B.T.,* Nov. 20, 1893; Mut., *M.B.T.,* Jan. 29, 1902, Feb. 14, 1894. McCurdy's prediction was $700,000,000 short of the actual 1940 total.

6. Maurice H. Robinson, "Government Regulation of Insurance Companies," *Proceedings of the American Political Science Association,* III (1906), 81; N.Y., *Test.,* II, 1840–1842; Hyde to Spencer H. Hazard, May 16, 1895, B5, Hyde Mss.; Perkins to Rev. Henry M. Ladd, Dec. 6, 1897, Perkins Mss.; Darwin P. Kingsley, "An Age of Belief," *Independent,* LIV (1902), 3081; Kingsley, "The Driving Power of Life Insurance," *Review of Reviews,* XXXII (1905), 552. Kingsley's *The First Business of the World, and Other Addresses and Papers* (New York, 1905), had in its frontispiece: "I believe that life insurance is a new evangel, whose church is the heart of man."

7. Stalson, *Marketing Life Insurance,* pp. 504–505; A.L.I.P. *Proceedings,* 1907, p. 9; Darwin P. Kingsley, "Life Insurance — Its Service and Its Leadership," *Independent,* LII (1900), 2827.

8. James M. Beck, "The Federal Regulation of Life-Insurance," *North American Review,* CLXXXI (1905), 201; John A. McCall, "The Life Insurance Business in 1899," *Independent,* LII (1900), 151; Woods, "Life Insurance and Social Progress," p. 1200; McCall, "Free Coinage and Life Insurance Companies," p. 136; Kingsley, "Driving Power of Life Insurance," p. 554; Hyde memo to McCall, March 5/7, 1891, A29, Hyde Mss.; Alexander, "Some Prejudices about Life Insurance," p. 19; Mut., *M.B.T.,* Jan. 29, 1902, Jan. 25, 1888.

9. Kingsley, "Life Insurance — Its Service and Its Leadership," pp. 2826–2828; Kingsley, "Age of Belief," p. 3082; McCall, "Life Insurance Business in 1899," p. 151. See also Kingsley, *First Business,* pp. 20–21, and his typescript, "The Great Value to Us as a People and as a Nation Growing Out of the Operations

of Our Life Insurance Companies in the Foreign Field," Perkins Mss.; and Elbert Hubbard article in Howard P. Dunham, comp., *The Business of Insurance* (New York, 1912), I, 409–415. For expressions of insurance leaders' antiwar sentiments, see John R. Hegeman to Stewart L. Woodford, Nov. 18, 1897, Met. Arch.; Mut., *M.B.T.*, Feb. 18, 1896; George W. Perkins to William E. Ingersoll, April 12, 1898, Perkins Mss.

10. Mut., *M.B.T.*, June 9, 1897; Perkins to Major E. W. Halford, June 21, 1894, Perkins Mss.; William C. Beer to Solicitor, Dept. of State, June 17, 1899, Misc. Let., State, Arch.; Hyde to McCurdy, Nov. 23, 1893, B3, Dec. 4, 1887, A26, Hyde to Homans, March 16, 1892, A30, Hyde Mss.; Kingsley statement July–Aug., 1897, Perkins Mss.

11. Woodford to Hegeman, Nov. 2, 1897, Met. Arch.

12. Alexander, "Some Prejudices about Life Insurance," p. 21, 23; Kingsley, "Insurance Supervision and National Ideals," *North American Review*, CLXXXIX (1909), 481–496; N.Y.L., *M.B.T.*, April 12, 1905.

13. Louis D. Brandeis, *Business — A Profession* (Boston, 1914), pp. 109–153.

CHAPTER IV. GROWTH AND THE CORPORATE STRUCTURE

1. N.Y.L., *M.B.T.*, Feb. 8, 1892.

2. May and Oursler, *Prudential*, pp. 104–105, 109; James, *Metropolitan*, p. 129; Clough, *Mutual*, pp. 204–205; on the Metropolitan, Grim, "Masters of Insurance Finance," p. 6214, and N.Y., *Test.*, III, 2685.

3. N.Y.L., *M.B.T.*, April 13, 1887, Feb. 14, 1889. New by-laws in 1892 created the office of comptroller. *Ibid.*, April 13, 1892.

4. Pru., *M.B.D.*, Oct. 12, May 13, 1891, July 8, 1889, Dec. 12, 1900; Pru., *M.E.C.*, Sept. 17, 1901; Pru., *M.B.D.*, Jan. 4, 1904.

5. N.Y., *Test.*, II, 1737–1738, VII, 6046; on Wells, N.Y.L., *M.B.T.*, Nov. 9, 1898. On regional makeup of boards, Hyde to Depew, Oct. 27, 1891, A30, Hyde Mss.; Mut., *M.B.T.*, May 26, June 9, 1886.

6. McCurdy to W. S. Candee, Dec. 1897, XIX, Mut. Lbs.; N.Y., *Test.*, I, 762. See also Douglass C. North, "Entrepreneurial Policy and Internal Organization in the Large Life Insurance Companies at the Time of the Armstrong Investigation of Life Insurance," *Explorations in Entrepreneurial History*, V (1952–53), 139–140.

7. On Equitable building, Buley, *Equitable*, pp. 59–60. On New York Life building, N.Y.L., *M.B.T.*, Nov. 13, 1889, Nov. 13, 1895, May 13, 1896, Hudnut. *Semi-Centennial History*, p. 315. On Mutual building Mut., *M.B.T.*, Feb. 24, 1892, Clough, *Mutual*, pp. 209–210, 362–363; N.Y., *Test.*, III, 2009–2012. On Prudential building, Pru., *M.B.D.*, Jan. 8, 1899. On Metropolitan building, Met., *M.F.C.*, Jan. 12, 1893, James, *Metropolitan*, pp. 100, 112, 174, "Some Things Gained," *Outlook*, LXXXIII (1906), 152. On John Hancock building, Schwab, *John Hancock*, pp. 42–44.

8. Hegeman to W. B. Staniland, April 19, 1898, Met. Arch.

9. N.Y., *Test.*, I, 19–80.

10. Hendrick, *Life Insurance*, pp. 83, 172–174; N.Y.L., *M.B.T.*, March 9, 1892.

11. N.J., *Test.*, p. 174; Met., *M.B.D.*, Feb. 11, 1902; N.Y., *Test.*, I, 118–124.

12. N.Y.L., *M.F.C.*, Dec. 20, 1900; James, *Metropolitan*, p. 97.

13. On McCurdy, N.Y., *Test.*, II, 1817–1818; on McCall, N.Y.L., *M.F.C.*, Dec. 20, 1900; on Hegeman, N.Y., *Test.*, III, 2558–2562, Met., *M.F.C.*, Jan. 23, 1900, April 26, 1904.

14. N.Y., *Test.*, II, 1834–1838.

15. Depew statement in N.Y., *Test.*, IV, 3193–3195; McCurdy in N.Y., *Test.*, II, 1894; Dryden in N.J., *Test.*, pp. 196–198, N.Y., *Test.*, VI, 4858–4862.

16. Hyde statement in N.Y., *Test.*, IV, 2890; May and Oursler, *Prudential*, pp. 157, 162; on Richard McCurdy, "Current," *Harper's Weekly*, XLVI (1902), 2005.

17. N.Y., *Test.*, V, 4416.

18. On capitalization, James, *Metropolitan,* pp. 90–91, 97, 121, 189; Met., *M.B.D.*, April 27, 1889, Jan. 27, 1891; N.Y., *Test.*, III, 2332–2333. On mutualization, Met., *M.B.D.*, Feb. 15, April 22, 1902; James, *Metropolitan,* pp. 187–191.

19. Frederick L. Hoffman, *History of the Prudential Insurance Company of America* (Newark, 1900), 117; N.Y., *Test.*, VI, 4833.

20. N.Y., *Test.*, VI, 4869; Pru., *M.B.D.*, Jan., years cited; *Massachusetts Ins. Rep.*, XLVIII (1903), xxviii; *Newark Evening News,* Aug. 12, 1909.

21. Pru., *M.B.D.*, July 11, Oct. 10, 1898, Jan. 17, 1901; N.J. *Test.*, pp. 184–185; Hegeman and Fiske to Dryden, July 21, Dryden to Hegeman and Fiske, July 22, in Met., *M.B.D.*, July 26, 1898; James, *Metropolitan,* pp. 133–134.

22. Pru., *M.B.D.*, Jan. 4, 1901.

23. Pru., *M.B.D.*, Aug. 12, 1901; N.Y., *Test.*, VI, 4816–4827, 4866–4874.

24. N.Y., *Test.*, VI, 4817, 4819, X, 323.

25. N.Y., *Test.*, VI, 4827; *W.U.*, LXVII (1902), 291–292, 338; *Massachusetts Ins. Rep.*, XLVIII (1903), xx–xxvii, XLIX (1904), x–xi; Pru., *M.B.D.*, May 9, 1904; *Wisconsin Ins. Rep.*, 1904, p. 32.

26. Fiske to Dryden, Oct. 22, 1902, Hegeman and Fiske to Dryden, Oct. 31, in Met., *M.B.D.;* James, *Metropolitan,* pp. 133–134; *Robotham v. Prudential,* 53 Atl. 842, 853 (N.J. Court of Chancery, 1903); May and Oursler, *Prudential,* pp. 126–129. See also printed documents, "The Prudential-Fidelity Merger," Met. Arch., and Thomas W. Lawson, *Frenzied Finance* (New York, 1905), pp. 447–452.

27. Pru., *M.B.D.*, Jan. 13, 24, Feb. 5, 1903; N.Y., *Test.*, X, 323–324; N.J., *Test.*, p. 152f.

28. Schiff remark in N.Y., *Test.*, II, 1312–1313; Met., *M.B.D.*, Feb. 11, 1902.

29. Text of trust agreement in N.Y., *Test.*, I, 148–157; Equit., *Report to the Board of Directors . . . of the* [*Frick*] *Committee Appointed April 6th, 1905, to Investigate and Report Upon the Present Management of the Society,* p. 15.

30. Buley, *Equitable,* p. 113; Equit., *Report to the Board of Directors . . . April 6, 1905,* p. 35; 'Q.P.,' "Life Insurance Corruption," *World's Work,* XI (1906), 7320–7322. See accounts of the Equitable fight in Buley, *Equitable,* chap. 4; Mark Sullivan, *Pre-War America* (*Our Times, III*) (New York, 1930), pp. 67–68, and Chap. XV below. It is suggestive that other management men, like John A. McCall and Darwin P. Kingsley of the New York Life, sympathized with Alexander rather than with "the Frenchman" and saw no reason to worry about "the poor stockholders." Kingsley to Perkins, Feb. 13, 1905, McCall to Perkins, Feb. 25, Perkins Mss.

31. Equit., *Report to the Board of Directors . . . April 6, 1905,* p. 14; N.Y., *Test.*, I, 188, X, 97; Buley, *Equitable,* pp. 104, 118.

32. Charles E. Russell, "Where Did you Get It, Gentlemen?" *Everybody's Magazine,* XVIII (1908–1909), 119–120.

33. Buley, *Equitable,* pp. 118–121; Charles P. Norcross, "Owners of America. IX. E. H. Harriman," *Cosmopolitan,* XLVII (July 1909), 160; D. T. Pierce, "Men of the Month. I. Thomas F. Ryan," *World To-Day,* IX (1905), 56–57, and "Thomas F. Ryan, Corporation-Saver," *ibid.*, 6616; Walter Wellman, "American Life Insurance on Trial," *Review of Reviews,* XXXII (1905), 460.

34. Pierce, "Thomas F. Ryan, Corporation-Saver," p. 14; Alfred H. Lewis, "Owners of America. II. Thomas F. Ryan," *Cosmopolitan,* XLV (1908), 144–146; N.Y., *Test.*, V, 4578–4580; Burton J. Hendrick, "Great American Fortunes and Their Making," *McClure's,* XXX (1908), 323–338.

35. Buley, *Equitable,* pp. 150–151. See George F. Parker, "Cleveland and the Insurance Crisis," *McClure's,* XXXIII (1909), 185, 188.

CHAPTER V. GROWTH AND THE BUSINESS TECHNIQUE

1. Mut., *M.B.T.*, Jan. 27, 1892, Dec. 28, 1898.

2. Ernest Howard, "The Next Step in Life Insurance," *International Quarterly,*

XII (1905), 146–147; N.Y., *Test.*, III, 2506, 2550; on smaller companies, N.Y., *Test.*, V, 4741–4744.

3. *Chronicle,* XLVIII (1891), 273; Mut., *M.B.T.*, April 22, 1891; McCurdy to Lewis May (chairman, committee on expenditure, board of trustees), Nov. 13, 1893, XV, Mut. Lbs.; Mut., *M.B.T.*, April 27, 1898; McCurdy to W. R. Gillette, etc., March 30, 1898, XX, Mut. Lbs.; Perkins to McCall, Aug. 24, 1900, Perkins Mss.

4. Richard McCurdy to Robert McCurdy, May 29, Aug. 28, 1900, to A. C. Fields, Aug. 21, 1900, to C. A. Hopkins, Oct. 5, 1900, XXI, Mut. Lbs.; Perkins to McCall, July 20, 1900, Perkins Mss.

5. N.Y., *Test.*, III, 2388; Dryden statement in N. J., *Test.*, p. 202.

6. Hendrick, *Life Insurance,* pp. 258–259; Alexander to Elizur Wright, Jan. 30, 1884, Wright Mss.; N.Y., *Test.*, V, 4747.

7. Frederick L. Hoffman, "Fifty Years of American Life Insurance Progress," *Publications of the American Statistical Association,* XII (1911), 747.

8. Clough, *Mutual,* pp. 141–144; McCurdy to Hyde, Feb. 3, 10, 1896, XVII, Mut. Lbs.

9. Met., *M.B.D.*, Oct. 22, 1901; James, *Metropolitan,* pp. 86, 338–339; Hoffman, *Prudential,* pp. 137, 207–211.

10. McCurdy to William H. Blackford, April 15, 1898, XX, to Charles H. Raymond, Dec. 23, 1895, XVII, Mut. Lbs.; Pru., *M.B.D.*, April 11, 1898; Hoffman, *Prudential,* p. 255; James, *Metropolitan,* p. 118; Perkins to McCall, March 12, 1898, Perkins Mss.

11. Beers statement in Ohio, *Report of Senate Committee Appointed . . . to Investigate Tontine Insurance* (Columbus, 1885), p. 43; Equit., *Report to the Board of Directors . . . April 6, 1905,* pp. 33–34.

12. N.Y., *Test.*, II, 1510, 1445; *C.F.C.*, LII (1891), 739, 623–624; *C.F.C.*, LXX (1900), 303–305. See also McCurdy to Theodore Roosevelt, Seth Low, etc., Nov. 1895, XVII, Mut. Lbs., offering 5 percent 20 Year Gold Bond Policies as "investments" for men of means.

13. Hendrick, *Life Insurance,* p. 155.

14. Mut., *M.B.T.*, April 25, 1888; Weeks statement in N.Y., *Test.*, II, 1149; Mutual actuary's statement in N.Y., *Test.*, III, 2501; James, *Metropolitan,* pp. 113–114.

15. Hendrick, *Life Insurance,* p. 159; *Papers Relating to Tontine Insurance Issued by the Connecticut Mutual Life Insurance Company, 1885–1888* (Hartford, 1888).

16. Buley, *Equitable,* p. 58; James W. Alexander to Wright, April 1, 1884, Oct. 24, 1885, Wright Mss.

17. N.Y.L., *M.B.T.*, May 9, 1883; Lawrence F. Abbott, *The Story of NYLIC* (New York, 1930), p. 104. On Mutual, *C.F.C.*, LII (1891), 700; *Insurance Monitor,* LIII (1905), 24.

18. N.Y.L., *M.B.T.*, May 11, 1898, Dec. 13, 1899, Oct. 14, 1896, May 12, 1897; McCurdy to John M. Cornell, June 4, 1896, XVII, Mut. Lbs.; McCurdy to Edward S. Savage, April 30, 1903, XXIII Mut Lbs.; *C.F.C.*, LXXVII (1903), 7–8.

19. George L. Amrhein, *The Liberalization of the Life Insurance Contract* (Philadelphia, 1933).

20. Hudnut, *Semi-Centennial History,* p. 305; Hyde to Tarbell, May 10, 1895, A33, Hyde Mss.; McCurdy to Hyde, Nov. 17, 1897, XIX, Mut. Lbs.; Clough, *Mutual,* p. 154; Henry S. Nollen, "Recent Fluctuations in Policy Loans," in "Some Statistical Reflections on the State of the Nation in 1921," A.L.I.P. *Proceedings,* 1921, p. 36. The conservative Jacob Greene of the Connecticut Mutual opposed policy loans. N.Y., *Test.*, II, 1438.

21. Wright and Wright, *Elizur Wright,* pp. 230–232; Clough, *Mutual,* pp. 67–68; Hudnut, *Semi-Centennial History,* p. 195.

22. James, *Metropolitan,* pp. 91–93; John R. Hegeman to Massachusetts in-

surance commissioner Smith, Jan. 25, 1888, Met. Arch.; N.Y.L., *M.B.T.*, Feb. 21, 1888.

23. McCurdy to Henry W. Smith, Jan. 8, 1894, XV, Mut. Lbs.; N.Y.L., *M.B.T.*, Dec. 13, 1893; Clough, *Mutual,* p. 156; Hudnut, *Semi-Centennial History,* pp. 343, 346.

24. Pru., *M.B.D.,* Jan. 14, 1897, Jan. 12, 1899; Buley, *Equitable,* p. 94; N.Y., *Test.,* II, 1403; Clough, *Mutual,* pp. 156, 274; Hyde to McCurdy, Nov. 19, 22, 1897, B6, Hyde Mss.; McCurdy to Hyde, Nov. 17, 1897, XIX, Mut. Lbs.; McCurdy to Emory McClintock, May 28, 1897, XVIII.

25. Mutual actuary's statements in N.Y., *Test.,* III, 2229–2247, 2352–2353; McCall's statement in N.Y., *Test.,* II, 1405.

26. James W. Alexander to James H. Hyde, March 25, 1904, P12, Hyde Mss. See the persuasive letter from a Mutual deferred dividend policyholder, N.Y., *Test.,* II, 1885–1891, which notes: "My dividend in 1885, on an investment of $214.05 was $16.85. My dividend in 1905, on an investment of $4,075.20 was $2.73."

27. N.Y.L., *M.B.T.*, Jan. 8, 1896, *M.F.C.*, Aug. 8, 1900.

28. Mut., *M.B.T.*, Nov. 22, 1893; McClintock statements in N.Y., *Test.,* III, 2435–2437, 2464, 2459. In 1894 the New York Life transferred $1,738,768.50 from its Individual Surplus Account to its Tontine Fund Account; in 1893 Mutual dividends were cut pending an improvement in the business outlook. N.Y.L., *M.F.C.,* Jan. 12, 1894; McCurdy to B. J. Mandlebaum, Feb. 9, 1894, XV, Mut. Lbs.

29. The classic description of the period is in Hendrick, *Life Insurance*; on early Equitable advertising, Alexander, *My Half-Century,* pp. 71–73.

30. McCurdy to Charlton Lewis, Dec. 8, 1897, XIX, McCurdy to James W. Alexander, Feb. 5, 1904, XXIII, Mut. Lbs.; *Insurance Times,* XXVIII (1895), 28–29.

31. Hyde to Homans, Feb. 20, 1888, A25, Hyde Mss.; Hyde to Gen. Stekel, Nov. 11, 1889, A28.

32. Hyde to James W. Alexander, Feb. 11, 1890, A28, June 15, July 9, 1888, A25, Hyde Mss.; on Mutual activities, John K. Duer to George L. Norton, June 3, 1890, XIII, Mut. Lbs.; on Smith, N.Y., *Test.,* III, 2280–2302. See Charles J. Smith, "Life Insurance and the Public," *The Eclectic Magazine,* CXLV (1905), 481.

33. Hyde to James W. Alexander, May 11, 1888, A25, Hyde Mss.; William C. Beer to John N. Parsons, Dec. 30, 1910, Beer Mss.; Perkins to John A. McCall, Aug. 3, 1900, Perkins Mss.

34. McCurdy to Thomas Tully, April 16, 1895, XVI, Mut. Lbs.; *Massachusetts Ins. Rep.,* XLVIII (1903), xliv.

35. N.Y., *Test.,* III, 2314–2317, Hegeman to W. G. Staniland, April 19, 1898, Met. Arch.; N.Y., *Test.,* VI, 5077; Pru., *M.E.C.,* July 23, 1895, Feb. 2, 1896; May and Oursler, *Prudential,* pp. 118–120; Buley, *Equitable,* facing p. 31.

36. N.Y., *Test.,* VII, 6308, IV, 3525, II, 1642, 1510; Hendrick, *Life Insurance,* pp. 263–264.

37. Mut., *M.B.T.,* Nov. 28, 1888. On the Dinkelspiels, Hendrick, *Life Insurance,* pp. 288–290; *New York Times,* Oct. 20, 1891; Hyde to McCurdy, Feb. 8, 1888, A24, Hyde Mss.

38. McCurdy to E. D. Mann, Nov. 17, 1896, XVIII, Mut. Lbs. On Nylic, Abbott, *Story of NYLIC,* pp. 144–152, James M. Hudnut, *History of the New York Life Insurance Company, 1895–1905* (New York, 1906), pp. 12–20.

39. Clough, *Mutual,* pp. 164–165; Pru., *M.B.D.,* Jan. 10, 1888; May and Oursler, *Prudential,* p. 111; Buley, *Equitable,* pp. 220, 95.

40. Beveridge to Perkins, Nov. 15, 1897, Perkins Mss.; Perkins to Beers, Feb.–March 1890, Perkins Mss.; Mut., *M.B.T.,* June 8, 1892; Hyde to Daniel R. Noyes, March 13, 1890, A28, to Holliday, Jan. 21, 1891, A29, to James W. Alexander,

June 11, 1892, D2, Hyde Mss.; William E. Ingersoll to McCall, Sept. 7, 1900, Perkins Mss.

41. McCurdy to Hyde, Nov. 9, 1893, to Charles H. Ferguson, Dec. 16, 1895, XVII, Mut. Lbs.; N.Y., *Test.*, IV, 3459–3474. The New York Life reciprocated by taking many of the Equitable's Buffalo agents in 1901. N.Y., *Test.*, II, 1270.

42. Hegeman to Dryden, Dec. 10, 1879, Knapp to Noah Blanchard, Jan. 25, 1881, Dryden to Knapp, Jan. 28, 1881, Met. Arch.; L. F. Blanchard to Dryden, Oct. 2, Sept. 21, 1883, G. Green to Dryden, July 2, 1883, Pru. Arch.

43. Hyde to Homans, Feb. 6, 9, 1888, A24, Hyde Mss.; to McCall, Feb. 5, 1887, A23; to James W. Alexander, April 5, 1887; to William Alexander, April 22, 1887, A23.

44. N.Y., *Test.*, VII, 6224–6232; Hendrick, *Life Insurance,* p. 197; Hyde to William Alexander, May 24, 1890, A28, Hyde Mss.; Perkins to Beers, Nov. 20, 1890, Perkins Mss.; Secretary, John Hancock, to J. S. Galvin, March 16, 1905, J.H., Secretary's Files, no. 080.

45. James, *Metropolitan,* p. 84; *W.U.*, XLVI (1892), 7; Hyde to McCurdy, March 28, 1892, Hyde to Homans, June 26, 1891, A30, Hyde Mss. Chauncey Depew claimed that he used his "relations and power and influence" to "bring about a harmony which would save for all the companies vast amounts of money." N.Y., *Test.*, IV, 3183.

46. Stalson, *Marketing Life Insurance,* p. 535; Hyde to Greene, Oct. 2, 1888, to James W. Alexander, July 14, Sept. 19, 1888, A25, Hyde Mss.; *Massachusetts Ins. Rep.*, XXXV (1890), xiv–xxv; Hyde to J. H. Nolan, Nov. 6, 1890, A29, Hyde Mss.; Richard McCurdy, "Insurance: The Root of the Rebate Trouble," *Independent,* XLIV (1892), 1414.

47. Clough, *Mutual,* p. 142; *W.U.*, XLV (1891), 310–311; Hyde to Isaac Vanderpoel, Feb. 23, 1893, B2, Hyde Mss.; N.Y., *Test.*, III, 2392–2395. See *Connecticut Ins. Rep.*, 27th (1892) and 29th (1894), and actuary David P. Fackler's N.C.I.C. address in N.J., *Test.*, 112, favoring limitation; and *New York Ins. Rep.*, XXXIV (1893), opposing it.

48. On 1891 meeting, *Chronicle,* XLVII (1891), 65; Hyde to Amzi Dodd and to McCall, Feb. 2, 1891, A29, Hyde Mss. On 1893 meeting, Hyde to McCall, Nov. 4, 1893, B3, Hyde Mss.; N.Y., *Test.*, IV, 3437–3439. On 1895 agreement, Perkins to Frank Block, Sept. 6, 1895, Perkins Mss.; *Insurance Times,* XXVIII (1895), 341–342; N.Y.L., *M.B.T.*, Nov. 13, 1895; Perkins to Reed, May 23, 1899.

49. Perkins to Darwin P. Kingsley, Aug. 31, 1896, Perkins Mss.; McCall to Perkins, Oct. 27, 1899, Perkins Mss.; Buley, *Equitable,* p. 95; Mut., *M.B.T.*, Dec. 28, 1898. See also *W.U.*, LIV (1896), *passim.; Insurance Times,* XXXI (1898), 156; *W.U.*, LXI (1899), 201; N.Y., *Test.*, IV, 3440; McCurdy to W. S. Candee, Dec., 1897, XIX, Mut. Lbs. On agent stealing, N.Y., *Test.*, II, 1277–1278. On other agreements, Hyde to McCurdy, Nov. 19, 22, 1897, B6, Hyde Mss.; James, *Metropolitan,* p. 121; N.Y., *Test.*, IV, 3492; James W. Alexander to Robert A. Granniss, June 24, 1898, B6, Hyde Mss.

50. McCurdy to E. D. Mann, Nov. 17, 1896, XVIII, Mut. Lbs.; Hyde to James W. Alexander, Sept. 19, 1888, A25, Hyde Mss.; Perkins to McCall, Nov. 30, 1899, Perkins Mss.; N.Y.L., *M.B.T.*, Feb. 10, 1892; Mut., *M.B.T.*, Feb. 24, 1892.

51. Hyde to McCurdy, Jan. 13, 1888, A24, Hyde Mss.; Hegeman statement in N.Y., *Test.*, III, 2340; N.Y., *Test.*, IV, 3522; McCurdy to Alexander, Feb. 3, 1898, XIX, Mut. Ibs.; Mut., *M.B.T.* Feb. 21, 1900; McCurdy to James H. Hyde, Nov. 3, 1898, XX, McCurdy to Theodore Roosevelt, Dec. 16, 1904, XXIII, Mut. Lbs.; James H. Hyde to James W. Alexander, July 25, 1904, P12, Hyde Mss.; McCurdy to Hegeman, Oct. 28, 1898, XX, Feb. 9, 1903, Jan. 14, 1904, XXIII, Mut. Lbs.; McCurdy to George T. Dexter, July 6, 1899, XX, Mut. Lbs. See also Perkins to James H. Hyde, May 12, 1899, Perkins Mss.

52. William A. Fricke to John McCall, n.d., N.Y.L. Arch.; *W.U.*, LXVI

(1902), 37, 46, LXVII (1902), 248. On Paris meeting, James W. Alexander to James H. Hyde, Sept. 12, 1901, P12, Hyde Mss.; Buley, *Equitable,* p. 104.

53. N.Y., *Test.,* III, 2441.

CHAPTER VI. THE DYNAMICS OF FOREIGN EXPANSION

1. *W.U.,* LXII (1900), 429–430.

2. Material on foreign business in N.Y.L. Arch., Equit. H.P.; on volume, N.Y.L., *M.B.T.,* April 11, 1900; Stalson, *Marketing Life Insurance,* pp. 434–440, 442, app. 25, 28.

3. U.S. Department of Commerce and Labor, Bureau of Manufactures, *Insurance in Foreign Countries,* Special Consular Reports, vol. XXXVIII (Washington, 1905), pp. 48, 20, 24; statement of Dr. Albert Ehrenzweig, in *The Spectator,* April 27, 1922, quoted in Abbott, *Story of NYLIC,* p. 140.

4. John A. McCall, "American Life Insurance Companies in Germany," *Harper's Weekly,* XLIII (1899), 1054; Mut., *M.B.T.,* Feb. 19, 1896; Stalson, *Marketing Life Insurance,* pp. 436–438. On foreign firms in U.S., Cleona Lewis, *America's Stake in International Investments* (Washington, 1938), pp. 110–112; U.S. Industrial Commission, *Reports* (Washington, 1901), XVII, 203; P. G. M. Dickson, *The Sun Insurance Office, 1710–1900* (London, 1960), 221–231. Statistics on insurance in force of European companies are from Spectator Co., *Insurance Year Book,* 1885 *et seq.*

5. McCall, "American Life Insurance Companies in Germany," p. 1054; U.S. Department of Commerce, *Insurance in Foreign Countries,* pp. 24, 49–51, 92.

6. U.S. Department of Commerce, *Insurance in Foreign Countries,* p. 51; Hudnut, *Semi-Centennial History,* p. 150; *New York Ins. Rep.,* XXXVII (1896), xxxix.

7. Stalson, *Marketing Life Insurance,* pp. 442–443; U.S. Department of Commerce, *Insurance in Foreign Countries,* p. 27; Buley, *Equitable,* pp. 52–54, 74–75; Secretary General for Europe file, "Information given by Mr. Schoofs to Miss Nortier, June, 1951," G. T. Wilson memo, Sept. 29, 1895, to Equit. Auditor, Dec. 14, 1897, H.P., Equit. For a comparison of British and American agency techniques see Henry Moir, "Divergent Developments of Life Insurance in Britain and America," *Transactions of the Actuarial Society of America,* XXIX (1928), 58.

8. Hudnut, *New York Life, 1895–1905,* p. 11; N.Y.L., *M.B.T.,* Sept. 13, 1899; N.Y., *Test.,* VIII, Ex. 216; McCurdy to Richard McCurdy, Dec. 10, 1897, XIX, Mut. Lbs. On the development of the Mutual's overseas agency force, see Clough, *Mutual,* pp. 164–165.

9. Hyde to James W. Alexander, Oct. 12, 1888, A25, Hyde Mss.; Hendrick, *Life Insurance,* p. 167; Stalson, *Marketing Life Insurance,* p. 443; William Alexander to Elizur Wright, March 14, 1885, Wright Mss.; Perkins to John A. McCall, Nov. 20, 1899, Perkins Mss.; U.S. Department of Commerce, *Insurance in Foreign Countries,* p. 69.

10. Hudnut, *Semi-Centennial History,* p. 145; Hyde to S. G. Goodrich, Dec. 10, 1880, A14, to James W. Alexander, Jan. 23, 1888, A24, to G. T. Wilson, July 6, 1894, B4, to ?, Feb. 9, 1884, A20, Hyde Mss.; on Paris conference, McCurdy-Hyde correspondence, Oct.–Nov. 1901, April 1902, miscellaneous material, Mut. Lbs.; McCurdy to Perkins, Sept. 6, Nov. 26, 1901, N.Y.L. Arch.; P12, Hyde Mss.; Buley, *Equitable,* pp. 95–96, 103–104.

11. N.Y., *Test.,* IV, 2936; March–May 1896, XVII, Mut. Lbs.; N.Y.L., *M.B.T.,* May 11, 1904; Buley, *Equitable,* p. 71; Hyde to Senators William M. Evarts and Anson McCook, March 13, 1888, A24, to Chauncey Depew, Feb. 27, 1889, A27, to Woodford, June 22, 1897, B6, Hyde Mss. William E. Ingersoll to William C. Beer, June 30, 1899 and K. Radkiewicz to John McCall (cable), July 12, 1901, Beer Mss., discussed consular appointments for New York Life men in Madrid and Warsaw.

12. Hyde to ?, May 18, 1882, A17, Hyde Mss., to Beers, Nov. 2, 1885; Mut., *M.B.T.*, July 25, 1888.

13. McCurdy to D. C. Haldeman, Feb. 12, 1895, to Colonel Thomas Tully, April 16, 1895, XVI, Mut. Lbs.; Perkins to Darwin P. Kingsley, April 25, 1895, Perkins Mss.; Hyde to John A. McCall, Feb. 27, 1889, A27, Hyde Mss., to E. W. Scott, Nov. 18, 1893, B3; N.Y.L., *M.B.T.*, Dec. 14, 1892; Alexander to G. T. Wilson, July 14, 1903, P12.

14. Hyde to James W. Alexander, Jan. 19, 23, 1888, A24, Hyde Mss.; Mut., *M.F.C.*, May 31, 1893; N.Y.L., *M.F.C.*, Aug. 5, 1901.

15. Lewis, *America's Stake*, p. 340; George W. Edwards, *The Evolution of Finance Capitalism* (New York, 1938), pp. 182–183; Alexander D. Noyes, *Forty Years of American Finance* (2nd ed., New York, 1909), pp. 280–283; Charles F. Spears, "Foreign Investments of the Nations," *North American Review*, CXC (1909), 86; Nathaniel T. Bacon, "American International Indebtedness," *Yale Review*, IX (1900), 276. See also Paul D. Dickens, "The Transition Period in American International Financing: 1897 to 1914" (unpubl. diss., George Washington University, 1933), pp. 9, 212; Matthew Simon, "The United States Balance of Payments, 1861–1900," in Conference on Research in Income and Wealth, *Trends in the American Economy in the Nineteenth Century* (Princeton, 1960).

16. *Paris Herald*, quoted in *W.U.*, LXVIII (1903), 42.

17. N.Y.L., *M.F.C.*, Nov. 25, 1890, June 8, 1899; N.Y., *Test.*, II, 1501; McCurdy to George Haven, April 7, 1898, XIX, Mut. Lbs.

18. N.Y., *Test.*, IV, 3751.

19. *W.U.*, LXIV (1901), 303; Perkins to John A. McCall, Nov. 10, 1899, Perkins Mss.

20. Edward J. Sullivan to State, Sept. 12, 1904, File No. 2775, B.C., Arch.

21. Mut., *M.B.T.*, Jan. 19, 1887, Oct. 30, 1889, Feb. 19, 1896; Clough, *Mutual*, pp. 162–63; McCurdy to Robert McCurdy, Feb. 9, 1894, XV, Mut. Lbs.

22. N.Y.L., *M.B.T.*, Dec. 14, 1892; Perkins to Major E. W. Halford, June 21, 1894, Perkins Mss. When Senator Albert Beveridge went to China and the Philippines in 1899, Perkins charged him to gather information on life insurance prospects in those areas. Perkins to Beveridge, March 17, 1899, Beveridge Mss.

CHAPTER VII. THE CHALLENGES OF NATIONALISM

1. *W.U.*, LXI (1899), 257; Mut., *M.B.T.*, July 25, 1888, Dec. 25, 1898.

2. *Chronicle*, XLVI (1890), 263; Abbott, *Story of NYLIC*, p. 122; McCurdy to William McKinley, March 31, 1895, Misc. Let., State, Arch. Estimates of the percentage of the Mutual's total outlay as compared to its foreign business ran from 23 percent in 1886 to 87 percent in 1887 to 27 percent in 1902–03. N.Y., *Test.*, VIII, Ex. 253.

3. Hyde to European representatives, Oct. 21–23, 1893, B3, Hyde Mss.; Hyde to Charles R. Flint, April 19, 1895, A33; Hyde to S. S. Schmey, Feb. 1, 1895; Hyde to chairman and local directors, Jan. 16, 1896, B5; Alexander to James H. Hyde, Oct. 11, 1901; Alexander to G. T. Wilson, July 14, 1903, P12; N.Y., *Test.*, IV, 3746–3753, V, 3950–3961, VIII, Ex. 512–514, IX, Ex. 925–927.

4. N.Y., *Test.*, II, 1571–1572, VIII, Ex. 212–214; N.Y.L., *A Temple of Humanity* (New York, 1909), p. 12.

5. Alexander to James H. Hyde, Oct. 10, 1900, P12, Hyde Mss.; McCurdy to George G. Haven, April 7, 1898, XIX, Mut. Lbs. On Australia, Hyde memo, July 13, 1896, A35; C. C. Taylor to G. T. Wilson, Feb. 15, 1897, Feb. 11, 1898, Equit., H.P. On interest rates, N.Y.L., *Annual Statements*, Schedule D.

6. *Connecticut Ins. Rep.*, XXVI (1891), XXVII (1892); *New York Ins. Rep.*, 33rd (1892); Abbott, *Story of NYLIC*, p. 126; Hyde to J. T. Hamilton, Dec. 17, 1895, B4, Hyde Mss.; N.Y.L., *M.B.T.*, Dec. 13, 1905.

7. *Very Old Opinions*, in Law Department, Equit., no. 112, June 26, 1888; *Chronicle*, XLV (1890), 293; *Docket Books*, II, in Law Department, N.Y.L.

8. New York superintendent quoted in *W.U.*, LIII (1895), 25; Great Britain, *Select Committee, Report,* p. 35; George W. Perkins testimony, *G.J.M.*, Beer Mss.; Hyde to James W. Alexander, Oct. 12, 1888, A25, Hyde Mss.; Root to McCurdy, July 7, 1905, Root Mss.

9. Howard K. Beale, *Theodore Roosevelt and the Rise of America to World Power* (Baltimore, 1956), p. 228.

10. On Japanese business, *List Compiled from William Mather's Record . . .*, H.P., Equit.; Clough, *Mutual,* p. 162; McCurdy to Kogara Takahira, April 29, 1902, to Sen. John Kean, April 30, XXII, Mut. Lbs.; N.Y.L., *M.B.T.*, May 13, 1903; on Japanese troubles, Japan, Dip. Des., Misc. Let., Nov. 1903–Feb. 1904, State, Arch.

11. Hudnut, *Semi-Centennial History,* p. 187; James W. Alexander to Elizur Wright, Feb. 5, 1884, Wright Mss.; Richard McCurdy to Fayette Brown, May 4, 1894, XVI, Mut. Lbs.

12. "Central & South America, Mexico, and Cuba," H.P., Equit.; N.Y.L., *M.F.C.*, May 14, Aug. 27, Sept. 3, Oct. 1, 1895; State to Equit., Sept. 28, Oct. 10, 1896, Dom. Let., State, Arch.; on Mutual, Office of Registrar, Division of Loans, Letters Sent, Aug. 14, 1902, Treasury Department, Arch.

13. N.Y.L., *M.B.T.*, June 19, 1891; Hudnut, *Semi-Centennial History,* pp. 276–278; on San Domingo incident, N.Y.L. to State (copy), Feb. 7, 1911, Beer Mss. The agent's fate is unrecorded.

14. Materials on Cuban case are in Beer Mss., 1909–12.

15. Details of the incident are in Uruguay, 1903–04, Dip. Des., State, Arch.; File No. 185, B.C., Arch.; *W.U.*, LXIX (1903), 31, 321; Washington (D.C.) *Times,* July 23, 1903.

16. Equit. to State, Dec. 22, 31, 1890, Misc. Let.; N.Y.L. to State, Feb. 15, March 7, 15, 1899, Misc. Let.; Argentina, no. 599, Jan. 7, 1899, no. 632, Feb. 9, 1899 (tel.), June 29, 1899, no. 716, July 3, 1899, Dip. Des., State, Arch.

17. *Chronicle,* XLV, XLVII (1891), 61, 314; Brazil, no. 407, Sept. 12, 1895, Dip. Des.; State to Equit., Aug. 27, Sept. 9, 1895, Dom. Let.; *Board of Trade Journal,* XIX (1895), 564.

18. Equit. to State, Jan. 28, July 15, 1902, Misc. Let.; McCall to William C. Beer (tel.), Oct. 8, 1902, Senator J. D. Willard to Beer, Oct. 8, 1902 *et seq.*, Beer Mss.; Brazil, no. 26, June 1, 1903, Dip. Des.

19. *W.U.*, XXXI (1884), 109, XXXIII (1885), 288; U.S. Department of Commerce, *Insurance in Foreign Countries,* p. 102; Hyde to J. B. Batterson, "Central & South America, Mexico, and Cuba." H.P., Equit.; Richard McCurdy to J. Y. Limantour, Oct. 25, 1897, XVIII, Mut. Lbs.; Mut., *M.B.T.*, Nov. 24, 1897; Darwin P. Kingsley–William C. Beer correspondence, Jan.–Feb., 1903, Beer Mss.

20. N.Y.L., *M.B.T.*, Aug. 10, 1898; Equit., *Very Old Opinions,* no. 110, Nov. 24, 1885; *W.U.*, XXVI (1882), 418, XXXVII (1888), 247; James W. Alexander to George T. Wilson, July 14, 1903, P12, Hyde Mss.

21. On Serbia: Equit. to State, May 22, 24, June 3, 28, 1893, Misc. Let., State to Equit., June 2, 1893, Dom. Let., State, Arch. On Spain: *W.U.*, XLIX (1893), 104; Buley, *Equitable,* p. 78; N.Y., *Test.*, II, 1436. On Portugal: Portugal, no. 58, Feb. 10, 1904, Dip. Des. On Turkey: N.Y.L. to State, April 17, 1902, Misc. Let., State to N.Y.L., July 12, 1902, Dom. Let. On Sweden: N.Y.L. to State, Jan. 4, March 8, 1898, Misc. Let., Sweden, no. 11, March 26, 1898, Dip. Des.

22. *W.U.*, XXXIV (1886), 208; Austria, no. 221, Dec. 20, 1896, Dip. Des.; Hyde to George T. Wilson, June 8, 1897, B6, Hyde Mss.; Buley, *Equitable,* p. 76; Austria, no. 215, Nov. 24, 1896, no. 221, Dec. 20, 1896, Dip. Des., State, Arch.; Richard McCurdy to John Tatlock, Sept. 29, 1898, XIX, Mut. Lbs.; Perkins to Darwin P. Kingsley, Aug. 14, 1896, Perkins Mss.; N.Y.L., *M.F.C.*, Sept. 29, 1896, July 13, Oct. 19, 1897.

23. Equit. to State, Nov. 2, 1889, Sept. 26, 1891, Misc. Let., State, Arch.;

Switzerland, no. 96, Oct. 23, 1891, Dip. Des.; N.Y.L. to State, Nov. 10, 1898, Misc. Let.; (tel.), Oct. 8, 1898, no. 102, Oct. 22, 1898, Dip. Des.

24. McCurdy to Gustav E. Kissel, Oct. 26, 1900, XXII, Mut. Lbs.; *Chronicle,* XLVIII (1893), 181; Germany, no. 353, Nov. 2, 1891, no. 400, March 11, 1892, no. 376, Oct. 2, 1895, Dip. Des., State, Arch.; Buley, *Equitable,* p. 172–173. Much of the ensuing story is drawn from the State Department Archives, Germany, Dip. Ins. and Dip. Des., 1892–1902.

25. McCurdy to William McKinley, March 31, 1895, Misc. Let.; Germany, no. 371, Sept. 21, 1895, Dip. Des., State, Arch.; Hyde to George T. Wilson, June 15, 1894, Hyde to Thomas Tully, Sept. 12, 1894, B4, Hyde Mss., McCall to Sec. State, Oct. 23, 1894, Misc. Let.

26. State to Mut., July 10, 1891, Dom. Let., State, Arch.; James D. Richardson, comp., *Messages and Papers of the Presidents* (Bureau of National Literature ed., New York, 1911–22), p. 6061; *Insurance Times,* XXVIII (1895), 405; *W.U.,* LIII (1895), p. 302; Mutual Foreign Department, memo, March 19, 1897, "Prussian Re-Entry" file, Mut. Arch.

27. *W.U.,* LIII (1895), 264; *Insurance Times,* XXVIII (1895), 332; McCurdy to Morton, Nov. 6, 1895, Feb. 14, 1896, XVII, Mut. Lbs.; *W.U.,* LIII (1895), 278–291; *Texas Ins. Rep.,* XXI (1895), 10–11; *Pennsylvania Ins. Rep.,* XXIII (1895), x–xi; *Missouri Ins. Rep.,* XXVII (1896), x–xi; *New York Ins. Rep.,* XXXIX (1896), xxxix f.

28. Bigelow–New York Insurance Department Correspondence, New York State Library Manuscripts and History Section; Germany, no. 469, Feb. 8, 1896, no. 488, Feb. 28, 1896, Dip. Des., State, Arch.

29. McCurdy to State, March 9, 1898, Misc. Let.; State to Mut., March 17, 1898, Dom. Let.; on Batchellor, James W. Alexander to Henry B. Hyde, July 13, 1892, Foreign Business, Miscellaneous Photostats, H.P., Equit.; N.Y., *Test.,* IV, 3269, V, 3905.

30. McCurdy to Carl F. von Gablenz, Jan. 18, 1895, XVI, Mut. Lbs.

31. McCurdy to Lewis, June 17, 1895, XVI, Mut. Lbs.; State to N.Y.L. (tel.), Jan. 23, 1897, Dom. Let.; *Insurance Times,* XXXI (1898), 265; Abbott, *Story of NYLIC,* p. 124; Perkins to William E. Ingersoll, May 27, 1898, Perkins Mss.; Perkins to Guido von Nimptsch, Sept. 5, 1899, Perkins Mss.; Hyde to McCurdy, Nov. 28, 1896, "Prussian Re-Entry" file, Mut. Arch.; on Prussian commissioners, N.Y.L., *M.B.T.,* June 14, 1899. On Perkins' negotiations with Germany, see Garraty, *Right-Hand Man,* pp. 61–64, 69–71.

32. Perkins-McCall correspondence, Oct.–Nov. 1899, Perkins Mss.; readmission terms in Hudnut, *New York Life, 1895–1905,* pp. 42–45; N.Y.L., *M.B.T.,* Nov. 8, 1899; Abbott, *Story of NYLIC,* p. 124; Richardson, comp., *Messages and Papers,* p. 6370.

33. Memo re German loan, Sept. 12, 1900, Perkins to Guido von Nimptsch, Sept. 14, 17, 18, 1900, New York newspapers, Sept. 15–18, Perkins Mss.

34. McCurdy to State, Sept. 28, 1900, McCurdy to Gustav E. Kissel, Oct. 26, 1900, XXII, Mut. Lbs.; Hanna to State, Oct. 11, 1900, Misc. Let.; McCurdy to Hanna, Oct. 18, 1900, XXI; Mut., *M.B.T.,* May 23, 1900; *W.U.,* LXII (1900), 408; Representative John S. Sherman to McCurdy, June 9, 1900, "Prussian Re-Entry" file, Mut. Arch., McCurdy to Sherman, June 4, 1900, XXI; Perkins to Joseph J. Hearns, June 5, 1900, Perkins to Darwin P. Kingsley, June 12, 1900, Perkins Mss.; Richardson, comp., *Messages and Papers,* p. 6428; McCurdy to Root, Oct. 24, 1901, XXII, Mut. Lbs.

35. Text of Imperial law in U.S. Department of Commerce, *Insurance in Foreign Countries,* pp. 31–48; Ernest J. Schuster, "State Supervision of Insurance Companies in Germany and Elsewhere," *The Economic Journal,* XII (1902), 561–573; on Mutual readmission, Germany, no. 1967, June 9, 1902, Dip. Des., State, Arch.; *New York Ins. Rep.,* 42nd (1901), 43rd (1902); McCall to Perkins,

Oct. 6, 1903, Perkins Mss.; U.S. Department of Commerce, *Insurance in Foreign Countries,* p. 29; Buley, *Equitable,* p. 74; Clough, *Mutual,* p. 163.

36. Abbott, *Story of NYLIC,* p. 132; *W.U.,* XXV (1886), 296; Equit. to State, Aug. 31, 1887, June 4, 1890, Misc. Let.; *Insurance Times,* XXIII (1890), 515; Buley, *Equitable,* p. 74.

37. Russia, Dip. Des., Dip. Ins., 1893–1894, *passim,* State, Arch.

38. Buley, *Equitable,* p. 75; John K. Duer to James W. Alexander, June 19, 1895, XVI, to Emil Phillipson, Dec. 17, 1897, XIX, to J. P. Morgan, Dec. 21, 1898, XX, to Richard McCurdy, Oct. 18, 1899, XX, Mut. Lbs.; N.Y.L., *M.F.C.,* Jan. 26, Feb. 26, 1897. See also Garraty, *Right-Hand Man,* pp. 64–68.

39. McCall to State (tel.), Oct. 6, 1899, Misc. Let.; Perkins to McCall, Nov. 30, 1899, Perkins Mss.; Herbert Feis, *Europe The World's Banker, 1870–1914* (New Haven, 1930), p. 210; Perkins to Edward N. Gibbs, Nov. 24, 1899, Perkins Mss.

40. Witte to N.Y.L. (transl.), Oct. 27, 1899, Perkins to McCall, Nov. 10, 1899, Perkins Mss.; N.Y.L., *M.F.C.,* Aug. 14, 19, 1901; on Morgan's Russian interests, copy of agreement between J. P. Morgan and Russian Finance Minister, Perkins Mss., William C. Beer to Perkins, Dec. 29, 1900, William I. Buchanan to Perkins, Nov. 23, 1904, Jan. 3, 1905, Beer Mss.; *C.F.C.,* LXXV (1902), 215–216.

41. Lewis, *America's Stake,* p. 337; N.Y.L., *M.F.C.,* April 14, 1902; Equit., *M.F.C.,* Resol. no. 49, in H.P., Equit.; N.Y., *Test.,* II, 1503; Perkins to Charles E. Hughes, Oct. 9, 1905, Perkins Mss.; Witte, *Memoirs,* p. 297; George T. Wilson to James W. Alexander, July 19, 1901, H.P., Equit.

42. *W.U.,* LIX (1898), 93; U.S. Department of Commerce, *Insurance in Foreign Countries,* p. 13.

43. *W.U.,* XXVII (1882), 125; Hyde to ??, Dec. 26, 1883, H.P., Equit.; "The Proposed French Corporation Law and Its Effect upon American Life Insurance Companies in France," July 1885, H.P., Equit.; McCurdy to State, March 9, 1898, Misc. Let., State, Arch.

44. France (tel.), Dec. 14, 16, 1904, Dip. Des., State, Arch.; N.Y., *Test.,* VIII, Ex. 359; Charles G. Loeb, *Legal Status of American Corporations in France* (Paris, 1921), pp. 55–56.

45. N.Y., *Test.,* IV, 2937, VIII, Ex. 359; "French Insurance Law of March 17, 1905" file, Dec. 12–13, 1904, H.P., Equit.; Buley, *Equitable,* p. 97; France (tel.), Dec. 1, 1904, Feb. 6, 1905, Dip. Ins.; text of law in U.S. Department of Commerce, *Insurance in Foreign Countries,* pp. 13–17; N.Y.L., *M.F.C.,* Feb. 23, 29, 1904; on Mutual (tel.), Dec. 9, 1905, Dip. Des.

46. France, no. 1373, Dec. 16, 1904, no. 46, Sept. 21, 1905, Dip. Des., State, Arch.; William I. Buchanan to Thomas A. Buckner, Dec. 7, 1905, "French Insurance Law of March 17, 1905" file, H.P., Equit.

47. John A. Nichols, *Germany After Bismarck: The Caprivi Era 1890–1894* (Cambridge, Mass., 1958); U.S. Senate, Committee on Interstate Commerce, *Control of Corporations, Persons, and Firms Engaged in Interstate Commerce* (Washington, 1913), pp. 1122–1123.

CHAPTER VIII. THE INVESTMENT ENVIRONMENT

1. Douglass C. North, "Capital Accumulation in Life Insurance between the Civil War and the Investigation of 1905" in William Miller, ed., *Men in Business* (Cambridge, Mass., 1952), pp. 238–253.

2. Lester W. Zartman, *The Investments of Life Insurance Companies* (New York, 1907), chap. 6, esp. p. 151; Equit., Law Department, *Very Old Opinions,* no. 76, July 3, 1880, no. 197, Sept. 11, 1879.

3. Dryden to W. H. Wells, Sept. 1884, quoted in "Atkinson's *History,*" chap. 3, p. 6, Pru. Arch.; Beers statement in W. S. Manning, comp., *The Condition of the Life Insurance Companies in the State of New York* (Albany, 1877), p. 271;

James, *Metropolitan,* pp. 103–104; Mut., *M.B.T.,* June 3, Oct. 21, 1885; Clough, *Mutual,* p. 185; Hyde to Fitzgerald, Feb. 8, 1888, A24, Feb. 25, 1889, A27, to James W. Alexander, Nov. 24, 1897, B6, Hyde Mss.; Buley, *Equitable,* p. 46; N.Y.L., *M.F.C.,* Jan. 19, 30, 1888, March 18, 1890.

4. New York statutes are summarized in Zartman, *Investments,* chap. 6, and Clough, *Mutual,* pp. 176–178; Dryden statement in N.J., *Test.,* 192; Laws of N.J., 1904, chap. 51.

5. Shaw Livermore, "The Success of Industrial Mergers," *Quarterly Journal of Economics,* L (1935), 68–69; Luther Conant, Jr., "Industrial Consolidations in the United States," *Publications of the American Statistical Association,* VII (1901), 207–226; Thomas R. Navin and Marian V. Sears, "The Rise of a Market for Industrial Securities, 1887–1902," *Business History Review,* XXIX (1955), 105–138; *C.F.C.,* LII (1891), 738–739.

6. Hyde to Fitzgerald, Aug. 24, 1894, A32, Jan. 7, 1889, A27, Hyde Mss.; McCurdy to Reverend G. Gottheil, Oct. 21, 1897, XVIII, Mut. Lbs., to John W. Auchincloss, May 23, 1895, XVI; Mut., *M.B.T.,* Dec. 28, 1898; Clough, *Mutual,* p. 368, quoting Mut., *M.F.C.,* Jan. 23, 1899; Report on Finance Committee, Perkins Mss.; N.Y.L., *M.F.C.,* March 12, 1895; Thomas W. Lawson, *Frenzied Finance* (New York, 1905), pp. 434–435.

7. James, *Metropolitan,* pp. 104–105; N.Y., *Test.,* III, 2335; Clough, *Mutual,* p. 183; Buley, *Equitable,* p. 66; Henry W. Lanier, "Investing a Million Dollars a Day," *World's Work,* IX (1904), 5478.

8. N.J., *Test.,* 192; Mut., *M.B.T.,* Jan. 29, 1902; Hyde to James W. Alexander, March 2, 1896, Hyde Mss.; Report on Finance Committee, Perkins Mss.; N.Y., *Test.,* V, 3888; on railroad bond defaults, Met., *M.F.C.,* July 25, 1893, Navin and Sears, "Rise of a Market," p. 106.

9. Mut., *M.B.T.,* June 3, 1891, *M.F.C.,* Jan. 25, 1893; Clough, *Mutual,* pp. 189, 191; N.Y., *Test.,* I, 194–195; Mut., *M.F.C.,* Nov. 4, 11, 1895, Dec. 15, 1897; on Equitable, N.Y., *Test.,* II, 1297–1305, 1318–1320, Buley, *Equitable,* pp. 66, 108.

10. On the New York Life Treasury, N.Y., *Test.,* I, 280–281, IV, 3892–3896; N.Y.L., *M.F.C.,* Aug. 4, 1896; N.Y.L., *G.J.M.,* 2, Beer Mss.; Pru., *M.F.C.,* Nov. 15, 1898; James, *Metropolitan,* p. 126.

11. Met., *M.F.C.,* Feb. 14, 1893, Oct. 23, 1896; N.Y.L., *M.F.C.,* Jan. 6, 1899; Pru., *M.B.D.,* April 12, 1897; N.Y., *Test.,* IV, 2246–2258 (Equitable); Abbott, *Story of NYLIC,* p. 95; Zartman, *Investment,* pp. 21–23; William F. Gephart, "Loans on Life Insurance Policies," *American Economic Review,* IV (1914), 332–339.

12. Hyde to McCall, March 6, 1890, to Albert Bierstadt, March 12, 1890, A28, to E. A. Merrill, Nov. 17, 1891, A30, Hyde Mss.; N.Y.L., *M.F.C.,* June 12, 1894; N.Y.L., *M.B.T.,* Feb. 10, 1904; Mut., *M.B.T.,* April 24, 1889.

13. Pru., *M.B.D.,* Oct. 27, 1888, June 8, 1903; James, *Metropolitan,* pp. 102–103, 106; N.Y.L., *M.F.C.,* May 29, 1893, March 22, 1892; McCurdy to William Babcock, Feb. 5, 1897, to William C. Little, March 8, 1897, XVIII, to Judge E. E. Farman, June 26, 1890, XIII, Mut. Lbs.

14. N.C.I.C. *Proceedings* (1892); Chicago *Dispatch,* July 3, 1895, in "Mud-Chicago and Other" folder, Met. Arch.; *Massachusetts Ins. Rep.,* 48th (1903), 175–177; L. A. Anderson, "Competition in Life Insurance," *Yale Review,* XIV (1905), 288; Charles J. Bullock, "Life Insurance and Speculation," *Atlantic Monthly,* XCVII (1906), 638; Louis D. Brandeis, *Business — a Profession* (Boston, 1914), pp. 109–153, esp. pp. 113, 117; Schiff statement in N.Y., *Test.,* II, 1362; N.J., *Test.,* 112–113.

15. James W. Alexander, "Some Prejudices about Life Insurance," *Atlantic Monthly,* LXXXVI (1900), 20; McCurdy to Charles Mellen, May 17, 1905, XXIII, Mut. Lbs.; N.Y.L., *M.F.C.,* Feb. 6, 1894, Dec. 31, 1895, Feb. 4, 1896, April 4, 19, 26, May 24, 1898.

16. John A. McCall, "Free Coinage and Life Insurance Companies," *Forum,* XXII (1896), 136–140; N.Y.L., *M.F.C.,* Dec. 16, 1890, May 18, 1892, March 28, 1893, Nov. 13, 1894, July 6, 21, 1896; Met., *M.F.C.,* Jan. 10, 24, 1893; Hyde to Gerald Brown, July 29, 1896, B5, Hyde Mss.; Buley, *Equitable,* p. 84; *C.F.C.,* LXIII (1896), 208–211; N.Y.L., *M.F.C.,* July 21, Sept. 29, Oct. 6, 1891.

CHAPTER IX. THE STRUCTURE OF INVESTMENT

1. Douglass C. North, "The Large Life Insurance Companies Before 1906" (unpubl. diss., University of California, 1952) makes the same point of a network of subsidiaries; Lawson, *Frenzied Finance,* p. 419. The material on other companies' investment practices collected by the Armstrong Committee (N.Y., *Test.,* VII, 6363–6483) suggests the gap in performance and in financial connections between the five subjects of this study and firms such as the Northwestern Mutual, the John Hancock, the Mutual Benefit, Penn Mutual, and Aetna. These companies had no bank or trust company holdings, and operated in an investment milieu of a lesser magnitude altogether.

2. N.Y., *Test.,* I, 639; Hendrick, *Life Insurance,* pp. 3, 246; Orson H. Hart, Jr., "A Study of the Investment Performance of the Eighteen Largest Domestic Life Insurance Companies" (unpubl. diss., Yale University, 1946), 102.

3. N.Y., *Test.,* III, 2099; Mut., *M.B.T.,* Jan. 27, 1892; Hyde to Fitzgerald, Nov. 7, 1888, A26, Hyde Mss.; Depew statement in N.Y., *Test.,* IV, 3181–3183; *Myers v. Mutual,* 54 N.E. 755 (Ind. 1899); N.Y., *Test.,* I, 640, 627–629, III, 2099–2100, I, 568–569. See also Douglass C. North, "Life Insurance and Investment Banking at the Time of the Armstrong Investigation, 1905–1906," *Journal of Economic History,* XIV (1954), 218, 224–227.

4. Cromwell and Harriman statements in N.Y., *Test.,* I, 628–629, VI, 5142; McCurdy to ?, Dec. 16, 1896, to Robert J. Lowrey, president, A.B.A., May 7/10, 1897, XVIII, to Carl F. von Gablenz, Jan. 18, 1895, XVI, Mut. Lbs.; Equit., *Report to the Board of Directors . . . April 6, 1905* (Frick Report), pp. 32–33.

5. *C.F.C.,* LII (1891), 738–739; McCurdy to *New York Commercial,* Dec. 27, 1898, XX, Mut. Lbs.

6. On Metropolitan, N.Y., *Test.,* III, 2764–2767, 2829–2830; on Hyde, *New York Ins. Rep.,* 47th (1906), 13f; Hyde to McCall, Feb. 7, 1888, A24, Hyde Mss., to Governor Oliver Ames, n.d., to William H. Beers, March 17, 1887, A23, to McCall, Dec. 17, 1888, A27; on surety companies, N.Y., *Test.,* III, 2718; Hyde to David B. Sickels, Dec. 2, 1890, A29; William C. Beer to M. B. Macfarlane, Dec. 10, 1897, Beer Mss.

7. Pru., *M.F.C.,* March 22, 1892, Feb. 28, 1893; N.Y., *Test.,* VI, 4832, 4991; Pru., *M.F.C.,* June 27, Sept. 6, 1893.

8. On Metropolitan, N.Y., *Test.,* III, 2754, 2782–2789, 2833–2835; James, *Metropolitan,* p. 105; on Mutual, N.Y., *Test.,* I, 609–616.

9. Hyde to James W. Alexander, Feb. 20, 1888, A24, Hyde Mss.; on Kuhn, Loeb, Buley, *Equitable,* pp. 102, 107, Cyrus Adler, *Jacob H. Schiff* (Garden City, N.Y., 1928), I, 185f; on Fanshawe, N.Y., *Test.,* I, 501–502, 739–740, V, 3840–3844, 3921–3933; on Morgan, miscellaneous material, Perkins Mss. During these years Kuhn, Loeb sold $31,000,000 worth of securities to the New York Life and $42,000,000 to the Mutual. The Equitable took $23,000,000 of $677,-000,000 offered by Morgan; the Mutual $31,000,000 of $556,000,000.

10. Charles J. Bullock, "The Concentration of Banking Interests in the United States," *Atlantic Monthly,* XCII (1903), 185–186; Margaret G. Myers, *The New York Money Market* (New York, 1931–1932), I, 240–242, 248; on trust companies, Alexander D. Noyes, "The Trust Companies: Is There Danger in the System?" *Political Science Quarterly,* XVI (1901), 248–261 and Redlich, *American Banking,* II, 177, 179; *C.F.C.,* "Bankers and Trust Supplement," Sept. 3, 1898, pp. 10–11, Sept. 16, 1899, pp. 75–76, Oct. 13, 1900, pp. 32–33, Oct. 26, 1901, pp. 42–43, and Oct. 21, 1905, pp. 127–129; Frederick D. Kilburn, "Control

and Supervision of Trust Companies," A.A.P.S.S. *Annals,* XXIV (1904), 31–32.

11. Lawson, *Frenzied Finance,* p. 458; *Massachusetts Ins. Rep.,* 48th (1903), xliii-xliv.

12. Buley, *Equitable,* pp. 44–45, 82–83, 106; Fritz Redlich, *The Moulding of American Banking* (Ann Arbor, 1940–51), II, 187.

13. Ives to Hyde, Jan. 20, 1894, A39, Hyde to Alexander, June 5, 9, 1897, to John E. Searless, June 8, 1897, to Albert Baldwin, June 25, 1897, B6, to Alexander, July 7, 1897, to Hanna, Dec. 9, 1897, B6, Hyde Mss.; Buley, *Equitable,* pp. 82–83, 104–105.

14. N.Y., *Test.,* I, 268–270; Mut., *M.B.T.,* Nov. 28, 1894, Jan. 29, 1902; N.Y., *Test.,* III, 2193; Mut., *M.B.T.,* Jan. 31, 1900; McCurdy to D. C. Haldeman, Dec. 24, 1896, XVIII, to Carl F. von Gablenz, Jan. 18, 1895, XVI, Mut. Lbs.

15. Mut., *M.F.C.,* Jan. 17, 1894, Feb. 6, 1895; Clough, *Mutual,* pp. 192–193; McCurdy to Senator William J. Sewall, Feb. 3, 1898, XIX, Mut. Lbs.; McCurdy to Hyde, Nov. 17, 1897, XIX, Mut. Lbs.; Mut., *M.F.C.,* July 19, 1893.

16. McCurdy to James W. Alexander, May 26, 1902, XXII, Mut. Lbs.; on International, N.Y., *Test.,* III, 2753; James K. Duer to Arthur J. Fraser, Jan. 28, 1898, XIX, Mut. Lbs.; Samuel McRoberts, "The Extension of American Banking in Foreign Countries," A.A.P.S.S. *Annals,* XXXVI (1910), 508; on Guaranty, McCurdy to Alexander, May 26, 1902, XXII, to James N. Jarvie, Jan. 5, 1897, XVIII, Mut. Lbs.

17. McCurdy to Arthur J. Fraser, May 26, 1899, XX, Mut. Lbs.; *C.F.C.,* LXIX (1899), 9, "Bankers and Trust Supplement," Oct. 26, 1901, p. 101, LXX (1900), 460, 564, 771, 774; N.Y., *Test.,* I, 237–240; on Morton's firms, Redlich, *American Banking,* II, 363–364.

18. Mut., *M.F.C.,* Jan. 18, June 21, 1893; McCurdy to James J. Hill, etc., Nov. 11, 1892, XV, to D. C. Haldeman, Dec. 9, 1898, XX, to A. J. Cassatt, May 9, 1900, XXI, Mut. Lbs.

19. McCurdy to ? Betts, Dec. 14, 1903, XXIII, Mut. Lbs.; on National Bank of U.S., N.Y., *Test.,* II, 1342, III, 2029–2031; on National Bank of Commerce, McCurdy to Alexander E. Orr, May/August 17, 1899, XX, Mut. Lbs.; N.Y., *Test.,* I, 587–595, III, 2087–2091; *C.F.C.,* LXVIII (1899), 1054–1055.

20. On Morristown Trust, N.Y., *Test.,* I, 209–211, 727–728, II, 1670–1671; McCurdy to Samuel Freeman, Dec. 28, 1893, XV, to Alexander E. Orr, May/Aug. 17, 1899, to Walter R. Gillette, Feb. 17, 1899, to George W. Young, Feb. 18, 1899, June 22, 29, 1899, XX, Mut. Lbs.

21. N.Y.L., *M.B.T.,* Feb. 11, March 11, 1885; *M.F.C.,* Jan. 24, Feb. 3, Jan. 10, 1893; Lee B. Durstine to William C. Beer, Nov. 11, 1903, Beer Mss.

22. N.Y.L., *G.J.M.,* pp. 262–263, 281–282, Beer Mss.

23. N.Y.L., *M.F.C.,* Jan. 24, Sept. 26, 1893; N.Y.L., *G.J.M.,* pp. 43–44, 48, 171–172, Beer Mss.

24. James, *Metropolitan,* pp. 126, 154–155; N.Y., *Test.,* III, 2749–2759.

25. Pru., *M.B.D.,* Feb. 10, 1902; May and Oursler, *Prudential,* pp. 117–118; Ransom E. Noble, Jr., *New Jersey Progressivism before Wilson* (Princeton, 1946), pp. 33–35; N.J., *Test.,* pp. 164, 167.

26. McCurdy to Joseph C. Hendrix, June 22, 1899, XX, Mut. Lbs.; N.Y., *Test.,* VI, 4826; Equit., *Supplemental Report . . . March 15, 1906,* p. 17; James W. Alexander to Hyde, Sept. 30, 1901, to W. H. McIntyre, July 22, 1903, McIntyre to Alexander, Dec. 20, 1901, P12, Hyde Mss.

27. Hyde to McCurdy, Oct. 29, Nov. 13, 1897, A37, B6, Hyde Mss.; James W. Alexander to James H. Hyde, Nov. 10, Dec. 22, 1903, P12; on Metropolitan offer, William Beer to McCall, June 8, 1903, Beer Mss.

CHAPTER X. THE INVESTMENT PERFORMANCE

1. N.Y., *Test.,* I, 532; Equit., *Report of Investigation . . . Jan. 30, 1906,* p. 187; N.Y.L., *M.B.T.,* July 2, 1906.

2. N.Y., *Test.*, VIII, Ex. 64; N.J., *Test.*, p. 161; Hughes to Mark Sullivan, Feb. 4, 1930, Hughes Mss. Yet losses and difficulties cropped up even from bank and trust company stock ownership. N.Y.L., *M.F.C.*, April 17, 1894, Hyde to Fitzgerald, Dec. 14, 1895, A34, Hyde Mss., and N.Y., *Test.*, I, 195–207, describe the Mutual's troubles with the Guaranty and Indemnity; Buley, *Equitable*, p. 82, and Equit., *Supplemental Report*, p. 21, discuss the Equitable's difficulties with the Mercantile Trust and the Western National Bank.

3. Equit., Law Department, *Old Opinions*, no. 501, Oct. 4, 1905. See also Douglass C. North, "Entrepreneurial Policy and Internal Organization in the Large Life Insurance Companies at the Time of the Armstrong Investigation of Life Insurance," *Explorations in Entrepreneurial History*, V (1952–53), 151.

4. N.Y., *Test.*, I, 539, 302; Mut., *M.F.C.*, Dec. 15, 1897; Alexander to General Thomas H. Hubbard, Sept. 8, 1902, P12, Hyde Mss.; Buley, *Equitable*, p. 82. The International Banking Corporation should not be confused with the earlier, unsuccessful International Banking Company.

5. N.Y., *Test.*, III, 2732.

6. McCurdy to Carl F. von Gablenz, Jan. 18, 1895, XVI, Mut. Lbs.; on Mutual deposit earnings, N.Y., *Test.*, VIII, Ex. 36, 63; on Metropolitan, N.Y., *Test.*, I, 531–532, III, 2749–2758; on Mutual, N.Y., *Test.*, I, 240.

7. N.Y., *Test.*, I, 208, III, 2151, I, 653; on Prudential, N.Y., *Test.*, VI, 4824–4826; on Equitable, Hyde to Fitzgerald, July 1, 1895, B5, Hyde Mss.; on New York Life, Randolph to Charles S. Fairchild, Jan. 25, 1902, Beer Mss. The Prudential earned 1.83 percent on its deposits in 1905. N.J., *Test.*, p. 211.

8. On Mutual, N.Y., *Test.*, I, 590, 253, 637–638; Alexander to James H. Hyde, Aug. 13, 1903, in Equit., *Report to the Board of Directors . . . April 6, 1905* (Frick Report), p. 32; to W. H. McIntyre, April 8, 1904, P12, Hyde Mss.; on Prudential, N.J., *Test.*, pp. 158, 161, 168. In 1904 the New York Life negotiated to free half of its $5,000,000 New York Security and Trust deposit on payment of a $25,000 surrender charge. N.Y.L., *M.F.C.*, June 23, 1904. In 1905 the Mutual reduced its deposits from more than $16,000,000 to $7,000,000. N.Y., *Test.*, VII, 6222.

9. Met., *M.F.C.*, Oct. 3, 1905; N.Y., *Test.*, VI, 5713; on Hegeman, N.Y., *Test.*, III, 2334–2343; on Equitable, N.Y., *Test.*, IV, 5714, 3205–3217.

10. James, *Metropolitan*, pp. 152–153; Perkins to Hegeman, April 18, 1895, Perkins Mss.; McCurdy to Walter G. Oakman, Nov. 25, 1895, XVII, Mut. Lbs.

11. N.Y., *Test.*, I, 509–512.

12. N.Y., *Test.*, III, 2721–2723, VIII, Ex. 350; James, *Metropolitan*, p. 127; Met., *M.F.C.*, Oct. 19, 1894; on Read arrangement, N.Y., *Test.*, VI, 5005–5007, Met., *M.F.C.*, April, Dec., 1905, Dec. 20, 1906.

13. Met., *M.F.C.*, Jan. 12, 1905; N.Y., *Test.*, III, 2790.

14. On Prudential–Fidelity Trust–Public Service arrangement, N.Y., *Test.*, VI, 4851–4852, N.J., *Test.*, p. 221, John F. Dryden to Jacob E. Ward, Jan. 9, 1906, Pru. Arch.; on stock bonuses, N.Y., *Test.*, VI, 4982–4984; N.J., *Test.*, 213–219, 224; on private arrangements, N.Y., *Test.*, VI, 4990.

15. N.Y., *Test.*, VII, 5788–5804, 6052–6063; Mut., *M.B.T.*, Dec. 27, 1905.

16. On Brooklyn Wharf, N.Y., *Test.*, II, 2111, 2135–2140, I, 728–729; Mut., *M.F.C.*, Jan. 30, Feb. 13, Aug. 5, 25, 1895; Clough, *Mutual*, p. 196. On Washington Traction, McCurdy to Depew, Feb. 14, 1900, XXI, Mut. Lbs.; N.Y., *Test.*, III, 2141–2148, 2317–2327.

17. Syndicate lists, 1904–05, in *Public Accountants' Report*, Mut. Arch.; Mut., *M.F.C.*, June 28, 1893; N.Y., *Test.*, I, 250, IX, Ex. 908; N.Y., *Test.*, I, 566–573 (Japanese bonds), 630–636 (Missouri Pacific), 561–562 (Pennsylvania).

18. Equit., *Report . . . of the Committee Appointed April 6, 1905* (Frick Report), p. 32.

19. N.Y., *Test.*, VIII, Ex. 219, IV, 297; on Speyer, VIII, Ex. 164; on Schiff, II, 1337; on masked accounts, II, 1168–1170, 1180.

20. N.Y., *Test.*, IV, 3110, 2956.

21. N.Y., *Test.*, II, 1045–1047 (Railroad Securities), 1106–1125, IV, 3345 (Chicago, Burlington, and Quincy); Alexander to Hyde, Aug. 13, 1903, P12, Hyde Mss.

22. N.Y., *Test., Report,* X, 141–143.

23. N.Y.L., *M.F.C.,* June 14, 1899, April 24, 1894, May 4, July 6, 1897, Dec. 31, 1895, Feb. 4, 1896.

24. Perkins statement in N.Y.L., *G.J.M.,* pp. 273–274, Beer Mss.; Garraty, *Right-Hand Man,* p. 85; N.Y., *Test.*, II, 1507.

25. N.Y., *Test.,* I, 735; N.Y.L., *M.B.T.,* April 12, 1905; N.Y., *Test.,* I, 737, 772.

26. "New York Life Syndicate Participations, 1895–1905," "Summary of Operations of New York Life Finance Committee, Jan. 1, 1901–Sept. 15, 1905," Perkins Mss.; N.Y., *Test.,* II, 1252–1253. N.Y.L., *M.F.C.,* May 8, 1905, had an analysis of finance committee operations from January 1, 1901, to date.

27. On joint accounts, N.Y., *Test.,* I, 739, 781, 908; Randolph statements in N.Y., *Test.,* I, 331–334.

28. On Atlantic Coast Line, N.Y., *Test.,* I, 289–302, 308. On St. Louis Terminal, N.Y., *Test.,* II, 1216–1230. On Treasury bonds, N.Y.L., *M.F.C.,* Oct. 9, 13, 23, 1902, Feb. 25, 1903. On Nylic transaction, N.Y., *Test.,* V, 3830–3859; "Mexican Central Railway Co. Bond Transaction," Perkins Mss.; Garraty, *Right-Hand Man,* p. 177.

29. Thomas R. Navin and Marian V. Sears, "A Study in Merger: Formation of the International Mercantile Marine Company," *Business History Review,* XXVIII (1954), 291–328; Perkins to Hanna, Nov. 15, 1900, "The $800,000 Interest in the Navigation Syndicate," "Statement Concerning the International Mercantile Marine," Perkins Mss.; "Material Relating to the IMM Syndicate," Beer Mss.; N.Y., *Test.,* I, 312–315, 766–770, 775, II, 1213–1214; Garraty, *Right-Hand Man,* pp. 171–172.

30. N.Y., *Test.,* V, 3879, 3791; "United States Steel Syndicate Transaction," Perkins Mss.

31. "Committee Report on New Orleans Railway Company Securities Matter," Perkins Mss.; N.Y., *Test.,* I, 473–486, 931–941, II, 1242, 1245–1247, V, 3922–3928; Garraty, *Right-Hand Man,* p. 173.

32. Randolph to J. S. Morgan, Ltd., Sept. 18, 1906, J. P. Morgan and Co. to J. S. Morgan, Ltd., Feb. 3, 1904, "United Collieries," Beer Mss.; N.Y., *Test.,* I, 368–369.

33. N.Y.L., *G.J.M.,* pp. 192, 24, 55, Beer Mss.; N.Y., *Test.,* I, 390. On unlisted bonus stocks, see N.Y., *Test.,* I, 406–413, 432–438. The muckraker Thomas W. Lawson accused the New York Life of secretly using $2,700,000 in unreported stock sales profits to pay off balances due agents and to cover real estate depreciation. Lawson, *Frenzied Finance,* p. 460; *Massachusetts Ins. Rep.,* (1902), 158–159.

34. N.Y.L., *M.F.C.,* Nov. 15, 1900; N.Y.L., *G.J.M., passim,* Beer Mss.; N.Y., *Test.,* I, 372–395; Garraty, *Right-Hand Man,* pp. 174–176.

35. N.Y., *Test.,* II, 1238, V, 3899–3901, 3914–3918.

CHAPTER XI. AN EXPERIENCE AT LAW

1. On early litigation, Charles K. Knight, *The History of Life Insurance in the United States to 1870* (Philadelphia, 1920), p. 158; Hyde statement in W. S. Manning, comp., *The Condition of the Life Insurance Companies of the State of New York* (Albany 1877), p. 13. *W.U.,* XXXVII (1887), 85–86, notes the small number of policy claims contested between 1882 and 1887.

2. See Morton Keller, "The Judicial System and the Law of Life Insurance, 1888–1911," *Business History Review,* XXXV (1961), 322–323, for the data supporting the analysis in this chapter. For similar conclusions derived from a

study of Wisconsin insurance litigation, see Spencer L. Kimball, *Insurance and Public Policy* (Madison, 1960), 209f; and Kimball, "The Role of the Court in the Development of Insurance Law," *Wisconsin Law Review* (1957), 520–561.

3. *Hillmon v. Mutual,* 79 Fed. 749 (C.C. Kan. 1897), *Hillmon v. New York Life,* 79 Fed. 749, *Metropolitan v. McNall,* 81 Fed. 888 (C.C. Kan. 1897), *Mutual v. Boyle,* 82 Fed. 705 (C.C. Kan. 1897); *Metropolitan v. New Orleans,* 205 U.S. 395 (1907), *Board of Assessors v. New York Life,* 216 U.S. 517 (1910); *New York Life v. Hardison,* 85 N.E. 410 (Mass., 1908); decisions of unconstitutionality compiled from N.Y.S.L.B., *Index to Legislation,* 1890–1908 and *Insurance Law Journal,* XVII-XXXVII (1888–1908).

4. *Robotham v. Prudential,* 53 Atl. 842 (N.J. Ch. 1903); on mutualization, *Lord v. Equitable,* 108 N.Y. Supp. 67 (1908), 87 N.E. 443 (1909), *People v. Equitable,* 101 N.Y. Supp. 354 (Trial Ct., 1906); on managerial problems, *Rennie v. Mutual,* 176 Fed. 202 (1st Circ., 1910); *Mutual v. McCurdy,* 103 N.Y. Supp. 840 (Sup. Ct. 1907); *Beers v. New York Life,* 20 N.Y. Supp. 254 (Sup. Ct. 1892); *Akers v. Mutual,* 112 N.Y. Supp. 254 (Trial Ct. 1908).

5. *People v. Formosa,* 16 N.Y. Supp. 783 (1891).

6. Thomas I. Parkinson, "Are the Law Schools Adequately Training for the Public Service?" *American Law School Review,* VIII (1935), 294.

7. William R. Vance, "The History of the Development of the Warranty in Insurance Law," *Yale Law Journal,* XX (1911), 533; George Richards, *A Treatise on the Law of Insurance* (3rd ed., New York, 1912), p. vii.

8. *Holly v. Metropolitan,* 11 N.E. 507.

9. George L. Amrhein, *The Liberalization of the Life Insurance Contract* (Philadelphia, 1933), pp. 196–237; L. G. Fouse, "Policy Contracts in Life Insurance," A.A.P.S.S. *Annals,* XXVI (1905), 219–221.

10. *Ritter v. Mutual,* 169 U.S. 139 (1898).

11. Roger W. Cooley, *Briefs on the Law of Insurance* (St. Paul, 1905), pp. 3740–3741.

12. Ellerbe W. Carter, "Suits for Accounting on Tontine Life Insurance Policies," *Virginia Law Review,* II (1914), 22–25; Herbert H. Reed, "Distribution of Surplus by Insurance Companies," *American Law Review,* XLII (1908), 12–24.

13. William R. Vance, *Handbook of the Law of Insurance* (St. Paul, 1904), pp. 298–305; Richards, *Treatise on the Law of Insurance* (1st ed., New York, 1892), p. 86; Charles B. Elliott, *A Treatise on the Law of Insurance* (Indianapolis, 1907), p. 138.

CHAPTER XII. THE STRUCTURE OF SUPERVISION

1. N.C.I.C., *Proceedings,* I (1871). On the development of insurance regulation, see Edwin W. Patterson, *The Insurance Commissioner in the United States* (Cambridge, Mass., 1926), pp. 519–537; Stalson, *Marketing Life Insurance,* pp. 296f; R. Carlyle Buley, *The American Life Convention, 1906–1952* (New York, 1953), I, 61f.

2. N.Y.S.L.B., *Digest of Governors' Messages,* 1879, 1883; *Missouri Ins. Rep.,* XXII (1891), XXVIII (1896), xxv f; *New Hampshire Ins. Rep.,* XXV (1894), xxix-xxx; XXXIV (1902), xxiv; *Connecticut Ins. Rep.,* XXXVII (1902), 192–194. Georgia in 1905 gave the duties of its insurance commissioner to the state treasurer. Ga. 1905, p. 76.

3. William E. Harvey to Wright, March 11, 1869, California insurance commissioner to Wright, May 5, 1876, Wright Mss.; *New York Ins. Rep.,* 10th (1869), cxxxii. When California law in 1874 required insurance firms to have resident agents with full company powers, the New York Life and twenty-eight other firms withdrew from the state. In 1878 the law was repealed, and the New York Life returned. Abbott, *Story of Nylic,* p. 75.

4. *Connecticut Ins. Rep.,* XXV (1890), lviii; *Missouri Ins. Rep.,* 22nd (1891), vii.

5. Patterson, *Insurance Commissioner,* p. 540; see also Miles M. Dawson, *Principles of Insurance Legislation* (New York, 1895).

6. N.Y.S.L.B., *Trend of Legislation, 1901,* pp. 418–419; N.Y.S.L.B., *Review of Legislation, 1905,* p. 283; N.Y. 1892, ch. 38; Charles B. Alexander, *Notes on the New York Law of Life Insurance* (New York, 1887).

7. These and ensuing observations on the nature of 1890–1905 insurance legislation are based on an analysis of all insurance laws summarized in N.Y.S.L.B., *Index to Legislation,* 1890–1905. By 1905 considerable legislation regulated the advertising of life insurance companies. Statutes held companies liable for false advertising, forbade false or misleading advertising, and required the publication of liabilities as well as assets. Equit., Law Department, *Old Opinions,* no. 271, May 18, 1905; Equitable to Alexander and Green, July 25, 1908. However, in 1902 Massachusetts and Ohio passed "important amendments" lessening insurance companies' examination expenses, and statutes occasionally waived the requirement to publish annual statements in newspapers. N.Y.S.L.B., *Review of Legislation, 1902,* p. 836.

8. Hudnut, *Semi-Centennial History,* p. 131; Equit., *Very Old Opinions,* no. 23, March 15, 1873; Harry G. Friedman, *Taxation of Corporations in Massachusetts* (New York, 1907), pp. 21–22, 155, 160–61; Joel R. Moore, *Taxation of Corporations in Illinois* (Urbana, Ill., 1913), pp. 78–87; *W.U.,* LXIX (1903), 5; *Kansas Ins. Rep.,* 34th (1904), 2.

9. *Northwestern Mutual v. Lewis and Clarke County,* 72 Pac. 982 (Mont., 1903), *State v. Insurance Company of North America,* 99 NW 35, 100 NW 405 (Neb., 1904); Home Insurance Company President John H. Washburn, in *Best's Insurance News,* IV (1903); John A. Finch, "The Law of Insurance in the Law School," A.B.A. *Reports,* XX (1897), 296; Equit., *Very Old Opinions,* no. 130, April 26, 1895; *Holliday* [Ind.] *v. State Board,* 150 Ind. 216 (1898); on Kansas tax, *Insurance Times,* XXXI (1898), 10; *Provident Savings v. Miller,* 179 N.Y. 227 (1904).

10. Colo. 1893, ch. 67; N.Y. 1902, ch. 437; *New Hampshire Ins. Rep.,* XXXIV (1902), xxiv; *New York Ins. Rep.,* XXXV (1894), xi.

11. On the department's origins, *W.U.,* XXII (1880), 201–202; *New York Ins. Rep.,* 51st (1910), pt. V, pp. xi f; on Barnes, *New York Ins. Rep.,* 3rd (1862), pp. vi, xxxvii; 4th (1863), p. vii.

12. *New York Ins. Rep.,* 11th (1870), pp. x, xxvii; 13th (1872), p. xxii.

13. Chapman, "A Theory of Supervision," *New York Ins. Rep.,* 15th (1874); *New York Ins. Rep.,* 17th (1876). A copy of Manning's book, *The Condition of the Life Insurance Companies of the State of New York. Revised Tabulated Edition of the Official Stenographer's Notes of the Investigation by the Assembly Committee* (Albany, [1877]), is in the New York Insurance Society Library.

14. On examination fees, Abbott, *The Story of NYLIC,* p. 105; on red ink, Hendrick, *Life Insurance,* pp. 212–214; on premium tax, *Nation,* LXXXI (1905), 436–437; N.Y., Special Legislative Committee, *Report* (1885), pp. 3–4; N.Y. 1890, ch. 400 (Attorney General law); N.Y. 1889, ch. 282 (antirebate law).

15. President Edward A. Temple of the Bankers' Life of Des Moines to William C. Beer, April 8, 1904, Beer Mss.; Maxwell statement in George S. Bixby Mss., HK 12136, Box 2, N.Y. State Library.

16. *New York Ins. Rep.,* 33rd (1892), 477–482; *Chronicle,* XLVII (1891), 82; N.Y., *Test.,* III, 1897; Hyde to Alexander, October 18, 1888, A26, Hyde Mss.; McCurdy to Pierce, March 19, 1894, XV, May 22, 1894, XVI, Feb. 13, 1893, XV, Duer to Pierce, Dec. 6, 16, 1893, XV, Mut. Lbs.

17. Payn statement in N.Y., *Test.,* VII, 5983; McCurdy to Payn, Feb. 8, 1898, to Gov. Black, April 26, 27, 1898, XIX, Mut. Lbs.; Harold F. Gosnell, *Boss Platt and His New York Machine* (Chicago, 1924); Elting E. Morison, ed., *The Letters of Theodore Roosevelt* (Cambridge, Mass., 1951–54), II, 1111f; on

Hendricks, "Insurance," *Independent,* LIII (1901), 399; N.Y., *Test.,* VI, 5632, VII, 5961.

18. *New York Ins. Rep.,* 37th (1896); N.Y., *Test.,* X, *Report,* 346f; N.Y., *Test.,* VII, 5856. On McCurdy, *Texas Ins. Rep.,* XXIV (1898); *Illinois Ins. Rep.,* XXXI (1899); W. H. Mabree to Lou Payn, May 25, 1898, XIX, Mut. Lbs.; McCurdy to Hoff and Robinson (tel.), Dec. 30, 1897, to James S. Hogg, June 24, July 6, Dec. 22, 1898, XIX, XX, Mut. Lbs. Payn statement in N.Y., *Test.,* VII, 5975–5980. McCurdy also called on Mutual general agents in Texas, Arkansas, Washington, and Minnesota to induce their state commissioners not to participate in this "joint raid" on the Eastern companies. McCurdy to Hogg and Robinson (tel.), Dec. 30, 1897, XIX.

19. N.Y.L., *M.B.T.,* June 13, 1894; McCall to commissioners, June 1, 1894, Merrill to McCall, June 25, 1894, "The Seven States Examination," I, N.Y.L. Arch.; *W.U.,* L (1894), 452, 471, LXIX (1903), 392.

20. *Insurance Times,* XXVIII (1895), 185; *Chronicle,* XLVII (1891), 11; *New Jersey Ins. Rep.,* 1893; N.J., *Test.,* I, *passim.*

21. Hyde to Merrill, Aug. 6, 1895, *et seq.,* A34, Hyde to Waddill, Sept. 1, 1896, Hyde to E. M. McPherson, Sept. 18, Hyde to Waddill, Nov. 30, D5, Hyde Mss.

22. *Pennsylvania Ins. Rep.,* XXI (1893), iii-iv, XXV (1897), vii, XXII (1894), iii, XXIII (1895), x-xi; "The Pennsylvania Insurance Department," *Outlook,* LXXXI (1906), 335–336; *W.U.,* LVI (1897), 398, 446; Samuel W. Pennypacker, *The Autobiography of a Pennsylvanian* (Philadelphia, 1918), pp. 385–387. The varying degree of the companies' control over the political organizations of the Eastern states may be measured by insurance taxation totals:

	1890	*1895*
Pennsylvania	$438,840	$684,888
New York	265,360	344,989
Massachusetts	429,398	535,345

N.Y.S.L.B., *State Finance Statistics, 1890 and 1895,* pp. 453–454.

23. *W.U.,* LVII (1897), 247; N.Y., *Test.,* IV, 3279–3288, V, 4206–4210.

24. McCurdy to Ohio superintendent William H. Hahn, May 16, 1895, XVI, to H. L. Remmel, May 12, 1903, XXIII, to Clarke, Feb. 4, 1896, XVII, Mut. Lbs.; Mut., *M.B.D.,* Dec. 28, 1898; *W.U.,* LVI (1897), 265; *Monthly Journal of Insurance Economics,* I (1899), 5; McCurdy to James S. Hogg, March 11, 1897, XVIII, Mut. Lbs.; N.Y., *Test.,* VI, 4841, VII, 5881.

25. *Chronicle,* XLVII (1891), 243; *W.U.,* XLIV (1891), 402. On North Carolina and Alabama, *Insurance Times,* XXVIII (1895), 86, 89; *W.U.,* LII (1895), 122; McCurdy to Alexander, Feb. 1, 1897, XVIII, Mut. Lbs. On Missouri, James W. Alexander to Charles B. Alexander, April 15, 20, 1898, Equit., *Old Opinions,* no. 169. On Nebraska, Perkins to McCall, Aug. 24, 1900, Perkins Mss. On Missouri, Arizona, and Wisconsin, Thomas Buckner to Andrew Hamilton, March 15, 1905, N.Y.L. Arch. On South Dakota, Perkins to McCall (tel.), Feb. 27, 1905.

26. *Texas Ins. Rep.,* XIX (1893), 22–23; Culberson to McCurdy, Dec. 28, 1896, John K. Duer to Hollingsworth, Jan. 5, 1897, McCurdy to Hogg, March 11, XVIII, to Hyde, Oct. 20, XIX, to Jefferson Johnson, Jan. 10, 1899, XX, Mut. Lbs.

27. On Hillmon case, Clough, *Mutual,* pp. 172–173; *W.U.,* LVI-LVIII (1897–98), *passim;* Buley, *American Life Convention,* I, 137–138; *Kansas Ins. Rep.,* XXVIII (1897), viii f; Perkins to McCall, March 8, 1897, Perkins Mss.; *W.U.,* LIX (1898), 274, LX (1899), 228–229; C. H. Luling to Edward O'Bryan, Oct. 28, 1904, N.Y.L. Arch.

28. On Fricke, N.Y., *Test.,* II, 1922; on Host, *Wisconsin Ins. Rep.,* 1903, p. xx, Robert S. Maxwell, *La Follette and the Rise of the Progressives in Wisconsin* (Madison, Wis., 1956), pp. 105–109; on Equitable, *Wisconsin Ins. Rep.,* 1904,

pp. 60f, L. A. Anderson, "The Distribution of Surplus in Life Insurance," A.A.P.S.S., *Annals,* XXVI (1905), 710–713, *Equitable v. Host,* 124 Wisc. 657 (1905); James W. Alexander to Gage Tarbell, July 8, 1904, P12, Hyde Mss., reporting the department's attitude; on contribution, *W.U.,* LXXIV (1906), 400, 440; on Prudential, Buley, *American Life Convention,* I, 140–141; *Wisconsin Ins. Rep.,* 1904, p. 32; N.Y., *Test.,* VI, 4847–4850. Even Host had his limitations. In 1905 he obtained a bill requiring that the state rather than the companies pay for departmental examinations; but Governor La Follette vetoed the measure. *Insurance Monitor,* LIII (1905), 261.

29. *Connecticut Ins. Rep.,* XXVI (1891), XXVII (1892); *Massachusetts Ins. Rep.,* XLIX (1904), xi–xii. A nice question might be raised here as to what constitutes "effective" regulation. Merrill, Cutting's predecessor, obviously was close to the Equitable. Because of this he sternly challenged the propriety of a newly devised New York Life policy in 1890 — so sternly, indeed, that the New York Life left the state for a while, and dropped the policy. Yet Cutting, generally considered a superior commissioner, may well have been influenced in his opposition to the Prudential-Fidelity merger by the fact that one of the large industrial firms, the John Hancock, had its home office in Massachusetts. *Chronicle,* XLV (Jan.–March 1890), *passim.*

CHAPTER XIII. THE RESPONSE TO REGULATION

1. Hyde to McCall, Dec. 5, 1889, A28, Nov. 17, 1890, A29, March 21, 1891, D1, May 18, 1887, A23; William H. McIntyre to Depew, March 22, 1896, A38, Hyde Mss.

2. On Coman, N.Y., *Test.,* IV, 3379–3385; on Platt, N.Y., *Test.,* IV, 3386–3391; on Husted, N.Y., *Test.,* IV, 3270–3278; Hill to Alexander, March 20, 1895, in N.Y., *Test.,* IX, Ex. 389; on Odell, N.Y., *Test.,* IV, 3005–3009, 3091–3093, 3143–3156.

3. On Lewis, Hendrick, *Life Insurance,* p. 227; on Platt, N.Y., *Test.,* IV, 3388; on Barnes, N.Y., *Test.,* III, 2659; on Pierce, N.Y., *Test.,* II, 1897; McCurdy to Hill, Nov. 21, 1893, XV, to James Speyer, Dec. 15, 1898, to Sewell, Dec. 30, 1898, XX, Mut. Lbs.

4. On Field, N.Y., *Test.,* II, 1484, 1919; on McClelland, N.Y., *Test.,* V, 3981–4024. The judgment of a state senator was that in the two decades before 1905 no member of the Insurance Committee had been unfriendly to the great firms. *New York World,* Sept. 17, 1905.

5. N.Y., *Test.,* II, 1748, 1378–1380; for Jordan memos, N.Y., *Test.,* VIII, Ex. 354–356. When a tax increase threatened in Texas McCurdy told Alexander that Fields "will at once take active measures to stop . . . the objectionable proceedings contemplated . . . at the fountain head." McCurdy to Alexander, Jan. 5, 1897, XVIII, Mut. Lbs. In the same year Fields was unable to attend to a Wisconsin legislative matter and McCurdy asked Alexander to look after the Mutual's interests there. McCurdy to Alexander, Jan. 7, 1897, XVIII.

6. Expenses in *New York Ins. Rep.,* 1895, 1900, 1904; N.Y., *Test.,* II, 1728, 1754.

7. On Edward McCall, N.Y., *Test.,* V, 3882, and author's interview with former New York Life actuary Arthur Hunter; on Buckley, Perkins to Thomas Buckner, April 23, 1897, Perkins Mss., N.Y., *Test.,* II, 1984; on Beer, Beer Mss., *passim;* on O'Bryan, Perkins to McCall, March 2, 1898, N.Y.L. Arch.; on Indiana tax, Perkins to Beveridge, April 5, 8, 1897, Beveridge Mss.; on Hamilton, N.Y., *Test.,* I, 788–789, Hamilton statement in N.Y., *Test.,* VII, 5861–5875; Payn quotation in N.Y., *Test.,* VII, 5983.

8. N.Y., *Test.,* II, 1365–1389, 1538, VII, 5873; McCurdy to General Agents Feb. 14, 1898, XIX; McCurdy to Alexander, Feb. 17, 1896, XVII, Dec. 30, 1897, XIX, Mut. Lbs.; Hyde to John C. Eisele, Jan. 23, 1895, B4, Hyde Mss.; on mortgage tax, N.Y., *Test.,* VI, 5509–5513.

9. McCall statement in N.Y., *Test.*, II, 1477; on use of policyholders, N.Y., *Test.*, IV, 3302–3306; Hamilton statement in N.Y., *Test.*, VII, 5864.

10. N.Y., *Test.*, VII, 5866; "Legal Expenses, Schedule and Recommendations," *Seven States' Examination,* I, N.Y.L. Arch.; "Special Report Concerning the Transactions of Andrew Hamilton," Perkins Mss.; N.Y.; *Test., Report,* X, 49–51.

11. N.Y.L., *M.F.C.*, March 5, 1895; McCall to Perkins, Oct. 27, 1902, Perkins Mss.

12. McCall statement in N.Y., *Test.*, V, 3862–3863; on various Hamilton arrangements, N.Y., *Test., Report,* X, 49–64. In his original arrangement with the company, Hamilton insisted on freedom from accountability in his expenditures; otherwise, he argued, it would be impossible to reach men who could not afford to have it known that they were "interested in insurance legislation." N.Y., *Test.*, VII, 5865.

13. Met., *M.B.D.*, Jan. 27, 1891, April 26, 1892, April 25, 1893, April 24, 1894, April 23, 1895, April 27, 1897, April 24, 1901; Marquis James, *The Metropolitan Life* (New York, 1947), pp. 121–124; N.Y., *Test.*, VI, 5060–5061; statements and correspondence on child insurance legislation, *Sundry Correspondence,* 1878–1898, Met. Arch.

14. Dryden to Hegeman, Dec. 9, 1885, Met. Arch.; N.Y., *Test.*, VI, 4841, 5003; on Prudential expenses, N.Y., *Test.*, VI, 4834; on Metropolitan, N.Y., *Test.*, II, 2870, Ex. 352; on John Hancock, Folder 221, Secretary's Office, J.H.; N.Y., *Test.*, VI, 5001–5004; Dryden statement in N.Y., *Test.*, VI, 4836; Met., *M.B.D.*, Oct. 22, 1901; on Massachusetts, N.Y., *Test.*, III, 2871; Met., *M.F.C.*, April 21, 1897.

15. N.Y., *Test.*, II, 1414–1415; Buley, *American Life Convention,* I, 134, 142–143; McCurdy to L. Anderson, Dec. 6, 1898, XX, Mut. Lbs.; Henry C. Lippincott, "The Essentials of Life Insurance Administration," A.A.P.S.S. *Annals,* XXVI (1905), 27. The president of the Home Insurance Company observed that "there is no business so hampered by legislation, so burdened with taxation, so treated with suspicion as is our own"; the chairman of the A.B.A. Insurance Committee declared: "No legitimate business is so constantly assailed, so cruelly burdened, so little understood." *Best's Insurance News,* IV (Oct. 1903); *American Agency Bulletin,* III (Sept. 1905).

16. William R. Vance, "Federal Control of Insurance Corporations," *Green Bag,* XVIII (1905), 86; chairman, A.B.A. Insurance Committee, in *American Agency Bulletin,* III (Sept. 1905); Hamilton statement in N.Y., *Test.*, VII, 5874; McCall statement in N.C.I.C., *Proceedings,* 1902; McCurdy to Ohio commissioner Hahn, June 3, 1895, XVI, Mut. Lbs.; Depew statement in N.Y., *Test.*, IV, 3200; N.Y., *Test.*, VII, 5879.

17. N.Y., *Test.*, VII, 5869, II, 1550–1552.

18. N.Y., *Test.*, III, 5869–5870; Perkins to Banta, July 11, 1893, Perkins Mss.; N.Y.L., *M.B.T.*, Jan. 25, Feb. 1, 1892; James K. Duer to Robert McCurdy, March 7, 1896, XVII, Mut. Lbs. On the hostile role of fire insurance companies, N.Y., *Test.*, II, 1560; on the impact of competing local firms on state legislation, correspondence on the role of the Minnesota Mutual and retaliatory legislation, Folder 226, Secretary's Office, J.H., and James A. Tinsley, "Texas Progressives and Insurance Regulation," *Southwestern Social Science Quarterly,* XXXVI (1955), 241–243, 245.

19. Perkins-McCall correspondence, Feb.–March 1900, William Buckley to Perkins, March 16, Perkins Mss. There is a full account of the fight in Garraty, *Right-Hand Man,* pp. 72–78.

20. Perkins to McCall, March 12, 1900, Perkins Mss.

CHAPTER XIV. THE COMPANIES AND NATIONAL POWER

1. McCurdy to Robert A. Maxwell, May 1, 1895, XVI, to Sewell, Dec. 9, 1897, XIX, to Edward Lyman Short, May 21, 1895, XVI, Mut. Lbs.; Perkins to

Major E. W. Halford, June 21, 1894, Perkins Mss.

2. Perkins to Darwin P. Kingsley, Aug. 10, 1893, Perkins Mss.; *W.U.*, L (1894), 376; Mut., *M.B.T.*, Feb. 14, 1894; N.Y.L., *M.F.C.*, May 14, 1895.

3. N.Y., *Test., Report,* X, 24, 63, 110. On the lesser firms, N.Y., *Test.*, VII, 6426, 6407, 6467, V, 4544–4545.

4. N.Y., *Test.*, VII, 6407; McCall statement in N.Y., *Test.*, I, 825–826; Metropolitan statement in N.Y., *Test.*, III, 2710. In July, the Metropolitan's directors had resolved not to make any political contributions. Met., *M.B.D.*, July 28, 1896. The New York Life refused to contribute to the 9th Regiment of the National Guard in April 1896, but by November was ready to support this bulwark of law and order. N.Y.L., *M.F.C.*, April 14, Nov. 4, 1896.

5. McCurdy to Thomas J. Finney, Oct. 13, 1896, to Hanna, June 29, XVII, Mut. Lbs.; Hyde to Hanna, Aug. 24, 1896, A35, Hyde Mss.; Buley, *Equitable,* p. 84.

6. Perkins to Thomas B. Reed, Oct. 3, 1896, to David B. Carse, Oct. 14, Perkins Mss.

7. Perkins to Beveridge, March 17, 1897, Perkins Mss.; Beveridge to Perkins, April 1, 1901, Beveridge Mss.

8. Perkins to William E. Ingersoll, April 12, 1898, to R. D. Bokurn (tel.), March 30, Perkins Mss.; McCurdy to Mahlon Pitney, April 13, 1898, XIX, Mut. Lbs.; Pru., *M.B.D.*, April 11, 1898; Hyde to Woodford, Nov. 1, 1897, B6, Hyde Mss.; Woodford to Hegeman, Nov. 18, 1897, Met. Arch.

9. Perkins to Samuel B. Platner, April 29, 1898, to Hans von Adelson, May 3, to Beveridge, May 5, 1898, Jan. 26, Feb. 28, 1899, Perkins Mss.

10. N.Y., *Test., Report,* X, 63; McCall to McKinley, n.d., in McKinley Mss.; Perkins to Frank Munsey, May 1, 1900, to Beveridge, May 21, to Dawes, May 9, 25, Sept. 24, Perkins Mss.; on questionnaire, Perkins to Dawes, Oct. 17, 1900; Perkins to McKinley (tel.), Nov. 6, 1900, to Roosevelt (tel.), Nov. 6, to Hanna (tel.), Nov. 7, Perkins Mss. See also Thomas Beer, *Hanna* (New York, 1941), pp. 628–643; Margaret Leech, *In the Days of McKinley* (New York, 1959), pp. 426–427.

11. Beer to C. S. Funk, Aug. 31, 1906, Millard to Beer, March 10, 1903, Long to Beer, Jan. 27, 1903, Curtis to Beer, April 17, Bristow to Beer, July 3, Beer to Foraker, Feb. 25, 26, Beer Mss.; on Department of Commerce, Roosevelt to Perkins, Dec. 26, 1902, June 26, 1903, Cortelyou to Perkins, April 17, 1903, McCall to Perkins, Oct. 22, Perkins Mss.; Beer, *Hanna,* p. 607n.

12. Alexander to Hyde, Sept. 17, 1901, P12, Hyde Mss.; on Equitable contributions, N.Y., *Test., Report,* X, 110, IV, 2916; McCurdy to R. D. Haislip, June 17, 1898, XIX, to Cornelius Bliss, Nov. 22, 1900, to Sewell, Feb. 8, 1901, on immigration, to Dryden, June 16, 1902, XXII, Mut. Lbs.; on campaign contributions, N.Y., *Test., Report,* X, 24; Duer to Roosevelt, Feb. 17, 1903, XXIII; Eugene S. Watson to Beer, Jan. 4, 1906, Beer Mss.

13. Lincoln Steffens, "New Jersey: A Traitor State (II)," *McClure's Magazine,* XXV (1905), 53; on 1904 campaign, N.Y., *Test.*, II, 1760, IV, 2916, II, 1555–1556, 1739–1742.

14. N.Y., *Test., Report,* X, 63–64; McCall statement in N.Y., *Test.*, II, 1472–1476; William Travers Jerome to Perkins, March 27, 1906, Perkins to Jerome, March 27, Perkins Mss.

15. On war tax, Met., *M.B.D.*, July 26, 1898, N.Y., *Test.*, I, 1553; Beer to ? Chance, Oct. 2, 1901, to U.S. pension commissioner H. Clay Evans, Sept. 24, 1901, Beer Mss.; N.Y., *Test.*, II, 1471.

16. James W. Hurst, *The Growth of American Law: the Law Makers* (Boston, 1950), pp. 227–229; Vice-President, Germania Fire Ins. Co., to Wright, March 20, 1865, Sheppard Homans to Wright, May 5, 1865, Wright Mss.; on Chamber, *U.S. Insurance Gazette,* XXVI–XXVII (1868), Stalson, *Marketing Life Insurance,* pp. 781–783; Winston to Wright, Nov. 6, 1866, Wright Mss.; *New York Ins. Rep.,* IX (1868), lx–lxi.

17. 8 Wall. 168; Wright quoted in William J. Graham, "The Romance of Life Insurance," *The World To-Day,* XV (1908), 1282; Homans to Wright, March 23, 1870, Lewis to Wright, Oct. 7, 1873, Wright Mss.; *New York Ins. Rep.,* XIII (1872), xxxiv, XV (1874), vi.

18. On abortive attempts at federal regulation in the 1870's and the 1880's, Maurice H. Robinson, "Government Regulation of Insurance Companies," *Proceedings of the American Political Science Association,* III (1906), 91; on Pattison bill, McCurdy to James W. Alexander, Aug. 31, 1892, XV, Mut. Lbs.; Solomon S. Huebner, "Federal Supervision and Regulation of Insurance," A.A.P.S.S. *Annals,* XXVI (1905), 683.

19. McCurdy to Secretary of War Daniel G. Lamont, to Cleveland, Nov. 8, 1895, XVII, Mut. Lbs.; Perkins to McCall, March 15, 1898, Perkins Mss.; on 1897 legislation, *W.U.,* LVII (1897), 337; McCurdy to Charlton Lewis, Dec. 8, 1897, XIX, Mut. Lbs.; Hyde to Sheppard Homans, June 22, 1896, A35, Hyde Mss. See also Sheppard Homans, "On Governmental Regulation of Life Insurance in the United States of America," *Journal of the Institute of Actuaries,* XXXIII (1897), 32–35.

20. Alexander to William H. McIntyre, April 26, 1904, P12, Hyde Mss.; James W. Alexander, "Some Prejudices about Life Insurance," *Atlantic Monthly,* LXXXVI (1900), 19; John K. Duer to Alexander, Nov. 22, 1901, XXII, McCurdy to *Spectator* editor Clifford Thompson, Dec. 14, 1904, XXIII, Mut. Lbs.; N.Y.L., *G.J.M.,* p. 321, Beer Mss.; on Dryden, N.Y., *Test.,* VI, 4992–5000. Buley, *Equitable,* p. 231, notes that the company never supported Federal regulation, but Alexander at least seems to have accepted the idea. See also *Moody's Magazine,* I (1906), 288f.

21. *New York Sun,* Aug. 17, 1905; N.Y., *Test.,* VII, 5872; *Spectator,* Dec. 22, 1904; Vance, "Federal Control," p. 86; Mutual lobbyist's statement in N.Y., *Test.,* II, 1559; A.B.A., *Reports,* XXVIII (1905), 112, 500f. John F. Dryden, "The Outlook for Federal Regulation of Insurance," *Independent,* LX (1906) 734, points to strong support for Federal regulation by academic and professional groups. Files NIR-16 and 2509, B.C. Arch., contain samples of the pronational regulation literature of the time.

22. Correspondence in Files 613, 617, 889–892, 942, 2103, 2509, and 3707, and Garfield, "Memoir of Conferences with Insurance Men," May 18 and 19, 1904, File 099.1, B.C. Arch.; on Roosevelt, Morton Keller, *In Defense of Yesterday* (New York, 1958), pp. 77–78, Appendix; Perkins to Roosevelt, Aug. 12, 1905, Perkins Mss.

23. Buley, *American Life Convention,* I, 146; *Insurance Monitor,* LIII (1905), 167; statement of William C. Johnson, File 2997, B.C. Arch.; *Massachusetts Ins. Rep.,* 51st (1906), xxvi–xxvii; *Moody's Magazine,* I (1906), 281–287.

24. A.B.A., *Reports,* XXVIII (1905), 112; *Moody's Magazine,* I (1906), 294–296; *Sun* quoted in "Life Insurance: Disclosures and Remedies," *Current Literature,* XL (1906), 30; *C.F.C.,* LXXXII (1906), 661–662; Brandeis quote in "Life Insurance: Disclosures and Remedies," p. 30; Roosevelt to Wayne MacVeagh, Sept. 23, 1905, in Morison, ed., *Letters,* V, 34.

25. Carman F. Randolph, "Federal Supervision of Insurance," *Columbia Law Review,* V (1905), 513, 518–519, 525–526. State bar association journals generally opposed Federal regulation.

26. Buley, *American Life Convention,* I, 145; Perkins to McCall (tel.), Feb. 27, 1905, Perkins Mss.; Roosevelt to Brandeis, Jan. 14, 1907, in Morison, ed., *Letters,* V, 551; U.S., *C.R.,* 59th Cong., 1st Sess., House, April 17, 1906, 5365; *District of Columbia Ins. Rep.,* 4th (1906), x. Congressman McCall of Massachusetts observed that the District's insurance code was procorporation enough to "make a New Jersey–man blush."

27. Garfield to Francis L. Stetson, Nov. 15, 1905, File 3551, B.C. Arch.: Smith to Nicholas R. Wall, Dec. 17, 1906, File 6412; Roosevelt to Governor John A.

Johnson, Nov. 27, 1905, Personal Lbs., Roosevelt Mss.; A.B.A., *Reports,* XXIX (1906), 552f, XXX (1906), 326f; "Insurance," *Independent,* LIX (1905), 112, 1425; Cravath to Morton, Feb. 5, 1906, in Robert T. Swaine, *The Cravath Firm,* (New York, 1946), I, 764–765; McCurdy to Frank Mebane, Nov. 13, 1905, XXIII, Mut. Lbs.

CHAPTER XV. 1905

1. Moody statement in Elting E. Morison, *Turmoil and Tradition: A Study of the Life and Times of Henry Lewis Stimson* (Boston, 1960), p. 105; *C.F.C.,* LXXX (1905), 2312; Johnson statement in Swaine, *Cravath Firm,* I, 753; Rufus W. Weeks, "The Insurance Conference," *Independent,* LX (1906), 471–472.

2. Thomas W. Lawson, *Frenzied Finance* (New York, 1905), pp. 413f; Morton Keller, *In Defense of Yesterday* (New York, 1958), p. 71; on Lawson's motives, James W. Alexander to James H. Hyde, Dec. 6, 1904, P12, Hyde Mss. Another pre-1905 attack was Henry S. Beardsley, "The Despotism of Combined Millions," *Era,* XIV–XV (1904–05).

3. *New York World,* Feb. 12, 1905 *et passim;* see above, Chapter IV.

4. N.Y., *Test.,* IV, 3119; *New York Ins. Rep.,* 47th (1906), pt. III, 13f; N.Y., *Test.,* VI, 5679, 5688; Perkins to John McCall, Feb. 25, March 2, 1905, Perkins Mss.

5. *Insurance Monitor,* LIII (1905), 118, 209; "Insurance," *Independent,* LVIII (1905), 451; "The Equitable Controversy," *Nation,* LXXX (1905), 147; Corporate Files and Frick Committee Correspondence, Secretary's Office, in H.P., Equit.; *Insurance Monitor,* LII (1905), 302.

6. N.Y., *Test.,* IV, 3011; Ryan and Harriman testimony in N.Y., *Test.;* on Root, Merlo J. Pusey, *Charles Evans Hughes* (New York, 1951), I, 141, Philip C. Jessup, *Elihu Root* (New York, 1938), I, 437–440; Swaine, *Cravath Firm,* I, 751–53; Root to Alexander, Feb. 21, March 30, 1905, to McCurdy, March 22, Root Mss.

7. N.Y., *Test.,* VI, 5154; William Beer to George Perkins, March 20, 1905, Perkins Mss. Armstrong was markedly obsequious to Harriman when the financier testified at the investigation. N.Y., *Test.,* VI, 5165.

8. Alfred H. Lewis, "Owners of America. II. Thomas F. Ryan," *Cosmopolitan,* XLV (1908), 150; Cravath to Frank Black, Aug. 11, 1905, in Swaine, *Cravath Firm,* I, 757 (his emphasis); McCall to Armstrong, Aug. 18, 1905, Perkins Mss.; Beer to Theodore Roosevelt, Nov. 8, 1907, Beer Mss., Arthur Hunter interview; *Insurance Monitor,* LIII (1905), 321; McCall to Perkins, March 27, 1905; McCurdy statement in Mut., *M.B.T.,* April 26, 1905.

9. On appointment, Pusey, *Hughes,* I, 140f; Armstrong to Choate, Aug. 15, 1905, Choate to Armstrong, Aug. 17, Choate Mss.; Hughes to Mark Sullivan, Feb. 4, 1934, "The Gas and Insurance Investigations," Beerits Memo, Hughes Mss. McKeen, Dawson, and Cox sketches in "Insurance Men, Past and Present," *International Insurance Encyclopedia* (New York and London, 1910), I. On Tully, James, *Metropolitan,* p. 211. For McKeen's gentle questioning of Mutual officers, N.Y., *Test.,* III, 2355, 2761–2762.

10. N.Y., *Test.,* I, 8–9; on Hughes technique, Ralph H. Gravis, "The Insurance Investigation and Its Results," *Harper's Weekly,* L (1906), 366–370, Lindsay Russell, "Charles E. Hughes," *Green Bag,* XVII (1905), 635–637, Burton J. Hendrick, "Governor Hughes," *McClure's,* XXX (1908), 531–532, Cravath to Frank Black, Aug. 29, 1905, in Swaine, *Cravath Firm,* I, 757; N.Y., *Test.,* I, 18. The committee's budget was only $50,000, and according to New York Life Treasurer Edward D. Randolph the stenographic reporting was sloppily handled. N.Y., *Test.,* I, 6; N.Y.L., *G.J.M.,* p. 36, Beer Mss. The companies may have adopted the technique of swamping Hughes with a seemingly indigestible mass of data; but Hughes and his staff digested it. Louis Filler, *Crusaders for American Liberalism* (Collier Books, New York, 1961), p. 189.

11. On Hamilton, William E. Ingersoll to Perkins, Dec. 21, 1905, Perkins Mss.; on McCurdy, N.Y., *Test.*, II, 1947, 1954f, 1966f; Perkins to Hamilton Cooke, Aug. 8, 1905; Beveridge to Perkins, Sept. 30, 1905, Perkins Mss.; N.Y., *Test.*, I, 729–731, 913–914. *The Philadelphia Press* of Sept. 19 welcomed Perkins' appearance on the stand: "He is the first of the younger generation of great financiers . . . to realize not only that this is a day of publicity, but that publicity is . . . the best policy."

12. Lawson, "The Black Flag on the Big Three," *Everybody's Magazine,* XIV (1906), 407, 411; N.Y., *Test., Report,* X, 282. Hughes himself commented: "I am impressed more with what we have failed to do than with what we have done." Pusey, *Hughes,* I, 165. In *The Brass Check* the Socialist Upton Sinclair claimed that corporation lawyer James B. Dill controlled the insurance revelations for the Morgan and Ryan interests, who were "taking away the control of life insurance money from irresponsible people like Jimmy Hyde, and bringing it under the control of people who were responsible — that is, responsible to Morgan and Ryan." When this goal was attained, said Sinclair, "the legislative investigations and the newspaper clamor stopped almost overnight." But the manifest thoroughness of the hearings, which looked critically at both Harriman and J. P. Morgan and Co., and the disagreement between Lawson and Sinclair over the true behind-the-scenes power (Standard Oil? Morgan?) militates against a conspiracy interpretation of the events of 1905.

13. Lawson, *Frenzied Finance,* p. 470; Charles B. Hubbell, "The Insurance Investigations," *Green Bag,* XVII (1905), 686; Ambrose Bierce, "Insurance in Ancient America," *Cosmopolitan,* XLI (1906), 555–557; *Outlook,* LXXXI (1905), 398–399, LXXXIII (1906), 152–153; pamphlet in Hughes Mss., no. 165. David Graham Phillips wrote a novel, *Light-Fingered Gentry,* inspired by the revelations.

14. *C.F.C.,* LXXXIV (1907), 1460–1462; *Ohio Ins. Rep.,* 1906, 3–7; *Massachusetts Ins. Rep.,* 52nd (1907), xxxviii; *Alabama Ins. Rep.* (1908), 12.

15. *New Jersey Ins. Rep.,* 1906, pt. II, pp. 15–16; N.J., *Test., passim,* esp. *Report,* pp. 14–26; Massachusetts, *Report of the Joint Special Committee on Insurance* (House Document 1085) (Boston, 1907); Louis D. Brandeis, "Savings Bank Life Insurance for Wage Earners," New York State Bar Association, *Proceedings,* XXX (1907), 103–117; Alpheus T. Mason, *The Brandeis Way* (Princeton, 1938), p. 174; *Ohio Ins. Rep.,* 1906; on Missouri, *Missouri Ins. Rep.,* XXXVII (1906), W. D. Vandiver, "The Responsibility of Insurance Officials," *World To-Day,* IX (1905), 1284; on Wisconsin, *Report of the Joint Committee of the Senate and Assembly on the Affairs of Life Insurance Companies* (Madison, 1907), Herman L. Ekern, "The Wisconsin Plan for State Life Insurance," *Case and Comment,* XX (1913), 8–10. The Michigan commissioner was friendly toward the companies. *Michigan Ins. Rep.,* XXXVI (1906). The Connecticut commissioner distinguished his state's firms from the New York companies, and committed the state to "its habitual policy of conservatism in matters of insurance legislation." *Connecticut Ins. Rep.,* 41st (1906), xxv–xxvi; 42nd (1907).

16. William J. Graham, "The Romance of Life Insurance," *World To-Day,* XIV (1908), 600; *Outlook,* LXXXI (1905), 249; *Louisiana Ins. Rep.,* 1905, vii; Roosevelt to Thomas D. O'Brien, Nov. 24, 1905, March 29, 1906, in Elting E. Morison, ed., *The Letters of Theodore Roosevelt* (Cambridge, Mass., 1951–1954), V, 93, 201–202, to Brandeis, Jan. 14, 1907, *Letters,* V, 551; *District of Columbia Ins. Rep.,* 5th (1906), xiii–xviii, Report of Committee of Fifteen in N.J., *Test.,* pp. 927–995. The actuary of an Eastern company complained that the committee was "easy in certain ways" to Southern and Western firms and "put restrictions on some of the Eastern companies." A. A. Welch to Herbert K. Smith, Dec. 3, 1906, File 2997, B.C. Arch.

17. N.Y.S.L.B., *Index to Legislation,* 1906–1908; N.Y.S.L.B., *Review of Legislation, 1908,* pp. 9, 311; Warren M. Persons, "Recent Insurance Legislation," *World To-Day,* XIV (1908), 45–50.

18. *Insurance Monitor,* LIII (1905), 131–132, 220; N.Y. 1906, ch. 326; N.Y.S.L.B., *Review of Legislation, 1906,* pp. 217–227; Hendrick, "Governor Hughes," p. 535.

19. *Massachusetts Ins. Rep.,* 51st (1906), xxvii; *Louisiana Ins. Rep.,* 1907, xiii; on Texas premium tax, *Texas Ins. Rep.,* XXXIII (1907–08), II. These observations are based on an examination of insurance laws reported in N.Y.S.L.B., *Index to Legislation,* 1906–1908, and *Insurance Enactments,* 1909–1910.

20. On Robertson Act, Texas 1907, ch. 170, and James A. Tinsley, "Texas Progressives and Insurance Regulation," *Southwestern Social Science Quarterly,* XXXVI (1955), 237–247; Thomas A. Crosson, "A History of the Robertson Law and Its Effect Upon Life Insurance in Texas" (unpubl. thesis, University of Pennsylvania, 1951), *Metropolitan v. Love,* 108 SW 821 (Tex. Sup. Ct. 1908).

21. N.Y., *Test.,* VII, 6036; New York, *Proceedings before the Senate . . . on . . . the Removal of Mr. Otto Kelsey, Superintendent of Insurance* (Albany, N.Y., 1908), "The Kelsey Removal," cont. 166, Hughes Mss.; Pusey, *Hughes,* I, 191–193, 206–207, 225; on Hotchkiss, A.L.I.P., *Proceedings,* 5th (1911), 37; on Hoey, Alfred Hurrell to Walton J. Crocker, Oct. 7, 1911, File 226, Secretary's Office, J.H.

22. "Notes on Current Legislation," *American Political Science Review,* III (1909), 401, IV (1910), 393–395; N.Y.L., *M.B.T.,* May 11, 1910; President's Report, Aug. 14, 1911, File 226, Secretary's Office, J.H.; "Notes on Current Legislation," VI (1912), 418.

23. Buley, *American Life Convention,* I, 407; "Notes on Current Legislation," III (1909), 401. *Bush v. New York Life,* 116 N.Y.S. 1056 (1909), upheld the law on business limits, the most controversial part of the Armstrong legislation.

24. Cleveland to Stephen Rhodes, Jan. 4, 1908, File H 080.2, Secretary's Office, J.H.; N.Y.L., *M.B.T.,* Jan. 9, 1907, Nov. 10, 1909; A. A. Welch to Herbert K. Smith, Dec. 15, 1906, File 2997, B.C. Arch.; Buley, *American Life Convention,* I, *passim.* In 1909 the American Institute of Actuaries was established as the Southern and Western counterpart to the Eastern-dominated Actuarial Society of America. Reinhard A. Hohans, "The Origin of the Society of Actuaries," *Transactions of the Society of Actuaries,* I (1949), 10–11.

25. Armstrong to McCall, March 3, 1906, Perkins to Beer, March 19, Perkins Mss.; Cravath to Armstrong, March 3, 1906, in Swaine, *Cravath Firm,* I, 761; William C. Beer to John N. Baldwin, Dec. 16, 1905, Buckner to Perkins, March 6, 1906, Beer to Perkins, March 10–17, Buckner to Perkins, March 12; *Outlook,* LXXXII (1906), 581.

26. Armstrong to McCall, March 3, 1906, Beer to Perkins, March 12, 14, 20, Perkins Mss.; on Hamilton, Buley, *American Life Convention,* I, 270; Cravath to Hughes, Feb. 28, 1906, to William A. Day, April 17, to Frank S. Black, March 5, in Swaine, *Cravath Firm,* I, 760–762; on Mutual, Thomas Buckner to Perkins, March 12, 1906, Perkins Mss.; James, *Metropolitan,* 167; Perkins to Colonel Alex A. Hawes, May 15, 1906, to Major F. A. Kendall, April 5, Perkins Mss. See also the criticism ("pure paternalism") in Paul Morton and Darwin P. Kingsley, "Life-Insurance Legislation," *North American Review,* CLXXXII (1906), 492–501.

27. McCall to Agents, Sept. 26, 1905, File 3703, B.C. Arch.; N.Y.L., *M.B.T.,* Oct. 11, 1905; McCurdy to W. C. Heimbuechar, Oct. 23, 1905, XXIII, Mut. Lbs.; Mut., *M.B.T.,* Nov. 16, 1905; N.Y.L., *M.B.T.,* Oct. 18, 1905; N.Y.L., *Annual* Reports, 1905–1907.

28. Beer to ? Moriarty, Dec. 18, 1905, Beer Mss.; Jessup, *Root,* I, 440; Darwin P. Kingsley, "Insurance Supervision and National Ideals," *North American Review,* CLXXXIX (1909), 482; *New York Life v. Deer Lodge County,* 231 U.S. 495 (1913); Elmer W. Sawyer, *Insurance as Interstate Commerce* (New York, 1945), 35–36; Herbert K. Smith to John F. Roche, Aug. 6, 1910, File 4676, B.C. Arch.; Charles A. Peabody to James M. Beck, Feb. 17, 1906, Mut.

Lbs. Elihu Root opposed Darwin P. Kingsley's appeal to the National Civic Federation for Federal regulation. *C.F.C.*, LXXXIX (1909), 1378, 1457.

29. Above, Chapter XI; case numbers from Guilford A. Deitch, comp., *Digest of Insurance Cases* (Indianapolis, 1910, 1915, 1920, 1925), XXII, XXVII, XXXII, XXXVII; on Met., Louis I. Dublin, *A Family of Thirty Million* (New York, 1943), 367–368; Howard P. Dunham, comp., *The Business of Insurance* (New York, 1912), III, 123.

30. Robert L. Cox, *Tracts on Life Insurance, 1908–13* (in Baker Library, Harvard University); Pru., *M.E.C.*, June 24, July 1, 1907; N.Y.L., *M.B.T.*, Dec. 11, 1907, March 11, 1908; on 1909 and 1913 acts, Pru., *M.B.D.*, July 12, 1909; Maurice H. Robinson, "The Federal Corporation Tax on Life Insurance," *American Economic Review,* II (1912), 172–173; Donald R. Childress, "The Taxation of Life Insurance Companies" (unpubl. diss., University of Pennsylvania, 1951), I; Buley, *American Life Convention,* I, 341–342, 421–423.

CHAPTER XVI. DISENGAGEMENT

1. *Massachusetts Ins. Rep.*, 55th (1910).

2. Louis G. Delafield to Perkins, March 7, 1906, Perkins Mss.; Garraty, *Right-Hand Man,* pp. 190–194; on Mutual, *Outlook,* LXXXIII (1906), 803; on Equitable, "Insurance," *Independent,* LXII (1907), 1283; James, *Metropolitan,* pp. 164–165.

3. N.Y.L., *M.B.T.*, Oct. 11, 1905, Jan. 3, April 11, 1906, March 13, June 5, 1907, Jan. 10, 1908; Buley, *Equitable,* pp. 142–143; Charles A. Peabody to Joseph H. Choate, Jan. 15, 1906, XXIV, Mut. Lbs.; *C.F.C.*, LXXXIX (1909), 1045, XC (1910), 1215; Mut., *M.B.T.*, Feb. 24, 1909, April 27, 1910; *New York Ins. Rep.*, 51st (1910), pt. V, pp. 711–748.

4. "The Insurance Revelations," *Arena,* XXXV (1906), 304; on Alexander, *Insurance Monitor,* LIII (1905), 321; Buley, *Equitable,* pp. 125, 128–129, 139, 143; Clough, *Mutual,* p. 231; May and Oursler, *Prudential,* pp. 148, 150, 155; Pru., *M.B.D.*, July 18, 1910; Hegeman to S. McDowell, June 13, 1907, Met. Arch.; James, *Metropolitan,* p. 192; Cromwell to Perkins, July 9, 1906, Perkins Mss.; John C. McCall to Charles E. Hughes, Jan. 5, 1906, N.Y.L. Arch.; N.Y.L., *G.J.M.*, p. 212, Beer Mss.; William C. Beer to Senator James H. Millard, Jan. 9, 1906. Other casualties of the period were Jacob Greene of the Connecticut Mutual (1905), the great pre-Armstrong adversary of the large companies, and the John Hancock's Stephen H. Rhodes (1909).

5. On new presidents, Buley, *Equitable,* pp. 121–122; Abbott, *Story of NYLIC,* p. 190; Clough, *Mutual,* pp. 231–232, 320–321; 'Q.P.,' "Changes in the 'Big Three' Companies," *World's Work,* XI (1906), 7388–7389; Peabody to D. C. Haldeman, Jan. 16, 1906, XXIV, Mut. Lbs.; Mut., *M.B.T.*, July 17, 1906.

6. Peabody to Herbert U. Williams, Feb. 10, 1906, XXIV, Mut. Lbs.; Clough, *Mutual,* p. 321; Buley, *Equitable,* pp. 128, 154, 156–169; Tarbell statements in N.Y., *Test.*, IV, 3583–3584; on Orr's eagerness to leave, N.Y.L., *M.B.T.*, April 11, 1906; on N.Y.L. management, Peabody to Emory McClintock, June 26, 1906, XXV, Mut. Lbs., Kingsley, "The Insurance Laws of New York," *Independent,* LXIV (1908), 244, A.L.I.P., *Proceedings,* 1st (1907), 51, N.Y.L., *M.B.T.*, May 11, 1910; May and Oursler, *Prudential,* p. 162, Pru., *M.B.D.*, Nov. 27, 1911; James, *Metropolitan,* pp. 173–174.

7. On I.P.C., "Insurance," *Independent,* LX (1906), 173, 821, "Democracy in Life Insurance," *Outlook,* LXXXIV (1906), 601–603; Thomas B. Wanamaker to Charles W. Fairbanks, Sept. 6, 1906, Fairbanks to George W. Perkins, Sept. 17, Perkins Mss.; *C.F.C.*, LXXXII (1906), 124–125; Beer to Perkins, March 20, 1906, Perkins Mss.; *Standard,* LIX (1906), 305.

8. N.Y.L., *M.B.T.*, April 11, July 25, 1906; Buckner to Perkins, March 6, 1906, Perkins Mss.; Beer to Cortelyou, Oct. 16, 1906, Beer Mss.; *New York Ins. Rep.*, 51st (1910), pt. V, p. 735; "Insurance," *Independent,* LXI (1906), 1189;

Mut., *M.B.T.*, June 25, 1906. Peabody (to Frank H. Hardison, Feb. 14, 1906, XXIV, Mut. Lbs.) denied using agents to corral proxies.

9. Mut., *M.B.T.*, April 23, 1907; Clough, *Mutual*, p. 232; "Insurance," *Independent*, LXI (1906), 1441, LXII (1907), 989; *C.F.C.*, LXXXVI (1908), 1369.

10. Lester Zartman, "Control of Life Insurance Companies," *Journal of Political Economy*, XV (1907), 531–541; Miles M. Dawson, "Mutualization of Life Insurance Companies," A.A.P.S.S. *Annals*, LXIX (1917), 62–76; James, *Metropolitan*, p. 190.

11. Buley, *Equitable*, pp. 150–152; on Stillman-Baker offer, *U.S. Money Trust Investigation*, pp. 1267–1268; Hotchkiss to Jerome J. Wilson, May 4, 1911, Letters in re Mutualization, Secretary's Office, Equit.; William A. Day to Thomas Spratt, May 10, 1911, *Report of Committee on Mutualization*, Feb. 15, 1912, Secretary's Office, Equit.; Buley, *Equitable*, pp. 161, 166–168.

12. Pru., *M.B.D.*, Feb. 10, 1908, Aug. 9, 1909, April 26, 1910; May and Oursler, *Prudential*, pp. 149–150, 153–157, 161–169, 253–257; cost estimate in *Report of Committee on Mutualization*, Secretary's Office, Equit.

13. James, *Metropolitan*, pp. 189–194.

14. On Fowler committee, N.Y.L., *M.B.T.*, April 11, July 2, 1906; on Truesdale committee, Mut., *M.B.T.*, Oct. 25, Nov. 16, 1905, and Clough, *Mutual*, pp. 223, 229–231; on salaries, N.Y.L., *M.F.C.*, Jan. 3, 1906, and Pru., *M.B.D.*, Jan. 8, 1912; *W.U.*, LXXVII (1907), 323; Clough, *Mutual*, p. 231n.

15. See controversy over dividend computation among Samuel B. Clarke, James McKeen, and William Trenholm, *American Law Journal*, XLI (1907), 161–196, 321–335, XLII (1908), 1–11, and "Life Insurance," *Journal of Accountancy*, I (1905), 142–144. The Prudential decided that the New Jersey laws made quarterly dividend valuations necessary, and the New York Life, to comply with a new Wisconsin statute, computed a separate valuation of first year premiums. Pru., *M.F.C.*, Nov. 26, 1906, *M.B.D.*, July 8, 1907; N.Y.L., *M.B.D.*, Dec. 11, 1907. On agency structure, Clough, *Mutual*, p. 277; Buley, *Equitable*, p. 137; N.Y.L., *M.B.T.*, Dec. 13, 1905, May 9, 1906; *W.U.*, LXXVI (1907), 104.

16. The Mutual's Peabody in 1910 set a voluntary business limit of $170,000,000 a year for his company. Clough, *Mutual*, p. 244n; Mut., *M.B.T.*, Oct. 25, Nov. 29, 1910. As New York Life Trustee Fowler saw it, the Armstrong investigation found "an overproduction of insurance . . . the rivalry between the companies has led to the writing of insurance that was not really wanted and that was soon dropped." N.Y.L., *M.B.T.*, July 2, 1906. On the rise of the other companies, "A New Era in Life Insurance," *World's Work*, XII (1906), 7598; Harold F. Williamson and Orange A. Smalley, *Northwestern Mutual Life* (Evanston, 1957), p. 113. Between the beginning of the Armstrong inquiry and January 1906, fifty new companies, a fifth of them in Indiana alone, were formed. *C.F.C.*, LXXXII (1906), 127–129.

17. Stalson, *Marketing Life Insurance*, p. 564; Perkins testimony in U.S. Senate, Committee on Interstate Commerce, *Control of Corporations, Persons, and Firms Engaged in Interstate Commerce* (Washington, 1913), p. 1133; "World-Politics," *North American Review*, LXXXI (1905), Peabody to Emory McClintock, June 26, 1906, XXV, Mut. Lbs.; J. C. Rocquet to William A. Day, June 1, 1909, "Society's Appeal" file, George T. Wilson to J. C. Rocquet, March 8, 1911, July 23, 1912, Secretary General for Europe file, H.P., Equit.

18. N.Y.L., *M.B.T.*, July 2, 1906, July 8, 1908; on Japan, no. 3442, Dec. 21, 1906, Numer. File, State Arch.; foreign business materials, N.Y.L. Arch.

19. Brazil, no. 87, Sept. 18, 1905, Dip. Des., State Arch.; Chile, no. 16030, Aug. 28, 1908, Numer. File, State Arch.; Simon G. Hansen, *Utopia in Uruguay* (New York, 1938), pp. 26–28; N.Y.L., *M.B.T.*, Feb. 9, 1911; Mexico, no. 812.5064/13, May 14, 1913, Dec. File.

20. Bulgaria, no. 3513, Dec. 5, 1906, Numer. File, State Arch.; on Serbia, N.Y.L., *M.B.T.*, Aug. 12, 1908, June 9, 1909; no. 4434, 1907, *passim*, Numer.

File; Italy, June 1911–Aug. 1912, Dip. Des.; on Spain, Equit. to State, no. 852.5064/29, April 4, 1910, Dec. File, State Arch., Buley, *Equitable,* p. 182.

21. *London Telegraph,* quoted in *Current Literature,* XXXIX (1905), 480; Great Britain, House of Lords, Select Committee on Life Insurance Companies, *Report* (London, 1906), pp. v–vi, 21, 61; E. Hilton Young, *Foreign Companies and Other Corporations* (Cambridge, 1912), pp. 237–238.

22. On Austria, State to N.Y.L., Sept. 20, 1905, Dom. Let., State Arch.; N.Y.L. to State, Oct. 16, 1905, Misc. Let.; on Russia, N.Y.L., *M.F.C.,* July 23, 1906; Rocquet to Wilson, Feb. 21, 1911, Paris File, H.P., Equit.; N.Y.L., *M.B.T.,* Oct. 13, 1910; Russia, no. 361.115/48, Oct. 13, 1910, Jan. 26, 1911, Numer. File, State Arch.

23. N.Y., *Test.,* VIII, Ex. 359; Adee to Buckner, Jan. 12, 1906, French Insurance Law File, H.P., Equit.; France, 1906, *passim,* Dip. Des., State Arch. The New York *Sun* noted, June 16, 1906, that State intercession "was only half-hearted, the insurance companies being actually frowned upon by . . . Washington."

24. McClintock statement in Great Britain, Select Committee, *Report,* p. 12; N.Y.L., *M.B.T.,* July 5, 1906; Buley, *Equitable,* pp. 143–148.

25. Abbott, *Story of NYLIC,* p. 205; correspondence of N.Y.L. and Mut. to State, 1914–17, Numer. File, State Arch.; France, no. 851.5064/11, Nov. 14, 1917, Dec. File, State. Arch.

26. "Reinsurance or Transfer of the Company's Foreign Business," N.Y.L. Arch.; Buley, *Equitable,* pp. 198–201.

27. Hotchkiss to Edward A. Woods, May 19, 1911, Letters in re Mutualization, Secretary's Office, Equit.; *C.F.C.,* LXXXVI (1908), 83; N.Y.L., *M.F.C.,* Feb. 27, 1908. *Morse v. Equitable,* 108 N.Y. Supp. 986 (Sup. Ct. 1908), allowed the Equitable to vote its Equitable Trust and Mercantile Trust stock on a merger question — as long as no control by the insurance company resulted.

28. N.Y.L., *M.F.C.,* Oct. 31, Nov. 7, 11, 1907; *New York Ins. Rep.,* 49th (1908), p. xi; 50th (1909), pt. I, pp. 281–308.

29. On Mutual, *W.U.,* LXXVI (1907), 119; Buley, *Equitable,* p. 172; Dryden to Jacob E. Ward, Jan. 9, 1906, Pru. Arch.; Pru., *M.B.D.,* Sept. 14, 1908; McCall to Perkins, Dec. 26, 1905, Perkins Mss. The Metropolitan's stock holdings were cut in half between 1906 and 1910. James, *Metropolitan,* p. 192.

30. On national investment patterns, Clough, *Mutual,* p. 188, Buley, *American Life Convention,* I, 351–352.

31. U.S., *Investigation of Financial and Monetary Conditions in the United States under House Resolutions Numbers 429 and 504* (Washington, 1913), *passim;* Brandeis quoted in William Z. Ripley, *Main Street and Wall Street* (Boston, 1927), p. 128.

CHAPTER XVII. THE END OF POWER

1. Pru., *M.B.D.,* Feb. 8, 1909; James S. Elston, "The Development of Life Insurance in the United States During the Last Ten Years," in *Readings in Life Insurance* (New York, 1934), I, 30.

2. A.L.I.P. *Proceedings,* 20th (1926), p. 17; George K. Gardner, "Insurance and the Anti-Trust Laws — A Problem in Synthesis," *Harvard Law Review,* LXI (1948), 247, 255–256.

3. *C.F.C.,* LXXXII (1906), 483–484, 656, LXXXVI (1908), 259; U.S., *Study of Legal Reserve Life Insurance Companies* [Investigation of Concentration of Economic Power, Monograph no. 28] (Washington, 1940), 371, 373–375.

4. Useful discussions of these developments are: "The Changing Pattern of Life Insurance Investments in the United States," *Transactions of the Society of Actuaries,* XI (1953), 216–249; Donald L. Kemmerer, "The Marketing of Securities, 1930–52," *Journal of Economic History,* XII (1952), 457–458; Haughton Bell and Harold G. Fraine, "Legal Framework, Trends, and Develop-

ments in Investment Practices of Life Insurance Companies," *Law and Contemporary Problems,* XVII (Winter, 1952), 45–85. On the major companies, see James, *Metropolitan,* chaps. 17, 19; Buley, *Equitable,* pp. 223–224, 229–231; Clough, *Mutual,* pp. 316–318.

5. Philip L. Gamble, *Taxation of Insurance Companies* [New York, Special Report of the State Tax Commission, No. 12] (New York, 1937); Cardozo statement in *Burnet v. Wells,* 289 U.S. 670 (1933); Magill statement in Daniel C. Knickerbocker, Jr., "Life Insurance and Federal Taxes," *Cornell Law Quarterly,* XLIII (1958), 423.

6. A.B.A. *Journal,* XII (1926), 96, 99, XIII (1927), 493, XVII (1931), 721; *U.S. v. South-Eastern Underwriters' Association,* 322 U.S. 473, 475 (1944). For a defense of the viewpoint embodied in the *South-Eastern Underwriters* decision see Robert L. Stern, "The Commerce Clause and the National Economy, 1933–46 (II)," *Harvard Law Review,* LIX (1946), 883–947; for criticism, see Thomas R. Powell, "Insurance as Commerce," *Harvard Law Review,* LVII (1944), 937–1008. For discussion of the effects of the decision and the McCarran Act, see Austin J. Lilly, "Insurance as Commerce: Five Years Under the SEUA Decision," *Maryland Law Review,* XI (1950), 81–99; James B. Donovan, "Regulation of Insurance Under the McCarran Act," *Law and Contemporary Problems,* XV (1950), 473–492; Joel B. Dirlam and Irwin M. Stelzer, "The Insurance Industry: A Case Study in the Workability of Regulated Competition," *University of Pennsylvania Law Review,* CVII (1958), 199–215; and Spencer L. Kimball and Ronald N. Boyce, "The Adequacy of State Insurance Rate Regulation: The McCarran-Ferguson Act in Historical Perspective," *Michigan Law Review,* LVI (1958), 545–578.

7. Stalson, *Marketing Life Insurance,* 636f; Richard C. Busse, "The History and Trend of the General Agency Contract in Life Insurance" (unpubl. thesis, University of Pennsylvania, 1950), p. 55; on uniform commissions, Clough, *Mutual,* pp. 281, 333; Pru., *M.E.C.,* Jan. 30, Feb. 20, 1911; on advertising, Ralph M. Hower, *The History of an Advertising Agency* (Cambridge, Mass., 1949), p. 95.

8. Frank W. Lewis, *State Insurance* (Boston, 1909); Hoffman, "Letters to the President," Pru. Arch.; Frankel and Dawson, *Workingmen's Insurance in Europe* (New York, 1910); Met., *M.B.D.,* Nov. 22, 1910; Buley, *Equitable,* p. 149.

9. Buley, *Equitable,* pp. 158–161, 181; James, *Metropolitan,* pp. 185f; Frankel, "Conservation of Life by Life Insurance Companies," A.A.P.S.S. *Annals,* LXIX (1917), pp. 77–91.

10. *New York Ins. Rep.,* 55th (1914), pt. V, pp. 654–658.

11. "1,700 Top Executives," *Fortune,* Nov. 1959, pp. 138–143, 307–308; C. Wright Mills, *The Power Elite* (New York, 1956), p. 137. David Bazelon, "Facts and Fictions of U.S. Capitalism," *The Reporter,* Sept. 17, 1959, pp. 43–48, is a discussion of modern corporatism that concentrates on the issues which once were particularly relevant to the large life insurance companies.

12. Adolf A. Berle, Jr., *The 20th Century Capitalist Revolution* (New York, 1954); John K. Galbraith, *American Capitalism, The Concept of Countervailing Power* (Boston, 1952). Berle has expressed concern over the dangers of stock control by institutional investors, among them life insurance companies. But the life firms have not exercised their investing power in any striking way. Berle, *Power Without Property* (New York, 1959), pp. 50–56, 160–161.

INDEX